GLOBAL CHINA

GLOBAL

CHINA

ASSESSING CHINA'S GROWING
ROLE IN THE WORLD

Edited by

TARUN CHHABRA
RUSH DOSHI
RYAN HASS
EMILIE KIMBALL

BROOKINGS INSTITUTION PRESS
Washington, D.C.

The Brookings Institution is a private nonprofit organization devoted to research, education, and publication on important issues of domestic and foreign policy. Its principal purpose is to bring the highest quality independent research and analysis to bear on current and emerging policy problems. Interpretations or conclusions in Brookings publications should be understood to be solely those of the authors.

Library of Congress Control Number: 2021937664

ISBN 9780815739166 (pbk)
ISBN 9780815739173 (ebook)

9 8 7 6 5 4 3 2 1

Typeset in Minion Pro

Composition by Elliott Beard

CONTENTS

Acknowledgments   xi

Introduction   1
TARUN CHHABRA | RUSH DOSHI | RYAN HASS | EMILIE KIMBALL

SECTION 1
DOMESTIC POLITICS

1 Hu's to Blame for China's Foreign Assertiveness?   25
RUSH DOSHI

2 Beijing's Nonmilitary Coercion—Tactics and Rationale   33
KETIAN ZHANG

3 Xi Jinping's "Proregress"   41
Domestic Moves toward a Global China
CHENG LI

SECTION 2
EAST ASIA

4 Trying to Loosen the Linchpin   53
China's Approach to South Korea
JUNG H. PAK

5 Lips and Teeth   60
Repairing China–North Korea Relations
EVANS J. R. REVERE

6 From Persuasion to Coercion   68
Beijing's Approach to Taiwan and Taiwan's Response
RICHARD BUSH

7 How China's Actions in the South China Sea   75
Undermine the Rule of Law
LYNN KUOK

8 The U.S.-China Nuclear Relationship   86
Why Competition Is Likely to Intensify
CAITLIN TALMADGE

SECTION 3
GREAT POWERS

9 China and the Return of Great Power   95
Strategic Competition
BRUCE JONES

10 U.S.-China Relations   102
The Search for a New Equilibrium
RYAN HASS

11 China, Japan, and the Art of Economic Statecraft   111
MIREYA SOLÍS

12 Managing China   120
Competitive Engagement, with Indian Characteristics
TANVI MADAN

13 Russia and China   132
Axis of Revisionists?
ANGELA STENT

14 Europe Changes Its Mind on China   140
THOMAS WRIGHT

SECTION 4
TECHNOLOGY

15 Preparing the United States for   151
the Superpower Marathon with China
MICHAEL BROWN | ERIC CHEWNING | PAVNEET SINGH

16 Navigating the U.S.-China 5G Competition   162
NICOL TURNER LEE

17 Managing China's Rise in Outer Space   171
FRANK A. ROSE

18 Dealing with Global Demand for   181
China's Surveillance Exports
SHEENA CHESTNUT GREITENS

19 Maintaining China's Dependence on Democracies   193
for Advanced Computer Chips
SAIF M. KHAN | CARRICK FLYNN

20 Artificial Intelligence and Autonomy in China's   209
Drive for Military Innovation
ELSA B. KANIA

21 China's Role in the Global Biotechnology Sector and
Implications for U.S. Policy   224
SCOTT MOORE

SECTION 5
REGIONAL INFLUENCE AND STRATEGY

22 China and Latin America   233
A Pragmatic Embrace
TED PICCONE

23 The Middle East and a Global China   241
Israel amid U.S.-China Competition
NATAN SACHS | KEVIN HUGGARD

Saudi Arabia's Relations with China   243
BRUCE RIEDEL

24 Great Expectations   247
        The Unraveling of the Australia-China Relationship
        NATASHA KASSAM

25 The Risks of China's Ambitions in the South Pacific   256
        JONATHAN PRYKE

26 China, the Gray Zone, and Contingency Planning   262
        at the Department of Defense and Beyond
        MICHAEL O'HANLON

27 All That Xi Wants   270
        China Attempts to Ace Bases Overseas
        LEAH DREYFUSS | MARA KARLIN

SECTION 6
THE GLOBAL ECONOMY

28 Reluctant Player   287
        China's Approach to International Economic Institutions
        DAVID DOLLAR

29 The Renminbi's Prospects as an International Currency   293
        ESWAR PRASAD

30 China's Digital Services
        Trade and Data Governance   297
        How Should the United States Respond?
        JOSHUA P. MELTZER

31 China's Influence on the Global Middle Class   309
        HOMI KHARAS | MEAGAN DOOLEY

32 The Global Energy Trade's New Center of Gravity   319
        SAMANTHA GROSS

33 Can the United States and China Reboot   326
        Their Climate Cooperation?
        TODD STERN

SECTION 7
GLOBAL GOVERNANCE

34 International Law with Chinese Characteristics   335
       Assessing China's Role in the "Rules-Based" Global Order
       ROBERT D. WILLIAMS

35 China's Expanding Influence at the United Nations—   353
       and How the United States Should React
       JEFFREY FELTMAN

36 China's Influence on the United Nations   359
       Human Rights System
       SOPHIE RICHARDSON

37 How to Curb China's System of Oppression in Xinjiang   367
       DAHLIA PETERSON | JAMES MILLWARD

       Contributors   381

       Index   397

ACKNOWLEDGMENTS

This initiative draws not only on Brookings' deep bench of China and East Asia experts, but also the tremendous breadth of the institution's experts in security, strategy, regional studies, technology, and economic development. A range of resident and nonresident Brookings scholars, as well as a few experts unaffiliated with Brookings, conducted rigorous research in an effort to provide an empirical baseline for understanding China's global role across wide-ranging geographic and functional areas. We are incredibly grateful to the scholars and research assistants who contributed to this project. It is because of them that this series exists. We would also like to thank the academics who provided anonymous peer review of the chapters. Their guidance and recommendations helped strengthen the reports.

We would like to thank Bruce Jones for his guidance in developing this project, and Will Moreland for his help in managing the project in the early stages of the series. A particular thanks goes to Michael O'Hanlon for reviewing an early draft of the volume, as well as Lindsey Ford for her orchestration and execution of a series of podcasts released alongside the briefs to help extend the reach of the research.

We appreciate the opportunities for intellectual exchange with a range of subject-matter experts within the United States government throughout this project. Even as many of these public servants would prefer not to be named,

their questions, comments, feedback, and curiosity about the research findings helped sharpen the analysis and connect it to the policy questions that
China's rise poses.

In all, the project released more than 70 research papers and 15 podcasts, some of which are highlighted in this edited volume. Preparing these
briefs for publication required herculean efforts from the Brookings Foreign Policy program communications team. We would like to thank Anna
Newby for her guidance to publish and promote the series, Ted Reinert for
his editing prowess, Suzanne Schaefer for her help with public events, and
Rachel Slattery for her phenomenal design and graphic work.

Several incredible colleagues helped proofread and edit the project and
research materials during various stages. They include Scarlett Ho, James
Haynes, Kevin Dong, Kizzy Dhaliwal, Nikhita Salgame, Samantha Diaz,
Holly Cohen, and India Daniel.

We are appreciative of the indispensable collaboration and partnership
of the Ford Foundation. This project would not have been possible without
their generous support throughout.

The generous support of David Rubenstein has also made possible the
broad collaboration of scholars from across the Foreign Policy program to
the Global China initiative.

Brookings is committed to quality, independence, and impact in all of
its work. Activities supported by its donors reflect this commitment and the
analysis and recommendations are solely determined by the scholars.

We are grateful to the team at the Brookings Institution Press who helped
shepherd the book to completion.

We remain thankful for the support of Brookings President John Allen
and for the leadership of Vice President and Director of the Foreign Policy
program Suzanne Maloney.

Introduction

TARUN CHHABRA
RUSH DOSHI
RYAN HASS
EMILIE KIMBALL

American assessments of China have changed dramatically in recent years. Once considered a potential "responsible stakeholder," China is now seen as America's principal "strategic competitor." With remarkable speed, U.S.-China relations have fallen to perhaps their lowest ebb since 1979. That trajectory has been further accelerated in the wake of the COVID-19 pandemic, which has seen views of China in most democracies around the world plummet, even as China—emboldened by its own response to the virus—has stoked nationalism at home and become more assertive in seeking to advance its interests abroad.

China has emerged as a truly global actor, impacting every region and every major issue area. To better address the implications for American policy and global order, Brookings scholars undertook a two-year project, titled "Global China: Assessing China's Growing Role in the World," of which this book is a part and for which this book is titled. The goal of this effort has been to furnish policymakers and the public with a new empirical baseline for understanding China's regional and global ambitions, particularly as Chinese president Xi Jinping heralds a "new era" for China.

This volume also comes at the start of a new American administration and a new Congress. Both the executive and the legislative branches are in the midst of evaluating the scale of China's ambitions, where those ambitions intersect with American interests, and how the United States can best protect and advance its objectives in the face of China's rise. This book is designed to speak to these questions across a wide spectrum of policy domains.

In the military domain, China's use of force against Indian soldiers during a 2020 border dispute has raised the possibility that it may do so against other American allies and partners in ways that could implicate American security commitments and potentially trigger a wider regional conflict. With respect to values, the mass incarceration and repression of ethnic minorities in the Xinjiang Uyghur Autonomous Region, the effective end of Hong Kong's autonomy, and China's exports of surveillance and censorship equipment have been unsettling to most democratic states. On the technology front, Beijing's desire to lead in the technologies of the "fourth industrial revolution" has shaken the confidence of advanced states in their own economic models and global economic position. Beijing's uses of economic incentives and disincentives to influence the choices of other countries across a range of issues has raised concerns about potential erosion of American influence. And with respect to the broader global economy, Beijing's retrenchment on economic reform, and Xi's calls for the state to play a larger role in the economy and to refocus China's growth on domestic drivers (what it calls dual circulation), have alarmed some in the business community. Finally, in the information space, China's efforts to influence politics and discourse in democracies have drawn growing scrutiny and concern. These same issues so frequently discussed in Washington are also driving debates among policymakers in capitals around the world.

To serve that increasingly global debate, this book seeks to illuminate the unprecedentedly complex picture of (1) China's activities on the global stage; (2) China's objectives, strategy, and reasons for strategic adjustment; and (3) the implications of China's growing global influence for the United States and the international system it established. Not all chapters can speak to these three questions independently, but taken together they make possible broad inferences that answer these questions and allow us to explore variation in the intentionality and implications of Chinese decisionmaking across an unprecedented range of regions and issue areas.

To provide additional analytical value, the project draws on Brookings's deep bench of China and East Asia experts, and also on the tremendous breadth of the institution's experts in areas of security, strategy, regional studies, and technological and economic development, among others. Several chapters are submitted by scholars from other institutions who are specialists in their fields. In this way, this work is a product of many scholars and practitioners from many different communities.

Together, the chapters suggest that China is increasingly and self-consciously global in its policy reach. In many cases, China has clear objectives and strategies to secure its interests, though in others its approach is more evolutionary than clearly purposeful. Many of the chapters demonstrate that Beijing is hardly the only power with agency, and that unique constellations of actors—from multinational companies to middle powers—have cleverly navigated for sometimes greater freedom of maneuver amid China's growing influence. Overall, they show that the implications for the United States and for the international system of a truly "global China" are enormous, and that formulating shared prescriptions for addressing the attendant challenges and for seizing the commensurate opportunities will be the defining foreign policy task of this decade and beyond.

The book's inquiry is structured across seven broad categories: domestic politics, East Asia, the great powers, technology, regional influence and strategy, the global economy, and global governance. Within each category, the book explores a broad framing question through a range of chapters. These sections and the findings of the chapters within them are summarized here.

SECTION 1. DOMESTIC POLITICS:
How Have Xi Jinping's Rise and Ambitions Shaped China's Foreign Policy?

Because the shift in U.S.-China relations has coincided with Chinese president Xi Jinping's consolidation of power, many in the United States associate the two closely with each other. The prevailing narrative in the United States is that President Xi is determined to take China in a new direction, a direction that many experts on China describe as increasingly illiberal at home and aggressive abroad. But this narrative has consequences. Whether President Xi and his consolidation of power bear responsibility for increased tensions, or instead, whether bilateral tensions are structural in nature rather than personality-driven has important implications for policy.

To critically assess President Xi's role in the breakdown in bilateral relations, we solicited contributions from Brookings colleagues and guest experts from both academia and the policy world.

Rush Doshi observes that high-level consensus among Chinese Communist Party (CCP) officials on China's grand strategy predates Xi's presidency, and that Beijing's former strategy of "hiding and biding" always had an expiry date because it was contingent on the Party's assessment of the international balance of power. Several apparently recent developments—including the departure from hiding and biding, a focus on power projection, more confident pursuit of territorial interests, and the launch of new international institutions—have clear roots in the tenure of Xi's predecessor, Hu Jintao. Doshi therefore cautions against attributing China's external assertiveness to Xi. Rather, the United States needs to build its China strategy with a clear-eyed recognition of China's long-standing commitment to its current path and the high-level Party consensus that underpins it.

Ketian Zhang also finds continuity in China's nonmilitary coercion. Zhang shows a consistent pattern between Beijing's response to the 2010 award of the Nobel Prize to Chinese dissident Liu Xiaobo, and the 2017 deployment by South Korea of the Terminal High Altitude Area Defense system (in response to heightened missile threats from North Korea). Zhang observes consistency in the tactics Beijing has employed for responding to such challenges, well before Xi assumed the presidency and since. These include economic sanctions on symbolic and visible areas of bilateral trade and the visible cutoff of high-level diplomatic engagement. She observes that the primary purpose of such actions is to signal disapproval and to deter similar moves by both the offending country and other countries as well.

Amid ongoing debates about whether President Xi Jinping is facing a backlash against his policy transformations at home and abroad, Cheng Li assesses recent domestic political and socioeconomic decisions and concludes that Xi has repositioned himself as a populist leader domestically while overseeing China's rise as a global power. Xi has drastically changed the composition of the key national and municipal leadership to include many of his confidants; significantly increased the budget to eliminate poverty in inland, rural areas; and generated policy incentives to establish "super megacities." Li warns against underestimating Xi's domestic power and the popular support for his foreign policy.

The contributions to this section of the book generally converge on the conclusion that Chinese foreign policy reflects more continuity than change under Xi's leadership, even if the consolidation of party control is transforming domestic politics and awakening the world to China's growing global ambitions.

SECTION 2. EAST ASIA:
How Is China Seeking to Reshape the Status Quo across East Asia's Hotspots, and How Are States within the Region Responding?

Viewed as a whole, the pieces in the East Asia section make a compelling case that China is no longer pursuing a narrowly defensive agenda of protecting its "core interests" on issues of sovereignty, political stability, and economic development. Rather, Beijing appears to be seeking revisions to the regional order to afford it greater influence over the outcome of events along its periphery, and ultimately, restoration of China as the leading power in Asia.

East Asia has become the region where U.S. and Chinese interests most clearly intersect. Importantly, it has also become the main growth engine of the global economy, a role for the region that is likely to continue well into the future. As such, how the United States and China navigate their competing interests in East Asia will go a long way toward determining how they will relate to each other as major powers in the international system.

Our contributors show that China is seeking adjustments to the status quo in each subregion of Asia, though staying at levels generally below the threshold of direct military conflict. Beijing's toolkit for incentivizing acquiescence to its aspirations for regional leadership includes both carrots and coercion. While Beijing's rapidly expanding military capabilities merit careful examination, so too does its use of economic rewards and disincentives to compel acquiescence—or nonopposition—to its regional agenda.

Likewise, Beijing has seemingly grown more comfortable with friction with the United States and other countries in the region as its power has expanded. Beijing has shown less sensitivity to reputational risk or pushback for taking bold measures to assert itself in the South China Sea, the East China Sea, or the Taiwan Strait, for example.

Together, these chapters raise fundamental questions about the kinds of actions or events that could plausibly induce Beijing to exercise restraint in pursuit of regional ambitions. They also highlight that the future direction of developments in the region is far from foregone. Regional countries have shown varying levels of dexterity in balancing between economic imperatives with China and their own security requirements, including by working among themselves—and with the United States—to respond to Beijing's advances.

Jung H. Pak observes that China seeks to drive a wedge between the United States and South Korea, which Beijing believes would weaken America's standing in Northeast Asia and increase Beijing's influence over outcomes on the Korean Peninsula. She notes, though, that China has undermined its own objectives with its aggressive opposition to South Korea's installation of an American missile defense system. Beijing's punitive response to Seoul's defensive measure revealed the divergence in interests between Beijing and Seoul on the Korean Peninsula. It also heightened South Korean concern about the risks of economic dependence on China. Pak concludes that the best counter that Washington and Seoul could provide to Beijing's efforts to drive wedges between them is to get on the same page about prioritizing regional stability, economic growth, and coordination on common challenges.

Evans J. R. Revere warns that China's identification of its interests will lead it to accommodate a nuclear-armed North Korea. For China, stability and avoidance of conflict are higher priorities than denuclearization. Revere argues that China and North Korea share similar goals, which include weakening the U.S.–South Korea alliance, removing U.S. forces from the Korean Peninsula, and reducing U.S. influence in Northeast Asia. As such, the United States must approach China with full awareness of the misalignment of each side's respective priorities on the Korean Peninsula. Washington must not base North Korea strategy on assumptions of Chinese support, and also must not mortgage leverage with Beijing in pursuit of cooperation on North Korean denuclearization, given the low likelihood of such cooperation materializing.

Richard Bush examines how China's approach to cross-Strait relations is colliding with Taiwan's democratic system of governance. He identifies three potential pathways for Beijing to pursue its goal of unification: (1) persuading the Taiwan people to accept "one country, two systems"; (2) using force; and (3) pursuing coercion without violence to wear down Taiwan's resistance to unification. Bush argues that the coercion without violence is the Goldilocks solution for Beijing between being too soft and too risk-acceptant in pursuit of unification. He judges that Beijing views the will of the Taiwan people as the center of gravity for deciding the future fate of Taiwan, and Beijing sees intimidation, pressure, and cooptation as the best means to exacerbate societal divisions within Taiwan and wear down the confidence of the Taiwan people in their own future. Bush suggests that Taiwan's societal cohesion and success provide the best counter to Beijing's efforts to achieve unification via coercion without violence.

Lynn Kuok argues that China's actions in the South China Sea to bolster its territorial and maritime claims have led to a weakening of the international law of the sea. Chinese actions of concern include encroaching on coastal states' exclusive economic zones, increasing its military presence around features, seeking to deny the United States and other countries navigational and other freedoms of the seas, and escalating its militarization of features it occupies. She argues that Beijing has established military advantages in the event of conflict and strengthened its ability in peacetime to deter other claimants from challenging China's claims. To respond to these developments, Kuok urges the United States to support economic development in Southeast Asia and also to find ways to strengthen Southeast Asian states' agency, not least in supporting the continuing applicability of international law.

Caitlin Talmadge examines the U.S.-China nuclear relationship and concludes that bilateral competition in this domain is likely to intensify. Two primary factors will drive this competition. First, the United States will be unwilling to abandon its nuclear advantages over China as Chinese forces grow larger and more sophisticated. Second, U.S. efforts to strengthen defenses against global nuclear threats may appear threatening to China, fueling further (if unintended) competitive dynamics. To manage this competition and reduce nuclear escalation risks, Talmadge highlights the importance of building off-ramps through direct crisis communication channels and proposes integrating China in an arms control framework that could encompass cyber, space, and other frontier technologies that affect nuclear stability.

SECTION 3. GREAT POWERS:
How Are the World's Great Powers Maneuvering amid U.S.-China Rivalry, and Is the International System Increasingly Bipolar or Multipolar?

For many in the strategic community, great power politics is primarily understood as a shorthand for the bilateral competition between the United States and China (or between the United States and Russia). But great power politics is in fact about much more, and the ties between both China or the United States and the other great powers—notably Europe, Japan, India, and Russia are of critical importance—have the power to shape U.S.-China competition and the international system.

The chapters in this book demonstrate that a key development in great power politics is the strong position of Washington and Beijing relative to the other great powers, which appears to be producing an order that is more bipolar than multipolar. Indeed, with both countries' economic and military strength and leadership in technologies like artificial intelligence, the United States and China are outpacing the other great powers—and that gap is growing. In light of this widening separation, it is increasingly clear that decisions made in Beijing and Washington will play a major role in questions regarding geopolitical stability, global and national economic growth, emerging technology, and international values and institutions. At the same time, the fast-deteriorating relationship between these two countries will also form the broad structure within which the other great powers maneuver.

The intensifying U.S.-China competition is an important factor affecting the policies of the other great powers. For China, stabilizing ties with other great powers provides a hedge against the downturn in relations with the United States. Given the Trump administration's unpredictability, trade protectionism, and limited reliability as a security partner, great powers like Japan and India seized on China's receptiveness as an opportunity for improved, albeit limited, ties. Tokyo, for example, has managed to achieve a thaw in the political and diplomatic relationship even as security and economic competition intensifies, indicating the sophistication of both governments in managing bilateral ties. For Delhi, a fatal China-India border crisis has reinforced the fundamentally competitive nature of relations, with the potential for conflict ever present, even as China and India both look for ways to prevent relations from tipping into outright enmity. These improvements are of course limited: for both India and Japan, concerns about status, China's growing regional role, and especially ongoing territorial disputes continue to constrain room for better relations and form part of the reason for their continued pursuit of strong bonds with the United States broadly.

China's other neighboring great power, Russia, has seen its ties with China improve. The growing and unmistakable convergence between Moscow and Beijing is among the most important trends reshaping the web of great power ties. China and Russia share a mutual interest in challenging a world order dominated by the United States. Russia provides China with military hardware, energy, and Arctic access; China is Russia's largest trading partner and provides capital, technical expertise, and a market for Russia to further develop its natural resources; both provide each other support in diplomatic bodies. The depth and duration of this trend of strengthening Sino-Russian ties will be a key feature to watch going forward. The chapters in this section of the book examine these dynamics and their implications for the international system in greater detail. They also offer policy options for the United States and other countries.

As Bruce Jones notes in a sweeping analysis of the ways great power politics intersects with international order, China's rise marks the first time since the creation of a global system that an illiberal power has the reach, capacity, and ambition to reshape the rules of the international order. Jones highlights several key features of the current system: the continued weight and scale of the United States; the new position and global policies of China; a layer of powers (the European Union, the United Kingdom, Russia, India, and Japan) vying for space and security; the wide and deep network of multilateral institutions; and the presence of an informed and active network of civil society, the private sector, and the general public. Among the most critical factors, he notes, is the growing power gap between China and the United States—the top two powers—and the rest. This fact will force the other powers to pay close attention to the preferences of both Washington and Beijing, as well as the tensions between them.

Jones also argues that the United States will be better able to shape the international order if it recommits to (but also retools) the alliance system and returns to a wider appreciation of the multilateral order. Washington will need to navigate the reality that China can claim a full seat at the table in certain domains. That, in turn, forces an uncomfortable choice between acceding to a sharing of power or driving a degree of economic decoupling— potentially leading to the emergence of two zones of globalization. If the United States and China continue to pursue strategic rivalry, and if their relationship continues to deteriorate, Jones suggests that a kind of bifurcated globalization will develop—two zones of technological, infrastructure, and commercial integration.

Ryan Hass explores the key force driving that possibility: the U.S.-China relationship. He argues that the relationship is deteriorating faster than at any point since 1979, when the two countries first established diplomatic relations. While several factors have contributed to the downturn in relations, Hass identifies four in particular: (1) Washington and Beijing's dissatisfaction with the regional security status quo; (2) China's emergence as a global rulemaker; (3) the growing centrality of technology competition in the bilateral relationship; and (4) the intensification of ideological and systems competition. Hass offers several recommendations to U.S. policymakers for restoring equilibrium to the U.S.-China relationship, including right-sizing the risk that China poses to U.S. interests; developing a shared framework between Washington and Beijing for understanding the nature and distribution of power in the U.S.-China relationship; relearning how to shape China's behavior; and focusing on national cohesion and American renewal. He concludes that the United States and China can coexist within a state of heightened competition as long as both countries recognize that their national conditions are linked—for good or ill—to the actions of the other, exercise restraint in addressing challenges with one another, and concentrate on addressing their own internal shortcomings.

Mireya Solís analyzes China's ties to Japan and demonstrates that geo-economics has become a critical frontier in their bilateral competition for Asian leadership. She argues that China and Japan are each pushing visions of regional integration and offering development finance to see them through, but that neither is pressing developing countries in Asia to make binary choices on overall relations. Even as this competition unfolds throughout the region and beyond, Beijing and Tokyo have improved bilateral ties as both cope with the unpredictability and protectionism of the United States, with leader-level exchanges increasing and some cooperation on economic matters. That thaw has had limits: China continues to pressure Japan on territorial disputes, while Japan is increasingly adopting economic defensive measures to guard against technological leakage vis-à-vis China.

Tanvi Madan explores China's relations with India, Asia's other great power democracy. Madan characterizes Delhi's approach to Beijing as "competitive engagement with Indian characteristics." She observes that India's management of its China relationship has involved two elements: one that seeks engagement with Beijing where possible, and another that involves competing with China both alone and in partnership with others. Madan argues that India's recent "reset" with China has thus far been limited, consisting of greater high-level interaction, efforts to improve economic and people-to-people ties, and the restarting of boundary and military dialogues. However, the persisting boundary dispute, China's support for Pakistan, concerns about China's increasing activities and influence in South Asia and the Indian Ocean region through the Belt and Road Initiative and beyond, and an unbalanced economic relationship have ensured that the Sino-Indian relationship remains a fundamentally competitive one. With its concerns about a rising China's intentions and actions, India has pursued deeper ties with the United States and a range of countries in the Asia Pacific/Indo-Pacific, notably Japan and, increasingly, Australia. Madan notes that a major Indian revaluation of its China approach is unlikely at this stage, but could conceivably occur because of domestic political or economic developments in India, doubts about America's role and commitment in the region and vis-à-vis India, or a sustained Chinese strategy to reassure India or assuage its concerns.

Angela Stent writes that the growing Sino-Russian partnership represents one of the most concrete and durable achievements of Russian president Vladimir Putin's foreign policy. The turning point in the bilateral relationship came in 2014 after the annexation of Crimea—Putin promoted ties with China to balance Russia's adversarial relationship with the United States and Europe, and China enabled Russia to avoid the isolation the West sought to impose on Russia. China is interested in access to Russia's oil and gas, its military equipment, and its Arctic waters. Russia has even assisted China in developing an early warning system against nuclear attacks and adopting China's telecommunications equipment, and both countries have coordinated in global institutions. Despite this convergence, Stent argues that Russia and China see some strains. For example, Russia has reasons to be concerned about China's Belt and Road Initiative, and the two countries are not entirely aligned on their visions of a post-Western global order. While the United States is unlikely to be able to drive the two countries apart, Stent argues it should be careful not to push them closer together.

Thomas Wright examines the shift in European policy away from one organized around economic engagement with China to one aimed at limiting China's influence in Europe based on strategic and security concerns. He writes that China's behavior is the driving force behind the EU's evolution to a strategy of balancing. This was already underway before the COVID-19 crisis, but it has accelerated since. Europe's approach is different in significant ways from that of the United States, but it is generally complementary to it. Because it is based on an understanding of how European interests are challenged by China, it may prove more durable than if it were simply at the behest of Washington. Wright emphasizes that EU-China relations are an important case study of Chinese reaction to a major power that is willing to engage with them.

SECTION 4. TECHNOLOGY:
China Aspires to Global Technology Leadership. Can It Achieve Its Ambitions? What Would the Impacts Be at Home and Abroad?

While the United States has maintained its position as the technologically dominant power for decades, China has made enormous investments and implemented policies that have accelerated its own progress in the technology domain. China's rapid technological advances have contributed significantly to its economic growth, increasing military capabilities, and expansion in global influence. These technological developments have also reflected and informed strategic competition between the United States and China.

The Chinese Communist Party's ambition to "catch up with and surpass" the West in advanced technologies is hardly new. It traces a lineage in Party guidance from Mao Zedong to Xi Jinping, with an emphasis on technology as a source of national power and a key domain of international competition, and "indigenization" as a top priority. As China's economic and political influence has expanded, so, too, have many of its technological ambitions and achievements.

The chapters in this section explore the broad dynamics of U.S.-China technology competition and assess China's progress in the development of fifth-generation (5G) wireless technology, weapons enabled by autonomy and artificial intelligence (AI), biotechnology, surveillance technologies, and space technology. They reveal critical linkages between foreign and domestic policy through the cross-border reach of domestic technology policy and regulation, as well as the impacts of global standard-setting initiatives.

Michael Brown, Eric Chewning, and Pavneet Singh argue that the United States is in a "superpower marathon" with China, an economic and technology race in which the United States must compete with—rather than contain—China. Technology and innovation will drive U.S.-China economic competition and the U.S. role in the world. The authors advocate a strategy designed to improve U.S. competitiveness and focus on long-term capability development. In particular, they propose larger investments in research and development (R&D), including a focus on engineering talent, an integrated U.S. economic strategy across government, and longer-term focus for U.S. businesses and capital markets.

Nicol Turner Lee narrates the intensifying competition between the

United States and China to deploy 5G wireless networks. In particular, she highlights the risks of a "split digital ecosystem worldwide" spurred by China's Belt and Road Initiative, and the potential for China to "lock in" other nations with its 5G technology. In the United States, rising national security concerns surrounding Huawei, China's dominant 5G player, are impacting the global supply chain. Despite China's slight lead in the areas of spectrum and equipment, the United States historically has maintained dominance over innovation and could make up for lost time with a more coordinated 5G strategy.

Frank A. Rose outlines how China has rapidly expanded its presence in outer space in both the civil and military arenas. China's People's Liberation Army has conducted a major reorganization to better integrate space, cyberspace, and electronic warfare systems with its other military capabilities. Rose argues that, in light of these developments, the United States will need to develop a strategy that deters China's advancing anti-satellite (ASAT) capabilities, while also addressing sustainability and safety concerns like orbital debris, space traffic management, and the rise of mega-satellite constellations.

Sheena Chestnut Greitens focuses on the growing adoption of China's public security and surveillance technology platforms around the world. Greitens finds that there is relatively little correlation between such platform adoption and the levels of democracy or freedom in adopting countries. While there are concerns about how these technologies could contribute to the entrenchment of authoritarian rule in some countries, or the weakening of democratic norms in others, many leaders in adopting countries also see potential for these platforms to address urgent public policy challenges, such as violent crime. U.S. policymakers must address Chinese technology companies' often quiet initiatives to shape the global regulatory environment. She recommends that the United States propose a set of standards for adoption of these technology-enabled surveillance platforms that are compatible with U.S. values—respect for human rights, civil liberties, privacy, and democracy.

Saif M. Khan and Carrick Flynn examine China's ambitions, achievements, and obstacles in developing an indigenous semiconductor industry. They argue that it is in the strategic interest of the United States and its democratic allies and partners for China to remain reliant on them for state-of-the-art computer chips. China is investing heavily to produce advanced chips that can power weapons systems which could threaten the United

States and its allies and partners, as well as techno-authoritarian surveillance platforms that violate human rights. Khan and Flynn recommend coordinated, multilateral export controls on semiconductor manufacturing equipment to slow, if not halt, China's progress toward producing advanced chips. Because the United States, Taiwan, and South Korea are currently the only economies with significant, near-state-of-the-art chip fabrication factory capacity, Khan and Flynn argue that the export controls they prescribe would, over the long term, shift a significant portion of the production of high-end chips to democracies.

Elsa B. Kania focuses on Chinese advancements in "intelligent" and autonomous weapons systems. The Chinese military and defense industries have undertaken major initiatives in research, development, and experimentation in autonomy and AI-enabled weapons systems, as part of China's efforts to leverage innovation in science and technology in pursuit of great power status. However, China's progress will be contingent on its ability to overcome significant hurdles to testing, training, and application in real-world scenarios. China will also need to address emergent safety, technical, legal, and ethical considerations in its development of technology-enabled weapons systems. The United States must closely monitor Chinese military and technological advancements and engage in dialogue with allies and partners as well as Chinese military counterparts to reduce the risk of unintended escalation.

Scott Moore explores China's trajectory in the global biotechnology sector. While the United States has been the dominant global player in developing and commercializing biotechnology for decades, China is determined to become a leading player and is investing heavily in the sector. Moore argues that although the United States is likely to remain ahead in most biotechnology fields, China's biotechnology sector can still be expected to produce significant innovations, some of which will have national security implications for the United States. China is already poised to become a critical player in policy and governance issues related to biotechnology, even as it works to overcome some of its own internal deficiencies, for example, in R&D and higher-risk financing. Moore identifies avenues for potential U.S.-China coordination, including in addressing the COVID-19 pandemic and in developing biosafety and biosecurity protocols that could open space for cooperation, much as shared concerns among major powers over nuclear security did in previous decades.

SECTION 5. REGIONAL INFLUENCE AND STRATEGY:
China Now Touches Virtually Every Region in the World—How Is China's Increasing Involvement Impacting South Asia, the Middle East, Latin America, and Elsewhere?

In the regional influence and strategy section, contributors explored where China is exercising initiatives to expand its presence, what factors are driving it to do so, and what tools it is relying on to advance its objectives. Viewed as a whole, the pieces push the discussion about China's ambitions beyond the long-standing debate over whether China seeks to consolidate leadership in Asia as a stepping-stone toward greater global leadership. The contributors in this section make clear that China is not waiting to consolidate its position in Asia before it asserts itself as a global actor. Rather, China is strengthening its presence in every corner of the world simultaneously.

China is now one of a small handful of countries with interests spanning the globe and the capacity to act on them. While its rapidly expanding military capabilities are supporting China's pursuit of its global ambitions, they are not Beijing's tool of first resort. For the moment at least, China is relying foremost on its economic statecraft, both in the form of incentives to attract support for its agendas and disincentives (withheld investments and curtailment of market access) for countries that challenge Beijing's plans.

The lack of a military presence at the leading edge of many of China's efforts around the world should not be mistaken for any lack of strategy, though. These chapters also highlight China's desire to strengthen its force projection capacity, its consideration of building overseas military bases, and its awareness of the need to have capabilities to counter threats to its interests abroad. So, in several regions where economic imperatives have outrun other features of China's growing global presence, it remains an open question whether a military footprint will follow.

Ted Piccone examines the tightening embrace between China and the Latin American and Caribbean region. He highlights how China has emerged as a dominant economic actor in the region, and the implications for the region's infrastructure, energy sector, and politics. Piccone argues that intensifying U.S.-China competition in the region should push the United States to articulate a comprehensive strategy that positions Washington as the partner of choice for tackling major regional challenges. An affirmative American agenda will have greater purchase than a defensive agenda that seeks to outspend China or obstruct China's inroads into various countries in the region.

Natan Sachs and Kevin Huggard examine Israel's relationship with China within the broader context of American and Chinese strategies in the Middle East. They observe that Israel finds itself torn between its diplomatic and economic incentives to work with China and its paramount interest in maintaining a close relationship with the United States. The net result has been to cause Israel to limit its engagement with Beijing and remain sensitive to security risks of deepening relations with China. Across the region, China's need for the secure flow of Middle Eastern energy means that its primary regional interests lie with oil-exporting states, not Israel. Even if Beijing does not intend to take on a more central role in regional security or politics, potential American retrenchment in the region could change its calculus over time. For Israel, though, China cannot serve as a substitute for the United States.

Bruce Riedel observes that China's relationship with Saudi Arabia is driven by access to oil. Aside from purchases of Saudi oil, there is little strategic cooperation between the two countries. Riyadh still views Washington as its main strategic partner; a majority of its arms purchases come from the United States. Washington is also far more aligned than Beijing on Iran, Saudi Arabia's regional rival. Even if U.S.-Saudi relations go through a downgrade, there will remain limits on China's ability to take advantage, given the narrow foundation on which China–Saudi Arabia relations have been built.

Natasha Kassam traces the causes of the deteriorating China-Australia relationship and its economic and security implications. Kassam highlights Beijing's rising tolerance for friction and Canberra's decision to reciprocate in kind. She observes that Beijing views Australia through the lens of U.S.-China competition. Seeing the relationship in this light has motivated Beijing to seek to create distance between the United States and Australia in order to weaken America's position in the western Pacific. She warns that China's growing pressure on Australia should not be seen as an aberration, but rather as a foretaste of how China will exercise its growing power to advance its strategic objectives. She warns that such conduct could backfire for Beijing, though, by betraying an aggressiveness that will be viewed unfavorably by other countries in the western Pacific.

Jonathan Pryke analyzes China's efforts to expand its influence in the South Pacific and the alarm that such efforts have triggered among the

United States and its allies. While observing that China's growing involvement in the local affairs of the island nations has had a corrosive effect on good governance through elite capture, corruption, and lack of transparency in commercial dealings, it may also prove to be a losing formula for Beijing. Pryke notes that China's increased activism has prompted Australia and New Zealand to up their diplomatic game in the region, raising questions of how far Beijing will be able to go in its efforts to build inroads in the South Pacific.

Michael O'Hanlon explores what issues could trigger conflict between the United States and China or Russia. He concludes that the greatest risk of a head-on and large-scale conflict would likely result from a Chinese assault on an island administered by Japan, or by a Russian attack on a Baltic state. Potential scenarios could involve a small-scale Russian or Chinese attack against a sliver of allied territory, designed less to seize land than to flex national muscles and challenge the U.S.-led global order. What should the United States and its allies do if China or Russia undertakes an aggressive action that is at once both minor in its physical scale and strategic in potential consequences? O'Hanlon argues that rather than rely on rapid military escalation, the United States and its allies will need to develop strategies of asymmetric defense and counterattack. An asymmetric defense would combine and interweave the economic instruments of statecraft and warfare into combat plans. The active elements of the strategy would center on economic warfare. Military responses would be important but would often function in a supportive role, to create a defensive line against any further enemy advance and perhaps to support the enforcement of economic sanctions.

Leah Dreyfuss and Mara Karlin analyze China's military basing and force projection strategies. They judge that in the near to medium term, China will likely maintain its posture of foregoing formal military alliances, instead seeking security partnerships entwined with Belt and Road Initiative projects that enable access in recipient countries. They conclude that China's reliance on imported energy and commodities, as well as its desire to protect overseas citizens and investments, are likely the key drivers of China's efforts to acquire greater access for its forces overseas. At the same time, Karlin and Dreyfuss warn that China's appetite could grow with the eating, leading it to pursue an expanding global military posture as its national power and force projection capabilities expand in the future.

SECTION 6. THE GLOBAL ECONOMY:
How Is China's Rise Reshaping Global
Economic Institutions and Affecting Progress
on Goals Like Poverty and Climate?

China's growing weight in the international economy is allowing it to gain greater influence over the key underpinnings of the global economic system. China's efforts to secure a larger role for itself in multiple international institutions, as well as its willingness to launch new institutions to rival existing ones, have generated questions about the scale of its ambitions and the tools it will use to advance them. On issues ranging from energy to trade, China has had some success in bending institutions, rules, and norms in its preferred directions. At the same time, in other areas, such as internationalization of the renminbi, China's aspirations continue to outpace its impacts. The chapters in this section explore the tension for Beijing between preserving its state-led economic model and exercising the type of influence it aspires to in the international economy. The chapters also examine the global ramifications of China's growing middle class, as well as the energy and climate implications of China's economic expansion for the rest of the world.

David Dollar details China's approach toward international economic institutions. While China has fulfilled its commitments to these institutions, it has been reluctant to take on greater responsibilities that typically befall developed countries. China's insistence on being treated as a developing country has generated tensions with developed countries. To preserve and adapt the global economic architecture, Dollar recommends that China and other developing countries should receive more weight in global economic decisionmaking in return for greater adherence in their initiatives to prevailing global norms and standards, such as on debt sustainability and environmental and labor safeguards.

Eswar Prasad articulates that while China has the second-largest economy in the world, its currency, the renminbi, is not commensurate with the country's weight in the world economy. Prasad argues that the renminbi's status has been impeded by the Chinese government's unwillingness to undertake a broad range of economic and financial system reforms to liberalize its exchange rate, to allow the currency's external value to be determined by market forces, and to fully open the capital account. According to Prasad, the renminbi's growing prominence has come at the expense of other currencies—the euro, the British pound sterling, and the Japanese yen—rather than the U.S. dollar. For the renminbi to become a safe-haven currency requires not just economic and financial reforms but also significant institutional reforms that the Chinese leadership has thus far proven unwilling to advance.

Joshua P. Meltzer explains that China's dominance in 5G infrastructure will further support China's digital economy, which is second only to that of the United States. The extensive online activity of Chinese netizens provides large amounts of data, which provides an advantage, particularly in developing AI-enabled capabilities. Yet China is largely closed to foreign competition given restrictions on digital services imports and a heavily regulated internet. China's actions toward foreign competition stand in contrast to its actions to shape the international environment and the development of norms and rules affecting data governance, including through China's Digital Silk Road. While the United States has been leading the charge for an open internet, more must be done to counter China's global efforts, lest the internet become bifurcated between the United States and China.

Homi Kharas and Meagan Dooley show how China has impacted the global middle class through its size and numbers, its increasing ability to set new middle-class trends, and its challenge to the values and attributes of what belonging to the middle class really means. China is in large part responsible for the ongoing fastest expansion of the global middle class the world has ever seen, reinforced by growth in India and other countries. Kharas and Dooley explore three challenges and costs for others around the world as China's middle class grows: (1) whether the world can sustain such a large consumer class within planetary boundaries, (2) whether China's middle class poses a competitive threat or is a positive force promoting global growth, and (3) how a growing Chinese middle class will change the country's politics.

Samantha Gross examines how China has become the center of gravity for global energy markets. As energy demand growth has slowed elsewhere, over the last decade China's energy demand has increased by nearly 50 percent. Gross explores the electricity and oil and gas industries separately to understand how China carves out a place in energy markets and how it might change its policies as it confronts the challenges of climate change and local pollution. China aims to lead in new energy technologies in electricity; it has succeeded in leading the world in its pace of solar and wind capacity buildout. However, China is still reliant on oil and gas imports because domestic production cannot keep up with demand. China has also contributed to climate challenges through its continued construction of coal-fired power plants. As demand for coal-fired plants slows in China, Beijing has financed coal-fired power projects abroad through the Belt and Road Initiative to maintain excess Chinese industrial capacity.

Todd Stern underscores the importance of U.S.-China coordination on climate change. He argues that there is no way to contain climate change worldwide without full engagement by both countries. As the U.S.-China bilateral relationship declines further, he urges U.S. policymakers to find ways to manage a relationship that permits both competition and collaboration. Without renewed U.S.-China climate cooperation, the United States and the world will face grave national security consequences. Stern underscores that reviving climate cooperation between the two countries will also require an adequate level of commitment from both China and the United States to tackle climate change and decarbonize their economies toward meeting the Paris agreement's best-efforts goal of holding global temperature rise to 1.5°C.

SECTION 7. GLOBAL GOVERNANCE:
How Is China Reshaping Global Governance, Human Rights Norms, and International Institutions?

From human rights to the rule of law and global multilateral bodies, China, by virtue of its size and initiative, is exercising an almost gravitational force on liberal values, pulling key institutions, rules, and norms in its preferred direction. The chapters in this section explore this trend by focusing on China's engagement with international law, its growing influence in the United Nations, its effort to reshape the global human rights system, and its egregious repression in Xinjiang. Even if China does not seek to evangelically "export" its system, the reality is that its actions and interests demonstrate a desire to alter global governance to better reflect its own illiberal preferences. These chapters critically examine where China might be able to advance its preferences, and where it might face obstacles in its attempts to do so.

Robert D. Williams examines China's history of engagement with international law and its mixed record in the areas of trade, maritime and territorial disputes, Hong Kong, human rights, climate change, and the emerging spheres of cybersecurity and autonomous weapons. He concludes that China takes a flexible and functional approach to international law, that China is seeking to shape legal norms in its favor across many domains of international relations, and that despite its considerable limitations, international law can influence the context for the choices of Chinese leaders and their perceptions of their interests. Williams urges the United States, in concert with allies and partners, to reengage with international law in a clear-eyed effort to shape rules that are more robust and more effectively enforced, as a tool for advancing U.S. interests and influencing Chinese behavior.

Jeffrey Feltman writes that China's growing influence at the United Nations is inevitable. Even so, he cautions that fears of China changing the UN from within are premature. The United States is still the UN's most powerful member state. The UN has largely served as a force multiplier for American values; yet Americans need to be realistic about the future as China assumes a larger global role and shifts its focus to peace and security work. Feltman suggests that having China operate within a system forged under U.S. leadership provides the United States with an advantage. Feltman warns, however, that the United States must join forces with others at the UN to push back against Chinese and Russian attempts to distort normative principles of the UN, and to prevent leadership vacuums from emerging that China will seek to fill.

Sophie Richardson argues that the Chinese government's greater engagement with international institutions is not a gain for the global human rights system, and highlights the ways Chinese authorities are trying to reshape norms and practices globally. Chinese domestic censorship now extends across borders and, at the United Nations, China seeks to manipulate procedures to minimize scrutiny of its conduct. Richardson outlines steps to reverse these trends, for example, urging academic institutions to prioritize academic freedom. Companies have a responsibility to respect human rights and should reject censorship. Noting that the spread of COVID-19 has triggered a wave of racist anti-Asian harassment, Richardson stresses that efforts to limit the Chinese government's threats to human rights should not penalize people from across China or of Chinese descent.

Dahlia Peterson and James Millward describe China's system of oppression in Xinjiang and offer a slate of policy recommendations for the United States and its allies to increase public awareness and challenge repressive behavior in Xinjiang. CCP policies toward Xinjiang have eroded Uyghur autonomy through forced ethnic assimilationism. Chinese and Western companies have provided surveillance technology to the Xinjiang public security and surveillance industry, and while some of these companies have been sanctioned by the U.S. Department of Commerce, sanctioning has not yet had a significant impact. Peterson and Millward argue that the United States must clearly articulate the intended aims of its policy actions on Xinjiang and strengthen refugee and cultural protection for Uyghurs.

CONCLUSION

This book marks a first step in the effort to understand what kind of global power China will be and how it will reshape global order. The COVID-19 pandemic has seemingly accelerated the urgency of these questions while at the same time putting China, the United States, and the global order in a state of flux that obfuscates the answers.

For researchers and practitioners, one of the most important lessons of a "global China" is the need for a shared pursuit of the answers. China is no longer the exclusive province of China and East Asia experts. As its influence extends into every regional and functional domain, the formulation of good China policy increasingly relies on experts of other fields to interpret, illuminate, and explain the various facets of China's new global profile.

DOMESTIC POLITICS

*How Have Xi Jinping's Rise and Ambitions
Shaped China's Foreign Policy?*

1

Hu's to Blame for China's Foreign Assertiveness?

RUSH DOSHI

As Sino-American ties descend to a new post–Cold War low, Western analysts increasingly place the blame on Chinese president Xi Jinping's aggressive international activism. But to what degree is this muscular foreign policy the product of one man versus the larger system in which he is embedded?

This is a question of profound importance to bilateral ties. Too often, analysts overpersonalize China's foreign policy by contrasting a supposedly weak and timid Hu administration with a bold and striving Xi administration. But the reality is far more complex, and Xi's power consolidation and cult of personality are overshadowing important ways in which his foreign policy exhibits continuity with past trends.

The link between Hu and Xi's foreign policy has meaningful policy stakes. Widening the lens with which we view present Chinese foreign policy helps bring into focus a strategy that appears to enjoy a high-level consensus among Chinese Communist Party (CCP) officials. Many aspects of an increasingly assertive Chinese policy that the United States finds disagreeable are not "bugs" introduced by Xi's unique power consolidation and aggressiveness but enduring "features" of that consensus.

THE DECLINE OF "HIDE AND BIDE"

In popular media, Xi Jinping often receives credit for moving Chinese grand strategy away from Deng Xiaoping's strategic guideline (战略方针) that China needed to "hide capabilities and bide time." That guideline, more precisely rendered as Tao Guang Yang Hui (韬光养晦), dated back to the end of the Cold War when the United States rose to become China's chief threat, prompting Deng Xiaoping to advise his successors to adhere to a strategy of nonassertiveness. The strategy was about more than avoiding the costs of international leadership; it was also about avoiding conflict with the United States, reducing the risk of encirclement by China's neighbors, and creating space for Chinese development.

While it is true that Xi had almost never mentioned Tao Guang Yang Hui during his tenure and that authoritative Party commentaries on his remarks have stressed his emphasis on China's need to "step out from Tao Guang Yang Hui," the formal shift away from this core strategic guideline clearly began under Hu, as recently published documents now make clear.

To understand how Xi's policy shares continuity with the past, it is important to recognize that for decades, China's leaders have been explicit in open sources that they never expected Tao Guang Yang Hui to be permanent. Deng, Jiang, and Hu's own speeches all conceded that adherence to the strategy was based on China's assessment of the "international balance of power" (国际力量对比) and (implicitly) that it would therefore one day expire.[1] Accordingly, when that balance of power finally shifted after the global financial crisis that began in 2008, China's strategy changed. In a 2009 speech the following year, then president Hu Jintao modified Tao Guang Yang Hui by stressing that China needed to "actively accomplish something" (积极有所作为).[2] This may seem a trivial semantic point, but Tao Guang Yang Hui and "accomplish something" were placed in a "dialectical relationship" in key Party texts. In lay terms, that meant they were basically opposite concepts. When Hu stressed one part of the dialectic, he was effectively departing from the other, thereby substantially revising Chinese strategy.

Some suggest that Hu was reluctant to depart from Tao Guang Yang Hui or that he was pushed into doing so by hawks, but there is no real evidence for this view, and it is clear that Hu's 2009 formulation was reiterated throughout his term.[3] Xi's departure from hiding and biding had roots in a Party consensus that emerged roughly a decade ago, and his predecessor's administration in many ways inaugurated the shift. Attributing it to Xi ignores this fact.

Finally, to the degree that Xi has shifted China's grand strategy, the departure from the past primarily occurred not at the dawn of his term but roughly five years into it in 2017 and in response to Brexit and the election of President Trump. Shortly after those events, Beijing declared that the world was experiencing "great changes unseen in a century" and that now was the time to push Chinese grand strategy in a more global direction. But given the continuity of so much of the present Chinese grand strategy with past preferences and behavior, it would be premature to attribute this shift entirely to Xi and not to the Party in which he is embedded.

THE RETURN OF "NATIONAL REJUVENATION"

Many scholars stress Xi Jinping's focus on "national rejuvenation" as if he were the originator of a new concept that increasingly guides Chinese behavior. History, however, shows that the concept has a long lineage that precedes Xi and that it has always been at the center of the Party's ambitions. As the scholar Zheng Wang notes: "The explicit goal of rejuvenation goes at least as far back as Sun Yet-Sen, and has been invoked by almost every modern Chinese leader from Chiang Kai-Shek to Jiang Zemin and Hu Jintao."[4] While the term has become a prominent feature of Chinese propaganda under Xi, it has never been far from the focus of the Party.

Similarly, Xi has also received attention for his focus on the "two centenary goals," but these too have analogues in Party history. The goals are essentially built around important 100-year anniversaries. The first goal seeks a moderately prosperous society by 2021, a century after the founding of the Communist Party; the second seeks a China that has fulfilled its national rejuvenation by 2049, a century after the founding of the People's Republic of China. While Xi stressed these goals after assuming leadership, they were in fact part of Jiang Zemin's 15th Party Congress Work Report in 1997[5] and appeared in several documents in less formalized terms even before that. Xi has undoubtedly brought greater attention to these concepts, but the fact that they were already key parts of the CCP's governing philosophy again demonstrates the way in which key attributes of his agenda have deep roots in the Party.

CHINESE MILITARY, ECONOMIC,
AND POLITICAL ACTIVISM

China's major military, economic, and political investments under Xi have clear roots in the tenure of Hu.

First, while Xi Jinping has pushed through a dramatic military reorganization, other landmark components often attributed to him—including China's turn to a blue-water navy—began well before his leadership. Indeed, it was President Hu's administration that inaugurated China's shift away from two decades of anti-access/area-denial capabilities that were intended to complicate U.S. intervention in favor of a new emphasis on power projection and amphibious capabilities. In 2003, nine years before Xi assumed leadership, President Hu announced China's "Malacca Dilemma"[6] and suggested that China needed the blue-water capabilities to protect the sea lines upon which it depends; the next year, he tasked the navy with "new historic missions" away from China's shore.[7] After the global financial crisis, Hu committed resources to these goals. In 2009, the Politburo Standing Committee reportedly approved work on refitting the former Soviet-carrier *Varyag* into a Chinese aircraft carrier.[8] Not long after, China began plans to construct a second and third carrier and to accelerate production lines on surface vessels. Ultimately, it was Xi's predecessor who announced the goal of becoming a "maritime great power," fulfilling missions in the "far seas," securing Chinese overseas interests and taking action to get there.[9] Overstressing Xi's role in this development discounts the degree to which the Party and its previous leadership shared his vision of a more global Chinese military presence.

Second, Xi's use of infrastructure and economic coercion as tools to bind the region to China has a long history. While there is no question that the Belt and Road Initiative (BRI) is a signature program associated with Xi Jinping, many of its high-profile projects began before Xi's tenure under Hu's "going out" policy, which produced port projects, including those in Pakistan, Sri Lanka, Myanmar, and Malaysia. More fundamentally, the very idea of using infrastructure to bind neighbors to China was part of Hu's important 2009 address. Presaging the BRI, Hu declared then that one component of "actively accomplishing something" was to use infrastructure to tie neighbors together: "In particular, we must actively participate in and vigorously promote the construction of surrounding highways, railways, communications, and energy channels in the periphery [i.e., neighborhood] to form a network of interconnected and interoperable infrastructure around China."[10] The conceptual (and literal) foundation for what became the BRI was laid before Xi even took office. Finally, China's discourse on economic statecraft and coercion shifted before Xi took power.[11] The decision to wield it against Japan (over the East China Sea), Norway (over the Nobel Prize), and the Philippines (over the South China Sea) precedes Xi's leadership.

Third, major Chinese multilateral initiatives—including its launch of the Asia Infrastructure and Investment Bank (AIIB) and its leadership of the Conference on Interaction and Confidence Building in Asia (CICA, a regional institution)—had antecedents in Hu's tenure. For example, AIIB was first proposed by the Central Party Research Office in 2009, discussed at the Bo'ao Forum that year, and then apparently approved for implementation at the 18th Party Congress when Hu was still the paramount leader, though admittedly Xi may have made the final decision.[12] Similarly, China's application for leadership of CICA was submitted as early as 2012 and probably decided sooner internally, and leaked preparatory documents contained the anti-alliance language that so many found objectionable in 2014 as early as 2010.[13]

TERRITORIAL DISPUTES

At first glance, China's territorial assertiveness seems to be a unique product of Xi's diplomacy. Indeed, Hu neither declared an air defense identification zone in the East China Sea nor engaged in land reclamation and militarization in the South China Sea, while Xi did both. Xi also had deep enough interest in these issues to have assumed leadership of the then newly created Maritime Rights Protection Leading Small Group (中央海洋权益工作领导小组) in mid-2012, shortly before taking office.[14]

Even so, the break between the two leaders is not quite so clear-cut. Hu's administration called for a reassessment of China's territorial approach in his 2009 Ambassadorial Conference address when, in language that starkly departed from previous addresses, he called for China to take a firmer line. China's subsequent handling of disputes in the East and South China Sea—including the 2009 *Impeccable* incident, the 2010 collision between Chinese and Japanese vessels, and the 2012 purchase of the Senkaku Islands by the Japanese government presaged a more assertive policy. When these actions are combined with Hu's authoritative remarks, the conclusion is that China's trajectory on regional disputes was moving in a hawkish direction before Xi assumed power—and well before he assumed leadership of the Maritime Rights Protection Leading Small Group. It seems reasonable to assume that even if Xi had not assumed power, China would still have pushed to consolidate its territorial interests under a different leader.

CONCLUSIONS AND PRINCIPLES FOR U.S. CHINA POLICY

Xi's personality cult and power consolidation likely give him considerable policy autonomy. But the fact that Xi has such autonomy does not mean he has defied the Party's consensus on foreign policy. Instead, Chinese grand strategy under Xi should be understood as an extension of underlying trends and policies, many of which began with his predecessor Hu Jintao's post–global financial crisis strategic shift. China's focus on blue-water capabilities, its infrastructure investments and economic coercion, its launch of AIIB and leadership of CICA, and its growing territorial assertiveness all have roots in Hu's tenure. More fundamentally, key Xi-era ideological phrases like "national rejuvenation" and "the two centenary goals" that are understood as suggesting a loose timetable for China's ascent themselves hearken back decades—and in the case of rejuvenation, a century.

This continuity has a few implications for the principles that guide U.S. China policy. First, those who view China's foreign policy through the narrow and highly personalized lens of the present miss important patterns and trends that connect today's behavior to yesterday's choices. The danger of such oversight is to write off China's strident international activism as a result of the whims of one paramount leader rather than the outgrowth of long-term Party planning and consensus. Once one understands the continuity in China's approach, it only increases the urgency of a similarly focused, coordinated, and long-term American strategic response.

Second, efforts to shift Chinese tactics on cyber theft or North Korea may well be successful in the short-term, but pushing China to abandon a more assertive and revisionist policy, especially in Asia, will be unlikely to succeed given its deep roots. Indeed, China would likely have embarked on a more assertive foreign policy even if Xi had not assumed his paramount position in 2012. Accordingly, the increasing tension in U.S.-China ties is likely to remain robust with changes in Chinese leadership, relatively unaffected by American concessions, and immune to efforts to reassure or socialize China. Instead, it is likely to endure into the future.

For these reasons, the United States should not allow overconfidence about its ability to change or shape the Party consensus to dissuade it from pursuing a competitive approach, nor should it allow misguided beliefs about whether tougher U.S. policies embolden "hard-liners" to deter it from protecting its economic and political interests. China's assertiveness in Asia is unlikely to disappear, and U.S. China policy must begin with a clear-eyed recognition of that fact if it is to secure American interests and successfully manage strategic competition.

NOTES

1. For example, see Jiang Zemin's 9th Ambassadorial Conference Address in 1998, Jiang Zemin [江泽民], *Jiang Zemin Selected Works* [江泽民文选]. Vol. 2 of 3. Beijing: People's Press [人民出版社], 2006, p. 195–206. See also Hu's remarks at a 2003 diplomatic symposium in Hu Jintao [胡锦涛], *Hu Jintao Selected Works* [胡锦涛文选]. Vol. 2 of 3. Beijing: People's Press [人民出版社], 2016, p. 93.

2. Hu Jintao [胡锦涛], *Hu Jintao Selected Works* [胡锦涛文选]. Vol. 3. Beijing: People's Press [人民出版社], 2016, no. 3: 234–246.

3. M. Taylor Fravel, "Revising Deng's Foreign Policy," *The Diplomat,* January 17, 2012, https://thediplomat.com/2012/01/revising-dengs-foreign-policy-2/.

4. Zheng Wang, "Not Rising, but Rejuvenating: The 'Chinese Dream,'" *The Diplomat*, February 5, 2013, https://thediplomat.com/2013/02/chinese-dream-draft.

5. Jiang Zemin [江泽民], "Hold High the Great Banner of Deng Xiaoping Theory for an All-round Advancement of the Cause of Building Socialism with Chinese Characteristics" into the 21st Century" [高举邓小平理论伟大旗帜，把建设有中国特色社会主义事业全面推向二十一世纪].

6. Ian Storey, "China's 'Malacca Dilemma,'" *China Brief*, April 12, 2006, https://jamestown.org/program/chinas-malacca-dilemma/.

7. James Mulvenon, "Chairman Hu and the PLA's 'New Historic Missions,'" *China Leadership Monitor*, no. 27 (January 2009), 1–11, https://media.hoover.org/sites/default/files/documents/CLM27JM.pdf.

8. Research Group of the Ocean Development Strategy Center [海洋发展战略研究所课题组], *China's Ocean Development Report 2010* [中国海洋发展报告2010] (Beijing: China Ocean Press [海洋出版社], 2010), p. 482.

9. http://cpc.people.com.cn/n/2012/1109/c349998-19530612.html.

10. For this address, see Hu Jintao [胡锦涛], "Firmly March on the Path of Socialism with Chinese Characteristics and Strive to Complete the Building of a Moderately Prosperous Society in All Respects [坚定不移沿着中国特色社会主义道路前进　为全面建成小康社会而奋斗]."

11. James Reilly, "China's Unilateral Sanctions," *Washington Quarterly* 35, no. 4 (October 2012): 121–133, www.tandfonline.com/doi/full/10.1080/0163660X.2012.726428.

12. David Dollar, "China's Transition at Home and Abroad" (Brookings Event,

Washington D.C., July 21, 2015), www.brookings.edu/wp-content/uploads/2015/07
/20150721_china_transition_transcript.pdf.

13. "Statement by H.E. Mr. Chen Guoping at CICA Meeting of Ministers of
Foreign Affairs" (CICA Meeting of Ministers of Foreign Affairs, Ankara, 2012),
www.s-cica.org/page.php?page_id=605&lang=1.

14. Bonnie Glaser, "China's Maritime Rights Protection Leading Small Group—
Shrouded in Secrecy," Center for Strategic and International Studies, September 11,
2015, https://amti.csis.org/chinas-maritime-rights-protection-leading-small-group
-shrouded-in-secrecy/.

2

Beijing's Nonmilitary Coercion— Tactics and Rationale

KETIAN ZHANG

As China has become a rising power, Chinese coercion—the use or threats of negative actions to force the target state to change behavior—has garnered the attention of foreign policymakers. Although China uses military coercion less in the post–Cold War period, it has become increasingly well versed in the use of nonmilitarized coercion, including diplomatic and economic sanctions.[1]

This chapter discusses the rationale and tactics of Chinese nonmilitary coercion in non–core interest issue areas, such as human rights and the deployment of Terminal High Altitude Area Defense (THAAD). President Xi Jinping's coming into power has not changed the rationale and tactics of Chinese coercion. China has continued to be a cautious bully. The chapter first discusses the breadth of Chinese core interests and demonstrates that China's definition of core interests has been stable despite leadership changes. It then examines Chinese nonmilitary coercion during the Hu Jintao and Xi Jinping administrations, using the 2010 Nobel Peace Prize in Norway and the 2017 deployment of THAAD in South Korea as cases. The chapter concludes by offering policy implications for the United States.

THE CONTINUITY OF CHINA'S CORE INTERESTS

The Chinese government definition of "core interests" has always been stable. Then Chinese state councilor Dai Bingguo stated in 2010 that the Chinese Communist Party's (CCP's) leadership, territorial integrity, and continuous economic and social development were China's core interests while also singling out Taiwan as a core interest.[2] This hierarchy of Chinese national interests remained unchanged even after Xi Jinping came into power.[3] Nevertheless, it is important to examine Chinese coercion regarding some of its non–core interest issues, including human rights and nuclear proliferation. These may not be core Chinese interests, but they may indeed be core interests of the United States.

CHINESE COERCION AGAINST NORWAY
REGARDING THE NOBEL PEACE PRIZE

China imposed sanctions on Norway after the Nobel Peace Prize was awarded to Chinese political dissident Liu Xiaobo. Immediately after the award, China imposed both diplomatic and economic sanctions. The immediate goal of Chinese coercion was to stop Norway from "meddling with China's internal affairs," according to former Norwegian diplomats based in Beijing.[4] The broader goal, however, was preventing other countries from following Norway and engaging in activities "that harmed Chinese national interests," as manifested by the Chinese Embassy in Norway's letters to other foreign embassies.[5] This suggests that the rationale of Chinese coercion goes beyond a particular target state: China also aims to deter other countries from engaging in similar activities in the future.

Regarding economic sanctions, China canceled exchange visits between the two sides, terminated trade negotiations, and froze the negotiation on free-trade treaties.[6] China also banned Norwegian salmon export to China—Norway's market for fresh salmon in China fell from about 90 percent in 2010 to under 30 percent in the first half of 2013.[7] Interviews with former Norwegian diplomats confirmed this ban on Norwegian salmon.[8] Former Norwegian diplomats further indicated that some fully or partially state owned enterprises from Norway had difficulty getting contracts in China.[9]

As for diplomatic sanctions, China denied a visa for a former Norwegian prime minister to visit China.[10] Also, starting in January 2013, all European countries except Norway became beneficiaries of the policy of non-visa transit.[11] As of 2014, diplomatic sanctions were still ongoing, and senior-level exchanges between Norway and China were stalled.[12] The manner through which China coerced Norway did not change, despite the leadership changes. Norway eventually relented. In May 2014, the Norwegian government publicly announced that the prime minister would not meet with the Dalai Lama.[13] In December 2016, the foreign ministers of China and Norway met in Beijing, and the Norwegian foreign minister stated that Norway "will not support any behavior that harms China's core and important interests while upholding the 'one-China' policy."[14]

This sanctions episode spanned from the Hu Jintao administration to Xi Jinping's reign. Yet the practices stayed the same, suggesting that there is continuity in China's sanctions rationale and tactics, about which several points are worth noting.

First, Chinese sanctions, in this case, are symbolic and serve as a signaling device. China was not a major salmon export destination for Norway.[15] Less than 2 percent of Norway's salmon went to China, even prior to this episode.[16] In other words, Norway could easily find alternative markets. Chinese sanctions were therefore symbolic and did not actually inflict damage on the Norwegian economy. What is interesting, however, is *how* China imposed the salmon ban.[17] According to Norwegian diplomats, Norwegian salmon was held up in Shanghai for "food safety" issues.[18] Norwegian diplomats noted that just as Airbus was the pride of Europe, salmon was a "national fish" and "national symbol" of Norway.[19] To imply that the salmon had "safety issues" was severely insulting to Norwegians.[20] Although China's sanctions were largely symbolic, they sent a clear signal to Norway and other countries that China wanted Norway to change its behavior.

Second, Chinese economic sanctions tend to be narrowly focused on sectors that are not of importance to the Chinese economy. For example, Norwegian diplomats noted that China needed Norway for its expertise in deepwater drilling, which was critical if China wanted to make advances in energy exploration in the South China Sea.[21] Consequently, a Chinese state-owned enterprise—Blue Star—bought a Norwegian hydro company in 2011 despite the cold bilateral relations.[22] In short, China was highly calculative and risk-averse in terms of what sectors to impose sanctions on, and the bottom line for China was to avoid economic loss. This explains why Chinese sanctions tend to be small and highly selective, especially if China depends on the target state for specific sectors.

Third, Chinese economic sanctions tend to target large state-owned enterprises or large private businesses, as former Norwegian diplomats noted.[23] China's tactics with Norway worked because the Norwegian business community had been pressuring the government to improve relations with China.[24]

CHINESE COERCION AGAINST SOUTH KOREA REGARDING THAAD

China has been systematically opposed to U.S. ballistic missile defense systems (known as THAAD) in South Korea. China has indeed imposed economic sanctions on South Korea for its agreement with the United States to install THAAD.[25] China's goals of coercing South Korea were clear: the Foreign Ministry repeatedly opposed THAAD and urged South Korea to stop the installation process and refrain from "venturing further into the wrong path."[26] Similar to the coercion episode against Norway, China's rationale was to prevent the target state or other states from engaging in behavior that further "harms" China's interests.

The sanctions episode against South Korea regarding THAAD is another example suggesting the continuity of China's sanctions practices regardless of who is in power. The sanctions were initiated during Xi Jinping's term, and although the issue was not about human rights but rather missile defense, China's rationale and tactics were similar to those used against Norway.

First, Chinese coercion in response to THAAD was symbolic and served as a signaling device. For example, China blocked the streaming of the latest South Korean music and dramas on Chinese websites and TV channels.[27] K-pop stars had to cancel their concerts in China.[28] The ban was not lifted until November 2017.[29] Similarly, by March 2017, China had closed more than twenty stores of Lotte Mart, a South Korea supermarket chain that operated stores in China and other Asian countries.[30] China cited "fire safety concerns" as the reason for the closures.[31] Lotte was eventually forced to abandon and sell all of its Lotte Mart stores in China.[32] Chinese coercion did not touch on major sectors of Sino-Korean economic relations.

Second, just as in the Norwegian case, China was calculative in what businesses it decided to coerce and did not impose sanctions on sectors that were important to China. Coercing Lotte Marts did not affect the Chinese retail industry because China had numerous foreign and domestic "exit options." Furthermore, China did not impose sanctions on electronics, industrial chemical products, and optical medical equipment, all of which China needed from South Korea.[33] Despite the THAAD episode, South Korean exports to China in 2017 actually increased by 14.2 percent, and South Korea enjoyed a surplus of U.S. $44.3 billion.[34] Put simply, China did not sanction the sectors that it needed the most.

Third, China exhibited a consistent pattern in coercing large private or state-owned businesses in the THAAD episode. The Lotte Group is South Korea's fifth-largest business conglomerate, and China was Lotte Mart's largest overseas investment destination.

POLICY IMPLICATIONS AND SUGGESTIONS FOR THE UNITED STATES AND ALLIES

Policymakers should be aware of China's logic and coercion tactics. Chinese coercion serves as a signaling device. Interestingly, China seems to have a rationale for using compellence to deter. At the same time, China is highly calculative and rarely utilizes coercion with great magnitude. When imposing economic sanctions, China singles out large state-owned or private businesses of the target state from which China has exit options, while making sure to avoid sectors of the target state that China needs the most, most of which are high-tech machinery or intermediary machinery products. Economic concerns play an important role in China's coercive calculation.

There are several policy implications for the United States. First, the United States can use its economic leverage against China to deter China from coercing the United States. Even though China has been emphasizing domestic consumption in recent years, it will be a long time before China transitions into an economy based on domestic consumption. The United States is still China's most important foreign market. China still needs the United States for technological transfers and high-tech products. Also, the United States has leverage in the realm of foreign direct investment, as China has been pushing its indigenous companies to be globally competitive. For the time being, China needs the United States more than vice versa. The United States should clearly signal its leverage to China, threatening economic sanctions, preferably in private, if U.S. national security interests are at stake, and reassuring China that there will be no sanctions if China complies. Using private channels for such communications may help to avoid affecting China's reputation for resolve. It is important to note that an all-out trade war that receives full media coverage will not be as effective as targeted economic pressure done privately. The United States could also further limit China's exit options by enlisting the help of U.S. allies, especially if the values and security interests of U.S. allies are in danger. If China can use carrots and sticks, so can the United States.

Second, the United States needs to stay at the cutting edge of technological advancement so that China continues to depend on the United States for technological transfers. The United States should commit to devoting sufficient resources and talent to technological development. As MIT's president L. Rafael Reif has noted, China's challenge can be America's opportunity.[35]

Third, to hedge against the potential risk of Chinese coercion, large U.S. businesses may consider strengthening alternative markets and investment destinations. This is a particularly viable option since the increase in labor costs in the Chinese market might begin to outweigh the benefit of investing in China. With cheaper labor costs, ASEAN countries, for example, have huge potential and would most likely welcome U.S. investment to counter Chinese influence.

Fourth, what should the United States do when China bullies U.S. allies? What should U.S. messages be to its friends and allies? U.S. policymakers first need to have in mind a clear hierarchy in terms of what the United States most values. Does the United States value alliance credibility enough that it is willing to bear the risk of a potential escalation of conflicts with China on behalf of its allies? Which allies and issue areas are important enough to justify the risk of escalation? In a sense, a healthy debate on U.S. grand strategy is much needed. Quietly and privately utilizing nonmilitarized tools of influence can lower the risk of escalation. As for U.S. messages to its allies, there is a danger of a "resolve dilemma" in that both China and U.S. allies want to establish resolve. Nevertheless, as is true for the United States, U.S. allies can benefit from quietly increasing the geopolitical pressure for China to avoid using military coercion. "Quiet rebalancing," therefore, might be a better option for both the United States and its allies.

NOTES

1. See, for example, Ketian Zhang, "Cautious Bully: Reputation, Resolve, and Beijing's Use of Coercion in the South China Sea," *International Security* 44, no. 1 (Summer 2019), 117–159.

2. Ibid.

3. Central Party School, *Xi Jinping guanyu zongti guojia anquan guan lunshu*

zhanbian [Xi Jinping's view on comprehensive national security](Beijing: Zhong-yang Wenxian Chubanshe, 2018), 40–48.

4. Interview, Beijing, June 12, 2014

5. Chinese Ministry of Foreign Affairs (Hereafter MFA) Press Conference, December 9, 2010, www.chinese-embassy.no/chn/zjsg/sgxw/t775762.htm.

6. Sewell Chan, "Norway and China Restore Ties, 6 Years After Nobel Prize Dispute," *New York Times*, December 19, 2016, www-nytimes-com.mutex.gmu.edu /2016/12/19/world/europe/china-norway-nobel-liu-xiaobo.html?_ga=2.131196047 .1045674104.1610037760-577618797.1610037760.

7. "Norway Penetrates China Blockage through Vietnam," *Nordic Page*, August 31, 2013, www.tnp.no/norway/economy/3936-salmon-norway-penetrates-china -blockage-through-vietnam.

8. Interview, Beijing, June 12, 2014.

9. Ibid.

10. MFA Press Conference, June 13, 2012, www.360doc.com/content/12/0614/ 01/5646261_218019392.shtml.

11. Ye Fan, "Beijing guojing mianqian, nuowei shoupaiji" [Norway was denied visa-free-transit trips to China], Voice of America, December 7, 2012, www.voa chinese.com/a/beijing-to-allow-visa-free-transit-trips-20121206/1559981.html.

12. Interview, Beijing, June 12, 2014.

13. Ibid.

14. MFA, "Wangyi yu nuowei waijiaodachen bulande juxing huitan" [Wangyi met with the Norwegian foreign minister], *Remin Net*, December 19, 2016, http:// world.people.com.cn/n1/2016/1219/c1002-28961518.html.

15. Interview, Beijing, June 12, 2014.

16. Ibid.

17. See also, Peter Harrell, Elizabeth Rosenberg, and Edoardo Saravalle, *China's Use of Coercive Economic Measures* (Washington, DC: CNAS, June 2018), www .cnas.org/publications/reports/chinas-use-of-coercive-economic-measures.

18. Interview, Beijing, June 12, 2014.

19. Ibid.

20. Ibid.

21. Ibid.

22. Ibid.

23. Ibid.

24. Ibid.

25. Jeongseok Lee, "Back to Normal? The End of the THAAD Dispute between China and South Korea," *China Brief* 17, no. 15 (November 22, 2017), https:// jamestown.org/program/back-normal-end-thaad-dispute-china-south-korea.

26. MFA Press Conference, March 6, 2017, www.fmprc.gov.cn/web/fyrbt_673021 /jzhsl_673025/t1443469.shtml; MFA Press Conference, March 7, 2017, www.fmprc .gov.cn/web/fyrbt_673021/jzhsl_673025/t1443750.shtml.

27. "Thaad Row: China Blocks Streaming of Korean Dramas," *Straits Times*, February 27, 2017, www.straitstimes.com/asia/east-asia/thaad-row-china-blocks

-streaming-of-korean-dramas; MFA Press Conference, March 1, 2017, www.fmprc
.gov.cn/web/fyrbt_673021/jzhsl_673025/t1442434.shtml.

28. Daniel Sanchez, "Lee Kwang Soo, BTS, EXO in Trouble after China-Korean
Conflict," *Digital Music News*, March 6, 2017, www.digitalmusicnews.com/2017/03
/06/china-korea-thaad-conflict-kpop/.

29. AKP Staff, "China's Ban on Korean Entertainment Lifted, MAMAMOO's
Performance in China Broadcast Live," *Allkpop*, November 3, 2017, www.allkpop.
com/article/2017/11/chinas-ban-on-korean-entertainment-lifted-mamamoos
-performance-in-china-broadcast-live.

30. MFA Press Conference, March 6, 2017.

31. MFA Press Conference, March 7, 2017.

32. "South Korea's Lotte to Abandon China Supermarkets Chain," *Financial
Times*, October 11, 2017, www.ft.com/content/647f8c04-ee3f-393b-9bb0-4beff1e
259fb.

33. Chinese Ministry of Commerce, "2017nian hangul huowu maoyi ji zhonghan
shuangbian maoyi gaiguang" [Country Report: an overview of Sino-Korean
bilateral trade in 2017], https://countryreport.mofcom.gov.cn/record/view110209
.asp?news_id=57568.

34. Ibid.

35. L. Rafael Reif, "China's Challenge Is America's Opportunity," *New York
Times*, August 8, 2018, www.nytimes.com/2018/08/08/opinion/china-technology
-trade-united-states.html.

3

Xi Jinping's "Proregress"

Domestic Moves toward
a Global China

CHENG LI

The 2018 Shanghai Biennale, a reputable, international contemporary art exhibition held in China's frontier city of global engagement, attracted public attention for its ingenious and thought-provoking thematic title in both English and Chinese. The English title was "Proregress," a word coined by the American poet E.E. Cummings in 1931, combining "progress" and "regress."[1] The word reflects the profound contradictions and anxieties that plagued both the imperative for transformation and the barriers of stagnation in the early decades of the twentieth century. Interestingly, the Chinese thematic title of the Biennale employed the rarely used term *yubu*, in reference to the mystical Daoist ritual dance of ancient China, where the dancer appears to be moving forward while simultaneously going backward, or vice versa.

While this symbolism can apply to various paradoxical phenomena and perhaps the global context in general, it is particularly valuable in assessing Chinese president Xi Jinping's consolidation of power and domestic socio-economic policies. Since ascending to the pinnacle of China's leadership in 2012, Xi has become known for solidifying the Chinese Communist Party (CCP) and his direct command over the People's Liberation Army (PLA), especially over the past few years. His administration has tightened restrictions on civil society and has fiercely enforced censorship of the internet and media.[2] Among his many unanticipated moves, the action that has arguably made the greatest waves was the abolishment of presidential term limits in March 2018. This move was widely critiqued as a step backward in the decades-long political institutionalization in the country—a "political regression" that effectively reversed Deng Xiaoping's experimentation with intraparty factional checks and balances as well as succession norms.[3]

Despite his crystal-clear inclination for strongman politics and his ambition to cement China's status as a global power, Xi has nevertheless also pursued a fragile balance through a number of important policy moves, including the following:

- Portraying himself as the inheritor of the legacies of both Mao Zedong and Deng Xiaoping, who represented two different styles of political leadership and socioeconomic policies

- Consolidating power based on both his communist "red nobility" status (princeling [*taizidang*]) and solidifying his legitimacy through populism and his understanding of "ordinary people"

- Promoting private-sector development and foreign investment in some aspects while asserting greater state control in others

- Showing willingness to compromise with the Trump administration on a trade deal while preparing for a technology war with the United States

- Offering contradictory clues regarding whether China seeks to be a revisionist power or to preserve the status quo in the post–Cold War international order

- Signaling willingness to change the official verdict on Dr. Li Wenliang (one of the most widely recognized whistleblowers during the initial outbreak of COVID-19 in Wuhan) and to regard him as a national hero, while continuing to tighten media control and suppress dissent

These *yubu,* or contradictory moves, by Xi Jinping—or proregress— can be attributed to several factors. In ruling the world's most populous country, full of divergent views and conflicting interests, Xi has realized the need to maximize public support by aligning with diverse constituencies and socioeconomic trends. Some of Xi's moves are primarily directed to benefit domestic audiences and may not make sense to international spectators. This is what Harvard professor Robert Putnam has described as "two-level games" in a general context.[4] Given that Xi needs to play two "games of chess" simultaneously (one domestic and the other foreign), his motives and objectives can be better understood if one observes both chess boards instead of just one.

Perhaps most importantly, national leaders in today's rapidly changing world must acknowledge and adjust to the political and economic realities of their time. Xi is no exception. Recently, for example, in the wake of both a domestic economic slowdown and a trade war (or even an all-encompassing decoupling) with the United States that have damaged the confidence of China's middle class, Xi has adopted tax cuts and more easily accessible bank loans to promote private-sector development and ease the anxieties of arguably the country's most important socioeconomic constituency. In recognizing the strong linkages between domestic concerns and international interests, one may reasonably argue that the former is more important than the latter simply because, from Xi's perspective, the former is the power base without which he cannot make an impact on the latter.

Xi Jinping's two most recent parallel domestic policy moves—shifting his identity from a princeling to a populist by launching an ambitious program for poverty elimination and enlarging the country's largest metropolis clusters as the new engines for economic growth—deserve particular attention among policymakers and analysts in Washington. This discussion can help avoid miscalculations, overreactions, or underestimations of Xi's power.

SHIFTING IDENTITIES AND POVERTY ELIMINATION

Arguably, the most important political maneuvering that Xi has employed has been the shift in his identity from a princeling to a populist leader. That shift has accompanied drastic changes in the composition of the national leadership and major policy moves. Xi Jinping was born "red"—the "princeling" son of Xi Zhongxun, a veteran revolutionary leader during the Communist takeover of China in 1949. When Xi Jinping was a young boy, his father was secretary general (chief of staff) of the State Council and was primarily responsible for assisting Chairman Mao and Premier Zhou Enlai with running the government.

When Xi Jinping assumed the party chairmanship in 2012, his background as a princeling loomed as a large part of his identity, not least of all because his most important political allies at the time were fellow prince-lings who collectively held unprecedentedly strong representation in both the civilian and military leadership.[5] In 2012, for example, four of the seven members of the Politburo Standing Committee (PSC), the most powerful decisionmaking body in the country, were princelings.[6] In the twenty-five-member Politburo, nine members (36 percent) were princelings. During his first term, Xi had no choice but to lean on these princelings to balance the power of Hu Jintao's protégés, who usually hailed from humble family backgrounds and advanced their careers from leadership positions of the then powerful competing faction—the Chinese Communist Youth League (known as *tuanpai* in Chinese).

When public criticism of rampant official corruption peaked at the time of the 18th Party Congress in 2012, Xi seemed to have acutely grasped these political tensions. Unsurprisingly, his foremost priority became fighting of-ficial corruption and implementing tight restrictions on the use of public funds by officials—political moves that not only helped obscure their own princeling identities but also helped present them as "leaders of the people." Given that Xi had successfully undermined the power of *tuanpai* in his first term, he had little remaining political incentive to rely heavily on prince-lings. Not surprisingly, Xi began distancing himself from princelings and drastically reducing their representation in the leadership. At the 19th Party Congress formed in 2017, the number of princelings in the Politburo dropped by more than half—from 9 in the 18th Party Congress to 4.[7] Figure 3-1 shows the significant decrease in the number of princelings on the 376-member Central Committee (CC) from 41 on the 18th CC to 20 on the 19th CC, a 50 percent drop. The 19th CC has the lowest number of princelings of the past four Central Committees.

These political moves have helped obscure Xi's princeling identity. But to bolster his reputation as a "leader of the people," Xi needed to deliver on his socioeconomic policies. Xi's pledge to eliminate poverty in China by 2020 has endeared him to the general public, particularly in the rural inland areas where Hu Jintao's protégés have traditionally had the upper hand in garnering support. In 2013, Xi coined the term "precise poverty alleviation" (*jingzhun fupin*) to suggest that he would take a more strident approach to eliminating impoverished conditions.[8] The Xi administration has substantially increased expenditures on poverty alleviation. Poverty al-leviation funds allocated under the central government budget amounted to 282.2 billion yuan (US$41.7 billion) during Xi's first term (2012–17), more

Figure 3-1. **Changes in the Number of Princelings in the Central Committee of the CCP, 2002–2017**

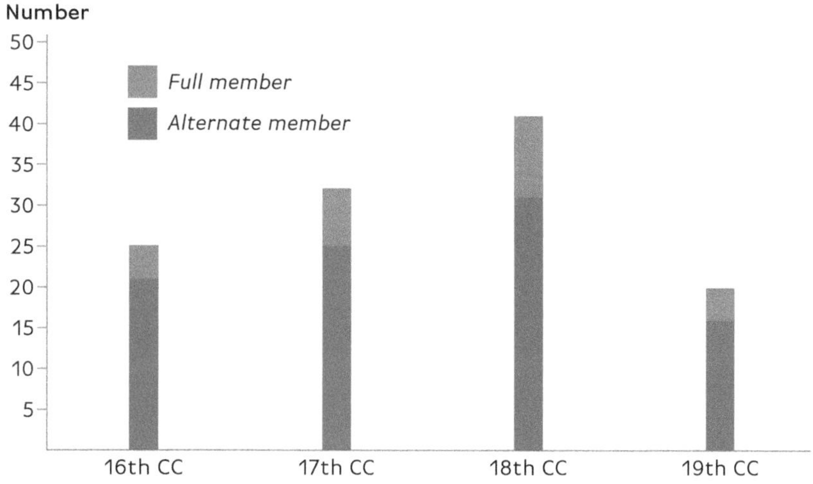

Source: Cheng Li's database

than double the level of the previous five years under the Hu Jintao-Wen Jiabao administration. Figure 3-2 shows that the annual funding dedicated to poverty alleviation in 2019 reached 126.1 billion yuan—6.4 times greater than the 19.7 billion yuan expended in 2009, and a sixteen-fold increase over the 7.8 billion yuan expended in 1999.

As recently noted by Bill Gates, approximately 800 million people have been lifted out of poverty in China over the past 40 years.[9] This figure is approximately ten times the population of Germany, the most populous country in Europe. Although Xi cannot claim credit for most of the poverty reduction in China, he has been fortunate to be sitting in power during the final push of this decades-long campaign. Xi's contributions toward poverty elimination may constitute some of the most important political capital he has accrued, which he can now utilize to overturn decades of Chinese political norms as a Mao-like figure and enhance China's (and his own) influence on the world stage.

Figure 3-2. **The Drastic Increase in Expenditures on Poverty Alleviation under Xi**

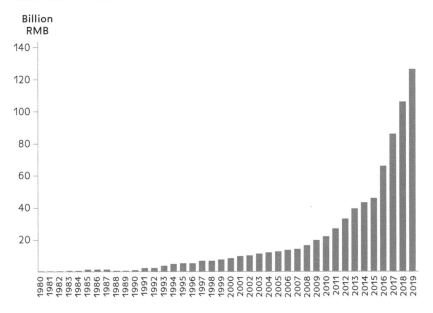

Source: 2019, http://www.gov.cn/xinwen/2019-05/17/content_5392632.htm; 2018, http://www
.gov.cn/xinwen/2018-05/04/content_5288150.htm; 2017, http://www.gov.cn/xinwen/2017-06
/08/content_5200771.htm

STRETCHING CHINA'S SIX SUPER METROPOLISES AND THE NEW ENGINE OF GROWTH

Xi's campaign for poverty alleviation has enhanced his popularity among the poor rural population primarily located in China's inland regions.[10] But what has driven China's economic growth is the country's middle class, the members of which disproportionately reside in coastal metropolises. The Xi administration has apparently grasped the strategic importance of Chinese urban development at a time when China is confronting not only an economic slowdown, due to major structural changes in the Chinese economy, but also the devastating effects of economic decoupling with the United States and the global economic repercussions from the COVID-19 pandemic.

In 2008, long before China's encounter with these new challenges, Liu He, then an economic adviser to the top leadership and now vice premier in charge of financial and economic affairs, called for the development of "megacity circles" (*teda chengshi qun*). Liu argued that the new wave of urbanization should center around metropolis clusters instead of a "small town development strategy" (*chengzhenhua*). Beijing, Tianjin, Shanghai, Chongqing, Shenzhen, and Guangzhou are the country's top cities in terms of contributions to the GDP, and the Chinese media have often branded them as the "six super megacities."[11] They have formed the four most important "megacity circles" across the country. According to a recent Chinese official report, China's top ten cities contributed almost a quarter of the GDP to the national total in 2018.[12] These cities are also the main indicators of China's middle-class consumption. Altogether, the total aggregate GDP of these cities was 15 trillion yuan (US$2.2 trillion) in 2018, roughly equivalent to the total GDP of Brazil in the same year, ranked eighth in the world. The development of these megacities is now closely linked to the new Chinese "dual circulation" (*shuang xunhuan*) strategy that emphasizes advancement of domestic consumption and innovation.

Xi's protégés now occupy the top political postings (party secretaries and mayors) in most of these six cities, which was often not the case during his first term. The party secretaries of the four major cities directly under central government control (Beijing, Shanghai, Tianjin, and Chongqing) routinely serve in the twenty-five-member Politburo. Shenzhen and Guangzhou, which do not have the same status, fall under the leadership of Guangdong Province, where the provincial party secretary, Li Xi, a protégé of Xi Jinping as well, also serves in the Politburo. Because the CCP leadership emphasizes administrative experience gained through serving as a major city party secretary during the reform era, these posts are pivotal steppingstones for aspiring entrants into top posts in the national leadership. Beijing party secretary Cai Qi, Shanghai party secretary Li Qiang, and Chongqing party secretary Chen Min'er all previously worked directly under Xi Jinping in Zhejiang Province, and they, along with Li Xi, are candidates for the next Politburo Standing Committee.

Under the leadership of Xi Jinping, these six super megacities have all recently adopted new strategic development blueprints with some distinct focuses. Given the fact that most of these top municipal leaders are his confidants, Xi apparently intends to grant them decentralized authority—and a much greater degree of autonomy, compared with other regions—to pursue somewhat different approaches in their respective metropolis clusters. These ambitious new plans, as listed here, will potentially lead to a new round of far-reaching economic reforms in the country that merit more international attention:

- The Beijing-Tianjin-Hebei (*Jing-Jin-Ji*) development strategy with new initiatives embracing Xiong'an as China's third special economic zone and making Tongzhou city an annex to Beijing

- The Shanghai and the Yangtze River delta economic integration plan with its concentration on an "entity economy" (*shiti jingji*) and the modern, high-tech manufacturing industry

- The Guangdong-Shenzhen-Hong Kong-Macau Bay Area strategy with its goal of strengthening urban connectivity through the flow of people, logistics, capital, and information in the Greater Bay Area

- The Chongqing-Chengdu corridor development scheme with plans to integrate megacity development with the establishment of so-called characteristic towns (*tese xiaozhen*)

In addition, Xi's appeal for green development is a nod to the widespread concerns and discontent by China's rising middle class over air, water, and soil pollution, and the environmental degradation that has resulted from China's breakneck economic growth. Although China has continuously confronted issues arising from serious environmental degradation, the recent efforts of Chinese authorities to shut down a large number of heavily polluting factories and promote clean usage through a variety of means, such as more energy efficient cars, seem to have yielded positive results. According to EcoWatch, among the twenty cities with the most air pollution in the world in 2018, fifteen were in India and two were in China.[13] Ten years earlier, in 2008, studies by both the World Bank and the Worldwatch Institute showed that sixteen of the world's twenty most air polluted cities were in China.[14]

DOMESTIC POLITICS, GLOBAL IMPLICATIONS

What does this analysis of Xi's consolidation of personal power and domestic major policy initiatives tell us about China's ongoing quest for global preeminence? What are the implications of Xi's performance on his domestic priorities for China's external activism? What is the political and strategic logic of Xi casting himself as a populist strongman leader in Zhongnanhai while at the same time advancing the goal of making China a global power?

Foreign analysts will continue to debate whether Xi's domestic political and socioeconomic moves in recent years reflect foresight or missteps and strengths or weaknesses, but this chapter argues that in many cases both are evident. Xi's insecurity, shared among the party elite as a whole, stems from the CCP's precarious hold on the country. The observations of this analysis—including drastic changes in the composition of the national and key municipal leadership, massive budget increases to eliminate poverty, and preferable policy incentives for super megacities—reveal the pragmatic and adaptive aspects of the leader who holds the reins of the preeminent emerging power in today's world.

China's ongoing global engagement undoubtedly has had a major impact on the international order. Most of these domestic initiatives are arguably driven by the need to respond to the challenges that Xi, the CCP, and China confront, and are not necessarily predetermined by their goal to undermine the status of U.S. supremacy in the world. Yet, the developments during the final year of the Trump administration—the devastating impact of COVID-19, the dire situation in American domestic politics exemplified in the insurrectionist attack on Capitol Hill, and the dangerous deterioration in the bilateral relationship that resulted in a surge of Chinese anti-U.S. nationalism—could reshape Beijing's domestic and foreign policies. To forecast China's future—and to develop a sound and balanced strategy for responding to this rising global power—a thoughtful empirical analysis of the interlocking political, economic, and social factors in the country is essential.

ACKNOWLEDGMENTS: The author thanks two anonymous reviewers, Alison Berman, Kevin Dong, Ryan Hass, James Haynes, Ryan McElveen, Anna Newby, and Amanda Oh for offering constructive criticism and suggestions for this chapter.

NOTES

1. Cuauhtémoc Medina, "Theme of the 12th Shanghai Biennale: Proregress: Art in an Age of Historical Ambivalence," 12th Shanghai Biennale website, www .shanghaibiennale.org/en/page/detail/308cw.html.

2. For more criticism of Xi's hardliner political moves, see Richard McGregor, *Xi Jinping: The Backlash* (New York and Sydney: Penguin Books Australia, 2019), and Susan L. Shirk, "China in Xi's 'New Era': The Return to Personalistic Rule," *Journal of Democracy* 29, no. 2 (April 2018): 22–36, www.journalofdemocracy.org/ articles/china-in-xis-new-era-the-return-to-personalistic-rule/.

3. For post-Deng political experimentation in "collective leadership" and institutionalized political succession, see Cheng Li, *Chinese Politics in the Xi Era: Reassessing Collective Leadership* (Washington, DC: Brookings Institution Press, 2016).

4. Robert D. Putnam, "Diplomacy and Domestic Politics: The Logic of Two -Level Games," *International Organization* 42, no. 3 (Summer 1988): 427–460, www .jstor.org/stable/2706785?seq=1#page_scan_tab_contents.

5. Princelings, by definition, are leaders born to (or married to the offspring of) the families of Communist Revolution veterans or other high-ranking officials, namely those at the level of vice minister, vice governor, PLA major general, or above.

6. Cheng Li, "Rule of the Princelings," *Cairo Review of Global Affairs*, no. 8 (Winter 2013): 34–47, www.thecairoreview.com/essays/rule-of-the-princelings/.

7. Cheng Li, *Chinese Politics in the Xi Jinping Era*, 270.

8. Xi Jinping, "Tan jingzhun fupin: Kai duile 'yaofang zi', caineng ba diao 'qiong genzi'" [On precision poverty alleviation: When you have found the right "medical formula," you can unplug the "poor roots"], *Renmin wang* [People's Daily], February 18, 2019, http://cpc.people.com.cn/xuexi/n1/2019/0218/c385474-30759690.html.

9. "Bill Gates tongguo xinhuashe fabu dujia shipin zanshang Zhongguo cujin quanqiu fazhan suozuo gongxian" [Bill Gates releases exclusive video through Xinhua News Agency praising China's contributions to promoting global development], Xinhua News Agency, February 13, 2019, http://xhpfmapi.zhongguowang shi.com/vh512/share/5697369.

10. When it comes to assessing Xi's popularity, we are constrained by the absence of independent polling in China. Nevertheless, reports based on those foreign observers who live in China's poverty-stricken regions have documented favorable public sentiment. See, for example, Matthew Chitwood, "For Rural Chinese, Economic Reform Is Worth the 40-Year Wait," Institute of Current World Affairs Newsletter, January 29, 2019, www.icwa.org/current-fellows/matthew-chit wood/?lcp_page0=3#lcp_instance_0.

11. Sha Lu, "Chaoda teda chengshi dafu zengjia luohu guimo" [Large megacities increase populations], *Xinjing bao* [Beijing News], April 9, 2019, http://news.163. com/19/0409/07/ECA8M0180001875N.html.

12. "Zhongguo qian shi chengshi GDP jin quanguo zong liang si fen zhi yi" [China's top ten cities constitute almost a quarter of national total GDP], *Sina*, January 22, 2018, http://finance.sina.com.cn/china/gncj/2018-01-22/doc-ifyqtycx1 482169.shtml.

13. Olivia Rosane, "The World's 20 Most Polluted Cities in 2018," *EcoWatch*, March 6, 2019, www.ecowatch.com/worlds-most-polluted-cities-2630812632.html.

14. "The World's 10 Worst Cities," *Popular Science*, June 23, 2008, www.popsci .com/environment/article/2008-06/worlds-10-dirtiest-cities/; "16 of World's 20 Most-Polluted Cities in China," Voice of America, October 31, 2009, www.voanews .com/archive/worldwatch-institute-16-worlds-20-most-polluted-cities-china.

EAST ASIA

*How Is China Seeking to Reshape
the Status Quo across East Asia's
Hotspots, and How Are States
within the Region Responding?*

4

Trying to Loosen the Linchpin

China's Approach to South Korea

JUNG H. PAK

China sees South Korea as a critical part of its effort to establish its pre-eminence in Northeast Asia. South Korea's status in the U.S. alliance architecture as the "linchpin" and its central role regarding North Korea issues, as well as its geographic proximity and economic dynamism, have underscored the country's importance to China's regional strategy. This strategy is driven by a desire to weaken Washington's alliance relationships, increase Beijing's influence on Korean Peninsula affairs, including North Korea's denuclearization, and shape the region to be more amenable to supporting its preferences.[1] Beijing perceives Seoul as the weakest link in the U.S. alliance network, given its perception of South Korea's deference and history of accommodating China's rise relative to other regional players, such as Japan, which considers China a long-term security threat.[2] As the strategic competition between the United States and China shows no signs of abating and China's leaders appear to have more tolerance for conflict with the United States, Beijing's pressure on Seoul will likely intensify and include a range of coercive tools.

BEIJING SEEKING TO EXPLOIT
PERCEIVED GAPS IN ALLIANCE

For most of the two decades following the normalization of bilateral relations in 1992, Beijing primarily employed its soft power—encouraging economic interdependence and people-to-people ties, emphasizing China's desire for peace and prosperity in the region, and highlighting its role as a "good neighbor," for example—to woo South Korea. China and South Korea upgraded the relationship at least five times, according to scholar Min Ye, from a "friendly cooperative relationship" in 1992 to a more robust "enriched strategic cooperative partnership" in 2014.[3] Trade data similarly attest to the upward trajectory. In 1992, bilateral trade totaled a little over $6 billion,[4] but by 2003, that number jumped to $63 billion, making China South Korea's largest trading partner, replacing the United States.[5] Twenty years after normalization, the total was $215 billion.[6]

Seoul has welcomed the blossoming of trade relations and further boosting security cooperation in large part because South Korean leaders view China's cooperation as vital to its North Korea policy, even as its leaders became increasingly wary about the implications of China's rise. But as the U.S.-China strategic competition has intensified, Beijing has made it clear that it is willing to use its growing economic, diplomatic, and military weight to take a more aggressive approach toward South Korea to make it yield to China's preferences.

Over the past several years, Beijing has tried to exploit the seams and gaps in perceived alliance weaknesses and is taking an approach that is a combination of positive assurances and public and private pressure and threats. Such an approach is aimed at demonstrating its regional leadership, while downgrading the U.S. presence and credibility in the region.

First, Beijing is trying to weave greater engagement with both Koreas to increase China's influence on the Korean Peninsula. Despite icy ties that had marked the first seven years of Kim Jong Un's rule, Xi Jinping has accelerated and intensified diplomatic engagement, including visiting Pyongyang in June 2019 for a summit with Kim, the first time a Chinese head of state had done so in fourteen years. With South Korea, Xi will probably use President Moon Jae-in's strong desire to make headway with Pyongyang during his single five-year term to loosen the sanctions regime against North Korea, in line with these leaders' belief that inducements rather than pressure would support their strategic interests, which are at odds with the

U.S. approach of sharpening the choice for Kim between nuclear weapons and economic development.

Second, Beijing is grabbing opportunities to demonstrate its regional leadership, calculating, as former senior State Department official and Brookings nonresident senior fellow Evans J. R. Revere has noted, "that U.S. influence in Northeast Asia is waning and that friction in the U.S.–South Korea alliance, the erosion of the U.S.–South Korea–Japan security cooperation, and a passive U.S. approach to its regional alliances give China a major opportunity to advance its interests."[7] For example, Chinese leaders convened a trilateral meeting with South Korea and Japan in late December 2019. With Chinese premier Li Keqiang hosting Moon and Abe and the three sides issuing a statement in support of dialogue with North Korea on nuclear issues, Beijing played the role of regional anchor.[8]

Moreover, as China has had success in taming the spread of the coronavirus, even as the death toll mounts in the United States, Xi has been using the pandemic as an opportunity to further cozy up to Moon and assert his coronavirus diplomacy. In mid-May, Xi in a phone call with Moon remarked, "Our countries have been a model for international cooperation on infectious diseases."[9] Beijing and Seoul have also started to open up business travel between the two countries to reinvigorate their economies, as China has attempted to shape the narrative globally about its benevolence in helping other countries tackle the pandemic. [10]

Third, these diplomatic moves have been accompanied by more coercive actions. When Washington in 2019 placed sanctions on Chinese telecommunications company Huawei and lobbied its allies to reject the firm's 5G technology, China reciprocated with stern admonitions to its neighbors. The Chinese government warned of unspecified consequences if they cooperated with the Trump administration's ban.[11] Given China's unofficial economic boycott against South Korea to punish it for the 2017 deployment of the Terminal High Altitude Area Defense (THAAD) after North Korea's fourth nuclear test in January 2016—the economic coercion cost South Korea $7.5 billion in losses in 2017 alone—the threat is ominous and hard to ignore.

Finally, more worrisome for their potential to spark an unintended military clash have been China's unauthorized intrusions into South Korean airspace in recent years, designed to test the strength of the U.S.-led security infrastructure and seeking to normalize a more aggressive maritime presence in the region.[12] In 2019, there were over two dozen breaches, including the first China-Russia air patrol in the region—over islands that are disputed by Tokyo and Seoul—sparking a brief military confrontation that involved China, Russia, South Korea, and Japan.[13]

HAZARDS AHEAD

South Korea's role as the linchpin the U.S. alliance architecture in Northeast Asia will continue to be a key target for China. The Moon administration, for its part, will try to avoid risking antagonizing Washington and Beijing—probably unsuccessfully—while taking actions to diversify South Korea's economic and foreign relations via the New Northern Policy and New Southern Policy, which aim to build stronger ties to Russia, Mongolia, and Central Asia, and Southeast Asia and India, respectively.[14]

Beijing's use of coercion to achieve its goals—with South Korea as well as other countries in the region—will probably limit, if not undermine, its attempt to wean Seoul away from Washington, while reinforcing for the Moon administration (and probably successive governments) the need for South Korea to build and cultivate cooperative partnerships with its neighbors, outside the framework of the U.S.-China strategic competition.

For example, despite its attempt to wield its significant economic heft for political influence against its much smaller neighbor in the THAAD case, Beijing found only limited success in shaping Seoul's security choices. Rather than finding a malleable partner in South Korea in its efforts to counter U.S. influence in the region, China's blunt use of coercive economic tools damaged its reputation with Seoul and the South Korean public, while doing little to prevent President Moon's decision to complete the deployment of THAAD antimissile defense units after North Korea's intercontinental ballistic missile tests in July 2017,[15] even as he sought to stabilize ties to Beijing, motivated by, among other issues, China's support for his more concessionary approach to North Korea.

China's actions have had a negative impact on South Korean public opinion. In March 2017, Xi's favorability rating in South Korea was at its lowest ever (at 3.01 out of 5.0), according to a poll conducted by the Asan Institute for Policy Studies.[16] That negative opinion had a long tail. The Chicago Council on Global Affairs polling from 2019 indicated that about 14 percent of South Koreans perceived China as a reliable future partner, compared to 33 percent in 2016 before the THAAD episode.[17] (Meanwhile, 95 percent of South Koreans interviewed by the Asan Institute in 2017 had a favorable view of the alliance with the United States.[18])

Washington must avoid falling into the same trap of viewing Seoul through the lens of competition with Beijing, rather than recognizing its interests and preferences outside the great powers paradigm and perceiving Seoul's actions as part of a zero-sum scorecard between the United States and China. More damaging for U.S. credibility has been its inability or unwillingness to provide assistance to Seoul as it faced Chinese retaliation for THAAD.

Meanwhile, Xi almost certainly sees opportunities to make progress on China's goals because of the significant fissures that have appeared in the U.S.–South Korea alliance under the Trump and Moon administrations. Trump's consistent criticisms of the alliance,[19] the contentious negotiations over his demand for a 400 percent increase in host nation support,[20] and the threat to launch a military strike against North Korea in 2017,[21] with apparent disregard for the devastating implications for the Korean Peninsula, have fueled South Korea's mistrust.

But it is never too late for Washington to heed the counsel of Asia defense expert and Brookings fellow Lindsey W. Ford, who has argued for a "deeper dialogue about the practical challenges that China's influence poses for alliance management." To do so, she adds, Washington "needs to think more creatively about how to help smaller allies and partners offset the risks they are likely to face when they do align with the United States on sensitive issues."[22]

At the same time, the United States should focus on linking Seoul's desire for regional stability, economic growth, and multilateral cooperation toward shaping Beijing's choices on security, governance, and the economy. Showing our decades-old ally greater American willingness to understand and incorporate its concerns seems like a reasonable minimum requirement to preserve a seventy-year-old relationship that since the 1950s has been a part of the "backbone of global security."[23]

Beijing clearly recognizes South Korea's strategic importance. It would behoove Washington to arrive at that conclusion as well.

NOTES

1. Yuan Jingdong, "China's Core Interests and Critical Role in North Korea's Denuclearization," *East Asian Policy* 11, no. 3 (July 2019): 29, https://ideas.repec.org/a/wsi/eapxxx/v11y2019i03ns1793930519000242.html.

2. Jonathan D. Pollack, *Order at Risk: Japan, Korea, and the Northeast Asian Paradox* (Washington, DC: The Brookings Institution, September 2016), www.brookings.edu/research/order-at-risk-japan-korea-and-the-northeast-asian-paradox/; Jae Ho Chung, "East Asia Responds to the Rise of China: Patterns and Variations," *Pacific Affairs* 82, no. 4 (Winter 2009/2010): 663, www.jstor.org/stable/25608969.

3. Min Ye, *China-South Korea Relations in the New Era: Challenges and Opportunities* (Lanham, MD: Lexington Books, 2017), 5; Jaeho Hwang, *The ROK's China Policy under Park Geun-hye: A New Model of ROK-PRC Relations* (Washington, DC: The Brookings Institution, August 14, 2014), 2–3, www.brookings.edu/research/the-roks-china-policy-under-park-geun-hye-a-new-model-of-rok-prc-relations/.

4. Jaeho Hwang, *The ROK's China Policy under Park Geun-hye*.

5. Mark Manyin, Emma Chanlett-Avery, Mary Beth D. Nikitin, Brock R. Williams, Jonathan R. Corrado, *U.S.-South Korea Relations* (Washington, DC: Congressional Research Service, May 23, 2017), 31, https://fas.org/sgp/crs/row/R41481.pdf.

6. Shannon Tiezzi, "It's Official: China, South Korea Sign Free Trade Agreement," *The Diplomat*, June 2, 2015, https://thediplomat.com/2015/06/its-official-china-south-korea-sign-free-trade-agreement/.

7. Evans J. R. Revere, *Lips and Teeth: Repairing China–North Korea Relations* (Washington, DC: The Brookings Institution, November 2019), www.brookings.edu/research/lips-and-teeth-repairing-china-north-korea-relations/.

8. Jing Xuan Teng, "China Shows Off Diplomatic Muscle at Trilateral Meeting with Japan and South Korea," *Japan Times*, December 25, 2019, www.japantimes.co.jp/news/2019/12/25/national/politics-diplomacy/china-japan-south-korea-nuclear-north-korea/#.XlKmp0pOnb0.

9. Yosuke Onchi, "Xi Eyes South Korea as Possible First Post-pandemic Trip in 2020," *Nikkei Asian Review*, May 14, 2020, https://asia.nikkei.com/Politics/International-relations/Xi-eyes-South-Korea-as-possible-first-post-pandemic-trip-in-2020.

10. Chun Han Wong, "China, South Korea Move to Revive Business Travel between Them," *Wall Street Journal*, April 29, 2020, www.wsj.com/articles/china-south-korea-move-to-revive-business-travel-between-them-11588168284.

11. Kate Conger, "China Warns Tech Giants to Defy Trump Ban," *New York Times,* June 9, 2019, www.nytimes.com/2019/06/08/business/economy/china-huawei-trump.html.

12. Jina Kim, "China and Regional Security Dynamics on the Korean Peninsula," in "Korea Net Assessment 2020: Politicized Security and Unchanging Strategic Realities," ed. Chung Min Lee and Kathryn Botto (Washington, DC: Carnegie Endowment for International Peace, March 18, 2020), 55–66, https://carnegieendowment.org/2020/03/18/china-and-regional-security-dynamics-on-korean-peninsula-pub-81235.

13. "Chinese warplane violates Korea's air defense again," Yonhap, November

29, 2019, https://en.yna.co.kr/view/AEN20191129006051325; Andrew Osborn and Joyce Lee, "First Russian-Chinese air patrol in Asia-Pacific draws shots from South Korea," Reuters, July 22, 2019, www.reuters.com/article/us-southkorea-russia-air craft/first-russian-chinese-air-patrol-in-asia-pacific-draws-shots-from-south -korea-idUSKCN1UI072.

14. Lee Jaehyon, "Korea's New Southern Policy: Motivations of 'Peace Cooperation' and Implications for the Korean Peninsula," The Asan Institute for Policy Studies, June 21, 2019, http://en.asaninst.org/contents/koreas-new-southern -policy-motivations-of-peace-cooperation-and-implications-for-the-korean -peninsula/.

15. When campaigning, Moon, who was from the opposition party, indicated that he would reexamine Park's decision, casting doubt on the fate of the THAAD system in South Korea, but he reversed course following Pyongyang's testing of intercontinental ballistic missiles in the fall of 2017. Park Byong-su, "President Moon's THAAD Flip-Flopping Continues with Call for Additional Launchers," *Hankyoreh*, August 3, 2017, http://english.hani.co.kr/arti/english_edition/e_nation al/805423.html.

16. Kim Jiyoon, "South Korean Public Opinion," The Asan Forum, February 27, 2018, www.theasanforum.org/south-korean-public-opinion/.

17. Chicago Council on Global Affairs, "Cooperation and Hedging: Comparing US and South Korean Views of China," October 15, 2019, www.thechicagocouncil .org/publication/cooperation-and-hedging-comparing-us-and-south-korean -views-china.

18. Kim Jiyoon, "South Korean Public Opinion."

19. William Gallo, "In South Korea, a Small but Notable Backlash against Trump," Voice of America, August 20, 2019, www.voanews.com/east-asia-pacific/ south-korea-small-notable-backlash-against-trump.

20. Nicole Gaouette, "Trump Hikes Price Tag for US Forces in Korea almost 400% as Seoul Questions Alliance," CNN, November 15, 2019, www.cnn.com/2019 /11/14/politics/trump-south-korea-troops-price-hike/index.html.

21. Karen DeYoung and John Wagner, "Trump Threatens 'Fire and Fury' in Response to North Korean Threats," *Washington Post*, August 8, 2017, www.wash ingtonpost.com/politics/trump-tweets-news-report-citing-anonymous-sources -on-n-korea-movements/2017/08/08/47a9b9c0-7c48-11e7-83c7-5bd5460f0d7e_ story.html.

22. Lindsey Ford, "Refocusing the China Debate: American Allies and the Question of U.S.-China 'Decoupling,'" The Brookings Institution, *Order from Chaos* (blog), February 7, 2020, www.brookings.edu/blog/order-from-chaos/2020/ 02/07/refocusing-the-china-debate-american-allies-and-the-question-of-us-china -decoupling/.

23. "Summary of the 2018 National Defense Strategy of the United States of America: Sharpening the American Military's Competitive Edge," Arlington, VA, U.S. Department of Defense, January 2018, https://dod.defense.gov/Portals/1/ Documents/pubs/2018-National-Defense-Strategy-Summary.pdf.

5

Lips and Teeth

Repairing China–North Korea Relations

EVANS J. R. REVERE

FROM "LIPS AND TEETH" TO "FIRE AND FURY"

Ties between the Democratic People's Republic of Korea (DPRK) and the People's Republic of China (PRC) are often described as being "as close as lips and teeth"—a reference to the amity of bilateral relations. But there has always been more to this phrase than meets the eye. It comes from the Chinese proverb, "If the lips are gone, the teeth will get cold," and was used to justify Chinese intervention in the Korean War out of fear that the defeat of North Korea (the "lips") would endanger China (the "teeth"). In this context, history tells us that North Korea has not only been a valuable buffer for China, it has also been a vulnerability. Today, that fact deeply informs PRC policy toward the DPRK.

In recent years, China has had ample reason to feel vulnerable. Since Pyongyang's first nuclear test in 2006, its pursuit of nuclear weapons, military provocations, and confrontation with the United States have escalated tensions on the Korean Peninsula. Tensions spiked in 2017 as Pyongyang demonstrated new, more dangerous capabilities, and as U.S. president Donald Trump and North Korean supreme leader Kim Jong Un traded threats and insults, including Trump's threat to unleash "fire and fury" against Pyongyang. The U.S. reaction intensified after North Korea detonated a 250-kiloton hydrogen bomb on September 3, 2017.

CHINA REACTS

As the crisis unfolded, Beijing saw its Korean ally stoking a conflict that could bring chaos, or worse, to China's border. Faced with this possibility, Beijing began to criticize and pressure Pyongyang, sending relations into a tailspin.

At their first summit in April 2017, President Trump pressed Chinese president Xi Jinping for support on North Korea. Following a Trump tweet suggesting Beijing's help would ease trade tensions and after a telephone conversation between the leaders, PRC official media began to criticize Pyongyang.[1]

On April 12, the state-affiliated *Global Times* declared, "China, too, can no longer stand the continuous escalation of the North Korean nuclear issue at its doorstep." The paper warned, "If the North makes another provocative move this month, the Chinese society will be willing to see the (U.N. Security Council) adopt severe restrictive measures that have never been seen before, such as restricting oil imports to the North."[2]

PYONGYANG RESPONDS

North Korea lashed out in response. The DPRK's official news agency accused Beijing of making "a string of absurd and reckless comments." The commentary declared, "China had better ponder over the grave consequences to be entailed by its reckless act of chopping down the pillar of the DPRK-China relations," adding that the DPRK "will never beg for the maintenance of friendship with China."[3]

Pyongyang's September thermonuclear test only deepened Beijing's anger. The test came just hours before Xi Jinping was scheduled to speak at a BRICS (Brazil, Russia, India, China, South Africa) summit in Beijing and undoubtedly embarrassed the Chinese leader.

CHINA'S SANCTIONS CARD

Beijing vented its anger by supporting a series of UN Security Council (UNSC) resolutions designed to punish Pyongyang. During 2017, China voted in favor of four UNSC resolutions, each significantly strengthening economic and trade pressure on North Korea.

China actually sought to water down some of the more aggressive measures sought by Washington, in keeping with Beijing's long-standing concern that excessive pressure on North Korea could cause its collapse. China's effort got it no credit from North Korea. Neither did the fact that, even as Beijing was voting in favor of sanctions, Chinese ships were continuing to transfer oil to North Korea in apparent violation of UNSC restrictions.

In August, North Korea's official news agency said China and Russia should "pay dearly" for supporting new UN sanctions and promised "physical action" by its military in response.[4] When the UNSC voted unanimously in December to strengthen sanctions and called for countries to expel North Korean workers, the DPRK foreign ministry criticized "the U.S. and its followers," implicitly including China and Russia. A defiant North Korea called the new measures "an act of war."[5]

2018: CHINA ON THE OUTSIDE

As 2018 began, PRC-DPRK ties were at their nadir. Beijing had shown Pyongyang the cost of undermining China's security interests. Importantly, China's support for sanctions may have contributed to Pyongyang's dramatic shift from confrontation to dialogue.

That shift, beginning during the February 2018 Winter Olympics in South Korea, led to remarkable change. Within weeks, the world witnessed a North-South summit, an offer by Kim Jong Un to meet the U.S. president, and President Trump's surprising acceptance of that invitation. By the time Trump and Kim met in Singapore in June, dialogue and diplomacy had become the prevailing trend.

These developments prompted both relief and concern in Beijing. For the first time in months, the possibility of U.S.–North Korea conflict was receding. However, the new North-South and DPRK-U.S. diplomacy provided no role for Beijing. China found itself on the outside looking in.[6]

Behind China's concern was a fear that Pyongyang, having defied Chinese efforts to prevent it from developing nuclear weapons, could now cut its own deals with Washington and Seoul.[7] As a senior Chinese official remarked in late 2018, "We were concerned that North Korea was drifting away, our influence in Pyongyang was declining, and our interests were not being protected."[8]

BEIJING SHIFTS INTO DIPLOMATIC OVERDRIVE

In response, China quickly sought to reassert its role in Korea-related matters and rehabilitate ties with Pyongyang.

Beijing launched its initiative with a visit by Kim Jong Un in March 2018, the first of five summits over a span of eighteen months. The March visit was Kim's first foreign trip since assuming the leadership in 2011. Coming only days after President Trump had accepted Kim's invitation to meet, and as Pyongyang and Seoul were planning an April summit, the timing of the Xi-Kim meeting was hardly coincidental. Each of the Xi-Kim meetings took place in close proximity to a U.S.-DPRK or inter-Korean summit, allowing Beijing to coordinate positions with and obtain readouts from Pyongyang.

The capstone of PRC-DPRK diplomacy was Xi Jinping's visit to North Korea in June 2019—the first visit by a Chinese leader in fourteen years. There had been previous visits by then president Hu Jintao but only after Pyongyang had agreed to the September 19, 2005, Six-Party denuclearization agreement. However, Pyongyang's violation of that agreement and its 2006 nuclear test began the downward slide in relations that Xi now sought to repair.

Xi's brief visit was highly successful. The optics of the visit confirmed that the two countries had put the dark days of 2017 behind them. The summit also showed Washington that, despite the collapse of the U.S.-DPRK summit in Hanoi in February, China intended to strengthen relations with Pyongyang regardless of the state of U.S.-DPRK diplomacy.

Xi's visit led to a flurry of exchanges that reinvigorated China–North Korea ties, including a visit by PRC foreign minister Wang Yi. In Pyongyang, Wang said, "China and the DPRK should communicate more, exchange more, understand each other, trust each other, support each other, and safeguard common interests and legitimate rights and interests." Wang assured Pyongyang that "China will always stand on the road as comrades and friends of the DPRK."[9]

CHINA–NORTH KOREA RELATIONS: AS CLOSE AS . . . ?

Beijing's reset of relations with Pyongyang clearly laid the foundation for a new atmosphere of diplomatic decorum that had largely disappeared in 2017. But it would be too much to say that ties are now fully on track. China's greatest worry—the potential for instability or conflict on its border—has eased. But the root cause of that concern—North Korea's pursuit of nuclear weapons—remains. Pyongyang is firmly wedded to its nuclear weapons program.

For China, North Korea is now a permanently nuclear armed neighbor. Nuclear weapons give Pyongyang useful leverage in its relations with its neighbors, including China. But Beijing's ability to influence North Korea is constrained by its unwillingness to use its considerable economic clout for fear of causing the precipitate collapse of the DPRK regime—China's long-time nightmare. Stability, avoiding conflict, and preserving North Korea intact, not denuclearization, have long been and continue to be Beijing's top policy priorities.

In fact, Beijing seems to have reconciled itself to the permanence of a nuclear-armed DPRK, although it officially continues to urge denuclearization. A prominent former senior Chinese official declared that Beijing would "never accept" North Korea as a nuclear-weapon state. However, he acknowledged, China will "tolerate" a nuclear-armed North Korea as long as Beijing can point to a negotiating process that offers some hope, however distant, for eventual denuclearization.[10] Maintaining a fictional goal of denuclearization meets China's needs.

Meanwhile, China's overall approach to the Korean Peninsula remains unchanged. Core goals of that approach include the following:

- Ensuring that China plays a central role in any future Korean peace mechanism

- Weakening the rationale for the U.S.–South Korea alliance

- Maintaining good relations with both Koreas

- Preventing the collapse of North Korea and the reunification of the peninsula under a U.S.-allied South Korea

- Reducing the threat posed by the U.S.–South Korea alliance and, if possible, ending that alliance

- Limiting the vulnerability caused by Pyongyang's possession of nuclear weapons and provocative behavior

Beijing has noticed how U.S.–South Korea friction, the erosion of U.S.–South Korea–Japan cooperation, and declining U.S. regional leadership could help it advance its interests. China may exploit its improved ties with Pyongyang to accelerate these trends.

Today, all may not be perfectly harmonious in PRC-DPRK relations, but bilateral ties are greatly improved, and the two allies share strategic goals. For China, even a problematic partnership with Pyongyang has great value. But it remains to be seen whether China's patience and tolerance of Pyongyang's nuclear weapons will continue if North Korea's actions again threaten China's interests.

IMPLICATIONS AND RECOMMENDATIONS FOR THE UNITED STATES

Renewed nuclear or ICBM testing could prompt Beijing to react strongly against the DPRK. But unless Pyongyang acts provocatively, China seems unlikely to support increased pressure on the regime. This seems particularly true as North Korea deals with the COVID-19 pandemic and as China works to keep its ally's economy afloat. Unlike in 2017, China has made clear its desire to ease sanctions on Pyongyang. Beijing also continues to violate both the letter and the spirit of existing international sanctions.[11] Meanwhile, the growing discord between Beijing and Washington may make it impossible to secure China's cooperation on North Korea. The "renormalization" of Beijing-Pyongyang ties poses a major challenge to Washington's ability to manage the DPRK issue. U.S. policymakers will therefore have to refine their approach to include the following:

- Future attempts to solicit Chinese cooperation against Pyongyang must convince Beijing that its own security is at stake.

- Securing Chinese cooperation against North Korea as U.S.-PRC relations deteriorate is unlikely. As a former senior Chinese official put it, Beijing will not do the United States a "favor" while Washington treats China with hostility.[12]

- Washington policymakers may not want to prioritize cooperation with Beijing on North Korea over other important issues. But the growing North Korean threat to America's allies and to the United States argues strongly for making North Korea an urgent priority with China.

- The United States should dissuade Beijing from offering uncoordinated or unilateral economic incentives to Pyongyang and should be prepared to impose sanctions on China and its firms if it does so.

- The United States should acknowledge China's role in the Korean Peninsula peace process, while understanding that Beijing may seek to exploit that process to undermine the rationale for the U.S.–South Korea alliance.

- As relations with China deteriorate, America's alliances, leadership, and determination to remain the region's central actor are more important than ever.

- The foundation of the effort to both denuclearize the DPRK and contend with China is close U.S.–Japan–South Korea cooperation. Washington must reverse the deterioration of that partnership.

Finally, U.S. policymakers must not underestimate the challenge posed by the shift in China's policy on North Korea. Over the years, the conventional wisdom was that, for all their differences, Washington and Beijing shared an interest in achieving Pyongyang's denuclearization. But China now shows signs of accommodating itself to a nuclear-armed North Korea, and the common goal that once inspired U.S.-China cooperation is disappearing. Difficult times lie ahead.

NOTES

1. Jane Perlez, "Xi and Trump Discuss Rising Tensions with North Korea," *New York Times*, April 12, 2017, www.nytimes.com/2017/04/12/world/asia/trump-china-north-korea-xi-jinping.html. See also Gerry Mulany, Chris Buckley, and David E. Sanger, "China Warns of 'Storm Clouds Gathering' in U.S.–North Korea Standoff," *New York Times*, April 14, 2017, www.nytimes.com/2017/04/14/world/asia/north-korea-china-nuclear.html.

2. "A Chinese State-Run Tabloid Has Warned North Korea against More Nuclear Tests," Reuters/*Time*, April 12, 2017, https://time.com/4735649/china-north-korea-nuclear-test/; Jane Perlez, "Xi and Trump Discuss Rising Tensions with North Korea."

3. David Brunnstrom, "North Korea Media Issues Rare Criticism of China over Nuclear Warnings," Reuters, May 4, 2017, www.reuters.com/article/us-northkorea-china/north-korean-media-issues-rare-criticism-of-china-over-nuclear-warnings-idUSKBN17Z1TA.

4. Dagyum Ji, "Russia, China Should 'Pay Dearly' for Passing UNSC Resolution: N. Korea," *NK News*, August, 8, 2017, www.nknews.org/2017/08/russia-china-should-pay-dearly-for-passing-unsc-resolution-n-korea/.

5. Amy B. Wang, "North Korea Declares Latest UN Sanctions an 'Act of War,'"

Washington Post, December 24, 2017, www.washingtonpost.com/news/worldviews/wp/2017/12/24/north-korea-declares-latest-u-n-sanctions-an-act-of-war/.

6. Jane Perlez, "China, Feeling Left Out, Has Plenty to Worry about in North Korea–U.S. Talks," *New York Times*, April 22, 2018, www.nytimes.com/2018/04/22/world/asia/china-north-korea-nuclear-talks.html.

7. Katie Hunt and Tim Schwarz, "China Fears Kim Is Moving Out of Its Orbit as South Korea, US Talks Loom," CNN, April 24, 2018, www.cnn.com/2018/04/24/asia/china-north-korea-intl/index.html.

8. Author's notes, meeting with senior PRC official, December 2018.

9. Oliver Hotham, "Chinese FM Meets Party Officials, Tours Factory on Final Day of Pyongyang Visit, *NK News*, September 5, 2019, www.nknews.org/2019/09/chinese-fm-meets-party-officials-tours-factory-on-final-day-of-pyongyang-visit/.

10. Conversation with author, October 8, 2019.

11. Stephanie Kleine-Ahlbrandt, "Maximum Pressure against North Korea, RIP," 38 North, October 7, 2019, www.38north.org/2019/10/skleineahlbrandt100719/.

12. Conversation with author, October 8, 2019.

6

From Persuasion to Coercion

Beijing's Approach to Taiwan and Taiwan's Response

RICHARD BUSH

In the external policy of the People's Republic of China's (PRC), Taiwan is unique. From its beginning in 1949, the regime has claimed the island as part of China's sovereign territory.[1] It was to Taiwan that Chiang Kai-shek and his Kuomintang (KMT)-led Republic of China (ROC) government retreated after his defeat on the mainland at the hands of Mao Zedong's communists. For Beijing, the civil war will not be over until the PRC flag flies over the island. China's leaders also recognize Taiwan's strategic value as a link in the western Pacific's first-island chain. Thus ending Taiwan's separate existence has been a core objective of the PRC regime.

UNIFICATION THROUGH PERSUASION

The Chinese Communist Party (CCP) leaders have never renounced the use of force concerning Taiwan. Yet by the late 1970s, they believed they

This chapter is based on and summarizes a longer report of the same title, disseminated in November 2019, and available at www.brookings.edu/research/from-persuasion-to-coercion-beijings -approach-to-taiwan-and-taiwans-response/. Funding from the Smith Richardson Foundation helped support the research on which the report was based.

might *persuade* Taiwan's leaders to accept an end to cross-Strait division. The PRC's international position had improved, and it became an attractive investment site for Taiwan companies. Beijing elaborated a blueprint for the postunification relationship between the island and the mainland, similar to what was proposed for Hong Kong. This blueprint was dubbed "one country, two systems" (1C2S).[2]

Based on how 1C2S was implemented in Hong Kong through 2015, it would have the following elements:

- The Republic of China would cease to exist.

- Taiwan would legally become part of the sovereign territory of the PRC, a "special administrative region."

- The PRC government would control Taipei's foreign and defense affairs.

- Economic and social life in Taiwan would continue.

- Taiwan's leaders would have autonomy to administer domestic affairs, but Beijing would control how those leaders were selected, excluding leaders and parties it mistrusted.[3]

In addition, the Taiwan military would still exist and People's Liberation Army (PLA) troops would not be deployed to the island. But Taiwan could not be a platform for the projection of U.S. power against China.

PRC leaders likely believed this formula could induce the KMT regime to agree to unification. Economic interdependence and the fact that most Taiwan people were ethnic Chinese would be positive incentives. A power balance gradually shifting in Beijing's favor would strengthen persuasion. Taiwan's leaders would recognize reality and settle. As the Chinese saying goes, "Once ripe, the melon drops from its stem" (*guashu diluo*).

STRATEGIC SETBACK: TAIWAN'S DEMOCRATIZATION

It didn't work out that way. The melon did not drop. For most of the last forty years, David has outplayed Goliath. Even as the economies of China and Taiwan have become more interdependent, Beijing has had no success in achieving unification through persuasion.

International factors, such as revitalized American support for Taiwan's security, had worked in Taiwan's favor. Most importantly, Taiwan's transition from a tough authoritarian system to a full democracy in the late 1980s and early 1990s created major obstacles to China's ambitions. It opened the door for new players, particularly the Democratic Progressive Party (DPP). A long-suppressed Taiwanese identity flowered.[4] The share of the population in favor of unification remained low, and around 80 percent of the population preferred the status quo.[5] Therefore, if political negotiations of any kind were to occur with China, the Taiwan public effectively had a seat at the table.

For China, Taiwan's democratization not only impeded unification but also increased its fear that Taiwan's leaders and citizens might move toward de jure independence. The DPP's 1991 charter favored creation of a "Republic of Taiwan."[6] Presidents Lee Teng-hui (1995–2000) and Chen Shui-bian (2000–2008) exploited Taiwanese and anti-China sentiment to win elections. Hence, during the latter part of the Lee administration and during all of Chen's, Beijing policy stressed "opposing independence."

THE MA YING-JEOU OPPORTUNITY

For China, the 2008 victory of KMT leader Ma Ying-jeou seemed to resume progress toward its ultimate objective. He was a mainlander by birth and a Chinese nationalist by temperament. In 2005, his party assured the CCP of its opposition to Taiwan's independence, and a consensus was forged to gradually develop cross-Strait relations. Easier, economic issues would come first and harder, political matters later. For Beijing, a return to persuasion was justified. There ensued the normalization, expansion, and institutionalization of cross-Strait economic relations.

Beijing rewarded Ma by allowing Taiwan modest, increased participation in the international community. But it insisted that further expansion would require the beginning of political talks, a move the Taiwan public and some in the KMT opposed. Beijing came to fear both Taiwan's independence and "permanent separation."

Moreover, Taiwan's political system was changing. Social movements emerged to promote a variety of causes. The Sunflower Movement of 2014 blocked legislative approval of an agreement with Beijing on trade in services, effectively bringing Ma's China engagement to a halt. It also helped sweep the DPP to power at the local and central levels of government. Tsai Ing-wen was elected president in 2016.

CHINA'S RESPONSE OPTIONS

For Beijing, the failure to realize the hopes that Ma's election had fostered posed the challenge of how to respond. Objectively, four options have existed.

First, Beijing could recognize that democratic Taiwan will never accept 1C2S and so make a more appealing offer. Yet its rigid adherence to 1C2S means this option is a nonstarter.

Second, PRC leaders could return to a persuasion-based approach. But they refused to try to coexist with Tsai Ing-wen, so they had to await the KMT's return to power and its adoption of acceptable policies. But in the 2020 election, Tsai handily defeated the KMT candidate Han Kuo-yu. The party has since struggled to simultaneously restore public support and formulate proposals that Beijing would accept. Its new leadership seems ambivalent and undecided about whether to endorse the "1992 Consensus," which Ma accepted and which remains the PRC bottom line.[7] Beijing's recent policy toward Hong Kong has eliminated any appeal 1C2S had for Taiwan and seriously handicapped the KMT.

Third, PRC leaders could order the PLA to undertake a limited military campaign to break the political will of Taiwan's leaders and public, and, if necessary, mount an invasion of the island. Since the late 1990s it has built capabilities to do exactly that, and to make it difficult for U.S. armed forces to intervene in support of Taiwan. In its March 2005 antisecession law, it stated ambiguously the circumstances under which it would use force.

Yet a military campaign is unlikely for the foreseeable future. Beijing takes seriously U.S. capabilities and probably works under the prudent assumption that Washington would intervene. Even if the PLA were successful, the economic, diplomatic, and reputational costs would be high. Governing an occupied Taiwan would be a daunting challenge.

Moreover, PRC leaders do not have a sense of urgency about Taiwan. Although Xi has said that "the long-standing political differences between the two sides of the Strait . . . should not be passed down generation after generation,"[8] he has not set an explicit deadline.

A Chinese policy of persuasion is low risk and low reward, and the use of force entails high risks and uncertain rewards. But an approach with modest risks and at least some chance of success, that is, a long-term campaign of intimidation, pressure, and cooptation of constituencies within Taiwan, seems to be a more optimal strategy and is the PRC's fourth option.

Beijing has used a wide range of tools to impose "coercion without violence" on Taiwan, keep it on the defensive, and wear down its psychological confidence. These tools include suspending interaction between the organizations that have conducted cross-Strait relations, creating difficulties for Taiwan companies whose leaders express sympathies for the DPP, snatching Taiwan's diplomatic allies, marginalizing Taiwan internationally, pressuring third-country companies and governments to employ PRC-friendly nomenclature about Taiwan, conducting military exercises in the area surrounding Taiwan, restricting PRC students from studying in Taiwan, restricting Chinese tourist travel to Taiwan, and limiting interaction between PRC scholars and pro-DPP scholars. It has also deployed incentives: purchases of Taiwanese products, especially from KMT-led jurisdictions, and "national treatment" for Taiwanese businesspersons, entrepreneurs, and students. (The incentives for companies may have come too late, after the cost of doing business on the mainland has already shifted against them. Nor is there any guarantee that young people who take advantage of educational opportunities will change their political attitudes.)

Beijing has also penetrated and interfered in Taiwan's politics through cyberwarfare, manipulating social media, controlling or influencing traditional media, and funneling money through cutouts to KMT campaign organizations. It is difficult for the Taipei government to conclusively prove that Beijing is behind these activities, so they will likely continue.

Beijing employed these various measures to punish the Tsai administration after it came into office and appears to be continuing them after her reelection. More importantly, intimidation can also socialize the Taiwan public toward the conclusion that the status quo is no longer sustainable and that it is time to settle on China's terms.

TAIWAN'S RESPONSE

Taiwan's democracy remains a significant barrier to China's demands. Negative public opinion regarding Beijing's policies and actions constrains leaders' freedom of action. Yet democracy also creates divisions, and not surprisingly Taiwan people have conflicting ideas on China policy. The DPP believes that Beijing's pressure campaign is real and reflects its malevolent intentions toward the island. The KMT believes that Tsai's refusal to accommodate China on the 1992 Consensus made PRC intimidation inevitable. Each party's internal splits complicate matters. The DPP pro-independence faction criticizes Tsai's policy moderation. Native Taiwanese in the KMT worry Ma's engagement of Beijing put Taiwan at risk. (Both parties do agree that U.S. support is vitally important.) These divisions and the larger dysfunction of Taiwan's political system work to Beijing's advantage. Intimidation, pressure, and selective cooptation target Taiwan's most serious point of vulnerability, the public's uncertainty about the future.

There are things Taiwan can do to respond to PRC "coercion without violence": strengthen cyberdefenses, rebut fake news, pursue a defense strategy appropriate to the PRC threat, improve ties with other economic partners, enhance youth employment, and increase government resources. Washington can and should help Taiwan in some of these areas. But the most important thing Taiwan can do is foster cross-party unity on China policy. Such a consensus would have to start with the premise that Taiwan is under threat, and then develop policies to effectively meet it. The stakes are too high to continue politics as usual. A more united Taiwan will be a stronger Taiwan. Continued and corrosive division only benefits China.

NOTES

1. The word "island" is used as a term of convenience. Actually, Taipei governs a number of small islands besides the larger island of Taiwan proper.

2. Note that the "two systems" were not political but economic—socialism and capitalism.

3. Richard C. Bush, *Hong Kong in the Shadow of China: Living with the Leviathan* (Washington, DC: Brookings Institution Press, 2016).

4. "Taiwan/Chinese Identity, 1992/06–2020/06," Election Study Center, National Chengchi University, July 3, 2020, https://esc.nccu.edu.tw/PageDoc/Detail?fid= 7800&id=6961. I limit the use of the word "Taiwanese" to refer to those residents of the island whose families migrated from southeast China in the early twentieth century. They are often known as "native Taiwanese." The word "mainlander" is usually applied to those people whose families came after 1945, when the ROC government took control from the Japanese. Because of the new regime's harsh rule over its new subject, the political cleavage between mainlanders and Taiwanese still persists in attenuated form. I use the word "Taiwan" as an adjective ("Taiwan people," "Taiwan companies") when the mainlander–Taiwanese cleavage isn't relevant.

5. "Taiwan Independence vs. Unification with the Mainland (1992/06–2020/ 06)," Election Study Center, National Chengchi University, July 3, 2020, https://esc .nccu.edu.tw/PageDoc/Detail?fid=7801&id=6963.

6. The DPP claims that more moderate resolutions about Taiwan's future, such as the one issued on May 8, 1999, have superseded the goal stated in the charter.

7. The 1992 Consensus embodied a commitment to one China but indicated no agreement on the legal and political relationship of Taiwan within that one China. In Taiwan, there is general agreement that the Consensus allows each side to offer its own interpretation of one China. Ma Ying-jeou asserted that his interpretation was the Republic of China. Beijing's official position is that the ROC ceased to exist in 1949.

8. "Working Together to Realize Rejuvenation of the Chinese Nation and Advance China's Peaceful Reunification," speech by Xi Jinping at the Meeting Marking the 40th Anniversary of the Issuance of the Message to Compatriots in Taiwan, January 2, 2019, website of the Taiwan Affairs Office of the State Council, www.gwytb.gov.cn/m/news/201904/t20190412_12155846.htm.

7

How China's Actions in the South China Sea Undermine the Rule of Law

LYNN KUOK

China's growing clout in East Asia has corresponded with a weakening of the international law of the sea. Its actions in the South China Sea, where it has aggressively pursued its territorial and maritime claims, undermine the rules-based order. International pressure on China has been inconsistent; periods of neglect have corresponded with further Chinese incursions. The erosion of the rule of law hurts all countries, including the United States and China, which have an interest in keeping competition, however fierce, within the parameters of the law to minimize the risk of conflict. Statements in 2020 by important Southeast Asian littoral states and the United States, Australia, the United Kingdom, France and Germany, and, in January 2021, Japan, point to progress in responding to China's incursions: parties are now clearly enunciating a common understanding of international law. This is a positive development, but promoting a rules-based order will require broad-based and sustained efforts.

THE DISPUTE

The South China Sea dispute concerns competing territorial and maritime claims. The maritime dispute has at its roots China's controversial nine-dash line, which made its first official appearance in a map Beijing submitted to the United Nations in 2009.[1] Beijing has never provided coordinates for the dashed line, but it appears to encapsulate much of the South China Sea. The line can be read as laying claim to everything within it or merely land features (features that are visible at high tide) and maritime zones compliant with the United Nations Convention on the Law of the Sea (UNCLOS). China's rhetoric and actions suggest that it adopts the former interpretation.

THE SOUTH CHINA SEA ARBITRATION

In January 2013, the Philippines brought a case against China over its expansive claims and activities in the South China Sea. The case was heard by an arbitral tribunal constituted under UNCLOS. The award, issued in July 2016, was a major victory for the Philippines. Its main significance was to clarify resource rights.

The tribunal ruled that insofar as China had historic rights to resources within the nine-dash line, such rights were extinguished by the entry into force of UNCLOS given incompatibility with the Convention's system of maritime zones.

The tribunal also found that, based on the geographic conditions laid out in UNCLOS, all features in the Spratly Islands and Scarborough Shoal are at most "rocks" entitled to a 12-nautical-mile territorial sea; none of the features are entitled to a 200-nautical-mile EEZ. In addition—and this is important for what appears to be China's latest basis for its expansive claims[2]—the tribunal also held that the Spratly Islands cannot be considered a unit from which maritime zones are generated (figure 7-1).

The upshot of these findings is that the Philippines and, by implication, the other littoral states of the South China Sea, enjoy exclusive economic rights in their EEZs unencumbered by China's nine-dash line or any claimed EEZ from features or groups of features in the Spratly Islands.

WORRYING DEVELOPMENTS

In the first year after the ruling, China's behavior, despite it decrying the tribunal decision as "null and void" and of "no binding force," was largely in keeping with the tribunal's decision.[3] Since then, however, China has continued to aggressively pursue its territorial and maritime claims. Despite the COVID-19 pandemic, China's activities in the South China Sea have not abated but have arguably intensified.

China has sought to strengthen its maritime claims and control around features. This has taken several forms. First, China has encroached on coastal states' EEZs, which flies in the face of the tribunal ruling. Second, it has increased its presence around features occupied or administered by other countries with vessels from its navy, coast guard, and maritime militia. Chinese presence around these features is not necessarily unlawful—user states have a right of innocent passage through any territorial seas and high sea freedoms outside them, but the numbers and persistence of Chinese vessels suggest that they are aimed at coercion and consolidating Chinese control. Third, China has objected to U.S. and other warships exercising innocent passage without prior authorization as well as navigation and other freedoms of the seas (in some cases engaging in dangerous, close encounters). Such behavior is inconsistent with the maritime rights and freedoms vested under UNCLOS, which China ratified in 1996 and the United States abides by as a matter of customary international law and domestic policy. At the end of January 2021, China passed a law permitting its coast guard to take "all necessary means," including the use of weapons, to conduct law enforcement operations in "waters under the jurisdiction of China," an area China interprets expansively.[4]

China also continues to consolidate its territorial claims, a pursuit begun at the end of 2013, when China began large-scale reclamation work on features it occupies, converting small rocks and reefs into large, artificial islands and building facilities on them. By the end of 2017, China effectively had operational naval and air facilities in the South China Sea.[5] Beijing's militarization of features escalated in 2018 and continues to date.[6]

Beijing repeatedly claims, as it did most recently in its 2019 Defense White Paper, that "China exercises its national sovereignty to build infrastructure and deploy necessary defensive capabilities on the islands and reefs in the South China Sea."[7] But sovereignty over features in the South China Sea is fiercely contested. Further, at least one feature in the Spratly Islands that China has built on, Mischief Reef, is clearly not China's territory. The international tribunal made clear in its ruling that Mischief Reef, like Second Thomas Shoal, is a low-tide elevation forming part of the EEZ and continental shelf of the Philippines and that the Philippines therefore has jurisdiction and control over it. The tribunal thus ruled that China's construction of an artificial island and installations at Mischief Reef violated the Philippines' sovereign rights and jurisdiction.

CHINA'S UPPER HAND

Beijing's aggressive militarization of the South China Sea is often dismissed as inconsequential in the event of outright conflict: naval experts say that installations and deployments are "extremely vulnerable to attack from [U.S.] ships, subs, and aircraft."[8] This has been disputed by those arguing that "China, not the United States, would control the sea and airspace of the South China Sea at the outbreak of hostilities thanks to its artificial island bases."[9] Whatever the case, we should not discount the advantages China has gained in situations short of outright conflict. Admiral Phil Davidson, then commander-designate of the U.S. Pacific Command, testified in April 2018 that China is now capable of controlling the South China Sea "in all scenarios short of war with the United States."[10] This overstates the extent of Chinese control in nonconflict situations—the United States and others continue to assert maritime rights and freedoms, but Davidson's statement underscores China's strong hand in the South China Sea.

A Japanese Ministry of Defense report found that China's naval and air facilities in the South China Sea allow for a more robust maritime presence.[11] This helps China realize its broader strategic goals: achieving strategic depth and reach to defend against adversaries, protecting access to the critical Strait of Malacca, and facilitating deployment of its embryonic submarine-based, second-strike nuclear capability. None of this, of course, precludes China from more ambitious strategic objectives in the future.

China has also gleaned *nonmilitary* advantages from its actions that are often overlooked. They have deterred other claimants from putting up strong resistance. Significantly, China's success in consolidating its position in the South China Sea has also undermined U.S. credibility in the region.

RESPONSES

Littoral Southeast Asian states have sought to resist Chinese incursions, but within limits. They are outmatched militarily and seek good ties with China. COVID-19 is increasing this imperative. Indonesia, Malaysia, and the Philippines are working with China on COVID-19 responses. We can expect ties to deepen as they seek to rebuild their economies after the pandemic, even if anti-China ground sentiment may complicate relations.

One area of progress in the South China Sea has been the emergence, prompted by Malaysia's extended continental shelf submission to the UN Commission on the Limits of the Continental Shelf in December 2019 and China's responses, of a clear sense that, apart from China, important players are operating under a common understanding of the law.[12]

The Philippines, Vietnam, Indonesia, and Malaysia have made clear through a series of diplomatic notes submitted to the United Nations that the UN tribunal ruling against China is an authoritative interpretation of the law and that China's asserted maritime rights to the South China Sea contravene UNCLOS. Together, these represent a chorus of disapproval for China's expansive claims in the South China Sea.

The United States, too, submitted a note to the UN in early June 2020, though it remained silent on the question of whether China can validly claim an EEZ from small individual islands in the South China Sea. This was followed by notes from Australia, the United Kingdom, France, Germany and, in January 2021, Japan.

U.S. silence on whether China can validly claim an EEZ from small individual islands in the South China Sea changed in July 2020 when U.S. secretary of state Mike Pompeo made a high-profile statement "aligning" the U.S. position on China's maritime claims in the South China Sea with the UN tribunal's decision.

Declaring that neither the Spratly Islands (individually or as a group) nor Scarborough Shoal was entitled to an EEZ, Pompeo went on to condemn as unlawful China's actions harassing Philippines fisheries and offshore energy development within its EEZ and any unilateral action on China's part to exploit these resources. Notably, Pompeo also declared any Chinese action to harass Southeast Asian states' fishing or hydrocarbon development or to carry out such activities within their EEZs as unlawful.

What this important clarification means for U.S. practice, particularly under a Biden administration, is still unfolding. Despite never previously endorsing the merits of the UN tribunal's decision, the United States had taken steps consistent with the ruling, such as, since 2019, condemning China's interference with oil and gas activities, including Vietnam's long-standing exploration and production activities.

But Pompeo's explicit endorsement of the tribunal ruling accords with earlier recommendations by this author to support coastal states' efforts to stand up to incursions into their EEZs and renew calls for China to abide by the tribunal ruling.[13] It is late, coming four years after the tribunal ruling, but is nonetheless a positive development for several reasons.

First, it goes toward reassuring Southeast Asian countries that the United States cares about their economic rights, even if no one is under the illusion that such concerns arise from anything other than escalating U.S.-China rivalry.

Second, actions that are explicitly in line with the tribunal judgment enjoy greater legitimacy and will help boost support for bilateral and multilateral efforts to defend the rules-based order. Although U.S. allies and partners may be persuaded to support the rule of law, most would shy away from an effort that appears aimed at containing China.

Third, recent U.S. statements help to counter China's false narratives. Accusations that "foreign powers are stirring up trouble in the South China Sea" ring hollow if those actions are clearly supported by international law. Further, while it is within a country's rights to construct and militarize facilities on its own territories, as China claims, sovereignty over land features in the South China Sea are hotly contested, and in the case of low-tide or submerged features, jurisdiction and control lie with the coastal state—a matter that the UN tribunal ruled on and which the United States has explicitly endorsed.

Finally, recent developments pave the way for stronger action against China, including sanctions. The day after Pompeo's statement, Assistant Secretary of State for the Bureau of East Asian and Pacific Affairs David Stilwell took aim at China's state-owned enterprises, highlighting China Construction & Communications Corporation (CCCC), which led the dredging for China's South China Sea military bases, and China National Offshore Oil Corporation (CNOOC), which encroached on coastal states' exclusive economic rights through various survey activities. Since then, the United States has followed up by adding numerous Chinese companies to its "Entity List," a sanctioned blacklist of entities believed to pose significant risk to U.S. national security or foreign policy interests, for their role in the South

China Sea. In August 2020, twenty-four Chinese companies, including several subsidiaries of CCCC, were added to the list for their role in building and militarizing artificial islands.[14] Seventy-seven Chinese companies were added to the list in December 2020 for transgressions that included supporting China's "militarization and unlawful maritime claims" in the South China Sea.[15] In January 2021, CNOOC joined the list for repeatedly harassing and threatening offshore oil and gas exploration and extraction.[16]

RECOMMENDATIONS

Some have argued that the "game" is over in the South China Sea and China has won. This argument is wrong. It is also dangerous: taking this stance could well be self-fulfilling. China has gained advantages, but the United States and its allies, through their assertions of maritime rights and freedoms, have thus far successfully pushed back against Beijing's attempts to assert control over the waters of the South China Sea. Moreover, while China has consolidated control over the features it occupies, it has not built on Scarborough Shoal, a rock located just over 200 miles from the Philippines' capital, despite China being in control of it since 2012. A Chinese base on Scarborough Shoal would hurt the interests of the United States and its allies since it would allow Beijing the third corner of a three-pronged security triangle in the South China Sea and one that sits close to a U.S. military facility in the Philippines.[17] This would complicate U.S. military planning.

The following are some suggestions for the United States and its allies and partners. The involvement of countries other than the United States helps to take the edge off U.S.-China rivalry and sends the important message that these countries care about maintaining open seas and that rules matter. It also helps debunk Beijing's claim that the dispute is one that only concerns claimants to territorial features and that other powers have no valid interests in the South China Sea.

First, continue to regularly assert maritime rights and freedoms. As a matter of law, regular assertions of maritime rights and freedoms ensure that rights are not lost through acquiescence to excessive maritime claims; as a matter of practice, they guard against the South China Sea becoming a Chinese lake.[18]

Second, persuade China that its interests as a fast-growing maritime power with economic and military interests that span the globe lie in upholding maritime rights and freedoms, rather than undermining them.[19]

While U.S. Freedom of Navigation Operations are essential, the United States should not neglect the other prongs of its Freedom of Navigation Program, including discussions to achieve greater uniformity in the interpretation of UNCLOS.[20]

Third, continue to hold bilateral and multilateral drills in the region. These are important, particularly in the context of the Code of Conduct negotiations wherein China seeks the agreement of parties to agree not to hold joint military exercises with countries from outside the region.[21]

Fourth, continue to boost regional capacity, particularly in the maritime domain. Increased capacity to monitor and patrol their EEZ will give coastal states greater confidence to shine a light on unlawful and coercive behavior.

Fifth, the United States should continue to strengthen ties with its regional allies and partners. In particular, Washington needs to foster better ties with the Philippines, an important Southeast Asian ally but one with which relations have been rocky.

Sixth, Washington should communicate to China that building on Scarborough Shoal will have serious repercussions. The Obama administration had privately warned China that building on Scarborough Shoal was a red line; there are no indications that the Trump administration issued similar warnings. The new administration should do so. While Scarborough Shoal does not technically fall within the U.S.-Philippines Mutual Defense Treaty since the tribunal did not rule on whether it is Philippines territory, and the United States takes no position on competing claims to sovereignty, a failure by the United States to act to stop China from building on Scarborough Shoal would nonetheless give the impression that the United States is a paper tiger and an unreliable ally.

Seventh, continue to support coastal states' efforts to push back against incursions into their EEZs and maintain calls for China to abide by the tribunal's ruling. Recent U.S. statements were quietly welcomed in the region[22]—whereas Washington had previously focused on championing open seas, for many Southeast Asian coastal states access to fish and oil and gas resources in their EEZs is their priority.

Eighth, the United States should demonstrate consistency in its support of the rule of law both within and outside the South China Sea. In this vein, it should accede to UNCLOS.

Finally, it should be remembered that events in the South China Sea cannot be viewed in isolation. Attempts to defend the rule of law in a region where development needs are high are likely to gain wider traction only if economic opportunities are afforded as well. While there is much talk about pushback against the Belt and Road Initiative, and Southeast Asian countries are cautious about Belt and Road projects, they remain open to it.[23] The United States must cooperate with its allies and partners to promote development, including ensuring viable options for infrastructure development and growth beyond Chinese money. In the wake of COVID-19, helping to support countries' health infrastructure will take on increased prominence.

All this, of course, assumes that the United States is interested in promoting a world where international law matters. This was called into doubt under a Trump administration; a Biden administration must demonstrate that this is a priority. The stakes are high: no countries matter more than the two superpowers in charting the future course of international law and regional and international stability. If international law is a casualty of their actions or omissions, a far less stable order may be expected—to the detriment of all.

NOTES

1. Note Verbale, CML/17/2009, Permanent Mission of the People's Republic of China to the United Nations, May 7, 2009, www.un.org/Depts/los/clcs_new/submis sions_files/mysvnm33_09/chn_2009re_mys_vnm_e.pdf.

2. See, for example, China, Communication to the UN dated December 12, 2019, www.un.org/Depts/los/clcs_new/submissions_files/mys85_2019/CML_14_ 2019_E.pdf.

3. Lynn Kuok, "Progress in the South China Sea?: A Year after the Hague Ruling," *Foreign Affairs*, July 21, 2017, www.foreignaffairs.com/articles/east-asia/ 2017-07-21/progress-south-china-sea.

4. Ronald Reagan, "United States Ocean Policy," National Oceanic and Atmospheric Administration, March 10, 1983, www.gc.noaa.gov/documents/031 083-reagan_ocean_policy.pdf.

5. Pia Ranada, "2018: Year of China Military Deployments in South China Sea—U.S. Think Tank," Rappler, December 26, 2018, www.rappler.com/nation/ 219458-gregory-poling-2018-chinese-military-deployments-south-china-sea.

6. Pia Ranada, "2018: Year of China Military Deployments in South China Sea— U.S. Think Tank."

7. State Council Information Office of the People's Republic of China, "China's National Defense in the New Era," July 24, 2019, http://english.www.gov.cn/archive /whitepaper/201907/24/content_WS5d3941ddc6d08408f502283d.html.

8. See, for instance, Robert Farley, "Would China's South China Sea Bases Be Wiped Out in a War?" National Interest, *The Buzz* (blog), May 9, 2019, https:// nationalinterest.org/blog/buzz/would-chinas-south-china-sea-bases-be-wiped -out-war-56577.

9. Gregory B. Poling, "The Conventional Wisdom on China's Island Bases in Dangerously Wrong," War on the Rocks, January 10, 2020, https://warontherocks.com/2020/01/the-conventional-wisdom-on-chinas-island-bases-is-dangerously-wrong/.

10. "Advance Policy Questions for Admiral Philip Davidson, USN Expected Nominee for Commander, U.S. Pacific Command," U.S. Senate Armed Services Committee, April 17, 2018, www.armed-services.senate.gov/imo/media/doc/Davidson_APQs_04-17-18.pdf.

11. This includes boosting China's intelligence, surveillance, reconnaissance, and other mission capabilities; runways for aircraft enable China to forward-deploy various aerial platforms, improving air power–projection capabilities and possibly allowing China to enforce an Air Defense Identification Zone (ADIZ) should it declare one in the future: "China's Activities in the South China Sea (China's Development Activities on the Features and Trends in Related Countries)," Japan Ministry of Defense, April 2019, pp. 22 and 23, www.mod.go.jp/e/d_act/sec_env/pdf/ch_d-act_201904b_e.pdf.

12. Lynn Kuok, "Southeast Asia Stands to Gain as US Hardens South China Sea Stance," *Nikkei Asia Review*, August 17, 2020.

13. Lynn Kuok, *How China's Actions in the South China Sea Undermine the Rule of Law* (Washington, DC: The Brookings Institution, November 2019), www.brookings.edu/research/how-chinas-actions-in-the-south-china-sea-undermine-the-rule-of-law/.

14. U.S. Department of Commerce, "Commerce Department Adds 24 Chinese Companies to the Entity List for Helping Build Military Islands in the South China Sea," August 26, 2020, www.commerce.gov/news/press-releases/2020/08/commerce-department-adds-24-chinese-companies-entity-list-helping-build.

15. U.S. Department of Commerce, "Statement from Secretary Ross on The Department's 77 Additions to the Entity List for Human Rights Abuses, Militarization of the South China Sea and U.S. Trade Secret Theft," December 18, 2020, www.commerce.gov/news/press-releases/2020/12/statement-secretary-ross-departments-77-additions-entity-list-human.

16. U.S. Department of Commerce, "Commerce Adds China National Offshore Oil Corporation to the Entity List and Skyrizon to the Military End-User List," January 14, 2021, www.commerce.gov/news/press-releases/2021/01/commerce-adds-china-national-offshore-oil-corporation-entity-list-and.

17. Seth Robson, "Facility for US forces Opens on Philippines' Main Island; Another Slated for Palawan," *Stars and Stripes*, January 31, 2019, www.stripes.com/news/pacific/facility-for-us-forces-opens-on-philippines-main-island-another-slated-for-palawan-1.566695.

18. For a discussion of the importance of asserting maritime rights and freedoms in the South China Sea, see Lynn Kuok, *The U.S. FON Program in the South China Sea: A Lawful and Necessary Response to China's Strategic Ambiguity* (Washington, DC: The Brookings Institution, June 2016), www.brookings.edu/research/the-u-s-fon-program-in-the-south-china-sea/.

19. For the lessons China should be taking from the Soviet approach to the law of the sea, see Lynn Kuok, "China Can Learn from Soviet Approach to the Law of the Sea," The Brookings Institution, *Order from Chaos* (blog), March 27, 2018, www .brookings.edu/blog/order-from-chaos/2018/03/27/china-can-learn-from-soviet -approach-to-the-law-of-the-sea/.

20. For a further discussion of this, see Lynn Kuok, "The U.S. FON Program in the South China Sea."

21. Carl Thayer, "A Closer Look at the ASEAN-China Single Draft South China Sea Code of Conduct," *The Diplomat*, August 3, 2018, https://thediplomat.com/2018 /08/a-closer-look-at-the-asean-china-single-draft-south-china-sea-code-of -conduct/.

22. Lynn Kuok, "Southeast Asia Stands to Gain as US Hardens South China Sea stance."

23. Lynn Kuok, "Shangri-La Dialogue: South-east Asia's Cautious Embrace of the Belt and Road Initiative," *Straits Times*, June 1, 2019, www.straitstimes.com/ opinion/s-e-asias-cautious-embrace-of-the-belt-and-road-initiative. For an in -depth discussion, see Lynn Kuok, "The Belt and Road Initiative and Southeast Asia," in *IISS Asia-Pacific Regional Security Assessment 2019: Key development and trends* (London: International Institute for Strategic Studies, May 2019), ch. 6. See also Lee Hsien Loong, "The Endangered Asian Century: America, China, and the Perils of Confrontation," *Foreign Affairs*, July/August 2020, www.foreignaffairs. com/articles/asia/2020-06-04/lee-hsien-loong-endangered-asian-century.

8

The U.S.-China Nuclear Relationship

Why Competition Is Likely to Intensify

CAITLIN TALMADGE

For decades, nuclear weapons have been largely peripheral to U.S.-China relations, but the nuclear relationship is now growing more competitive as both countries pursue major programs to modernize their forces. China's efforts to strengthen its relatively small nuclear arsenal seem largely oriented toward improving survivability and do not appear to constitute a shift away from the country's long-standing no first use policy.[1] Nevertheless, the improvements are provoking anxiety in Washington, which has long resisted acknowledging a state of mutual nuclear vulnerability with China.[2]

The core U.S. concern is that improvements in China's nuclear arsenal, even if intended only to improve survivability, will reduce the U.S. ability to limit damage in the worst-case scenario of an all-out nuclear war with China. The U.S. pursuit of damage limitation—through missile defenses that can intercept adversary nuclear launches and counterforce capabilities that can disable or destroy such adversary nuclear weapons prior to launch—should not be taken to mean that the United States intends to start a nuclear war or that it believes it could emerge from a nuclear war unscathed. Rather, the likely U.S. objective is to make it clear to China that if *China* starts a crisis or conflict that raises the risks of nuclear escalation, the United States will have a higher tolerance for bearing the risks than China will, because the United States has a relatively greater ability to limit the damage it would suffer in an all-out nuclear exchange. Advocates of damage limitation believe that such a capability would deter China from initiating conflict in the first place—even conflict well below the nuclear threshold—and would endow the United States with bargaining advantages in any effort to coerce China if a crisis or war did break out.[3]

Rightly or wrongly, this preference for damage limitation is likely why the United States perceives China's ongoing improvements to the survivability of its nuclear arsenal as threatening. China has made the most significant strides with respect to the land-based missile force, which has traditionally formed the backbone of its arsenal, and is also pursuing a sea-based deterrent capability.[4] The overall result of these changes is a force that is gradually growing larger and becoming more capable of penetrating U.S. missile defenses, better able to hold at risk U.S. cities, quicker to fire, and more easily concealed from U.S. intelligence, surveillance, and reconnaissance assets vital to any counterforce campaign. In short, China's modernization is raising the bar for any U.S. attempt to meaningfully limit damage, although where exactly that bar lies depends on the subjective perceptions of both Chinese and U.S. decisionmakers.

Classic deterrence theory of course would suggest that the mutual presence of secure second-strike forces would stabilize the U.S.-China relationship and reduce the likelihood of conflict due to the fear of escalation.[5] But U.S. policymakers may reasonably worry that if China turns out to be a highly revisionist actor with growing local conventional military advantages, improvements in its nuclear arsenal could embolden rather than inhibit Chinese aggression, in line with the so-called stability-instability paradox.[6] It was precisely this sort of fear that led to U.S. pursuit of a damage limitation capability versus the Soviets during the Cold War, even though the condition of mutually assured destruction seemed much more entrenched than it is now with China.[7]

The United States tends to view any erosion of its perceived position of nuclear advantage as cause for alarm. Understandably, however, China is also very unlikely to stop seeking a more survivable arsenal, even if its strategic aims are in fact limited and its nuclear doctrine remains static. As a result, nuclear competition between the United States and China is almost certain to intensify.

This is especially likely given that China is not the only nuclear-armed state of concern to the United States. Even if the United States wanted to eschew nuclear competition with China, U.S. nuclear policy choices with respect to other nuclear states would make it difficult to signal this choice credibly to China. For example, the United States might reasonably decide that damage limitation capabilities are an important part of preparation for worst-case scenarios vis-à-vis Russia and North Korea—states that clearly do reserve the right to use nuclear weapons first, unlike China. But these capabilities are likely to appear highly threatening to China even if they are aimed elsewhere, and they may propel a more competitive dynamic even if that is not the intent.[8]

Ultimately, a more competitive U.S.-China nuclear relationship could raise the risk that either side might actually use nuclear weapons, especially if Chinese fears of a U.S. damage limitation capability create rational pressures for it to use nuclear weapons early in a crisis or war.[9] Furthermore, as critics of damage limitation point out, the pursuit of damage limitation capabilities can itself generate suspicions that make crises or wars more likely to arise.[10] China's anxieties about the U.S. pursuit of damage limitation are evident in its repeated protestations of U.S. missile defenses in the region; they offer a glimpse into how this issue has affected China's broader assessment of U.S. intentions.[11]

What should policymakers do to manage this emerging nuclear rivalry? First, U.S. policymakers should acknowledge, at least to themselves, the trade-offs inherent in a more competitive nuclear relationship with China.[12] U.S. refusal to acknowledge mutual vulnerability, when combined with continued development of capabilities relevant to damage limitation and a worsening bilateral relationship, makes China relatively more likely to adopt an ambitious nuclear strategy than would otherwise be the case. It could create rational incentives for China to potentially move away from its no first use pledge, for example. If and when China does so, the United States should then recognize the role that its own policy choices may have played in that decision, rather than interpret such change as entirely a function of aggressive Chinese intentions. Of course, this is not an all-or-nothing equation, and it is not meant to downplay China's own motives, but the key point is simply to recognize that China will react to U.S. choices.

Second, even in a more competitive nuclear relationship, the United States can work to reduce the danger of nuclear escalation. Even if the United States believes that there are some deterrent or coercive advantages to be gained in a competitive nuclear relationship with China—advantages that depend on credible threats of escalation—the United States can still work with China to build off-ramps in the event of a crisis or war. The United States might seek to develop what RAND analysts in the Cold War once called "an optimal amount of instability": "enough to deter the [adversary] from precipitating a crisis, but not enough to cause a crisis to spiral out of control should it occur."[13] Fostering robust, direct crisis communication channels between high-level policymakers, and especially high-ranking military officers, is important in this regard, despite the challenges that such efforts face.[14]

Finally, the United States should consider engaging in arms control with China, bearing in mind that arms control in the future will probably look different from how it evolved in the Cold War. As Thomas Schelling and Morton Halperin noted decades ago, arms control can be conceptualized broadly, "to include all the forms of military cooperation between potential enemies in the interest of reducing the likelihood of a war, its scope and violence if it occurs, and the political and economic costs of being prepared for it." It requires only "the recognition that our military relation with potential enemies is not one of pure conflict and opposition, but involves strong elements of mutual interest."[15]

As former assistant secretary of state Frank Rose has argued, there are a variety of credible and creative means by which the United States might begin to integrate China into an arms control framework: convening bilateral strategic stability talks with China, expanding talks with Russia to include China, developing a bilateral pre-launch missile notification regime with China, inviting China to observe a New START inspection, establishing a link between the U.S. Nuclear Risk Reduction Center and a Chinese counterpart, and even building on Obama administration progress with China to develop norms for outer space.[16]

Arms control is not an end in itself, of course. It has to serve U.S. strategic objectives.[17] In the Cold War, the United States used arms control both to cap the arms race and, at times, to channel it into areas of competition more favorable to the United States. Although current prospects for arms control with China are dim, the U.S. relationship with the Soviets was adversarial too. The two sides still found common ground in transparency that reduced the likelihood of dangerous misperceptions in a crisis and that constrained some of the costs of peacetime competition. Despite China's long-standing resistance, the United States should continue trying to engage China in both government-to-government and nongovernmental dialogue on nuclear issues, with an eye toward developing an arms control framework over the longer term.

ACKNOWLEDGMENTS: For feedback on earlier drafts, I thank Fiona Cunningham, Brendan Green, Alex Lennon, Austin Long, Frank Rose, and an anonymous reviewer. For related conversations that sharpened my thinking, I thank Elbridge Colby, Owen Cote, Taylor Fravel, Charles Glaser, Avery Goldstein, Hans Kristensen, Keir Lieber, Vipin Narang, Michael O'Hanlon, Philip Saunders, and my students. Any errors or shortcomings are my responsibility alone.

NOTES

1. Taylor Fravel and Evan Medeiros, "China's Search for Assured Retaliation: The Evolution of Chinese Nuclear Strategy and Force Structure," *International Security* 35, no. 2 (Fall 2010): 48–87; Taylor Fravel, *Active Defense: China's Military Strategy Since 1949* (Princeton, NJ: Princeton University Press, 2019), ch. 8; Avery Goldstein, *Deterrence and Security in the 21st Century: China, Britain, France, and the Enduring Legacy of the Nuclear Revolution* (Stanford, CA: Stanford University Press, 2000); and Vipin Narang, *Nuclear Strategy in the Modern Era: Regional Powers and International Conflict* (Princeton, NJ: Princeton University Press, 2014), ch. 5.

2. Michael Pompeo and Marshall Billingslea, "China's Nuclear Buildup Should Worry the West," *Newsweek*, January 4, 2021; Robert Ashley, "Russian and Chinese Nuclear Modernization Trends," remarks at the Hudson Institute, Washington, DC, May 29, 2019, www.dia.mil/News/Speeches-and-Testimonies/Article-View/Article/1859890/russian-and-chinese-nuclear-modernization-trends/; Bill Gertz, "Stratcom: China Rapidly Building Up Nuclear Forces," *Washington Free Beacon*, August 1, 2019; and *Nuclear Posture Review Report 2018*, U.S. Department of Defense, February 5, 2018, https://dod.defense.gov/News/SpecialReports/2018NuclearPostureReview.aspx.

3. Austin Long, "U.S. Nuclear Strategy toward China: Damage Limitation and Extended Deterrence," in *America's Nuclear Crossroads: A Forward-Looking Anthology*, ed. Caroline Dorminey and Eric Gomez (Washington, DC: Cato Institute, 2019), 47–55; and Brendan Green and Austin Long, "Correspondence: The Limits of Damage Limitation," *International Security* 42, no. 1 (Summer 2017): 196–199. For a critical view, see Glaser and Fetter, "Should the United States Reject MAD? Damage Limitation and U.S. Nuclear Strategy Toward China," *International Security*, vol. 41, issue 1 (Summer 2016): 49–98.

4. Hans Kristensen and Matt Korda, "Chinese Nuclear Forces, 2019," *Bulletin of the Atomic Scientists* 75, no. 4 (2019): 171–178; and *Annual Report to Congress:*

Military and Security Developments Involving the People's Republic of China 2019, Office of the Secretary of Defense, 2019, https://media.defense.gov/2019/May/02/2002127082/-1/-1/1/2019_China_Military_Power_Report.pdf.

5. Robert Jervis, *The Meaning of the Nuclear Revolution: Statecraft and the Prospect of Armageddon* (Ithaca, NY: Cornell University Press, 1989).

6. Glenn Snyder, "The Balance of Power and the Balance of Terror," in *The Balance of Power*, ed. Paul Seabury (San Francisco: Chandler, 1965), 184–201.

7. Austin Long and Brendan Green, "Stalking the Secure Second Strike: Intelligence, Counterforce, and Nuclear Strategy," *Journal of Strategic Studies* 38, no. 1 (2015): 38–73; and Brendan Green, *The Revolution That Failed: Nuclear Competition, Arms Control, and the Cold War* (Cambridge: Cambridge University Press, 2020).

8. Glaser and Fetter, "Should the United States Reject MAD?" 49–50.

9. Avery Goldstein, "First Things First: The Pressing Danger of Crisis Instability in U.S.-China Relations," *International Security* 37, no. 4 (Spring 2013): 49–89; Caitlin Talmadge, "Would China Go Nuclear? Assessing the Risk of Chinese Nuclear Escalation in a Conventional War with the United States," *International Security* 41, no. 4 (Spring 2017): 50–92; and Caitlin Talmadge, "Beijing's Nuclear Option," *Foreign Affairs* 97, no. 6 (November/December 2018): 44–50.

10. Glaser and Fetter, "Should the United States Reject MAD?" 49–98; and James M. Acton, "Escalation through Entanglement: How the Vulnerability of Command-and-Control Systems Raises the Risks of an Inadvertent Nuclear War," *International Security* 43, no. 1 (Summer 2018): 56–99.

11. Elizabeth Shim, "Kim Jong Un Is Willing to Denuclearize, Xi Jinping Says," UPI, June 27, 2019, www.upi.com/Top_News/World-News/2019/06/27/Kim-Jong-Un-is-willing-to-denuclearize-Xi-Jinping-says/2591561644322/; and Fiona Cunningham and Taylor Fravel, "Assuring Assured Retaliation: China's Nuclear Strategy and U.S.-China Strategic Stability," *International Security* 40, no. 2 (Fall 2015): 7–50.

12. I thank the anonymous reviewer for making this point.

13. Glenn Kent and David Thaler, *First-Strike Stability: A Methodology for Evaluating Strategic Forces* (Santa Monica, CA: RAND, 1989), 5.

14. Scott Harold, "Optimizing the U.S.-China Military-to-Military Relationship," *Asia Policy* 14, no. 3 (July 2019): 145–168.

15. Thomas Schelling and Morton Halperin, *Strategy and Arms Control* (Washington, DC: Pergamon Press, 1985), 1–2.

16. Frank Rose, "The Future of Global Strategic Stability" (remarks at the Sasakawa Peace Foundation Book Launch, Tokyo, Japan, July 19, 2019), 5, available from the author.

17. Robert Joseph and Eric Edelman, "New Directions in Arms Control," *National Review*, April 29, 2016.

GREAT POWERS

How Are the World's Great Powers Maneuvering amid U.S.-China Rivalry, and Is the International System Increasingly Bipolar or Multipolar?

9

China and the Return of Great Power Strategic Competition

BRUCE JONES

China's rise to the position of the world's second-largest economy, its largest energy consumer, and its number two defense spender, has unsettled global affairs. Beijing's shift in strategy toward a more assertive posture is amplifying a change in international dynamics from patterns of cooperation toward a pattern of competition. We are entering, or have entered, a phase of rivalry between the great and major powers.

While several states and actors have agency in this unfolding dynamic, the choices made by the United States and China will matter more than those of others. The interplay between those two countries' choices will shape the prospects for peace, especially in East Asia and the Western Pacific; for prosperity, globally; for the way technology plays into the next phase of social and economic dynamics; and for the role and space accorded to democracy and human rights in international affairs.

On American and Chinese choices hinge three scenarios. We could face the "return of the jungle"—a period of increasingly unchecked rivalry between the world's top powers, with risk of military conflict growing apace.[1] In a more ideal scenario, all powers could exercise a degree of respect for the key treaties and provisions of the multilateral system, and the existing order could hold. Between these two extremes, we could see the emergence of a period defined by sharp competition but not outright hostility—one in which the risk of conflict is present but not dominant, and in which the major liberal powers work together in new arrangements to defend key interests and key values. America should prefer that outcome, and the obvious policy implication for the United States is to bolster its alliances and defend the core precepts of the multilateral order. Instead, in recent years, America has turned to unilateralism.

BACKDROP: AN EVOLVING INTERNATIONAL ORDER

It is commonplace to hear American pundits and policymakers talk about a seventy-five-year tradition of American foreign policy premised on defense of a "liberal international order." In point of fact, both the nature of international order and America's role in it have evolved considerably.

The first phase was brief and more aspirational than actual—an effort to design U.S.-Soviet cooperation on international security and in the reconstruction of Europe. That quickly collapsed and gave way to the Marshall Plan, NATO, and the start of the Cold War. The five decades of the Cold War were oriented toward deterrence and great power competition, though they had moments of cooperation (on global health and proliferation) as well as a sustained focus on arms control.

At the end of the Cold War, much of the rhetoric and some of the patterns of earlier periods continued, but in reality, the basic structure of international relations changed: the collapse of the Soviet Union left the United States alone atop international affairs.[2] The first decade that followed saw the United States exercise its hegemonic power in large part by advancing multilateral arrangements for trade and security, and inviting formal rivals to join those institutions.[3] It was a period of widening prosperity and relative comity in great power relations—not free of conflict or tensions but largely free of a risk of large-scale military clashes among the top powers.[4] This post–Cold War dynamic was interrupted by the al-Qaida attacks of September 11, 2001, and the start of what would become nearly two decades of sustained American warfare in the wider Middle East. And then the Arab Spring, the global financial crisis, and the growth of the "rising powers" conspired to bring this phase of American unipolarity to a close.

What followed was a confused and turbulent decade. Key markers of the uncertainty of the times came in Russia's seizure and annexation of Crimea from Ukraine; in U.S.-U.K. dithering over Syria; in China's decision to install military facilities initially on Woody Island in the South China Sea;

and in the failure of multiple rounds of negotiations of the World Trade Organization. These dynamics of deterioration were alleviated by episodes of successful cooperation, but they were not reversed by these more positive developments.

And all that was before the Brexit referendum and the election of Donald Trump brought skeptics of integration to power in London and Washington—the two key architects and managers of the postwar international system. And before COVID-19 cast grave doubt on the ability or willingness of the world's two largest economies to cooperate even on major transnational threats.

FIVE FEATURES OF THE WORLD THAT THE UNITED STATES AND CHINA CONFRONT

This brings us to the present, and the choices that Washington and Beijing confront. Five features of the present order seem most consequential.

The first is the continued scale and weight of the United States. For all the talk of decline and all the retreat to semi-isolationist instincts, the United States remains the world's largest individual market, has the largest and most powerful armed capacity in the world, and has a network of global bases and security relationships that is eroded but far from eclipsed. The United States retains huge power in international affairs.

The second is the evolving posture of China. Many elements of Chinese strategy are debatable, but few would query the notion that China under Xi Jinping has shed its "peaceful rise" (together with the more subtle "hide and bide") in favor of a more assertive, more nationalist, and more ideological approach.[5] The United States has also become more ideological in its response.

The third feature is the sizeable gap between the power of the top two players and all the rest. Several other players have a world-leading capacity in one issue space, but only the United States and China now have genuinely global economic, technological, and political influence, with the United States also having global military capacity—and China potentially catching up on that score.

The fourth feature of the contemporary order is a layer of major powers vying for space and security. These are the European Union (especially Germany), Britain, Russia, India, and Japan. Each of these countries or entities has a major population, substantial economic weight, or military heft—but none have all three. Together, and with others in the G-20 or that make major multilateral contributions, they are a consequential fact of international affairs. Within this realm, U.S. allies constitute a powerful contingent—*if* they can be wielded in new, more nimble ways.

Last, least, but not inconsequential is the continued existence of a wide and deep network of multilateral institutions, commitments, and mechanisms that bind together large parts of the rest of the world, and in which deep habits of cooperation have been forged. The major multilateral mechanisms are frayed and fragile, but not yet abandoned or broken, and COVID-19 has reminded us of their salience.[6]

WHAT CHOICES DO THE GREAT POWERS HAVE?

In the context of these features, if the United States more deeply abandons its alliance commitments or more fully alienates its core allies, the first effect of this will be to make the world safer for Russian adventurism and Chinese ambition. Some have argued differently, making the case that it is the very fact of the alliance structure that is provoking Chinese and Russian behavior and that a retreat from its forward posture in Asia and Europe will lead to more stable self-help arrangements among our former allies.[7] While the point needs to be argued country by country, the early evidence is not encouraging. Turkey could have taken diminished U.S. interest in the Middle East as an opportunity to deepen ties with Berlin and Brussels; instead it has turned toward Moscow. Japan and South Korea could have taken their growing concern about the credibility of America's commitment in Asia as an opportunity to bury the hatchet and join hands in blunting the effect of Chinese pressure; instead their relationship is in its worst state in decades. Europe could be treating an inward turn in America as grounds for deeper cooperation in fiscal and military affairs: instead we see Brexit and the resurgence of far-right parties across the European landscape. Each of these dynamics is adding to disorder and the risk of conflict.

However, even as the United States renews its focus on the alliance structure and multilateralism, it will confront some uncomfortable realities. First among them is the simple fact that the economic and technological weight of China—now, not in the future—means that China will be able to claim a full seat at the table in the writing of the next phase of the rules of the international trade, financial, and technological order. Will the United States accede? The values costs to doing so would be high. If not, we are likely to see some areas of economic decoupling accelerate (at substantial economic cost to both), and perhaps the emergence of two zones of globalization.

China confronts uncomfortable realities as well. Although Xi Jinping conveys a sense of exuberance about China's new status, the fact is that he confronts a degree of elite discontent at home, and a deteriorating reputation in the West (and in some parts of the developing world). For all the displeasure of European elites and publics about American political unilateralism, few are so gullible as to confuse their unhappiness about contemporary American policy with sympathy for China's own brand of increasingly assertive unilateralism (let alone Russia's recklessness, which China not only tolerates but indirectly enables).

What is more, China confronts an unenviable international structure, most notably in the form of the immediate presence on its eastern borders of a network of U.S. allies. It may, over time, succeed in weakening the alignment of some of those allies, like the Philippines or South Korea. But not others—there are few historically credible scenarios that see Japan or Australia fall into the Chinese camp. It also confronts a United States that even in a moment of deep internal division has forged a growing elite and social consensus about the problem of China (though not about a strategy).

An obvious move for China is not to confront the United States but to seek to erode its influence. This could be accomplished by supplanting the United States in the developing world (providing loans on attractive terms, technological and financial know-how, and noninterference on domestic policy); filling gaps left by U.S. myopia in shaping the work of multilateral institutions; and imposing substantial financial and political costs on countries in its own neighborhood if they align with the United States. Washington will be hard pressed to respond effectively to such a strategy, absent policy shifts and a deeper engagement with allies in Asia, Europe, and Latin America.

One key variable in all this is the prospect for deeper Russia-China cooperation. When American analysts debate the prospect for an "alliance" between Russia and China, many of them are quick to dismiss such an idea, pointing to a difficult history, a lack of trust, and the fact that Moscow would chafe at the role of junior partner. But this may be imposing too much of a Western sensibility on the framework that Moscow and Beijing would use to assess their options. We could see the emergence of a "tactical concert" between Russia and China—two rivals who set aside some of their differences for the greater gain of weakening the top power, or breaking the alliance.

Indeed, we are already seeing something of this behavior in Central Asia, in the Middle East, in the Arctic, and in the Western Pacific.

WHAT LIES AHEAD?

If China and Russia were to reach a concert arrangement of this sort, and if American unilateralism drives a deeper wedge between itself and its allies, we could rapidly find ourselves in a world characterized by two more equal blocks of military competitors and a situation brimming with risks of direct military confrontation between the two. This scenario, and variants on it, although not as yet baked in, is now solidly within the world of the feasible.

Another scenario is that both Washington and Beijing, pushed by their allies/neighbors and aware of the substantial costs to themselves of direct confrontation, instead pursue a path of strategic competition. This would still entail substantial risk, but less quickly and less directly. It would involve a military focus on deterrence, and an arms race, but combined with a willingness to invest in arms control mechanisms or deconfliction and de-escalation arrangements. It would involve some degree of continued economic engagement, although it would also be compatible with the emergence over time of a kind of bifurcated globalization—the emergence of two zones of technological, infrastructure, and commercial integration, one that has Beijing as its hub and for which Beijing sets the rules of the game, and the other revolving around Washington and its core allies.

Between these two options, many in DC now hope that the United States can construct a third scenario—oriented toward the democracies. This would involve pulling the major economies of Asia and Europe together into a wider "partnership"—a kind of wider-than-the-West concert of free societies (or largely free societies), which would work together to deter China, Russia, and others that would erode the core structures of stability and trade. Tom Wright has argued a "free world" version of this approach; an alternative is a form of "democratic multilateralism." It would require important shifts in the global supply chain, but not unmanageable ones. It might result in two globalizations—one Chinese led, one American led—but not to the breakdown of globalization itself. It would constrict China, and occasionally confront China, but it would not have to be organized in the first instance to engage in conflict with China. It would not obviate cooperation with China on issues like poverty reduction, infectious disease and public health, ocean science and ocean pollution, and climate change.

Should the United States seek to pursue such a strategy, it would be required to shed both the unilateralist instinct of President Trump and President Obama's aversion to the use of coercive power as a tool of diplomacy. It would require American strategic elites to restore political ties with NATO while reorienting American strategic policy away from its trans-Atlantic habits toward a wider set of partnerships. And above all—especially after the disastrous mismanagement of the American response to COVID-19 and the turmoil surrounding police oppression and the Black Lives Matter moment—it will require the United States to demonstrate a willingness to engage in serious reform of its own flawed and divided democracy.

One way or another, great power competition between the United States and China seems set to be the Archimedean point in contemporary international affairs.

NOTES

1. Robert Kagan, *The Jungle Grows Back: America and Our Imperiled World* (New York: Penguin Random House, 2018).

2. For different accounts of this moment, see Michael Mandelbaum, *The Case for Goliath: How America Acts as the World's Government in the 21st Century* (New York: Public Affairs, 2005); Andrew J. Bacevich, *American Empire: The Realities and Consequences of U.S. Diplomacy* (Cambridge, MA.: Harvard University Press, 2002); and Hal Brands, *Making the Unipolar Moment: U.S. Foreign Policy and the Rise of the Post–Cold War Order* (Ithaca, NY: Cornell University Press, 2016).

3. See G. John Ikenberry, *Liberal Leviathan: The Origins, Crisis, and Transformation of the American World Order* (Princeton, NJ: Princeton University Press, 2011).

4. Thomas J. Wright, *All Measures Short of War: The Contest for the 21st Century and the Future of American Power* (New Haven, CT: Yale University Press, 2017).

5. See inter alia Alexander Sullivan, Andrew Erickson, Elbridge Colby, Ely Ratner, and Zachary Hosford, *More Willing and More Able: Charting China's International Security Activism* (Washington, DC: Center for a New American Security, May 19, 2015), www.cnas.org/publications/reports/more-willing-and-able -charting-chinas-international-security-activism.

6. Bruce Jones, Jeffrey Feltman, and Will Moreland, *Competitive Multilateralism: Adapting Institutions to Meet the New Geopolitical Environment* (Washington, DC: Brookings Institution Press, September 2019), www.brookings.edu/research/ competitive-multilateralism/.

7. See inter alia Chris Preble, *The Power Problem: How American Military Dominance Makes Us Less Safe, Less Prosperous, and Less Free* (Ithaca, NY: Cornell University Press, 2009).

10

U.S.-China Relations

The Search for a New Equilibrium

RYAN HASS

In recent years, the U.S.-China relationship has undergone a rapid deterioration. Left unchecked, the relationship appears poised to continue traveling a sharply downward trajectory, even in spite of the considerable risks that would accompany an intensification of rivalry between the world's two most capable powers.

This chapter argues that leaders in both countries need not—and should not—accept the reductive logic of unavoidable enmity or conflict. To escape such an outcome, policymakers in both countries will need to reprioritize efforts to find an equilibrium to the relationship that allows both to coexist within a state of heightened competition. Such a process will not come naturally or easily to a relationship as badly battered as the present-day U.S.-China rivalry. Nevertheless, such efforts will be necessary for both powers to be able to free up resources and attention needed to promote the security and prosperity of their own peoples.

THE FORCES DRIVING THE DOWNWARD TRAJECTORY OF RELATIONS

It has become popular in the United States to argue that the downturn in U.S.-China relations is attributable to Xi Jinping, or at a minimum, to China's shift in policy orientation under Xi. At the same time, Chinese counterparts routinely argue that the United States is acting like an anxious declining power grasping for opportunities to slow the rise of its foremost competitor. The common thread tying both arguments together is that they each are used in respective capitals to justify the current policy course. The uncomfortable reality is that there are much deeper forces at work than either of these superficial arguments suggest.

Dissatisfaction with the Regional Security Status Quo

The first structural discontinuity is that the United States and China both are dissatisfied with the regional security status quo. This was not previously the case. For several decades following the formal establishment of diplomatic relations, there was a division of labor between both countries in the Asia-Pacific region. Although they were not generally codified in writing, the understandings were largely accepted by policymakers in both countries. The basic understanding was that the United States would use its predominant power to deter conflict, preserve a relatively stable security order, and push to open markets. China would defer external ambitions and focus mostly on lifting up its own people. Additionally, neither side would abandon the diplomatic framework for managing differences over Taiwan, as enumerated in three U.S.-China joint communiques.

Now, both the United States and China hold each other in violation of these understandings and show no interest in working to update them. The United States is increasingly pursuing a more formal relationship with Taiwan as a counter to China's tightening squeeze there. Meanwhile, Beijing is investing massive sums in military modernization and is deploying its growing capabilities in ways that appear intended to signal to America's closest allies and partners in Asia that it will always be nearby and active, and that there is risk in crossing China and then counting on the United States for security (figure 10-1).

China's Emergence as a Global Rulemaker

China is becoming the first non-Western power in the modern international system with the weight and ambition to reshape the rules of the international order.[1] While the Soviet Union posed its own challenges to the international order, it did not actively seek to build global institutional order in the way China has sought, nor did it have the capabilities to do so. Since its inception at the end of World War II, the modern system of rules, norms,

Figure 10-1. **China's Military Spending**

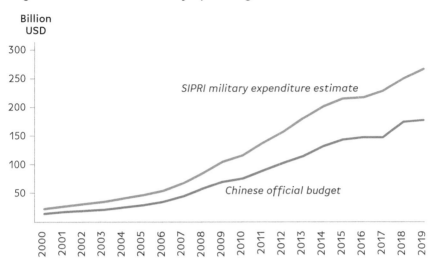

Billion
USD

Source: "SIPRI Military Expenditure Database," Stockholm International Peace Research Institute, www.sipri.org/ databases/milex; National Bureau of Statistics of China, www.stats .gov.cn/english/Statisticaldata/AnnualData/; Ministry of National Defense of the People's Republic of China, www.mod.gov.cn/.

and institutions has never been static, but it has also never come up for broad-scale reevaluation.

Now, questions abound about the continuing efficacy of the international system. Some of the questions result from a prevalence of antipathy in the United States toward international institutions, which some Americans view as limiting America's ability to exercise power advantages over all other countries on the world stage. Beijing has also sought to exploit leadership vacuums created by American retreat, whether on climate change, human rights, public health, or Iran. China has also worked to cultivate international support for its normative approach on issues such as internet governance, the relative importance of social stability over individual liberties, as well as the limited role for international institutions in addressing human rights issues within countries. More broadly, China is working to secure international acceptance of (or nonhostility toward) its state-led economic model and Leninist political model.

The Growing Centrality of Technology
Competition in U.S.-China Relations

In the span of recent decades, China has transformed itself from a low-wage assembly line for the manufacture of American-engineered products to a near-peer competitor of the United States in the innovation frontier. The speed and scale of China's technological ascent has triggered American concerns about implications for its own security and prosperity in a globalized twenty-first-century economy. These concerns have been intensified by China's use of state funds to subsidize production costs and undercut global competition, as was the case with solar panels and, more recently, Huawei's efforts to secure the commanding heights of global 5G networks.

China's technological progress is also placing stress on American national security. U.S. officials are concerned that China could leverage technological breakthroughs in foundational technologies, such as machine learning, to gain advantages over U.S. forces.[2]

Intensifying Ideological and Systems Competition

There are also concerns that China no longer remains content nurturing its governance system at home and now seeks to encourage other countries to replicate its political model. President Xi fanned this debate when he told the 19th Party Congress in 2017 that "China offers a new option for other countries and nations who want to speed up their development while preserving their independence." Xi's statement sparked a wave of commentary in the United States about the reemergence of ideological competition.[3] The U.S. intelligence community similarly sounded the alarm, writing in the 2019 Worldwide Threat Assessment that "China's leaders will increasingly seek to assert China's model of authoritarian capitalism as an alternative—and implicitly superior—development path abroad, exacerbating greatpower competition that could threaten international support for democracy, human rights, and rule of law."[4]

Even if China does not seek to export its governance model, its practices nevertheless offer an example for other countries to emulate. In recent years, Beijing has promulgated measures to limit civil society and curb dissent at the same time as it has made available for export technologically advanced surveillance and monitoring platforms. As more countries embrace Chinese laws and technologies in their pursuit of strengthened social control, the effect is to "normalize" China's domestic social stability practices.

Taken together, these four discontinuities in the U.S.-China relationship suggest that the relationship is not merely navigating another cyclical down-swing, as it did in 1989, 1996, 1999, or 2001,[5] in the wake of unanticipated events. Rather, the relationship is encountering deeper structural stresses as both countries adjust to shifts in the relative power dynamics between them.

POLICY RECOMMENDATIONS FOR THE UNITED STATES

The work of rebalancing the U.S.-China relationship toward a more durable equilibrium that enables both countries to coexist within a state of height-ened competition will require efforts from both sides. Since I am a former American policy practitioner working at an American think tank, I will focus my comments on the U.S. side of the ledger. I would be remiss if I did not stress, however, that unless China moderates its behaviors that are ag-gravating nearly every important American political constituency simulta-neously, there will be limited political space for future American leaders to chart a more constructive path for the relationship.

Right-Size the Risk That China Poses to U.S. Interests
With its dynamic economy, technologically advanced military, geographic positioning, and ambitious national goals, China poses the most significant challenge to American leadership in the twenty-first century. At the same time, China also faces significant challenges. These include, but are not lim-ited to, the social, health, and economic shocks resulting from the ongoing COVID-19 pandemic; energy and food insecurity; demographic headwinds; a heavy debt overhang; declining rates of productivity growth; acute ethnic and social divisions; and a sclerotic political system. China's economy is ex-periencing a long-term declining growth rate.

Externally, it should not be taken as given that China is on an unbreak-able path toward eclipsing the United States for influence on the world stage. Diplomatically, China's recent actions have done more to repel than to at-tract international support. Recent Pew Research polling shows that majori-ties or pluralities in nearly every country surveyed say the future would be better if the United States rather than China remains the world's leading power.[6]

From a strategic perspective, China's military remains relatively constrained in its ability to project force beyond its immediate periphery. There are no future guarantees that China will successfully marry power projection with political and economic influence on a global scale—definitional features of a global superpower.

Furthermore, China will likely encounter greater budgetary constraints on its massive overseas initiatives going forward. With an aging society, an underdeveloped social safety net, a cooling economy, an ongoing rebalancing of distribution of tax revenues between central and local governments, and an end to its era of current account surpluses, there will be intensifying competition for central government resources.[7]

Finally, American leaders will need to right-size the challenges posed by China's efforts to influence American public discourse and steal intellectual property. This will require moving beyond sweeping statements about "whole of society" threats that risk a resurgence of "Yellow Peril" racism, and instead relying on lawful tools to disrupt Chinese government–directed activities of greatest concern.

Develop a New, Shared Framework for the U.S.-China Relationship
Bereft of a shared logic, enmity and anxiety have come to define the U.S.-China relationship. Even so, neither side is capable of imposing its will on the other, short of risking catastrophic conflict. With both countries serving as the twin engines of the global economy and simultaneously trading over $600 billion in goods and services between them, it defies imagination to conceive of a scenario whereby one country rises while the other one falls, even as both countries strive to secure their own supply chains for sensitive technologies.[8] By the same token, it is also difficult to conceive of progress being achieved in addressing any of the most pressing transnational challenges—such as climate change, nonproliferation, public health, closing the development gap—if the world's two largest actors are out of sync in their responses. The failure of Washington and Beijing to coordinate on the common threat from the COVID-19 pandemic serves as a painful reminder of the costs and consequences of dysfunctional U.S.-China relations. A shared rejection of the inevitability of conflict along with a recognition of the mutual benefit of sharing the burden in addressing common challenges would provide an identifiable logic for both sides to work toward developing a more durable and productive relationship.

Revive Efforts to Influence China's Behavior

In recent years, a sense of fatalism has set in regarding America's inability to influence China's choices. A view took hold within the Trump administration that China stood too far apart from American interests or values to be influenced by traditional diplomacy; therefore, the only way to alter China's choices is through unilateral exertion of pressure. This approach failed to influence China's calculus, as Secretary Pompeo's consistent complaints about worsening Chinese behavior made clear. The Trump administration's reliance on negative reciprocity (e.g., taking something away and then demanding concession to return it) inflamed resentments without delivering results.

In the past, the United States has had some success, albeit limited, in influencing Chinese behavior. For example, persistent and focused American diplomacy pushed China to shift from being the world's leading proliferator to working with other major powers to halt proliferation. At America's urging, China cut its current account surplus, helping to fuel global economic expansion over the past decade. The United States also nudged China from being a problem to a partner in spurring global action on climate change, and pushed China off the sidelines in responding to the Ebola outbreak in 2014. It will need to adapt lessons from these experiences for addressing present challenges in the relationship.

Focus on Restoring Sources of Comparative
Advantage in Competition with China

In recent years, the United States has been undermining its own strengths in its competition with China. Washington has been treating its security alliances as areas of unrealized profit, instead of as platforms for addressing twenty-first-century challenges. This transactional approach has led to a degradation of America's global alliance network. To improve its ability to influence the strategic environment in which China pursues its interests, the United States will need to reprioritize efforts to aggregate the power and influence of its alliances and partnerships.

The United States has also been bleeding international prestige and leadership. While there has always been tension between values and interests in American foreign policy, that tension has mostly dissipated in favor of interests in recent years, to the detriment of America's image as a principled leader on the world stage.

At the same time, the United States has also been experiencing an erosion of national cohesion and accompanying political gridlock. The twin shocks of a demographic transition and a fourth industrial revolution have provided fertile ground for populism and nationalism to sprout. As they have done so, hyperpartisanship has intensified.

While the prescriptions for reinvesting in alliance relationships, restoring America's international prestige, and overcoming domestic political divisions are beyond the scope of this chapter, the upshot is that all of these challenges are self-induced, and all of them are fixable.

CONCLUSION

A key challenge for the United States is regaining confidence that if it lives up to its own potential, it can protect its vital interests in its competition with China. Confidence fosters steadiness, and steadiness signals the durability of strategy. China's perceptions of the durability of any American undertaking are fundamental to their calculations of how seriously to factor in America's concerns when evaluating their own approach.

The United States does not need to defeat China, but it does need to maintain the capability to deter China, constrain the export of the more malign aspects of its system, and strengthen its own global competitiveness and attractiveness. The more credibly Washington signals its determination on these fundamental issues, the better the odds that it will be able to work with Beijing to develop a new equilibrium that allows both countries to coexist within a state of heightened competition. This process could take years, and it could take decades. Establishing a new equilibrium will not come quickly and will not be easy for either side to accept. But it will remain vastly preferable to the available alternatives.

NOTES

1. Bruce Jones, "China and the Return of Great Power Strategic Competition," (Washington, DC: The Brookings Institution, February 24, 2020), www.brookings .edu/research/china-and-the-return-of-great-power-strategic-competition/.

2. Kathrin Hille, "Washington Unnerved by China's 'Military-Civil Fusion,'" *Financial Times*, November 8, 2018, www.ft.com/content/8dcb534c-dbaf-11e8-9f04 -38d397e6661c.

3. Hal Brands, "China's Master Plan: Exporting an Ideology," Bloomberg, June 11, 2018, www.bloomberg.com/opinion/articles/2018-06-11/china-s-master-plan -exporting-an-ideology.

4. Daniel R. Coats, "Statement for the Record: Worldwide Threat Assessment of the US Intelligence Community" (Washington, DC, Office of the Director of National Intelligence, January 2019), www.dni.gov/files/ODNI/documents/2019-ATA -SFR---SSCI.pdf.

5. Referring respectively to tensions over the Tiananmen Square tragedy (1989), the Chinese military intimidation against Taiwan in the run-up to its election (1996), the U.S. bombing of the Chinese embassy in Belgrade during NATO's operation against Yugoslavia in the Kosovo War (1999), and the collision of a U.S. EP-3 signals intelligence aircraft and a Chinese fighter jet off Hainan (2001).

6. Richard Wike, Bruce Stokes, Jacob Poushter, Laura Silver, Janell Fetterolf, and Kat Devlin, "Trump's International Ratings Remain Low, Especially among Key Allies" (Washington, DC, Pew Research Center, October 1, 2018), www.pewresearch .org/global/2018/10/01/trumps-international-ratings-remain-low-especially -among-key-allies/. See section 4, "Most Prefer That U.S., Not China, Be the World's Leading Power," www.pewresearch.org/global/2018/10/01/most-prefer-that-u-s-not -china-be-the-worlds-leading-power/.

7. Paula Campbell Roberts and Ken Mehlman, "What Does Population Aging Mean for Growth and Investments?" KKR, February 13, 2018, www.kkr.com/global -perspectives/publications/what_does_population_aging_mean_for_growth_ and_investments.

8. "The People's Republic of China," Office of the United States Trade Representative, accessed January 8, 2021, https://ustr.gov/countries-regions/china-mon golia-taiwan/peoples-republic-china.

11

China, Japan, and the Art of Economic Statecraft

MIREYA SOLÍS

To some observers, Asia is moving toward a long, familiar past—a China-centric regional order. While the jury is still out on the outcome of rekindled strategic rivalry between China and the United States (an extraregional actor enjoying primacy during the past seven decades), most believe it is game over when it comes to Asian great power competition. The conclusion seems obvious to most: China has eclipsed Japan. However, a focus on economic statecraft—purposive state action closely linking economic and security goals and leveraging material wealth to achieve influence abroad—renders this judgment premature.

BUILDING A REGION, DEFINING THE WORLD

Economic engagement has been at the heart of Japan's and China's bids for international leadership. In the twenty-first century, the task for Japan has been to exert influence with dwindling resources (official development assistance [ODA] budgets have been slashed for years) and avoid becoming a legacy power banking on the economic footprint built during its days of glory. For China, the major burst in material capabilities has purchased great influence, but significant challenges loom ahead in ensuring the long-term sustainability of Belt and Road Initiative (BRI) projects and preventing a backlash in recipient countries out of concern with onerous lending terms or undue political influence.

Comparing the muscle behind each country's economic statecraft is an inexact exercise at best given the paucity of Chinese data. A useful source of information is the AidData project, which uses public information sources on specific projects to track China's economic footprint. It estimates that between 2000 and 2014, China's official finance commitments (ODA and other official flows [OOF], such as export and investment credits) amounted to $354 billion.[1] During the same period, Japan's official finance (ODA plus OOF gross disbursements) amounted to $305 billion, with an additional $83 billion disbursed between 2015 and 2017, according to Organization for Economic Co-operation and Development (OECD) data.[2] The bulk of China's development finance centers on infrastructure with close to 60 percent of funds concentrated in energy, transport, and communications projects. The same is true for Japan. Figure 11-1 shows that Japan alone has provided 43 percent of all ODA committed to economic infrastructure projects by industrialized nations for the past four decades. And Japan's lead among Development Assistance Committee nations intensified in the twenty-first century, a time when the country suffered deflation and domestic contraction and was buffeted by the global financial crisis and the March 2011 triple disaster (earthquake, tsunami, and nuclear accident). When it comes to the mobilization of state resources to finance economic infrastructure abroad, only Japan is in serious competition with China.

How do China's and Japan's economic footprints measure up in Southeast Asia, a region at the center of great power competition? When it comes to infrastructure finance, Japan is ahead according to a widely noted report by Fitch Solutions, with $367 billion in pending projects across six ASEAN nations (Indonesia, Malaysia, Philippines, Singapore, Thailand, and Vietnam). Fitch Solutions puts the value of Chinese pending infrastructure projects in Southeast Asia at $255 billion.[3] Figure 11-2 reveals an interesting contrast regarding the weight of ASEAN's trade and investment flows with the world's three largest national economies. On the left side of the graph appears the well-known dominance of China as the region's top trading partner. On the right side, it is clear that China still lags behind Japan and the United States in terms of foreign direct investment flows to the region.

Leadership does not materialize without a compelling vision. China's flagship initiative, the Belt and Road Initiative, has captured the world's

Figure 11-1. ODA Commitments in Economic Infrastructure

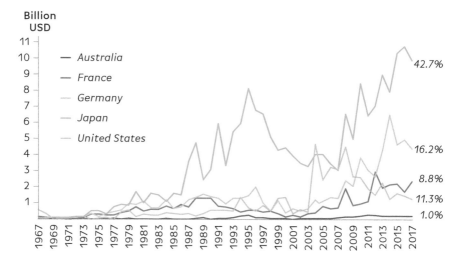

Note: Percentages reflect country shares of cumulative total, 1967–2017.

Source: OECD QWIDS Database.

Figure 11-2. ASEAN's Trade and Investment by Selected Partner Country (2010–2018)

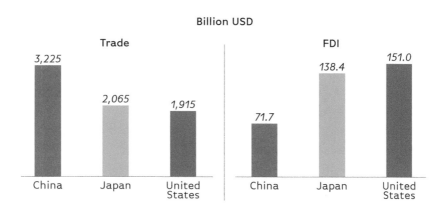

Source: ASEAN Stats Data Portal.

imagination with its promise to channel a trillion dollars toward the construction of economic corridors on land and at sea across Eurasia. In the past few years, however, China has learned that the road to becoming a titan of development finance is full of opportunity and risk. China supplied a commodity keenly desired in the region—capital to ameliorate the infrastructure finance gap choking economic growth. Relying on policy banks that are less constrained by exacting lending standards of multilateral development banks, but offer credit on less concessional terms, the Chinese state extended loans for infrastructure projects, animated by a mix of objectives. The motivations have ranged from the purely economic (nurturing domestic industries, disposing of excess capacity, promoting the regional integration of hinterland provinces) to the strategic (expanding its political influence in recipient countries, gaining access to ports across the region that ease Chinese concerns over maritime chokepoints, etc.).[4]

However, concerns over onerous lending terms, have brought greater international scrutiny, and in some instances, loan renegotiations as evidenced in Malaysia's East Coast Rail project. Looking at data on external debt relative to gross national income, David Dollar concludes that among BRI recipients in Southeast Asia, only Laos is at risk of insolvency.[5] Even if unsustainable debt is not as widespread as commonly asserted, China is aware that fragile BRI projects will siphon away precious financial resources at a time when its domestic economy is slowing down, and could backfire in terms of deepening ties with target countries. Hence the Chinese leadership recalibrated during the second Belt and Road Forum in the spring of 2019 (at least rhetorically) by adopting the concept of "quality infrastructure"— long Japan's calling card in this field.

For the first time, Japan has offered an ambitious blueprint for regional development and stability, coining the Free and Open Indo-Pacific construct with a whole-of-government approach. Its animating principles are rule of law, democratic values, freedom of navigation, and economic connectivity (through quality infrastructure finance and a free trade architecture that provides rules for free flows of data and governance of the digital economy).[6]

Rising and established powers (China, India, and the United States) have been important reference points in the evolution of this landmark Japanese initiative. Japan has coped with China's growing ambitions and capabilities by stretching the boundaries of the region beyond East Asia to include Australia, New Zealand, India, and the United States in regional institutions and collaborative efforts, such as the East Asia Summit and the Quad. Bilateral ties between Japan and India have deepened with the establishment of a 2+2 dialogue between each country's foreign and defense ministers, Japan's participation in the U.S.-Indian Malabar military exercises, and plans for an acquisition and cross-servicing agreement for military supplies. Importantly, India has refrained from partaking in the BRI for geostrategic reasons, giving Japan an important advantage in Asia's third-largest economy.

Japan has keenly felt competition with China. Tokyo abstained from joining the Asian Infrastructure Investment Bank as a founding member, citing concerns over the new bank's internal governance and worried about weakening the clout of the Asian Development Bank. Instead, in the spring of 2015, Prime Minister Shinzo Abe announced the Partnership for Quality Infrastructure in Asia with a commitment of $110 billion, later expanded globally to $200 billion, to be disbursed in five years. Tokyo embarked on a diplomatic campaign to codify its quality infrastructure standards across a broad set of platforms: Asia-Pacific Economic Cooperation, the OECD, the G-7, and, most recently, the G-20. These principles (open access to infrastructure services, transparency of procurement, debt sustainability, and economic efficiency over the life cycle of the project) are geared to highlight Japan's competitive assets in development finance.

How much political capital are China and Japan deriving from their vigorous programs of development finance? Traditionally, this question has focused on the ability to use economic inducements to create relations of trust with recipient countries. By this measure, Japan is far ahead. A recent ISEAS–Yusof Ishak Institute survey has Japan in the lead on "trust" rankings with 61.2 percent in positive responses, and China at the bottom with 16.1 percent.[7] Donor-to-donor relations are a second avenue to cultivate political capital. Coordinated action in infrastructure finance can serve as an opportunity to showcase shared development and foreign policy priorities and to develop habits of cooperation among implementing agencies. Individual donors may also be interested in pooling efforts for reputational benefits, to assure both recipients and fellow donors about underlying motivations and the soundness of lending practices. Thus many have called for China to multilateralize the BRI in order to instill confidence in its development finance push. However, the challenge for China is steep, as noted by Brad Parks. China has not taken full responsibilities as a member of the Paris Club for creditor nations and has chosen not to abide by the OECD's export credit guidelines. Furthermore, the opaqueness of BRI loans prevents cooperation with other international development finance agencies.[8] In fact, Japan is better poised to multilateralize its Partnership for Quality Infrastructure to signal a commonality of purpose with fellow donors. Tokyo has launched coordinated infrastructure funds with the United States, Australia, India, and the European Union. And the Abe cabinet has also opened the door for cooperation with China on infrastructure projects in third countries, provided China adopts Japan's quality infrastructure standards, as part of a campaign to improve Sino-Japanese relations.

ON THE LIMITS OF SINO-JAPANESE RAPPROCHEMENT

The Trump presidency has been a major factor behind the visible thaw in Sino-Japanese relations with a reactivation of bilateral political dialogue since 2018. Growing uncertainty about the role of the United States created a powerful incentive for Asia's great powers to stabilize their relationship after years in deep disrepair. Beijing is reeling from a bruising trade war, which is perceived as just the first chapter of a wider strategic contest with the United States; Tokyo is seeking to improve its external environment at a time when the American president is critical of trade agreements and host-nation support arrangements for U.S. military bases, and may compromise with the North Korean leader on missile and nuclear capabilities at the expense of Japan's security.

The improvement of Japan-China ties, however, is no prelude to a reordering of Asian geopolitics. There is no seismic change in security alignments at work. If anything, the trendline of the past decade continues: China exerting pressure on Japan's administrative control of the Senkaku Islands, and Japan investing in deterrence capabilities with China foremost in mind, betting on the alliance with the United States (with forays into collective self-defense, concessions on trade, and Abe's personal diplomacy with Trump), and fostering security partnerships with like-minded democracies.[9] Rather, the current rapprochement is interesting for what it reveals about the ability of Chinese and Japanese leaders to make pragmatic adjustments to new realities in international politics, and the keen sensitivity displayed by the Asian powers to an unpredictable United States. But it is also indicative of the difficulties in executing limited collaboration among them—official blessings aside.

The pandemic has added strain to Japan-China relations. President Xi Jinping's state visit to Japan (originally planned for spring 2020) was suspended and may not come to pass anytime soon. China's assertiveness in the

East China Sea and the harsh line it took with Hong Kong's national security law have weakened support in Japan for hosting Xi. Additionally, Tokyo has launched a $2.2 billion subsidy plan to avoid overdependence on China by returning some production back to Japan or diversifying into Southeast Asia. The subsidies do not amount to a decoupling effort—they are small compared to the stock of Japanese investment in China—but they do speak of a desire to hedge against a growing China risk.

Going forward, other arenas of economic statecraft, however, are likely to pose a harder edge for Sino-Japanese competition. China's technological push (with research and development investments that far surpass Japan's), its industrial policy goal of achieving 70 percent domestic content in core materials and components with a central role to state-owned enterprises (SOEs) and generous public subsidies in targeted sectors, and the 2017 Cybersecurity Law giving the state greater reach into telecommunications have brought an acute quandary to Tokyo's doorstep: how to balance economic internationalism and economic security. Japan's concerns with technological leakage, such as weak intellectual property protection in China and pressure on Japanese companies to surrender proprietary knowhow to enter the Chinese market, are long-standing. The novelty lies in the fact that Japan has catapulted to a leading role in drafting international trade and investment rules. Japan's proactive stance is evident not only in the Comprehensive and Progressive Agreement for Trans-Pacific Partnership (CPTPP), but also in the tripartite effort with the United States and the EU to codify new disciplines on market-distorting policies (forced technology transfer, investment restrictions, unfair advantages to SOEs, lack of transparency on subsidies, etc.). Hence Japan's planned contribution to World Trade Organization reform aims to curtail the very same practices that China has used or will continue to rely on in its technology upgrading bid.

Another major thrust of action has emerged: defensive measures to prevent technology flows that could harm national security. The Japanese government recently embarked on greater integration of economic policies with national security, establishing an economic division in the National Security Secretariat. Japanese officials have worried that the tightening of investment and export controls in the West could make Japan a soft target for the acquisition of critical technology that could be diverted to military use. Revisions to Japan's Foreign Exchange Law approved at the end of 2019 mandate that foreign investors need to receive prior approval for stock acquisitions above 1 percent in designated sectors, whereas the prior threshold was 10 percent. Exemptions to the approval process can be granted if the foreign investor forgoes a board position or access to critical technology in the company.

Japan is, therefore, entering unfamiliar terrain on how to reconcile globalization with national security. Such tradeoffs are only likely to grow. The U.S.-China technological rivalry is intensifying; Japan itself has deemed Chinese telecommunications firms a cybersecurity risk, effectively banning them from government 5G contracts; and internationalized Japanese firms will have to navigate not only tightened domestic regulations but also forthcoming American export controls on foundational and emerging technologies. Economic security is fast becoming the new frontier of Asian power competition.

NOTES

1. See "China's Global Development Footprint," AidData, accessed January 3, 2020, www.aiddata.org/china-official-finance; Axel Dreher, Andreas Fuchs, Bradley Parks, Austin M. Strange, and Michael J. Tierney, "Aid, China, and Growth: Evidence from a New Global Development Finance Dataset" (Williamsburg, VA: AidData, October 10, 2017), www.aiddata.org/publications/aid-china-and-growth -evidence-from-a-new-global-development-finance-dataset.

2. OECD, "Dataset: Total Official Flows by Country and Region (ODA+OOF)," OECD.Stat, accessed December 17, 2019, https://stats.oecd.org.

3. Fitch Solutions data cited by Michelle Jamrisko, "China No Match for Japan in Southeast Asia Infrastructure Race," Bloomberg, June 22, 2019, www.bloomberg .com/news/articles/2019-06-23/china-no-match-for-japan-in-southeast-asia -infrastructure-race.

4. Carla P. Freeman and Mie Ōba, "Bridging the Belt and Road Divide" (Washington, DC: Carnegie Endowment for International Peace, October 10, 2019), 2, https://carnegieendowment.org/2019/10/10/bridging-belt-and-road-divide-pub -80019.

5. David Dollar, *China and the West Competing over Infrastructure in Southeast Asia* (Washington, DC: The Brookings Institution, April 2020), www.brookings. edu/research/china-and-the-west-competing-over-infrastructure-in-southeast -asia/.

6. Kei Koga, "Japan and Southeast Asia in the Indo-Pacific," in *Implementing the Indo-Pacific: Japan's Region Building Initiatives*, ed. Kyle Springer (Perth: Perth USAsia Centre, August 2019), 25, https://perthusasia.edu.au/events/past -conferences/defence-forum-2019/2019-indo-pacific-defence-conference-videos/ keynotes-and-feature-presentations/pu-134-japan-book-web.aspx.

7. Tang Siew Mun, Hoang Thi Ha, Anuthida Saelaow Qian, Glenn Ong, and Pham Thi Phuong Thao, *The State of Southeast Asia: Survey Report 2020* (Singapore:

ISEAS-Yusof Ishak Institute, January 16, 2020), www.iseas.edu.sg/images/pdf/ TheStateofSEASurveyReport_2020.pdf.

8. Brad Parks, "Chinese Leadership and the Future of BRI: What Key Decisions Lie Ahead?" (Washington, DC: Center for Global Development, July 24, 2019), www.cgdev.org/publication/chinese-leadership-and-future-bri-what-key-decisions -lie-ahead.

9. See Jeffrey Hornung, "Japan's Pushback of China," *Washington Quarterly* 38, no. 1 (Spring 2015): 167–183, www.tandfonline.com/doi/full/10.1080/0163660X .2015.1038187; and Adam P. Liff, "Unambivalent Alignment: Japan's China Strategy, the U.S. Alliance, and the 'Hedging' Fallacy," *International Relations of the Asia -Pacific* 19, no. 3 (September 2019): 453–491, https://doi.org/10.1093/irap/lcz015.

12

Managing China

Competitive Engagement, with Indian Characteristics

TANVI MADAN

In October 2019, Chinese leader Xi Jinping and Indian prime minister Narendra Modi stood hand in hand in a seaside temple town near Chennai. Behind them loomed a large boulder, precariously poised atop an incline.[1] In many ways, it was an apt reflection of the relationship between the two Asian giants—one that has involved some efforts to cooperate, but with major challenges looming across the spectrum that could overshadow that engagement. Since that summit, the COVID-19 pandemic and a fatal China-India boundary crisis have done just that. Those developments have reinforced and demonstrated that despite the cooperative elements developed over the last two decades, China-India relations remain fundamentally competitive, with the potential for conflict ever present.

INDIA'S APPROACH

Given the cooperative and competitive dynamics over the last two decades, Delhi's approach to managing its China relationship has involved two broad elements. The first element has entailed engaging with Beijing where possible. The second element has meant competing with China where necessary, alone and in partnership with others.

India's approach, which has had mixed success, has been designed to stabilize the relationship, take advantage of it where possible, incentivize certain kinds of Chinese behavior and deter other kinds, as well as prepare for the scenario of Beijing breaking bad. It also aims to expand India's leverage, recognizing various Chinese points of leverage vis-à-vis India.

India's sources of leverage include its market, to which China and its companies want access. Another is the presence of Tibetan leaders and refugees in India, and, to some extent, India's position on Taiwan. A third is Delhi's ability to complicate Beijing's interests—and exploit its vulnerabilities—in the Indian Ocean. A fourth is India's partnerships—especially, but not only, with the United States.

China's points of leverage include its ability to pressure India on the boundary. It can also complicate India's internal security situation (particularly in India's northeast as it did in the past), as well as Delhi's regional options given Beijing's expanding ties with India's territorial and maritime neighbors. Furthermore, China can use its relationship with Pakistan as a tool to pressure—or reassure—India. Beijing can also be helpful or harmful to Indian interests as a result of its membership in key international bodies, especially the UN Security Council. Finally, while China's ability to use economic coercion with India is relatively limited because of the nature and extent of their investment ties, there are areas Beijing could target—for instance, critical infrastructure, or India's pharmaceutical sector, which is dependent on imports of active ingredients from China.[2]

ENGAGEMENT

There are multiple reasons why India has sought to keep its China relationship stable. One, it would allow Delhi to focus on its socioeconomic objectives, not require diversion of expenditure from development to defense, and buy time to enhance Indian capabilities and close the gap with China. Second was the possibility that India's economy could benefit from China's.[3] Third, Delhi believed that engagement could incentivize Beijing to respect Indian sensitivities or offer India opportunities. Finally, a more stable equilibrium with China would diminish the Indian need to deepen its ties with and depend on other partners—important for a country that prizes its strategic autonomy and believes partners can be unreliable.

Thus, following the June–August 2017 Doklam crisis during which the two countries' militaries faced off in the Bhutan-China-India tri-border area, India got the engagement part of its China approach back on track.

Beijing had its own reasons for stabilizing the relationship. It could open the door to opportunities for Chinese companies to benefit from the Indian economy and facilitate cooperation on some global issues. It could also limit Delhi's activism in opposing Chinese initiatives like the Belt and Road Initiative (BRI). And it could shape India's decisions vis-à-vis partnering with the United States and others in ways that would be favorable to China. This had been particularly important once the "Mar-a-Lago spirit" in China-U.S. relations had dissipated and the Trump administration began advocating for a coalition of democracies—Australia, India, Japan, and the United States—to tackle malign Chinese behavior.[4]

The Sino-Indian engagement track included a higher frequency of visits by senior policymakers, the revival of a number of dialogues that had been put on hold, as well as improved communication between the two countries' defense officials and personnel. In addition, India tempered its tone toward China (for instance, with less explicit criticism of BRI), and generally avoided what China would consider provocations. The government became more circumspect about participation in Tibet-related activities, and avoided commenting on developments in Xinjiang and Hong Kong. State-run airline Air India acquiesced to the Chinese demands to change its listing from "Taipei, Taiwan."[5]

Spurred by pressure and persuasion, China, in turn, lifted its long-standing hold on the designation of Pakistan-based Jaish-e-Mohammed (JeM) leader Masood Azhar as a terrorist in the UN Security Council Resolution 1267 sanctions regime committee.[6] It also allowed Pakistan to be placed on the "grey list" of the Financial Action Task Force (FATF) for taking insufficient action against terrorist financing and money laundering, which subjects the country to financial restrictions and potentially punitive action.[7]

There was also some progress on the bilateral economic front. Trade, which had stalled, increased by 25 percent from 2016–2017 to 2017–2018.[8] The stock of Chinese investment in India went from negligible amounts a few years ago to estimates of over $12 billion (plus pledges worth $16 billion).[9] In addition, Indian authorities gave the Bank of China a license to open a branch in Mumbai, and allowed Huawei to showcase its 5G capability at the India Mobile Congress in 2019.[10]

On the public diplomacy front, Beijing allowed the resumption of the pilgrimage for Indians through the Nathu La mountain pass to Tibet's Mount Kailash and Lake Mansarovar, which had been suspended during the Doklam crisis.[11]

Beyond the bilateral sphere, the Russia-India-China trilateral resumed in December 2017 and met twice at the leader level on the sidelines of multilateral summits.[12] India also continued to participate in organizations where China played a founding role, such as the Shanghai Cooperation Organization and the Asian Infrastructure Investment Bank.

COMPETITION

But despite this engagement, none of India's fundamental differences with China have been resolved, and some Indian concerns have grown in recent years.

These differences include the boundary dispute, which has involved four major standoffs—in 2013, 2014, 2017, and 2020—since Xi came to power. Beijing did not heed Modi's suggestion in 2014 to resume dialogue to clarify the Line of Actual Control that divides the two countries. Delhi dismissed China's proposal for a code of conduct—in part due to the concern that it would limit India from upgrading its infrastructure and capabilities near the boundary, as China has already done.[13]

Related to this is the issue of Tibet. China remains suspicious of the presence of the Dalai Lama and Tibetan refugees in India. Beijing also disapproves of U.S. government engagements with Tibetan leaders in India that are unlikely to occur without the acquiescence of the Indian government.[14] And China and India have different views of how the successor to the 14th Dalai Lama, now 85 years old, should be chosen. Delhi does not buy Beijing's assertion that the Dalai Lama's reincarnation would require Chinese concurrence and should involve no role for other countries.[15]

Another problem involves the Brahmaputra River that flows from China to India. Delhi has concerns about Chinese dam construction, potential river diversion, the erosion of its usage rights, as well as Beijing potentially using its upper riparian status to coerce India in the future.

Rather than alleviating bilateral differences, economic ties have also added to them. Indian complaints include India's trade deficit with China (one-third of its total trade deficit), lack of reciprocity, intellectual property theft, forced technology transfer, Beijing's influence over Chinese companies, and the potential use of economic coercion for strategic and political ends. Relatedly, in 2019, India declined to join the Beijing-backed Regional Comprehensive Economic Partnership, with the Indian home minister citing "adverse effects that Chinese interests could have caused."[16] Beijing, in turn, has complained about restricted market access for its companies in certain sectors and regions.

Then there is China's long-standing strategic relationship with Pakistan, which has deepened in part due to the China-Pakistan Economic Corridor (CPEC). Delhi believes Beijing has helped build its other rival's military, missile, and nuclear capabilities, and provided cover and support for Pakistan in international institutions like the UN Security Council and FATF.[17]

Beyond that, India has watched with concern as China's political, economic, and military ties with its other neighbors (Bangladesh, Maldives, Myanmar, Nepal, Sri Lanka) have grown. Policymakers are concerned about the impact on the neighbors' political and economic landscapes, and particularly on their strategic choices. There is a sense that Beijing has not respected India's redlines and is creating the space for—if not encouraging—these countries to do the same. These concerns, and the fact that some CPEC projects are in territory that India claims, have led to Indian opposition to BRI.[18]

China's forays into the Indian Ocean region have only added to Delhi's anxieties. It recognizes that a China which has global interests will seek a global presence. But it worries that Beijing's behavior elsewhere (e.g., the East and South China Seas) suggests that it might not be a rule-follower in this region either.[19] And it is skeptical about the reliability of Chinese assurances about its intentions, with the Indian foreign secretary pointing out to parliamentarians that "a number of steps, that the Chinese hitherto had said they would not do, are being done," including establishing bases and sending forces abroad.[20]

Globally, Delhi has seen little to change its belief that China seeks to limit India's space and prevent its rise. Beijing has continued to resist Indian membership in the UN Security Council, as well as the Nuclear Suppliers Group.

All these differences have caused India to maintain a second track—a competitive one—in its approach to China. This has involved internal balancing, including trying to enhance India's defense and security capabilities as well as its infrastructure. And it has involved external balancing through establishing or enhancing partnerships in India's extended neighborhood, as well as with like-minded major and middle powers. Greater attention to India's South and Southeast Asian and Indian Ocean neighbors has meant increased diplomatic presence and exchanges (both bilateral and regional), defense and economic diplomacy, and capacity building, as well as improved connectivity.[21]

As for partnering with like-minded balancing powers that also have concerns about China's capabilities, intentions, and actions, these are seen as (1) helping enhance India's capabilities across the board—crucial given the widening China-India gap, (2) contributing to capacity building and providing alternatives in the Indo-Pacific region, (3) helping shape Chinese behavior and a favorable balance of power in the region, and (4) serving as leverage for India with China.

Washington has been a crucial partner for Delhi in this regard. Over the last few years, India has particularly deepened defense and security cooperation with the United States, as shown in table 12-1.

Furthermore, India's network of partnerships also includes American allies like Australia, France, and Japan (and to some extent South Korea and the United Kingdom). The European Union is seen as a partner from an economic, technological, and global governance perspective. And, to a degree, India also sees Russia as important (especially as a supplier of military equipment, technology, and parts) despite Moscow's close ties with Beijing.

Over the last few years, India has deepened these relationships, particularly in the defense and security sphere. It is engaging with these countries bilaterally, trilaterally, and even quadrilaterally (in the case of Australia, Japan, and the United States). And it is cooperating and coordinating with these partners in third countries, as well as regional and global institutions. India's efforts with these countries have been focused on acquiring defense equipment and technology, increasing maritime domain awareness and information sharing, improving interoperability, facilitating regional capacity building and connectivity, and expanding India's reach.

RECENT DEVELOPMENTS AND THE IMPACT ON THE U.S.-INDIA RELATIONSHIP

Two developments have reinforced and even increased the competitive aspects of India's China perception and approach: (1) unilateral attempts by the People's Liberation Army since early May 2020 to change the status quo along the Line of Actual Control, the disputed de facto border between the two countries, which led to the first fatal clash in forty-five years between the two militaries; and (2) China's approach to the novel coronavirus pandemic.[22]

They have accelerated concerns in India about China's lack of transparency, its uncertain commitment to the rules-based order, as well as its

Table 12-1. Select US-India Diplomatic, Defense, and Security Cooperation since 2017

Agreements

Communications Compatibility and Security Agreement
Basic Exchange and Cooperation Agreement
Industrial Security Annex
Logistics Exchange Memorandum of Agreement implemented
HOSTAC program implemented
DTTI Standard Operating Procedure

Dialogues (new)

2+2 (ministerial + intercessional)
DTTI industry collaboration forum
Defense innovation units
Development assistance organizations
Defence cyber
Counterterrorism designations
US-India-Japan upgraded
Quadrilateral dialogue restarted

Quadrilateral ("Quad")

Dialogue at ministerial & working levels
Counterterrorism table-top exercise
MALABAR 2020 maritime exercise
Cyber experts' meeting
Embassy officials' meetings
Development organizations dialogue*
Quad-plus COVID-19 discussions

Liaisons

India at NAVCENT
US at India's Info Fusion Center-IOR
Additional liaisons*

Exercises

Cope India air force exercise revived
New Tiger Triumph multiservice
Vajra Prahar (special forces), Yudh Abhyas (army) continue
Naval PASSEX
Indian participation in AFRICOM's Cutlass Express
US observers at Australia-India naval exercise
Indian observers at Australia-US military exercise
Japan observers at Cope India
US-India-Japan-Philippines group sail through South China Sea

Defense Trade

C-17 transport aircraft
AH-64E Apache helicopters
MH-60R multirole helicopters
SIG716 Sig Sauer rifles
Extreme cold weather gear
M777 howitzers inducted
DSCA approvals: MK54 torpedoes, Harpoon missiles, Integrated Air Defense Weapon System, CBRN support equipment
Offered: F-21 and F/A-18 fighter aircraft, Sea Guardian Unmanned Aerial System

Other

Strategic Trade Authorization-1
US-India joint training of peacekeepers from African & Indo-Pacific countries
American P-8 maritime reconnaissance aircraft refueling on India's Andaman islands
US International Development Finance Cooperation office in Delhi
Space situational awareness information sharing*

*proposed.

Note: DTTI = Defense Technology and Trade Initiative

Source: Governments of India and the United States.

growing influence in the Indo-Pacific and in international institutions. The boundary crisis in particular has hardened views of China among the Indian public, strategic community, and, significantly, the government. Delhi has made clear that it sees Chinese actions as a "violation of the bilateral agreements and protocol[s] which ensured peace and tranquility in the border areas for close to three decades."[23] And the Indian foreign minister has reminded people that it was adherence to those agreements that allowed the broader relationship to "move . . . forward in other, different spheres, including the economic one."[24]

There have been tangible effects from the shift, particularly the intensification of Indian concerns in 2020 about (1) economic overdependence on and exposure to China; (2) inroads that Chinese companies, particularly those with close links with the state, have made into certain Indian sectors that are sensitive; and (3) avenues of Chinese influence in the country. This has led to a slew of measures that will restrict or scrutinize Chinese activities in the economic, technology, telecommunications, public diplomacy, and education sectors. These are also a sign of how China's actions have weakened the hands of those in Indian policymaking circles that argued for more engagement with China or for the idea that economic and civil society ties would help alleviate political strains.

China's recent behavior has also had an impact on Indian perceptions of America's importance as a partner. It has led to calls for India to be less cautious about relations with the United States and to double down on and even accelerate that partnership.[25] There has also been an apparent increase in Delhi's willingness to work with Washington at the bilateral, minilateral, and multilateral levels on issues like post-COVID recovery, building resilience, and defense and security cooperation. It has participated in two sets of Quad-plus dialogues (one with Brazil, Israel, and South Korea at the secretary of state level, and the other with New Zealand, South Korea, and Vietnam at the deputy secretary of state level).[26] And it has taken steps that it might have avoided at another time in the midst of a China crisis: conducted a maritime exercise with the United States (and separately Australia and Japan), allowed a U.S. maritime reconnaissance aircraft to refuel in the Andaman and Nicobar Islands, hosted the U.S. secretaries of state and defense for a 2+2 meeting, signed a geospatial data sharing agreement with the United States, participated in a Quad ministerial meeting, and invited Australia to participate in the India-Japan-U.S. maritime exercise Malabar.[27]

Even if China and India find a way to de-escalate the situation at the boundary, it is unlikely that the relationship will return to business as usual, as Beijing has been seeking.[28] The Indian ambassador to China has emphasized the considerable damage to India's trust in China, which was already at low levels.[29] This intensified Indian concern about China could present opportunities for the United States, but also challenges—for instance, Delhi's desire to reduce its economic dependence on China could benefit American companies. But if this leads to broader Indian protectionism, it could adversely affect American economic interests.

Moments like the current one can be clarifying for India, including in terms of which of its partners are reliable. The crisis will mean that it will closely watch how broader U.S. policy toward China evolves. And it will also assess Washington's approach to the crisis. American responsiveness and support could facilitate a closer Indian alignment with the United States in the future. However, if Delhi sees Washington as pushing it into decisions or choices, or as taking advantage of the boundary crisis, it could be unhelpful, if not counterproductive.

NOTES

1. Indian Ministry of External Affairs (MEA), Twitter, October 11, 2019, https://bit.ly/3mubquA.

2. This is something the Indian government has flagged as a concern. See Press Trust of India, "Dependence on Imported APIs Is Worrisome: Nirmala Sitharaman," *Economic Times*, February 5, 2016, https://economictimes.indiatimes.com/news/economy/foreign-trade/dependence-on-imported-apis-is-worrisome-nirmala-sitharaman/articleshow/50865195.cms.

3. Ananth Krishnan, "Modi Courts Chinese Investment, Showcasing the 'Gujarat Model,'" *The Hindu*, November 9, 2011, www.thehindu.com/news/international/modi-courts-chinese-investment-showcasing-the-gujarat-model/article2612458.ece; Atul Aneja, "China-India ties poised for an 'orbital jump,' says Doval," *The Hindu*, September 9, 2014, www.thehindu.com/news/national/chinaindia-ties-poised-for-an-orbital-jump-says-national-security-adviser-ajit-doval/article6395047.ece.

4. Rex Tillerson, "Defining Our Relationship with India for the Next Century" (remarks at Center for Strategic & International Studies, October 18, 2017), https://bit.ly/346W1IX.

5. Ananth Krishnan, "Air India Buckles to China's Pressure, Removes 'Taiwan' from Website," *India Today*, July 4, 2018, www.indiatoday.in/india/story/air-india-buckles-to-china-s-pressure-removes-taiwan-from-website-1277403-2018-07-04.

6. Press Trust of India, "China Lifts Technical Hold on Listing Masood Azhar as

Global Terrorist," The Hindu Business Line, May 1, 2019, www.thehindubusinessline
.com/news/china-lifts-technical-hold-on-listing-masood-azhar-as-global-terrorist
/article27002967.ece.

7. Kay Johnson and Drazen Jorgic, "Global Watchdog to Put Pakistan Back on
Terrorist Financing Watchlist: Sources," Reuters, February 23, 2018, www.reuters
.com/article/us-pakistan-militants-financing/global-watchdog-to-put-pakistan
-back-on-terrorist-financing-watchlist-sources-idUSKCN1G70X7; Pranab Dhal
Samanta, "Pakistan on FATF's Grey List: How India Convinced China & Pak Shot
Itself in the Foot," ThePrint, February 23, 2018, https://theprint.in/defence/pakistan
-fatfs-grey-list-india-convinced-china-pak-shot-foot/37751/.

8. Figures from Indian Ministry of Commerce and Industry's Export Import
Data Bank: "Export Import Data Bank Version 7.1—Tradestat," Government of
India, Ministry of Commerce & Industry, Department of Commerce, https://
commerce-app.gov.in/eidb/.

9. Estimates are from Ananth Krishnan, *Following the Money: China Inc's
Growing Stake in India-China Relations* (New Delhi: The Brookings Institution
India Center, March 2020), /www.brookings.edu/wp-content/uploads/2020/03/
China-Inc%E2%80%99s-growing-stake-in-India-China-relations_F.pdf.

10. "Huawei to Present 5G Use Case at India Mobile Congress," *The Hindu*,
October 10, 2019, www.thehindu.com/business/Industry/huawei-to-present-5g
-use-case-at-india-mobile-congress/article29634481.ece.

11. Anirban Bhaumik, "Post-Doklam, Indian Pilgrims Start Kailash Mansarovar
Yatra," *Deccan Herald*, June 11, 2018, www.deccanherald.com/national/year-after
-doklam-face-indian-pilgrims-start-travelling-kailash-mansarovar-china-674435.

12. After a planned April meeting did not materialize, reportedly because of
Chinese disapproval of a visit by the Dalai Lama to Arunachal Pradesh, which
China claims (Beijing denied that was the reason). Press Trust of India, "Dalai
Lama Not the Reason for Foreign Minister Declining to Attend RIC Meet in India:
China," *New Indian Express*, May 5, 2017, www.newindianexpress.com/world/2017
/may/05/dalai-lama-not-the-reason-for-foreign-minister-declining-to-attend-ric
-meet-in-india-china-1601440.html.

13. Ananth Krishnan, "It Took China Just Three Weeks since PM Modi's Visit to
Snub His Efforts to Clarify the LAC. The Neighbours Now Face Yet Another
Stalemate in Resolving the Boundary Issue," *India Today*, June 11, 2015, www.
indiatoday.in/magazine/the-big-story/story/20150622-china-india-lac-modi-visit
-xi-jinping-border-dispute-819865-2015-06-11; Manoj Joshi, "The Wuhan Summit
and the India–China Border Dispute" (New Delhi: Observer Research Foundation,
June 26, 2018), www.orfonline.org/research/41880-the-wuhan-summit-and-the
-india-china-border-dispute/.

14. Press Trust of India, "US Diplomat on Religious Freedom Meets Dalai Lama
at Dharamshala," NDTV, October 29, 2019, www.ndtv.com/india-news/sam
-brownback-us-diplomat-on-religious-freedom-meets-dalai-lama-at-dharamshala
-himachal-pradesh-2123833; Ken Juster (@USAmbIndia), Twitter, November 8,
2019, https://twitter.com/USAmbIndia/status/1192818698563866624?s=20.

15. Press Trust of India, "Next Dalai Lama Must Be Chosen within China; India Should Not Intervene: Chinese Authorities," *Economic Times*, July 14, 2019, https://economictimes.indiatimes.com/news/politics-and-nation/next-dalai-lama-must-be-chosen-within-china-india-should-not-intervene-chinese-authorities/articleshow/70215668.cms.

16. Amit Shah, "By Saying No to RCEP, PM Narendra Modi Has Kept India First," *Economic Times*, November 13, 2019, https://economictimes.indiatimes.com/news/economy/foreign-trade/view-by-saying-no-to-rcep-pm-modi-has-kept-india-first/articleshow/72028437.cms.

17. "China Denounces FATF Members for Pursuing Political Agenda against Pakistan," *Express Tribune*, October 29, 2019, https://tribune.com.pk/story/2089153/3-china-denounces-fatf-members-pursuing-political-agenda-pakistan/.

18. Indian MEA, "Response to a Query on Participation of India in OBOR/BRI Forum," May 13, 2017, https://bit.ly/2VAsmmM.

19. Arvind Gupta, "Chinese ADIZ in East China Sea: Posers for India," Institute for Defence Studies and Analyses, December 2, 2013, https://idsa.in/idsacomments/ChineseADIZinEastChinaSeaPosersforIndia_agupta_021213; Dipanjan Roy Chaudhury, "India to Resist Curbs on Navigation & Flight in South China Sea," *Economic Times*, July 12, 2018, https://economictimes.indiatimes.com/news/defence/india-to-resist-curbs-on-navigation-flight-in-south-china-sea/articleshow/48930379.cms.

20. Foreign Secretary Vijay Gokhale's testimony to Parliamentary Committee on External Affairs, February 16, 2018. See "Ministry of External Affairs, Demand for Grants (2018–19), Twenty First Report," Committee on External Affairs (2017–18), Sixteenth Lok Sabha, New Delhi, Lok Sabha Secretariat, March 2018, 65, http://164.100.47.193/lsscommittee/External%20Affairs/16_External_Affairs_21.pdf.

21. See Dhruva Jaishankar, "Act East: India in the Indo-Pacific" (New Delhi: The Brookings Institution India Center, October 24, 2019), www.brookings.edu/research/acting-east-india-in-the-indo-pacific/; and Constantino Xavier, "Bridging the Bay of Bengal: Toward a Stronger BIMSTEC" (New Delhi: Carnegie India, February 22, 2018), https://carnegieindia.org/2018/02/22/bridging-bay-of-bengal-toward-stronger-bimstec-pub-75610.

22. For more details, see Tanvi Madan, "China Is Losing India," *Foreign Affairs*, June 22, 2020, https://fam.ag/34sJb9E, and Testimony at Hearing on "U.S.-China Relations in 2020: Enduring Problems and Emerging Challenges," U.S.-China Economic and Security Review Commission, September 9, 2020, https://bit.ly/3kQFGzz. This section also draws from those texts.

23. Indian MEA, "Readout by the Official Spokesperson on India-China LAC Issue," September 3, 2020, https://bit.ly/3jwUjq4.

24. Shishir Gupta and R. Sukumar, "Interview with Dr. S. Jaishankar," *Hindustan Times*, August 30, 2020, https://bit.ly/31PK4rf.

25. See former Indian ambassador to China Ashok Kantha's comment in "Is the Quad Rising after China's Challenge at the LAC?" *The Hindu*, September 18, 2020, https://bit.ly/2Ty0fob.

26. Indian MEA, "Foreign Secretary's Conference Call with Counterparts from Indo-Pacific Countries," March 20, 2020, https://bit.ly/2HEA5gS; Indian External Affairs Minister S. Jaishankar, Twitter, May 11, 2020, https://bit.ly/3e5Vtrl.

27. Rahul Singh, "8 Indian, US Warships Conduct Maritime Drills in Indian Ocean," *Hindustan Times*, July 21, 2020, https://bit.ly/3muw9OS; Snehesh Alex Philip, "US Military Aircraft Refuels at Indian Base for First Time under Defence Pact," *The Print*, October 2, 2020, https://bit.ly/2J7J4b0; "US-India 2+2: Crucial Defence Deal Signed," *BBC News*, October 27, 2020, https://bbc.in/3muwJfw; Indian MEA, "2nd India-Australia-Japan-USA Ministerial Meeting," October 6, 2020, https://bit.ly/3e44MZ3; Indian Ministry of Defence, "Malabar 2020 Naval Exercise," October 19, 2020, https://bit.ly/3oysdhP.

28. Wang Qingyun, "India Urged to Recall Troops in Incursion," *China Daily*, September 2, 2020, https://bit.ly/2R1KuEZ; PRC Embassy in India, "Video Remarks by H.E. Sun Weidong on Current China-India Relations," July 10, 2020, https://bit.ly/31Tonq8.

29. KJM Varma, "India Warns China That Attempts to Alter Status Quo Will Have 'Ripples, Repercussions'" (interview with Indian ambassador to China Vikram Misri), *Press Trust of India*, June 26, 2020, https://bit.ly/32RrGNZ.

13

Russia and China

Axis of Revisionists?

ANGELA STENT

The China-Russia relationship has since 2014 evolved into a pragmatic strategic partnership, representing a significant new development on the global
stage. Recently, the COVID-19 pandemic has made Russia more dependent
on China, further solidifying their ties. Despite the asymmetries in the relationship, China and Russia share a number of core interests and a suspicion
and resentment of the United States. They may not be natural allies, but they
have, in the last decade, worked together to challenge the United States. This
chapter examines the drivers of the relationship, the effectiveness of their
bilateral ties, and the extent to which the United States can influence this
relationship going forward.

Since Russia's 2014 seizure and annexation of Crimea and the West's
subsequent attempts to isolate Russia, Putin has increasingly turned to
China. Sino-Russian economic and energy ties are expanding. China is economically more important to Russia than vice versa and is Russia's number
one trading partner and the second-largest purchaser of Russian military
hardware. Sino-Russian cooperation in the military and high-tech fields
continues to grow. Their joint military exercises and air patrols, as well as
joint work on artificial intelligence and biotechnology, pose new potential
threats to U.S. interests.

Their relationship is, however, far from balanced. There are significant asymmetries in the relationship beyond population (China has almost ten times more people than Russia), and mutual mistrust remains, especially in Russia's sparsely populated Far East, where Chinese traders and entrepreneurs are abundant. Nevertheless, Russia appears to have accepted its role as a junior partner to China. This is in part because China, unlike the United States, is not perceived to represent a threat to Vladimir Putin's rule.

Russia and China come together today as revisionist powers seeking to create a "post-West" world order—one where the United States can no longer dominate and determine the financial and political contours.[1] Both aim for a world order more supportive of authoritarian regimes that prize sovereignty and noninterference in each other's domestic affairs. Thus those who believe that Russia would be willing to distance itself from China and align itself with Washington against Beijing underestimate the extent to which China's unequivocal support of Russia's domestic system is an existential issue for the Putin regime. Moreover, the twin U.S. policies of sanctioning Russia and pursuing a trade war with China have pushed the two countries closer together. "Peeling Russia away from China," as some in the United States suggest, would involve a significant modification of current U.S. policy toward Russia at a time when Russia has become a toxic subject in U.S. politics following Moscow's interference in the 2016 and 2020 presidential elections.

KEY DRIVERS OF THE RELATIONSHIP

Sino-Russian relations have come a long way since 1969, when the USSR and China engaged in a brief shooting war on their border. Ties began to warm once the USSR collapsed, but the turning point came in 2014, as Russia's relations with the West sharply deteriorated after the onset of the Ukraine crisis. The imposition of U.S. and EU sanctions and other attempts to isolate Moscow increased Russia's dependence on China.

The close ties between Vladimir Putin and Xi Jinping are based on a mutual interest in challenging the current world order and in maintaining domestic stability and preventing "color" revolutions at home. Both leaders support each other's foreign policies. Putin and Xi share a common set of grievances, a conviction that their countries were unfairly treated by the West in the past. They are critical of the current U.S.-dominated international order, which they believe was imposed on them without consultation and disregards their legitimate interests.

Putin and Xi never criticize publicly each other's internal policies. China

and Russia promote models of internet governance and censorship condu-
cive to authoritarianism.[2] They both favor influence and interference operations that seek to affect the political processes of other countries in ways
amenable to their interests. While differing in their targets and approaches,
Chinese and Russian influence operations increasingly draw upon similar
tools (e.g., social media, state media, and co-opting media outlets in target
countries) to induce instability in democratic societies.[3]

The Sino-Russian economic relationship is evolving from relatively
modest to more dynamic, largely because of both countries' deteriorating
ties with the West. Since 2009, China has been Russia's largest trading partner. Their bilateral trade rose to $110 billion in 2019, with the governments
planning to boost it further to $200 billion in 2024.[4] The structure of bi-
lateral trade largely resembles that between a developing and a developed
country. Mineral products and hydrocarbons make up 73 percent of Russian exports to China. Machinery and transport equipment constitute 52
percent of Chinese exports, with textiles and footwear at 15 percent.[5]

China's main economic interest in the relationship is Russia's oil and gas.
As China has modernized and its economy has grown, its demand for energy
has increased exponentially. Russia has plentiful oil and gas reserves, but most
of its energy exports have traditionally gone to Europe. Since the Soviet collapse, Russia has sought to diversify its energy exports. The new $400 billion
Power of Siberia gas pipeline will increase bilateral energy interdependence.
Russia vies with Saudi Arabia as the top source of China's oil imports.[6]

The latest area for energy cooperation is in the Arctic. China can provide the capital, technical expertise, and markets needed to develop Russia's
natural resources. Russia in turn facilitates Chinese economic goals in the
region—particularly through the development of natural resources and the
use of shipping routes controlled by Russia.[7] China envisions a "Polar Silk
Road" as part of its Belt and Road Initiative (BRI) and is increasingly showing interest in commercial navigation via the Northern Sea Route, which
runs along the Russian Arctic coast.

MILITARY AND HIGH TECH COOPERATION

Russia and China have also notably intensified their military ties since the
onset of the Ukraine crisis. The three main areas of the bilateral defense relationship are military exercises, military-technical cooperation (including
arms sales), and high-level military-to-military contacts.[8] In 2015, as part

of the post-Crimea intensification of ties, Russia agreed in a $3 billion deal to sell China Su-35 fighter jets and S-400 surface-to-air missiles, which will upgrade China's missile defense capabilities and could jeopardize Taiwan's aerial defenses.[9]

The geographic scope of Sino-Russian military exercises has been expanding. In September 2018, China participated for the first time in Vostok (East) 2018, the largest Russian military exercise since 1981, held in Siberia and the Russian Far East. China participated to demonstrate that Russia and China stood together and to test its own military restructuring efforts.[10]

In 2019, the People's Liberation Army participated in another large-scale Russian military exercise, Tsentr (Center) 2019, held in western Russia and in Kyrgyzstan. The principal aim of the exercise was to simulate a response to possible security threats in Central Asia—including fending off terrorist threats, but also repelling conventional military forces from an imaginary "terrorist state" to the southwest of Russia.

In 2017 Russia and China adopted a three-year plan for military cooperation through 2020. Both sides have now said that they will negotiate a new military agreement reflecting broader cooperation, including joint aviation patrols. Moscow is also helping Beijing develop its own ballistic missile defense system, meaning that Russia is collaborating with China on technology related to strategic nuclear arsenals. This represents a new level in Sino-Russian military ties.[11] The Chinese ambassador to Russia has emphasized that Beijing wants to deepen military cooperation with Moscow: "China is prepared to strengthen [military] contacts with Russia at a high level, to cooperate in such areas as joint exercises; wargames; military preparedness; training; military-technical cooperation; counterterrorism and stability operations; increasing strategic cooperation on fundamental international and regional issues; jointly opposing unilateralism, protectionism, and hegemonism; supporting both countries' interests in security and development; and supporting peace and stability around the world."[12] Nevertheless, at the same time, Russia is also expanding its defense cooperation with other countries in the region that view China as a threat, such as India and Vietnam.

Russia and China have recently strengthened their technological cooperation, including fifth-generation telecommunications, artificial intelligence, biotechnology, and the digital economy. This is in response to increased U.S. pressure on both countries to limit their respective engagements in the global technological ecosystem through sanctions and export controls.[13]

The ongoing battle between the United States and China over the tech giant Huawei has also pushed Russia and China closer together. Huawei has expanded its engagement in Russia, looking to work more closely with Russian scientists. It has announced plans for a fourfold increase in its research and development staff in Russia and the creation of the Huawei Innovation Research program there. Sberbank and Huawei have formed a strategic partnership to provide cloud services for Russian businesses, extending the reach of Russia's largest bank into the country's digital economy.[14]

POLITICAL TIES

Whereas at the highest political levels Sino-Russian relations are improving, the situation in Russia's economically depressed and depopulated Far East (which two centuries ago was part of China) is more complex. There are 6.3 million Russians in the areas bordering China, facing 109 million Chinese on the other side of the border.[15] Russians remain suspicious of the Chinese, who often dominate local commerce. They are also wary of China's designs on their land. The Russian embassy in Beijing posted a video on Weibo of a party held to celebrate the 160th anniversary of the founding of Vladivostok, whose name in Russian means "ruler of the East." There was a swift reaction from Chinese diplomats, journalists, and internet users, reminding readers that the territory whose capital is Vladivostok was part of the Manchurian homeland of the Qing Dynasty and was annexed by Russia in 1860 in an "unequal treaty" after China's defeat in the Second Opium War.

Russia and China have created multilateral fora in which they cooperate actively. The first is the Shanghai Cooperation Organization (SCO), founded in 2002 to manage Sino-Russian relations in their shared neighborhood, Central Asia, and to combat the "three evils" of terrorism, separatism, and religious extremism.[16] Its eight members account for 80 percent of Eurasia's landmass, 43 percent of the world's population, and a quarter of global GDP. In terms of geographic coverage and population size, it is the largest regional organization in the world.[17]

Up till now, Russia and China have successfully managed their competition in Central Asia. Russia remains the predominant outside influence in the area, given the enduring linguistic, cultural, and personal ties between Moscow and many Central Asian elites. But China has emerged as the predominant economic power in Central Asia, given its energy needs and investment projects. The SCO provides a multilateral forum to regulate relations between Central Asian countries and their larger neighbors, but ultimately regional leaders understand that they have to balance China against Russia if they want to prosper and to retain their sovereignty.

Yet the disparity in the respective capabilities of the two countries and lingering mutual mistrust suggest a series of ongoing challenges to the relationship. The first is the impact that China's ambitious BRI will have on Russian political and economic interests. Putin launched the Eurasian Economic Union (EAEU) in January 2015. Two years earlier, in 2013, China announced its intention to construct a "Silk Road Economic Belt," now known as the Belt and Road Initiative, which will eventually link China with Europe, involving a network of transportation and construction projects, including multiple-billion-dollar investment deals in Central Asia. Whereas the Central Asian countries were generally enthusiastic about these projects, Russia was more reticent because it viewed BRI as a direct competitor to the EAEU. Seeking to assuage these concerns, Xi and Putin signed an agreement on the integration of the EAEU and BRI projects in May 2015. However, the two initiatives are quite different. The BRI transportation corridors will largely bypass Russia to the south, so it is uncertain how Russia will benefit from these massive infrastructure projects.[18] The BRI will promote globalized trade, financing, and infrastructure, and it will develop markets for Chinese goods. It will certainly expand Chinese geopolitical influence—all under the rubric of "connectivity."

The asymmetries that currently exist between the two countries will only grow. China is a rising power, economically and militarily. Russia can project military power effectively on the world stage, but it remains an exporter of arms and raw materials and a country with low rates of growth that has failed to modernize its economy. It is the junior partner in this relationship, a status that it appears to have accepted because it believes it can maintain and increase its global reach by partnering with the ascendant power in an era of U.S. withdrawal. As long as China treats Russia as an equal, never criticizes it publicly, and is careful about not challenging it directly in their shared neighborhood, the partnership will continue to meet both sides' interests.

IMPLICATIONS FOR U.S. POLICY

The major drivers of U.S. policy toward Russia and China differ from each other considerably. The key determinant of U.S.-Russian relations is the fact that the two countries are the world's two nuclear superpowers. Between them, they possess over 90 percent of the world's nuclear weapons. The United States and Russia have a limited economic relationship, since the United States does not need Russia's two major exports— hydrocarbons and military hardware. The key factor in the U.S.-Chinese relationship, by contrast, is the fact that they are the world's two economic superpowers and are economically integrated. Security issues have traditionally taken a secondary role to trade and investment questions, although they are becoming more salient as China becomes competitive in advanced technologies, its nuclear arsenal grows, and it asserts its sovereign claims to islands in the East and South China Seas and aims for unification with Taiwan.

Regardless of the imbalances and strains in the Chinese-Russian relationship, the two countries have compelling reasons to strengthen their partnership. Their shared suspicion of the United States and commitment to maintaining their authoritarian regimes will continue to bind them together. What remains unknown is the extent to which both countries might join forces in the cyber area to undermine U.S. interests in the future.

Given these realities, it is doubtful that a U.S.-Russian rapprochement would persuade Russia to distance itself from China and reverse the momentum in Sino-Russian military, technological, and economic cooperation. While there are sound arguments for the United States to seek more productive engagement with Russia, one cannot assume that this would lead to a cooling in Sino-Russian ties. Going forward, it would be prudent for the United States to carefully reassess policies and actions that could drive the two countries even closer together.

NOTES

1. "Lavrov Calls for Post-West World Order, Dismisses NATO as Cold War Relic," Deutsche Welle, February 18, 2017, www.dw.com/en/lavrov-calls-for-post -west-world-order-dismisses-nato-as-cold-war-relic/a-37614099.

2. Alina Polyakova and Chris Meserole, *Exporting Digital Authoritarianism: The Russian and Chinese Models* (Washington, DC: The Brookings Institution, August 2019), www.brookings.edu/research/exporting-digital-authoritarianism/.

3. "Chapter 4 Section 2—An Uneasy Entente: China-Russia Relations in a New Era of Strategic Competition with the United States," in *2019 Annual Report* (Washington, DC: U.S.-China Economic and Security Review Commission, 2019), 315–358, www.uscc.gov/annual-report/2019-annual-report.

4. Keegan Elmer, "China, Russia Set to Double Trade to US$200 Billion by 2024 with Help of Soybeans," *South China Morning Post*, September 18, 2019, www.scmp

.com/news/china/diplomacy/article/3027932/china-russia-set-double-trade-us200 -billion-2024-help-soybeans.

5. Tatiana Sidorenko, "Cooperación económica entre Rusia y China: alcances y perspectivas" [Economic Cooperation Between Russia and China: Scope and Prospects], *Problemas del Desarrollo* [*Development Issues*] 45, no. 176 (January– March 2014): 31–54, www.probdes.iiec.unam.mx/index.php/pde/article/view/ 43806.

6. "Russia Remains China's Largest Crude Oil Source for 3rd Year: Report," *Global Times*, March 24, 2019, www.globaltimes.cn/content/1143223.shtml.

7. "Chapter 4 Section 2–An Uneasy Entente."

8. Ethan Meick, "China-Russia Military-to-Military Relations: Moving toward a Higher Level of Cooperation" (Washington, DC: U.S.-China Economic and Security Review Commission, March 20, 2017), www.uscc.gov/research/china-russia -military-military-relations-moving-toward-higher-level-cooperation.

9. "S-500 in 2016?" Russian Defense Policy, April 18, 2016, https:// russiandefpolicy.wordpress.com/2016/04/18/s-500-in-2016/.

10. Zi Yang, "Vostok 2018: Russia and China's Diverging Common Interests," *The Diplomat*, September 17, 2018, https://thediplomat.com/2018/09/vostok-2018 -russia-and-chinas-diverging-common-interests/.

11. Michael Kofman, "Towards a Sino-Russian Entente?" Riddle, November 29, 2019, www.ridl.io/en/towards-a-sino-russian-entente/.

12. RIA Novosti,Китай готов развивать военно-техническое сотрудн- ичество с Россией [China Is Ready to Develop Military-Technical Cooperation with Russia], July 30, 2020, https://ria.ru/20200730/1575171586.html.

13. Samuel Bendett and Elsa Kania, "A New Sino-Russian High-Tech Partnership" (Barton, Australia: Australian Strategic Policy Institute, October 29, 2019), www.aspi.org.au/report/new-sino-russian-high-tech-partnership.

14. Reuters, "Russia's Sberbank Partners with China's Huawei on Cloud Services, March 3,2020, www.reuters.com/article/us-russia-sberbank-tech/russias -sberbank-partners-with-chinas-huawei-on-cloud-services-idUSKBN20Q2HX.

15. Dragoş Tîrnoveanu, "Russia, China and the Far East Question," *The Diplo- mat*, January 20, 2016, http://thediplomat.com/2016/01/russia-china-and-the-far -east-question/.

16. "Fighting Three Evils," InfoSCO, February 11, 2011, http://infoshos.ru/en/? idn=7678.

17. "The Evolution of the Shanghai Cooperation Organisation" (London: International Institute for Strategic Studies, June 2018), www.iiss.org/publications/ strategic-comments/2018/shanghai-cooperation-organisation.

18. Nathan Hutson, "Проект «Один пояс, один путь»—кто в выигрыше, и насколько?" [The "One Belt One Road" Project: Who Is Winning and by How Much?], Россия сегодня [Russia Today], December 22, 2017, https://inosmi.ru/ economic/20171222/241057172.html.

14

Europe Changes Its Mind on China

THOMAS WRIGHT

Over the past few years, the European Union and a handful of other European countries have reluctantly moved away from a China policy organized around economic engagement toward a policy of limiting China's influence in Europe for strategic and security reasons. This is a distinctly and uniquely European style of balancing, which involves marshaling Europe's internal power and working to build unity across member states. It has almost nothing to do with kinetic military power and is instead focused on technology, diplomacy, economics, and politics.

The driving force behind this shift is China's behavior—its refusal to end practices of intellectual property theft and forced technology transfers, its failure to enhance market openness for European companies, its use of coercive economic tools and political influence in Europe, and its illiberalism on the world stage. In some ways, the European shift has occurred despite American pressure, not because of it. If China were a responsible stakeholder, U.S. pressure would very likely lead to Europe hedging against the Trump administration and increasing engagement with Beijing. After all, most Europeans were profoundly worried by President Donald Trump, and China seemed well poised to take advantage of this with adroit diplomacy to weaken the trans-Atlantic bond. That it utterly failed to do so shows how badly Beijing has bungled its Europe policy.

With all of that said, Europe is far from united behind this strategic shift.

There are Europe-wide divisions, differences between countries, and within them. German chancellor Angela Merkel remains the most important figure on the pro-engagement side. But unless China's behavior becomes more benign, Europe's evolution toward balancing looks set to continue.

2015–2019: EUROPE CHANGES ITS MIND

In the first half of the last decade, the dominant approach in Europe was to see China as a challenging economic partner with whom engagement would produce positive results. European policymakers rejected the American view of China as overly securitized and believed that China was well on its way to becoming a responsible stakeholder in the international order. Germany took the lead, framing its relations with China as "a comprehensive strategic partnership" in 2014. U.K. prime minister David Cameron and his chancellor of the exchequer George Osborne declared the beginning of a "golden era" in Britain's relations with China when Xi Jinping made a state visit to their country in 2015.[1] They wanted to make China Britain's second-largest trading partner after the EU by 2025 and rejected U.S. concerns that they were too close to Beijing. These goals shaped and restricted Europe's behavior.

When Trump became U.S. president, Europeans looked set to continue to engage Beijing, especially when Xi publicly positioned himself as a champion of multilateralism as the United States was turning against the international order.[2] The Trump administration would subsequently put considerable pressure on Europe to limit its engagement with China, particularly on sensitive matters like the role of Chinese telecoms giant Huawei in European 5G wireless infrastructure. However, European governments, including the staunchly Atlanticist U.K., largely ignored this pressure, judging the economic benefits from engagement with China to outweigh the risks. The U.K. would press ahead with Huawei involvement in its 5G networks even as it sought a closer relationship with the Trump administration beyond Brexit. Italy's populist government, which included the right-wing (and pro-Trump) League, signed a memorandum of understanding with Beijing on the Belt and Road Initiative (BRI), becoming the first G-7 country to join the initiative.[3] Czech president Miloš Zeman declared that the Czech Republic hoped to become "an unsinkable aircraft carrier of Chinese investment expansion" in Europe.[4] In 2019, Greece joined China's "16+1" forum with central and eastern European nations—including eleven European

Union member states and an additional five Balkan countries, and largely seen as divisive by the EU—turning it into the 17+1.[5]

The primary driver of Europe's increased skepticism of China was economic. In *Foreign Affairs*, German Marshall Fund scholar Andrew Small summed it up as follows: "Europe has lost hope that China will reform its economy or allow greater access to its markets, and at the same time, China's state-backed and state-subsidized actors have advanced in sectors that Europe considers critical to its economic future."[6] Beijing's Made in China 2025 plan was particularly important in this regard. It proposed to use the power of the state, through subsidies, acquisitions, and other policies, to catch up and pass Western powers in key technologies such as 5G, advanced robotics, clean energy, and artificial intelligence.[7] China would reduce its dependence on foreign technology and promote Chinese manufacturers internationally—achieving 70 percent independence by 2025 and being globally dominant by 2049, the 100th anniversary of the founding of the regime. Beijing then doubled down on this with an announcement of a six-year, $1.4 trillion investment in technology to accelerate realization of those ambitions.[8]

European business demanded a response. In 2017, the European Union Chamber of Commerce in China called Made in China 2025 "highly problematic" and "suggests that Chinese policies will further skew the competitive landscape in favour of domestic companies."[9] The German Federation of Industries (BDI) also grew skeptical of China. In a highly influential strategic paper in January 2019, the BDI warned that a "competition is emerging between our system of a liberal, open and social market economy and China's state-dominated economy."[10] It urged a united European response and for the EU to work with like-minded allies. Meanwhile, some central and eastern European countries—including Poland and the Czech Republic—that had engaged with China in the hopes of an economic reward also became disillusioned. The promised investment never arrived, and they ended up with little to show for their cooperation with Beijing through the 17+1 and BRI.[11]

European governments began to tighten investment controls and sought strength through unity, although that proved to be difficult given the adroitness of China's economic power. China's efforts to divide Europe through the 17+1 and other bilateral engagements worried EU leaders, including Merkel. The problems were not just economic. China began to flex its muscles, trying to extend its powers of censorship to Europe by imposing a political or economic cost for any criticism of the regime by governments, organizations, or individuals. China was also associated with hacking efforts to steal industrial and political secrets. Beijing's treatment of Uighur Muslims in Xinjiang and its response to the pro-democracy protests in Hong Kong drew condemnation from European leaders.[12]

This shift dramatically manifested itself in 2019, when the EU published the document "The EU and China: A Strategy Outlook," which stated the following:

> China is, simultaneously, in different policy areas, a cooperation partner with whom the EU has closely aligned objectives, a negotiating partner with whom the EU needs to find a balance of interests, an economic competitor in the pursuit of technological leadership, and a systemic rival promoting alternative models of governance.[13]

French president Emmanuel Macron declared, "The time of European naïveté is ended. For many years we had an uncoordinated approach and China took advantage of our divisions."[14]

Nevertheless, Europe remained divided and conflicted. On the critical issue of 5G, European governments seemed determined to press forward with allowing Huawei to build their infrastructure. Merkel still spoke of the need to engage China. But the balance appeared to have shifted.

THE COVID-19 CRISIS

In the early days of the COVID-19 crisis it appeared as if the deterioration in Europe's relations with China might be slowed or even reversed. Europe refrained from criticizing China and quietly sent aid. Macron reportedly said that Chinese officials would remember Europe's support in the future. The arrival of the virus in Europe coincided with an ebbing of the crisis in China. China saw an opportunity to score a diplomatic win by positioning itself as the provider of assistance and expertise, based on its "success" in containing COVID-19. China set up a call between its medical experts and European nations, starting with the 17+1 format on March 13, 2020, and then moving on to the rest of Europe a week later.[15] There was little European solidarity or coordination in the first month of the crisis in Europe, and some national officials, most notably Italian foreign minister Luigi Di Maio, praised China's role.[16]

However, Beijing quickly moved to a more overt and controversial strategic approach. A study by the European Think-tank Network on China (ETNC) of EU-China relations during the pandemic identified four "key messages" in China's differentiated approaches across Europe:

(1) highlighting solidarity and aid; (2) calling for international unity; (3) promoting China's fight against Covid-19 as a success story, and in some cases (for instance in France) blaming Western democracies for their poor management or even responsibility in the spread of the pandemic; (4) countering narratives critical of China, including through sowing doubt about the origins of Covid-19.[17]

From March on, Chinese diplomacy became more assertive in parts of Europe. It was quickly labeled "Wolf Warrior diplomacy" after a popular Chinese action movie. Various Chinese ambassadors spread conspiracy theories about the origins of the virus, engaged in direct criticism of France's and Sweden's responses to the pandemic, and downgraded its presence at an EU-led forum on international cooperation on a vaccine.[18]

There were worrying signs that the EU was buckling under Chinese pressure. In early May, ambassadors to China from all twenty-seven EU member states published an op-ed in *China Daily*, another Chinese Communist Party (CCP)-controlled newspaper, calling for cooperation between the EU and China. The op-ed was overwhelmingly positive, with little criticism of Beijing on any front. However, it was soon alleged that the Chinese government had agreed to let the article be published only after it had deleted text on its handling of COVID-19. It also refused to let the article be published in Mandarin.[19] A week earlier, the EU high representative for foreign affairs and security policy Josep Borrell faced charges that his department had watered down a report on China by removing references to its disinformation campaign and to the Chinese Embassy in Paris's comments that the French had neglected the elderly in nursing homes.[20]

There was a visceral reaction to China's assertiveness. Norbert Röttgen—the chair of the German parliament's Foreign Affairs Committee and a candidate for the leadership of Merkel's party, the Christian Democratic Union—tweeted about the censorship of the *China Daily* op-ed, "I am shocked not once but twice: First the #EU ambassadors generously adopt #Chinese narratives & then the EU representation on top accepts Chinese censorship of the joint op-ed. Speaking with one voice is important, but it has to reflect our shared European values and interests!"[21] In a revealing interview, Borrell said, "We Europeans support effective multilateralism with the United Nations at the center. . . . China, on the other hand, has a selective multilateralism that wants, and is based on, a different understanding of the international order."[22] In the U.K., the chair of the House of Commons Select Defense Committee, Tobias Elwood, said the government was experiencing a "mindset change" toward China, "not least because of the attitude, the conduct of China throughout COVID-19."[23] Prime Minister Boris Johnson's government indicated a shift away from allowing Huawei to develop a share of the U.K.'s 5G infrastructure. The EU and individual member states have also taken steps to limit Chinese influence in its economies as they seek to recover from the economic fallout of the pandemic.[24]

After the U.S. election of 2020, in which Joe Biden defeated Donald Trump, the EU–China relationship took a surprising turn. China made a number of significant concessions in negotiations on a Comprehensive Agreement on Investment (CAI) and a deal seemed imminent. Jake Sullivan, Biden's National Security Advisor, signaled that Biden would prefer if the EU waited until after he took office so the allies could consult with each other on how to best handle China collectively.[25] The EU, with Germany at the helm given that it held the presidency of the Council, decided to go ahead anyway, in the face of criticism from the United States and quite a few dissenting voices in Europe. The episode underscored that even as Europeans become more skeptical of China, it remains a topic of heated debate.

ANALYZING EUROPE'S ROLE IN
THE U.S.-CHINA COMPETITION

European skepticism of China grew at a time when the EU was increasingly estranged from the United States. A number of European leaders proposed that the EU and the United States work together on China but were rebuffed by Trump, who reportedly said, "The EU is worse than China only smaller."[26] American heavy-handedness on 5G also aggravated EU governments and the U.K., which sought a middle road. Nevertheless, the EU and the U.K. continued along the path of skepticism because of Chinese behavior, and to some degree in spite of U.S. pressure. Now, with a U.S. president who will seek European cooperation on China, the proposition that the EU has evolved will be put to the test.

The European response will likely have several elements over time: (1) a continued effort post-CAI to strengthen investment controls and other economic measures to protect European companies and intellectual property from predatory Chinese behavior, (2) greater unity among the EU-27 and NATO to better resist Chinese coercive power, and (3) working with like-minded democracies to uphold liberal norms globally, including within international institutions like the World Health Organization. This is a form of balancing, albeit of a nonmilitary variety. European nations will not have the ability or will to materially affect the balance of power in East Asia, but they will play a crucial role in countering China's power and influence globally.

The United States should help facilitate the continuation of this process in the coming years with a light touch and by preserving an open trans-Atlantic economy so as to reduce the attractiveness of an economic partnership with China. Washington should be very selective about where it exerts pressure on Europe to more fully align with American policy. There are occasions—like 5G—where it is justified and effective but on other occasions it could be counterproductive. An EU policy based on its broad interests is preferable to one based exclusively on the narrower lure of economic gain.

The EU case is particularly important because it constitutes a natural experiment of sorts as to how China reacts when dealing with a major power that is inclined to engage and work with it. The evidence from the past five years strongly suggests that China does not respond in kind by making difficult compromises and increasing the net levels of cooperation on shared challenges. Instead, Beijing hardened its economic policy and sought to take advantage of divisions and weaknesses inside the EU, pushing the EU into a tougher position. These lessons are likely to have wider ramifications outside the EU-China relationship.

ACKNOWLEDGMENTS: The author would like to thank Filippos Letsas, Sam Denney, and Agneska Bloch for research assistance, Ted Reinert for editing, and Emilie Kimball for managing the project.

NOTES

1. Tom Phillips, "Britain Has Made 'Visionary' Choice to Be China's Best Friend Says Xi," *The Guardian*, October 18, 2015, www.theguardian.com/uk-news/2015/oct/18/britian-has-made-visionary-choice-to-become-chinas-best-friend-says-xi.

2. Xi Jinping, "Jointly Shoulder Responsibility of Our Times, Promote Global Growth" (speech, Davos, Switzerland, January 17, 2020), https://america.cgtn.com/2017/01/17/full-text-of-xi-jinping-keynote-at-the-world-economic-forum.

3. Giovanna Di Maio, *Playing with Fire: Italy, China, and Europe* (Washington, DC: The Brookings Institution, May 2020), www.brookings.edu/research/playing-with-fire/.

4. David Barboza, Marc Santora, and Alexandra Stevenson, "China Seeks Influence in Europe, One Business Deal at a Time," *New York Times*, August 12, 2018, www.nytimes.com/2018/08/12/business/china-influence-europe-czech-republic.html.

5. Emilian Kavalski, "China's '16+1' Is Dead, Long Live the '17+1,'" *The Diplomat*, March 29, 2019, https://thediplomat.com/2019/03/chinas-161-is-dead-long-live-the-171/.

6. Andrew Small, "Why Europe Is Getting Tough on China," *Foreign Affairs*, April 3, 2019, www.foreignaffairs.com/articles/china/2019-04-03/why-europe-getting-tough-china.

7. "'Made in China 2025' Plan Issued," State Council, People's Republic of China, May 19, 2015, http://english.www.gov.cn/policies/latest_releases/2015/05/19/content_281475110703534.htm.

8. Liza Lin, "China's Trillion Dollar Campaign Fuels a Tech Race with the U.S.," *Wall Street Journal*, June 11, 2020, www.wsj.com/articles/chinas-trillion-dollar-campaign-fuels-a-tech-race-with-the-u-s-11591892854.

9. "China Manufacturing 2025: Putting Industrial Policy Ahead of Market Forces" (Beijing: European Union Chamber of Commerce in China, 2017), http://docs.dpaq.de/12007-european_chamber_cm2025-en.pdf.

10. "Partner and Systemic Competitor—How Do We Deal with China's State-Controlled Economy?" (Berlin: Federation of German Industries, January 2019), www.wita.org/wp-content/uploads/2019/01/201901_Policy_Paper_BDI_China.pdf.

11. Alicja Bachulska and Richard Turcsanyi, "Behind the Huawei Backlash in Poland and the Czech Republic," *The Diplomat*, February 6, 2019, https://thediplomat.com/2019/02/behind-the-huawei-backlash-in-poland-and-the-czech-republic/.

12. Nick Cumming Bruce, "China Rebuked by 22 Nations over Xinjiang Repression," *New York Times*, July 10, 2019, www.nytimes.com/2019/07/10/world/asia/china-xinjiang-rights.html.

13. "EU-China—a Strategic Outlook" (Brussels: European Commission, March 12, 2019), https://ec.europa.eu/commission/publications/eu-china-strategic-outlook-commission-contribution-european-council-21-22-march-2019_en.

14. Michael Peel, Victor Mallet, and Miles Johnson, "Macron Hails 'End of Europe Naïveté' towards China," *Financial Times*, March 22, 2019, www.ft.com/content/ec9671ae-4cbb-11e9-bbc9-6917dce3dc62.

15. John Seaman, "Introduction: China as Partner, Competitor and Rival amid Covid-19," in *Covid-19 in Europe-China Relations: A Country-Level Analysis*, ed. John Seaman (Paris: European Think-tank Network on China, April 29, 2020), 7, www.ifri.org/en/publications/publications-ifri/ouvrages-ifri/covid-19-europe-china-relations-country-level-analysis.

16. Andrew Small, "The Meaning of Systemic Rivalry: Europe and China beyond the Pandemic" (London: European Council on Foreign Relations, May 13, 2020), www.ecfr.eu/publications/summary/the_meaning_of_systemic_rivalry_europe_and_china_beyond_the_pandemic.

17. John Seaman, "Introduction," 8.

18. Ambassade de Chine en France (@AmbassadeChine), Twitter, March 23, 2020, https://twitter.com/AmbassadeChine/status/1242011628608118786; Marc Julienne, "France: Between Healthcare Cooperation and Political Tensions with China amid Covid-19," in *Covid-19 in Europe-China Relations: A Country-Level Analysis*, ed. John Seaman (Paris: European Think-tank Network on China, April 29, 2020), 23, www.ifri.org/en/publications/publications-ifri/ouvrages-ifri/covid -19-europe-china-relations-country-level-analysis; Björn Jerdén, "Sweden: Not Quite Friends in Need with China amid the Covid-19 Crisis," in *Covid-19 in Europe-China Relations: A Country-Level Analysis*," ed. John Seaman (Paris: European Think-tank Network on China, April 29, 2020), 69, www.ifri.org/en/publications/publications-ifri/ouvrages-ifri/covid-19-europe-china-relations-country-level -analysis.

19. Yew Luan Tian, "EU Envoy Says Removal of Phrase in Op-ed in China Newspaper 'Regrettable,'" Reuters, May 7, 2020, www.reuters.com/article/us-health -coronavirus-china-eu/eu-envoy-says-removal-of-phrase-in-op-ed-in-china -newspaper-regrettable-idUSKBN22J1G3.

20. Jennifer Rankin, "EU 'Watered Down' Report on Chinese Disinformation on COVID-19," *The Guardian*, April 27, 2020, www.theguardian.com/world/2020/ apr/27/eu-watered-down-report-on-chinese-disinformation-about-covid-19.

21. Norbert Röttgen (@n_roettgen), Twitter, May 7, 2020, https://twitter.com/ n_roettgen/status/1258313682842537984?lang=en.

22. Louise Guillot, "Europe Has Been 'Naïve' about China Says Josep Borrell," Politico, May 3, 2020, www.politico.eu/article/europe-has-been-naive-about-china -josep-borrell/.

23. Laurens Cerulus, "UK Undergoing Mindset Change toward Beijing Says Leading MP," Politico, May 6, 2020, www.politico.eu/article/uk-undergoing -mindset-change-toward-beijing-says-tobias-ellwood/.

24. Valentina Pop, "EU Moves to Shrink Chinese, U.S. Influence in Its Economy," *Wall Street Journal*, June 17, 2020, www.wsj.com/articles/eu-moves-to-shrink -chinese-u-s-influence-in-its-economy-11592393124.

25. Jake Sullivan, Twitter, December 21 2020, https://twitter.com/jakejsullivan/ status/1341180109118726144

26. John Bolton, *The Room Where It Happened* (New York: Simon and Schuster, 2020), p 70.

TECHNOLOGY

China Aspires to Global Technology Leadership. Can It Achieve Its Ambitions? What Would the Impacts Be at Home and Abroad?

15

Preparing the United States for the Superpower Marathon with China

MICHAEL BROWN
ERIC CHEWNING
PAVNEET SINGH

Today, the United States is in a superpower marathon with China—an economic and technology race likely to last multiple generations for which we are not fully prepared. If we are to prevail, we must *compete with* rather than *contain* China. While this competition has many geopolitical dimensions—including military, diplomatic, and ideological ones—the crux of the competition is geoeconomic. We focus here on the foundation of that economic competition—technology and innovation—which has significant implications for future military advantage and, ultimately, for commercial prosperity.

SIMILARITIES WITH THE COLD WAR

The similarities with the Cold War are why many reach for this historical analogy as this competition with China is the national security threat of *our* generation. With President Xi Jinping's launch of the Belt and Road Ini-

---

The views reflected in this chapter are the personal views of the authors and not necessarily the views of the Department of Defense or of the United States government.

tiative in 2013, the competition became global in terms of political influence, investments, and trade. This is also an ideological conflict since the Chinese Communist Party (CCP) does not value individual freedom and views the rule of law as well as freedoms of speech and press as existential threats.[1] And, just as in the Cold War, there is a propaganda war being waged by China to make the world safe for authoritarianism and highlight what makes the Chinese model great.

In the space race, political and economic commitment to developing advanced technology determined the winner. Similarly, there will be large spillover effects to the economy as technology creates new industries and future economic prosperity. Investment in science and basic research enabled the United States to lead the world economically and militarily for decades by building on technology from the Cold War, such as the internet, space-based communications and geolocation, semiconductors, software, and computer processing. The culmination of these technologies—command-and-control capability through GPS (the Global Positioning System), encrypted communications and battlefield domain surveillance, night vision, stealth, and precision-guided munitions—provided the U.S. military overmatch for a generation. In winning the *geoeconomic* battle, the West also won the military competition.

NOT A NEW COLD WAR

There are five key differences, however, that make the Cold War and containment a poor analogy and prescription for a twenty-first century Sino-American competition.

China's Economic Scale
The Soviet Union at its peak was never more than 57 percent of the U.S. economy, with some experts calculating numbers as low as 43 percent.[2] Contrast that with China's economic growth from a tenth of the U.S. economy in the 1970s to the world's second-largest economy. By purchasing power parity, China is already 25 percent larger than the United States.[3]

China's Integration in the Global Economy
In the Soviet Union, trade was not a major factor in its relatively closed economy.[4] Compare that with China, with "more than 1 million Chinese

nationals working overseas, 140 million Chinese traveling abroad every year, some 40,000 Chinese enterprises around the globe, and overseas property and investment of $7 trillion."[5] The degree of economic integration is a key reason why a containment strategy is futile.

China's Desire and Ability to Manipulate Global Institutions

Xi has called for his nation to "lead the reform of the global governance system."[6] By creating new international institutions like the Asian Infrastructure Investment Bank and New Development Bank as well as expanding its influence in existing international organizations, Beijing is proving very adept at shaping the multilateral system to suit its desired outcomes. Through its China Standards 2035 project, Beijing aims to control the global standards–setting bodies to ensure that its information technology and telecommunications standards are favored.[7]

China's Embrace of Civil and Military Technology Fusion

By actively promoting the fusion of its military, civilian industrial, science, and technology sectors, Beijing's military-civil fusion strategy strives to build the country into an economic, technological, and military superpower while ensuring that overall control remains firmly in the hands of the CCP.

Insufficient Consensus among Western Allies

Unlike during the Cold War, there is insufficient consensus among Western allies on how to respond to China. America's political leadership now agrees that past policies with China have not worked and a more aggressive posture is necessary. While a broad-based, bipartisan coalition to better prepare ourselves for the competition with China has emerged, it is unclear if this will hold for multiple administrations in the same way that containment endured as the dominant U.S. grand strategy during the Cold War. Furthermore, many of America's traditional allies have thus far been reticent to publicly challenge China where economic issues are concerned.

CHINA TRANSFORMING TO FUEL ITS ECONOMY

China aims to surpass the United States, with a singular focus on technology leadership in transforming its economy. Most members of the Politburo are scientists and engineers who highly value the role that science can play in building a productive society and prosperous economy. In fact, China is executing a multidecade plan to transfer technology to increase the size and value-add of its economy.[8]

Beijing has directed academia, business, and the government to collaborate on sixteen "major special projects"[9] that are akin in size and scope to the Manhattan Project; the aim of these endeavors is grand-scale technology innovations in quantum communications, next-generation broadband wireless mobile communications (5G), bioinformatics, high-resolution Earth observation, and manned space flight.

China's economic nationalism is supported by all elements of state power. Specifically, China employs many mercantilist tools to overwhelming advantage in its trading relationships, including currency manipulation, dumping, limiting market access to foreign firms, forcing joint ventures to capture foreign firms' intellectual property, and providing state subsidies of land and capital.[10]

Additionally, guided by industrial policy, China invests in future-oriented economic activity, which is technology intensive. China details plans for increasing technological progress and import substitution, which, if successful, will transfer global market leadership to China in many markets, such as semiconductors, computer hardware and software, networking and communications, automobiles, and genetic engineering. The benefits of this industrial policy are most notable in the successful national champion firms, such as Baidu, Huawei, and Alibaba, which build large economies of scale before competing globally.

PREPARE FOR A SUPERPOWER MARATHON

We must envision a new paradigm for a multigeneration competition. U.S. strategy should be designed to improve U.S. competitiveness no matter what the future brings for China, and we should anticipate a long-term coexistence with China rather than a definitive conclusion as we had with the Cold War.[11] Technology—and especially commercial technology—will almost certainly play a more important role in fueling economic competition than in the Cold War.

Is the U.S. Government Ready to Compete?
When the U.S. government has unity of purpose, the combination of military, economic, and scientific tools at its disposal ensure military and eco-

nomic preeminence. During the Cold War, the U.S. government fostered an unparalleled scientific enterprise that aspired to moonshots and breakthroughs at national laboratories and universities. The private sector then commercialized many of these technologies, creating a virtuous cycle of innovation for both national and economic security.

Tomorrow's battle space will involve asymmetric technologies designed to neutralize U.S. advantages. Many are dual-use technologies.[12] Therefore the Department of Defense (DOD) faces a modernization challenge of the highest order: simultaneously modernizing existing platforms, such as the nuclear triad, while also changing the force composition by investing in technologies such as artificial intelligence (AI), space, cyber, and small drones. Fortunately, Congress and the DOD are aligned in creating new methods of acquisition, such as a fast lane (Outlined in Section 804 of the Fiscal Year 2016 National Defense Authorization Act) and Other Transaction Authority (OTA), which allow for rapid prototyping. Additionally, the Pentagon established the Defense Innovation Unit to accelerate adoption of commercial technology into the military and broaden the base of military suppliers to include companies with leading-edge technology. Similarly, U.S. Army Futures Command and U.S. Air Force Ventures are adopting commercial technology more rapidly. However, in total, these innovation activities influence only 1 or 2 percent of Pentagon procurement, which is insufficient to motivate investors or entrepreneurs to design with defense needs in mind.

Is Academia Ready to Compete?

It was through our world-class university system that the wellspring of ideas, experimentation, and talent played a signature role in ending World War II and buttressed the space program in the 1960s. Today, there is a decline in STEM (science, technology, engineering, and mathematics) graduates, whereas China now graduates six to eight times the number of STEM students that the United States does. University programs are financially strained and must seek higher-paying foreign students—often Chinese nationals—to fill the ranks. But the U.S. immigration system does not allow these students to stay in the United States after graduating. For similar financial reasons, universities are exploring partnerships with foreign sources of funding, often Chinese.

Is the Private Sector Ready to Compete?

Given the importance of *commercial* technology to the competition, the United States needs a private sector ready to join the U.S. government and allies in ensuring industrial capacity in critical sectors. But an even larger challenge for the private sector is shifting the balance from short-term profits to long-term capability development. Since the shareholder revolution of the 1980s, companies increasingly focus on return on capital at the expense of long-term R&D and technology development. With the increase in institutional ownership of companies, capital markets reinforce efficiency of capital in stock price performance.[13]

The CCP has a contrasting view focused on technology development for the long term. China's national science and technology plans mean hundreds of billions of dollars are invested to shift leadership in technology industries from semiconductors to satellites away from the West and toward China. In fact, this *is* the end-state of Made in China 2025.

In recent years, the growth of activist investors amplified the focus on near-term shareholder returns as their business models rely on improved returns. Corporations have become increasingly short-term oriented as CEOs must focus on *quarterly* earnings as a key metric, in part to avoid takeover or activist interest. We institutionalized our focus on short-term profits and capital efficiency rather than balancing these goals with research investments for long-term capability development.

Another response to the drive for higher returns is the erosion of U.S. manufacturing through offshoring and outsourcing to lower-cost geographies. One little understood consequence has been that as manufacturing expertise moves offshore, so do design skills and design-for-manufacturability expertise.

Two more trends accelerated U.S. manufacturing erosion: first, globalization moving manufacturing assets and jobs offshore and, second, the U.S. tax code, which until 2017 provided a potential 40 percent improvement in after-tax earnings for U.S. business income sheltered offshore.

Still another response to boosting financial returns was shedding hardware businesses, leaving just software and services firms. Entire ecosystems of suppliers moved offshore such that the United States does not, for example, build printed circuit boards or flex circuits—integral components of all electronic devices—in any volume, nor does it package or fabricate semiconductor wafers at global scale. From a national security standpoint, this is acceptable as long as the United States has access among our allies.

However, since we rely on China in so many instances, we have inadvertently created a glaring national security risk.

Finally, an additional response to boosting financial returns is the corporate share buyback—companies using their cash balances or even borrowing to repurchase shares to boost earnings per share. In the last decade alone, $3.8 trillion has been spent on share buybacks.[14]

The culmination of these trends resulted in "the destruction of America's once vibrant military and commercial industrial capacity in many sectors [that] has become the single biggest unacknowledged threat to our national security."[15] As a glaring example, Americans are reminded as the COVID-19 crisis unfolds that 80 percent of the ingredients to make our medicines and 97 percent of our antibiotics come from China.[16] Bottom line, to be an effective competitor with a country that has a long-term plan—fifty years instead of a few quarters—and values strategic technology advantage more than financial returns, we need a longer-term focus in our capital markets and corporations that rewards R&D and risk taking in technology development.

HOW IS THE UNITED STATES FARING IN THE TECHNOLOGY COMPETITION?

China already leads the United States in the deployment of hypersonics, small drones, quantum communications, 5G, facial recognition software, e-commerce and mobile payments, electric vehicles, clean power technology, high-speed rail, and the world's largest database of genetic engineering data. China challenges U.S. technology leads in AI, genetic engineering, quantum computing, and quantum sensors. China's goals are clear—in Xi's words, "catch up and surpass" the United States.[17]

RECOMMENDATIONS FOR COMPETING IN A SUPERPOWER MARATHON

While we are not fully prepared today in government, the private sector, or academia to compete, some critical work has already begun. America's guiding national security documents, the National Security Strategy and the National Defense Strategy, clearly signal a shift toward great power competition with China. The Department of Defense is developing new warfighting concepts and plans, making modernization investments in new technologies such as hypersonics, AI, and quantum a budget priority, and aggressively reforming its acquisition process to better leverage commercial sector innovations. Bipartisan support in Congress funded the largest R&D investment in DOD's history, passed legislation to modernize CFIUS to counter investment-driven technology transfer, and created the Space Force, a new military service whose raison d'être is winning the military competition in space. The U.S. Trade Representative (USTR) documented examples of Chinese intellectual property theft and initiated aggressive trade actions. The Department of Justice, through its China Initiative, has made prosecuting Chinese corporate espionage a prime concern, and the State Department is waging a global campaign to counter China's influence. Illustrating the level of bipartisan support, at the 2020 Munich Security Conference, both Trump administration Cabinet officials and Speaker of the House Nancy Pelosi pressed NATO allies on Huawei's presence in Europe's 5G infrastructure.

While all of this is necessary, it is not sufficient to catch up in a marathon that has already begun. Our next steps should focus on the following four areas: bolstering investment in basic R&D, investing in human capital in STEM fields, develop and build an integrated economic statecraft strategy, and focus on the long term in business and capital markets.

Bolster Federal Investment in Basic R&D

Most important of all these recommendations, the United States must recommit to excellence in science and basic research to develop new technologies, particularly in AI, quantum, genetic engineering, autonomous systems, cyber, and space. These technologies are key to the superpower marathon, and we cannot lose momentum in any of them. In recent years, federally funded R&D declined to 0.7 percent of GDP, down from 2 percent at the height of the Cold War. To stimulate business R&D, we need incentives and tax policies to reinforce long-term commitments to R&D to support emerging hardware businesses and a manufacturing renaissance. Increases in the federal R&D tax credit would likely stimulate corporate research budgets.[18] Together, we should aspire to create many "moonshots" in the technologies critical to this superpower marathon, bringing government, business, and academia together toward common goals of national purpose.

Attract, Develop, and Retain Human Capital in STEM Fields

Along with the increases in federally funded research and moonshots, we need a generational commitment to STEM education. We should provide financial incentives to study STEM fields, such as government internships that lead to employment offers, partial student loan debt forgiveness for study in STEM fields, and corporate tax credits to hire more engineers.

Additionally, we want to encourage the best foreign talent in the world to come to the United States to study but also ensure a clear path to green cards and citizenship so those we educate—especially in STEM fields—remain to contribute to our economy

Develop an Integrated Economic Statecraft Strategy
and Build the Institutional Capacity to Execute It
The political-military tools the U.S. government employs to address geopolitical concerns are largely concentrated in the Departments of Defense and State. By contrast, the authorities associated with the use of geoeconomic instruments are diffused across the federal government and the private sector. The first step in integrating these perspectives is the development of a whole-of-government strategy for economic statecraft. The core aim of this strategy is growing a vibrant U.S. economy with the free flow of capital, talent, and ideas among allies in the context of a coherent plan for competing with China.

Focus on the Long Term in Businesses and Our Capital Markets
Perhaps most difficult among these recommendations, we need to shift our thinking to a longer time horizon in businesses and in our capital markets. Reforms must be jointly agreed to by corporate management *and* institutional investors, which own the majority of total equity. First, the investment horizon and corresponding benchmark metrics must move away from a quarter or a year to a longer timeframe, such as a decade. Second, we should encourage long-term engagement from owners as well as longer holding periods of stocks.[19] From a policy perspective, this could be supported by tax incentives to hold equity positions longer and disincentives for momentum trading, which encourages turnover. Third, we should discourage financial engineering that does not create long-term value.

COMPETING FOR THE FUTURE

While China faces significant problems of its own in the coming years its authoritarian system also brings beneficial dimensions: stability and decisiveness of political direction, long-term planning horizons, and the coordination of government, commercial, and military sectors to achieve national aims. Given China's growing economy, investment in science and technology, and coercive power over its people, the winner of this superpower marathon is by no means certain. The stakes, however, are paramount given China's ideological differences and technology capability fueling an economy that is on a path to eclipse our own. As a result, we must strengthen our resolve and discipline in improving our competitiveness, benefiting from one of the only issues to enjoy strong bipartisan support among policymakers and legislators in Congress. We must prepare now for this superpower marathon or resign ourselves to becoming a second-rate power while the world looks up to a new global leader with strikingly different values and views.

NOTES

1. Chris Buckley, "China Takes Aim at Western Ideas," *New York Times*, August 19, 2013, www.nytimes.com/2013/08/20/world/asia/chinas-new-leadership-takes-hard-line-in-secret-memo.html.

2. There is debate about whether official U.S. intelligence assessments overstated the performance of the Soviet economy during the Cold War. Angus Maddison calculates that the Soviet GDP stood between 35 and 43 percent of U.S. GDP between 1950 and 1973. Angus Maddison, *Contours of the World Economy, I-2030 AD* (Oxford: Oxford University Press, 2007). U.S. intelligence reports assessed that the GDP of the Soviet Union fluctuated between 49 and 57 percent of U.S. GDP from 1960 to 1975 but fell backward to 52 percent by 1984. "A Comparison of the U.S. and Soviet Economies: Evaluating Performance of the Soviet System" (McLean, VA: U.S. Directorate of Intelligence, October 1985), www.cia.gov/library/readingroom/docs/DOC_0000497165.pdf.

3. Kurt M. Campbell and Jake Sullivan, "Competition Without Catastrophe: How America Can Both Challenge and Coexist with China," *Foreign Affairs* 98, no. 5 (September/October 2019): 99, www.foreignaffairs.com/articles/china/competition-with-china-without-catastrophe.

4. Russia did not join the World Trade Organization until 2012.

5. Zhou Bo, "The Future of the PLA," *Foreign Policy,* August 6, 2019, https://foreignpolicy.com/2019/08/06/the-future-of-the-pla/.

6. "Xi Urges Breaking New Ground in Major Country Diplomacy with Chinese Characteristics," Xinhua, June 24, 2018, http://xinhuanet.com/english/2018-06/24/c_137276269.htm.

7. Patrick Jenevein, "'China Standards' Promotion Foundational Campaign in Beijing's Global Expansion Strategy," Pointe Bello, November 2019, www.pointebello.com/briefs/china-standard-2035/. (Full report available by request to Pointe Bello.)

8. As related in Xinhua, Xi said that "China should establish itself as . . . a leading innovator by 2030 before realizing the objective of becoming a world

-leading [science & technology] power . . . by 2049." See Xinhua, "Xi Sets Targets for China's Science, Technology Mastery," *People's Daily*, May 30, 2016, http://en.people.cn/n3/2016/0530/c90785-9065418.html.

9. Tai Ming Cheung, Thomas Mahnken, Deborah Seligsohn, Kevin Pollpeter, Eric Anderson, and Fan Yang, *Planning for Innovation: Understanding China's Plans for Technological, Energy, Industrial, and Defense Development* (Washington, DC: U.S.-China Economic and Security Review Commission, July 28, 2016), www.uscc.gov/research/planning-innovation-understanding-chinas-plans-technological-energy-industrial-and-defense.

10. Huawei received as much as $75 billion in tax breaks, financing, and cheap resources as it became the world's top telecom vendor. Chuen-Wei Yap, "State Support Helped Fuel Huawei's Global Rise," *Wall Street Journal*, December 25, 2019, www.wsj.com/articles/state-support-helped-fuel-huaweis-global-rise-11577280736.

11. Kurt M. Campbell and Jake Sullivan, "Competition Without Catastrophe," 97.

12. Peter Levine, "If You Want More Defense Innovation, Spend Less on Legacy Platforms," War on the Rocks, August 20, 2018, https://warontherocks.com/2018/08/if-you-want-more-defense-innovation-spend-less-on-legacy-platforms/.

13. Corporate focus on shareholder returns as an exclusive measure of success has become so extreme that the U.S. Business Roundtable recently announced a return to a more balanced view of the interests of all stakeholders, including customers, employees, and the communities in which they serve, in a public statement signed by 181 CEOs. "Statement on the Purpose of a Corporation," Business Roundtable, August 19, 2019, https://opportunity.businessroundtable.org/ourcommitment/.

14. Jerry Useem, "The Stock-Buyback Swindle," *The Atlantic,* August 2019, www.theatlantic.com/magazine/archive/2019/08/the-stock-buyback-swindle/592774/.

15. Matt Stoller and Lucas Kunce, "America's Monopoly Crisis Hits the Military," *American Conservative*, June 27, 2019, www.theamericanconservative.com/articles/americas-monopoly-crisis-hits-the-military/.

16. Yanzhong Huang, "U.S. Dependence on Pharmaceutical Products from China," Council on Foreign Relations, August 14, 2019, www.cfr.org/blog/us-dependence-pharmaceutical-products-china.

17. Julian Baird Gewirtz, "China's Long March to Technological Supremacy," *Foreign Affairs*, August 27, 2019, www.foreignaffairs.com/articles/china/2019-08-27/chinas-long-march-technological-supremacy.

18. The conclusion from a recent group of quantitative studies is that R&D spending is elastic: "A 10% fall in the tax [adjusted] price of R&D results in at least a 10% increase in R&D in the long run." Nicholas Bloom, John Van Reenen, and Heidi Williams, "A Toolkit of Policies to Promote Innovation," *Journal of Economic Perspectives* 33, no. 3 (Summer 2019): 170, https://pubs.aeaweb.org/doi/pdfplus/10.1257/jep.33.3.163.

19. Dominic Barton and Mark Wiseman, "Focusing Capital on the Long Term," *Harvard Business Review*, January–February, 2014, https://hbr.org/2014/01/focusing-capital-on-the-long-term.

16

Navigating the U.S.-China 5G Competition

NICOL TURNER LEE

The United States and China are in a race to deploy fifth-generation (5G) wireless networks, and the country that dominates will lead in setting technical standards, filing patents, and building global supply chains. Some analysts have argued that the Chinese government appears to be on a sprint in the race to achieve this goal, largely due to its ability to quickly relax regulatory burdens imposed on state-run telecom companies.[1] U.S. government leaders and the private sector seem to be more on a marathon to network deployment, especially as they have more to do to cut the red tape of local and regional government bureaucracies, update restrictive and outdated regulations, and make more spectrum available for commercial use. The United States faces another challenge, which is the lack of current U.S. commercial competition to Chinese equipment suppliers in the development of 5G networks.

While both countries may ultimately deploy large-scale 5G networks at the same time, how they internally manage their respective spectrum policies, network deployment costs, and expectations around the anticipated 5G revenue models will ultimately position their global leadership. U.S. leaders must organize around a strategic and coordinated call to action for faster and improved access to infrastructure assets, as well as more reasonable expectations of the global supply chain to compete with the Chinese government.

This chapter argues that the positioning of 5G global competitiveness in the United States entails more flexible, robust, and timely spectrum policies; scalable replacement alternatives to Chinese 5G equipment; and long-term planning, inclusive of increased research and development (R&D) spending. Taken together, these actions will, at minimum, help the United States maintain global leadership in mobile markets.

SETTING THE 5G STAGE

Compared to 4G Long-Term Evolution (LTE), 5G mobile networks are expected to have peak download speeds as high as 20 gigabits per second and lower latency that will enable specialized and precise functions, including the Internet of Things, remote medicine, connected cars, as well as augmented and virtual realities (AR/VR). A recent World Economic Forum report concluded that 5G networks will contribute $13.2 trillion in economic value globally and generate 22.3 million jobs from direct network investments and residual services.[2] In the United States alone, 5G networks and their related applications are expected to add 3 million jobs and $1.2 trillion to the economy.[3]

China has assessed the economic potential of its own 5G networks, reporting more than 200 million subscribers before the full deployment of the technology and upward of 3 million jobs over a five-year period.[4] Chinese hardware manufacturers and software companies also predict generous earnings from a 5G-enabled economy.[5] However, the Chinese government's goals may be tempered by the federal bans being imposed on Huawei and ZTE by the previous administration of President Donald J. Trump amid accusations related to trade secrets and possible espionage.[6] The Trump White House also demanded similar alignment from allies, like the United Kingdom and Germany, who continue to do business with Chinese telecom companies. Despite such backlash, Huawei and ZTE continue to be global, low-cost alternatives for 5G equipment.[7] China's 5G aspirations are also part of the government's overall Belt and Road Initiative, which is a strategy to increase its global power.[8]

Compared to the involvement of the Chinese government, the U.S. private sector has largely driven the capital investments in national mobile infrastructure, with companies successfully lobbying Congress for more spectrum (the airwaves needed for 5G networks) and timely elimination of barriers to network build-outs. In 2019, the Federal Communications Commission (FCC) launched the 5G FAST Plan to deliver a range of spectrum assets, update existing infrastructure policies, and modernize outdated regulations that impact 5G delivery.[9] Additional initiatives have followed, including a $9 billion rural 5G fund, to expand services nationwide in 2020.[10]

A critical component of 5G networks is its unique architecture of both macro- and small-cell base stations with edge computing capabilities that require thousands of large cell towers and tens of thousands of small-cell antennae be deployed in local communities and cities. The Chinese government has exercised authority around the placement of these assets via mandates. Recently, the United States has sped up its siting and permitting processes, which are often slowed down by state or municipal laws. The federal government has also adopted blanket preemption of local and state laws or offered municipal redress on a case-by-case basis to maintain urgency around approvals of 5G small cells.[11]

Less than 10 years ago, the United States dominated the 4G LTE marketplace after falling behind in 3G to European adoption. The widely adopted "sharing economy" enabled by 4G LTE cultivated a range of new companies, including Lyft, Uber, Airbnb, and cloud-based services. However, what the future holds under 5G in terms of the next "killer apps" is largely unknown, except for the technology's known support of the latest innovations in artificial intelligence (AI) systems, AR/VR, and autonomous vehicles.

For the United States to maintain global leadership, stakeholders must find consensus around *spectrum management*, *network supply chain*, and *plans for anticipated innovations*. Each component is discussed below.

SPECTRUM

Electromagnetic spectrum is one of the key ingredients of advanced wireless networks and is a highly valued asset as the demands from mobile users increase. In the early stages of 5G development, the Chinese government opted to rely on low- and mid-band spectrum for its networks. Low-band spectrum, which travels in the 600 megahertz (MHz), 800 MHz, and 900 MHz bands, can cover longer distances, penetrate through walls of buildings, and provide superior coverage over large geographic areas. Mid-band spectrum, which is in the 2.5 gigahertz (GHz) and 3.5 GHz range, provides more balanced coverage and capacity due to its ability to cover a several-mile radius with 5G, despite needing more cell sites than lower-tiered spectrum bands.

The Chinese government looked mainly to sub-6 mid-band spectrum over higher frequencies, like mmWave, which travels between the 24 GHz and 300 GHz bands. As a result of this decision, Chinese telecom companies, including China Mobile, China Telecom, and China Unicom, have long been experimenting in the low- to mid-band ranges as they develop a suite of 5G products and services. The Chinese government also cleared "C-Band" spectrum around the same time, which at 3.7 GHz to 4.2 GHz brings even more geographic 5G coverage to its state-owned telecom companies. Compared to mmWave, which cannot travel long distances or through the walls of buildings, C-band supports high-capacity broadband and enables advanced applications like AR and VR, without the line-of-sight challenges.

On the other hand, U.S. companies started with reliance on mmWave, or higher-frequency spectrum. Both AT&T and Verizon, which focused their initial 5G deployments in this band, cite its viability when in use at stadiums and for localized private networks. However, mmWave's technical limitations make it less useful over wider coverage areas, especially in rural areas.

More recently, U.S. telecom companies have sought to deploy a mix of low-, mid-, and high-band spectrum to facilitate 5G service, a strategy already enacted by the Chinese government.[12] For example, Sprint, which was acquired by T-Mobile, launched its early 5G service using mid-band, and the company's acquisition will add their low-band tiers to the new wireless company's 5G service, which will cover more rural and remote areas.

The moral of the story here is that early U.S. decisions on spectrum have created some fragmentation between the private sector and the federal government in the requests for more commercial spectrum.[13] For example, the FCC was lauded in 2020 by the majority of wireless carriers for the release and auction of C-band assets, though this was long after the Chinese government's deployments and risks legal challenges from the satellite companies who primarily license this band for delivering television programming to most U.S. households.[14]

Congress has also been slow to repurpose government spectrum for commercial 5G use. For example, legislators introduced the Mobile Now Act, which was written to reduce the red tape associated with the procurement of gigabit wireless services like 5G. It took two years for it to be adopted.[15] The bill was reintroduced in 2017 after being presented in 2016. The Senate adopted the legislation as part of the Repack Airwaves Yielding Better Access for Users of Modern Services Act of 2018.[16]

GLOBAL SUPPLY CHAIN

Since 1987, Chinese equipment supplier Huawei has grown to be a leader in information and communication technologies and most recently in 5G equipment and services. Despite the U.S. ban of Huawei in federal deployments as part of the 2019 National Defense Authorization Act and threats to withhold intelligence from countries that use Huawei equipment, few governments have followed suit at this time.[17] In January 2020, the U.K. imposed a partial ban on Huawei products. In July 2020, the country banned all of Huawei from the 5G network products on grounds of cost and the risk management capacity.[18]

There have been similar attacks on Huawei by the Dutch, who pushed Huawei products out of the Netherlands' 5G core network to avert any potential threats of espionage.[19] In January 2020, the European Union also proposed a risk-based model for partner countries to provide a security baseline for 5G networks but stopped short of a complete ban on equipment and software.[20] On some level, network interdependence and reasonable cost concerns of other countries have staved off the United States' call for full bans.

African countries are perhaps more challenged to initiate any type of withholding in their mobile infrastructure. Africa has also long negotiated bilateral trade relationships with China through the Belt and Road Initiative and, without wireless access, would regress in its own digital advancements. In 2017, smartphone connections in Africa were at 250 million and are expected to be at 440 million by 2025.[21]

However, the public bullying by the Trump administration on the use of Huawei and ZTE products may potentially backfire for the United States without coordination with other countries or competitors, such as Nokia or Ericsson, who make up the global 5G supply chain.[22] Further, a complete ban on Chinese equipment makers from U.S. systems could also impose future global network dependency issues, which could impact user experiences of a more global internet.

While it could be perceived that the Trump administration's action to ban Chinese telecom providers would not generate similar results as Japan's somewhat closed-off mobile markets, the United States could box itself out of mainstreamed global expansion. In November 2019, before the United States officially added Huawei to the Department of Commerce's Bureau of Industry and Security List, about 290 American companies requested exemptions from the adopted ban of the company's equipment from domestic networks.[23] U.S. trade associations like CTIA, which represents a range of incumbent mobile providers, have generally supported the Huawei ban, but urge the federal government to present compelling evidence on data security concerns.[24]

INNOVATION

What is clear to many is that the United States will maintain its dominance over innovation, particularly in the applications and software enabled by these advanced mobile networks, despite China's slight lead on commercial spectrum availability and equipment.[25] Each generation of mobile technology has enabled a new suite of functional innovations for users and the economy.[26] Mobile voice communications eventually took on mobile messaging, or short message services, with the introduction of 2G. Smartphone technologies, high-definition video, and other robust multimedia applications were made possible through 3G and 4G.

The promise of 5G's faster data transmission speeds, lower latency, and wider coverage areas (depending on the spectrum band) will encompass virtual and augmented realities, autonomous vehicles, and other AI systems. Combined 5G and existing 4G LTE networks will lead to a more robust digital sharing and networking environments able to accommodate applications where these mobile attributes matter.

Under the leadership of President Xi Jinping, the Chinese government has made a recent attempt to upgrade their industrial strength as part of the Made in China 2025 strategic plan, which is targeting resources and political prowess toward "innovation-driven development." While some have argued that this initiative is unsettling against the former administration's Make America Great Again economic aspirations, China is positioning itself to become a competitor in the high-tech industries, including AI. According to a report issued by the Carnegie Endowment for International Peace, "China has eclipsed the U.S. as the world's largest overall (public and private) R&D investor."[27] However, some analysts are finding that these large tech investments are not automatically translating into success for Chinese companies. Last year, the *Los Angeles Times* reported that newly launched companies in the self-driving cars business, like Baidu, Inc., Pony.ai, and Tencent, are early in their implementation of this new technology,[28] whereas U.S. companies, including Alphabet Inc.'s Waymo, General Motors, and Tesla, have been at this since 2014, working on road tests, integrated technology systems, and increased research and development.[29]

What is important here is that attempts by the Chinese government to outspend the United States (and potentially the rest of the world) in digital platforms and services will largely come from its own consumers and businesses in the tech sector. There is also the possibility that Chinese officials will export their own technology to specific countries, creating a split digital ecosystem worldwide. Without forward-thinking leadership and some cooperation with the Chinese government, the United States and the private sector might miss out on a greater market share within the innovation economy, especially without some interoperability between next-generation global networks.

CONCLUSION

The mobile services that consumers are highly dependent on today are due to American ingenuity that ultimately contributed to a host of new businesses, expanded enterprises, applications, and consumer engagements. The worldwide deployment of 5G will lead the scope and direction of new applications and services, ushering in a period of catch-up for other countries. These and other issues should be of great importance to President Joe Biden and his administration.

But as the 5G marketplace quickly matures, the United States has lost some time in its attention to a range of regulatory and legislative directives that, at times, have constrained activities. If the country is going to maintain global standing in areas that drive the next wave of mobile innovations—standards, patents, applications, and software—a more coordinated call to action that also involves more strategic spectrum management and attention to the global supply chain will be required. This approach must engage stakeholders at all levels—from the public and private sectors to the most appropriate levels of federal and local governments. Surpassing the Chinese government in 5G will better position the United States for rapid digitization and, if strategically managed, increased competition in domestic and international markets.

ACKNOWLEDGMENTS: The author would like to thank Jack Karsten and Darrell West. Ted Reinert edited this chapter.

NOTES

1. Elsa B. Kania, "Securing Our 5G Future: The Competitive Challenge and Considerations for U.S. Policy" (Washington, DC, Center for a New American Security, November 7, 2019), www.cnas.org/publications/reports/securing-our-5g-future.

2. *The Impact of 5G: Creating New Value across Industries and Society* (Geneva: World Economic Forum, January 2020), www3.weforum.org/docs/WEF_The_Impact_of_5G_Report.pdf.

3. Roslyn Layton, "On C-Band Spectrum, Auction Speed Is All That Matters," *Forbes*, November 13, 2019, www.forbes.com/sites/roslynlayton/2019/11/13/on-c-band-spectrum-auction-speed--is-all-that-matters/.

4. Ma Si, "China to Boast over 20m 5G Subscribers by 2020," *China Daily*, November 21, 2019, www.chinadaily.com.cn/a/201911/21/WS5dd67360a310cf3e355 7917b.html.

5. "China Is Poised to Win the 5G Race: Key Steps Extending Global Leadership" (London: EY, 2018), www.ey.com/Publication/vwLUAssets/ey-china-is-poised-to-win-the-5g-race-en/$FILE/ey-china-is-poised-to-win-the-5g-race-en.pdf.

6. Bojan Pancevski, "U.S. Officials Say Huawei Can Covertly Access Telecom Networks," *Wall Street Journal*, February 12, 2020, www.wsj.com/articles/u-s-officials-say-huawei-can-covertly-access-telecom-networks-11581452256.

7. Juan Pedro Thomas, "ZTE Has Racked Up 46 5G Commercial Contracts Globally." RCR Wireless, February 25, 2020, www.rcrwireless.com/20200225/5g/zte-already-secured-46-5g-commercial-contracts-globally. See also Ma Si, "Huawei Secures Most 5G Contracts around World," *China Daily*, February 22, 2020, http://global.chinadaily.com.cn/a/202002/22/WS5e50491ea3101282172796b9.html.

8. "China's Belt and Road Initiative in the Global Trade, Investment and Finance Landscape," in *OECD Business and Finance Outlook 2018* (Paris: OECD, 2018), www.oecd.org/finance/Chinas-Belt-and-Road-Initiative-in-the-global-trade-investment-and-finance-landscape.pdf.

9. Alan Hearty, "Overview of the FCC's FAST Plan," *National Law Review*, February 20, 2019, www.natlawreview.com/article/overview-fcc-s-5g-fast-plan.

10. Bevin Fletcher, "FCC Floats Options for Proposed $9B 5G Rural Fund," Fierce Wireless, April 1, 2020, www.fiercewireless.com/regulatory/fcc-floats-options-for-proposed-9b-5g-rural-fund.

11. "In the Matter of Accelerating Wireless Broadband Deployment by Removing Barriers to Infrastructure Investment: Declaratory Ruling and Third Report and Order," Federal Communications Commission, September 27, 2018, https://docs.fcc.gov/public/attachments/FCC-18-133A1.pdf.

12. Sarah Krouse, "U.S. Telecom Giants Take Different Paths to 5G," *Wall Street Journal*, April 12, 2020, www.wsj.com/articles/u-s-telecom-giants-take-different-paths-to-5g-11586556074.

13. Milo Medin and Gilman Louie, "Clearing the Air on 5G," War on the Rocks, March 13, 2020, https://warontherocks.com/2020/03/clearing-the-air-on-5g/.

14. Ajit Pai, "Chairman Pai Speech Announcing the C-Band Proposal" (speech, Washington, DC, February 6, 2020), www.fcc.gov/document/chairman-pai-speech-announcing-c-band-proposal.

15. Making Opportunities for Broadband Investment and Limiting Excessive and Needless Obstacles to Wireless Act, S. 19, 115th Cong. (2017), www.congress.gov/bill/115th-congress/senate-bill/19.

16. Repack Airwaves Yielding Better Access for Users of Modern Services Act of 2018, H.R. 4986, 115th Cong. (2018), www.congress.gov/bill/115th-congress/house-bill/4986.

17. Julian E. Barnes and Adam Satariano, "U.S. Campaign to Ban Huawei Overseas Stumbles as Allies Resist," *New York Times*, March 17, 2019, www.nytimes.com/2019/03/17/us/politics/huawei-ban.html.

18. Max Colchester, "U.K. Allows Huawei to Build Parts of 5G Network, Defying Trump," *Wall Street Journal*, January 29, 2020, www.wsj.com/articles/u-k-allows-huawei-to-build-parts-of-5g-network-11580213316.

19. Toby Sterling, "No Huawei Ban in Dutch 5G Rollout: Government," Reuters, July 1, 2019, www.reuters.com/article/us-netherlands-telecoms-idUSKCN1TW2V8.

20. Jon Porter, "EU Supports Huawei Use in 5G Networks in Defiance of US," The Verge, January 29, 2020, www.theverge.com/2020/1/29/21113289/european-union-eu-huawei-5g-networks-national-infrastructure-ban-usa.

21. Elo Umeh, "Three Reasons Why African Mobile Connectivity Is Misleading," The Africa Report, June 27, 2019, www.theafricareport.com/14567/three-reasons-why-african-mobile-connectivity-is-misleading/.

22. Brian Fung, "How China's Huawei Took the Lead over U.S. Companies in 5G Technology," *Washington Post*, April 10, 2019, www.washingtonpost.com/technology/2019/04/10/us-spat-with-huawei-explained/.

23. Todd Shields, "Rift between U.S. and European Carriers Opens over Huawei," Bloomberg, February 19, 2019, www.bloomberg.com/news/articles/2019-02-19/huawei-issue-opens-rift-between-u-s-european-mobile-carriers.

24. Kelly Hill, "Industry Associations Push Back on FCC Move to Ban Chinese Equipment Vendors," RCR Wireless News, July 3, 2018, www.rcrwireless.com/20180702/policy/industry-associations-push-back-on-fcc-move-to-ban.

25. Stella Soon, "Here's How the US Can Beat China in the Race for Dominance in Next Generation Networks," CNBC, November 26, 2019, www.cnbc.com/2019/11/26/5g-race-how-the-us-can-beat-china-in-the-competition-for-dominance.html.

26. Nicol Turner Lee, *Enabling Opportunities: 5G, the Internet of Things, and Communities of Color* (Washington, DC: The Brookings Institution, January 9, 2019), www.brookings.edu/research/enabling-opportunities-5g-the-internet-of-things-and-communities-of-color/.

27. James L. Schoff, *Competing with China on Technology and Innovation* (Washington, DC: Carnegie Endowment for International Peace, October 10, 2019), https://carnegieendowment.org/2019/10/10/competing-with-china-on-technology-and-innovation-pub-80010.

28. Yan Zhang, "China Is Way behind the U.S. in Driverless Vehicles. It's Determined to Catch Up," *Los Angeles Times*, May 16, 2019, www.latimes.com/business/la-fi-hy-china-autonomous-vehicles-20190516-story.html.

29. Ibid.

17

Managing China's Rise in Outer Space

FRANK A. ROSE

The utilization of outer space helps us warn of natural disasters, facilitate navigation and transportation globally, expand our scientific frontiers, monitor compliance with arms control treaties and agreements, provide global access to financial operations, and scores of other activities worldwide. However, today's outer space environment is evolving rapidly, presenting the United States and the entire international community with several key challenges to the sustainability, safety, stability, and security of the outer space environment. Some of these challenges include the growth of orbital debris, which represents an ever-increasing threat to both human and robotic space flight, the emergence of mega constellations of small satellites, and the development and deployment of anti-satellite (ASAT) capabilities.

China's increasing activities in outer space lie at the heart of these challenges. Over the past several decades, China has rapidly expanded its presence in outer space in both the civil and military arenas. As a January 2019 report by the U.S. Defense Intelligence Agency noted, "China has devoted significant economic and political resources to growing all aspects of its space program, from improving military space applications to developing human spaceflight and lunar exploration programs."[1] This chapter discusses the key challenges facing the outer space environment; provides an overview of Chinese civil and military space programs; and shares pragmatic recommendations on how the United States can effectively manage China's rise in outer space.

CHALLENGES TO THE OUTER SPACE ENVIRONMENT

The Growth of Orbital Debris

Decades of space activity have littered Earth's orbit with defunct satellites and pieces of orbital debris. As activities in outer space continue to grow, the chances of a collision increase. The United States is currently tracking approximately 26,000 pieces of orbital debris 10 centimeters or larger in various Earth orbits. Approximately 2,218 of these objects are active satellites.[2] Other objects in orbit include spent rocket bodies, inactive satellites, a wrench, and even a toothbrush! Additionally, as many as 600,000 pieces of orbital debris smaller than 10 centimeters exist that we currently do not have the capability to track but which could still cause significant damage if a collision occurred. Experts warn that the current quantity and density of humanmade debris significantly increases the odds of future collisions, either as debris damages space systems or as colliding debris creates more space debris.

Because of the high speeds in which these objects travel in space—17,500 miles per hour—even a submillimeter piece of debris could cause a problem for human or robotic missions. This serious problem is continually growing as more debris is generated by routine operations as well as by accidents and mishaps, such as the 2009 collision between a Russian Cosmos satellite and a commercially operated Iridium satellite. Other debris is a result of deliberate acts, like China's 2007 destructive test against one of its own satellites. That single test created over 3,000 pieces of debris larger than 10 centimeters that will stay in low Earth orbit for potentially hundreds of years, presenting an ongoing threat to the space systems of all nations, including that of China itself. Over the past several years there have been hundreds of occasions when debris from China's 2007 ASAT test has come close to their own satellites. Indeed, these two events alone are responsible for approximately one-third of all the debris in low Earth orbit. Figure 17-1 illustrates the dramatic growth in the amount of orbital debris since the dawn of the Space Age in 1957.

The United States has been working to address the orbital debris challenge in several ways. First and foremost, it is improving space situation awareness capabilities, which allow us to track, characterize, and catalog objects in outer space. This mission is currently performed by the U.S. Department of Defense through the U.S. Air Force's 18th Space Control Squadron, based at Vandenberg Air Force Base in California.[3] The 18th Space Control

Figure 17-1. **Growth of Orbital Debris, 1957–2015**

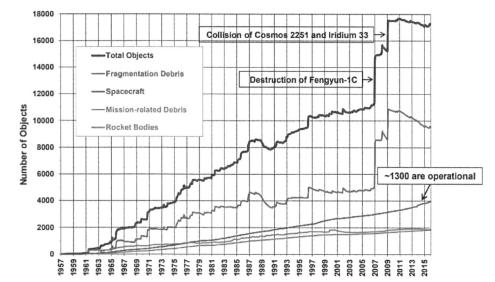

Source: National Aeronautics and Space Administration, Jer-Chyi Liou, "Orbital Challenges for Space Operations," presentation, ICAO/UNOOSA Symposium, Abu Dhabi, March 15–17, 2016, https://ntrs.nasa.gov/archive/nasa/casi.ntrs.nasa.gov/20160002047.pdf.

Squadron currently publishes a catalog of space objects and warns global space operators, including foreign governments and commercial operators, of potential collisions free of charge.[4] However, at some point in the future, this mission will transfer to a civilian agency to allow the Pentagon to focus more on its traditional warfighting mission.

Over the last several decades, the United States has also worked within several international forums like the Interagency Debris Coordination Committee, which consists of representatives from the world's major space agencies, and the United Nations Committee on the Peaceful Uses of Outer Space (UNCOPUOS), to develop international guidelines to improve the safety and sustainability of the outer space environment. Since 2007 these groups have developed and approved several important agreements, such as the U.N. Debris Mitigation Guidelines (2007) and the UNCOPUOS Long-Term Sustainability Guidelines (2016 and 2019), designed to address the orbital debris challenge.

According to data from Space-Track.Org,[5] the United States and Russia are responsible for the largest number of objects in Earth orbit, which includes active satellites, spent rocket bodies, and orbital debris. This is primarily due to their long history of outer space operations dating back to the 1950s. However, China is quickly catching up and is now the country with the third-largest number of objects in orbit. Some of these objects are satellites and spent rocket bodies, but the majority is debris from China's 2007 ASAT test. And as Chinese activities in outer space continue to grow, the number of its objects in space are almost certain to increase, making it critical that we find a way to constructively engage China on orbital debris.

Mega Constellations of Small Satellites

The second key challenge facing the outer space environment is the development of "mega constellations" of small satellites. According to press reports, several U.S. and European entities have plans to launch mega constellations in the coming years. The Federal Communications Commission (FCC) approved a request by SpaceX to construct, deploy, and operate a new very low Earth orbit constellation of more than 12,000 Starlink satellites using V-band frequencies.[6] These satellites will be used to improve broadband communications globally. And SpaceX has asked the FCC to approve an additional 30,000 satellites, resulting in a total of 42,000.[7] Other companies, such as OneWeb, have begun to deploy similar constellations, though not as large as Starlink.[8] While these mega constellations will improve space-based capabilities, they will also contribute significantly to the congestion of low Earth orbit.

But U.S. and European entities aren't the only ones who are developing mega constellations: several Chinese entities are also developing similar systems. For example, in December 2018, Aerospace Dongfanhong, a Chinese state-owned satellite manufacturing company, launched the first demonstration satellite for the Hongyan communications constellation of small satellites.[9] The Hongyan constellation will ultimately consist of 320 satellites and is expected to be fully operational by 2025.[10] Though this constellation is significantly smaller than the Starlink constellation proposed by SpaceX, it is likely only a matter of time before China's approach to mega constellations becomes more ambitious, making it imperative that the United States begin a discussion with China on this important issue.

The Growing Anti-satellite Threat

A third key challenge to the outer space environment is the growing threat from ASAT weapons. Throughout the Cold War, both the United States and the Soviet Union developed limited numbers of ASAT weapons but never moved forward with large-scale deployment of these weapons given concerns about the damage ASAT weapons could do to the sustainability of the outer space environment.[11] With the end of the Cold War, development of ASAT weapons declined significantly, but that changed in 2007 when China conducted a direct assent ASAT test "deliberately hitting and destroying one of its own aging weather satellites at an altitude of 865 kilometers."[12] Other nations, including India and Russia, are also developing ASAT capabilities.

What prompted this renewed interest in ASAT capabilities by China and other countries? From this author's perspective, interest is driven by the increasing importance that space-based systems play in military operations. This applies particularly to military operations conducted by the United States. Potential U.S. adversaries understand that space-based assets are key to the United States' ability to project power globally. For example, satellites enable the U.S. military to detect and target adversaries, as well as provide command and control for its own forces. Denying the United States access to space-derived data would provide potential adversaries significant military advantage.

As then U.S. director of national intelligence Daniel Coats noted in testimony before Congress in 2019, the U.S. Intelligence Community assesses that "China and Russia are training and equipping their military space forces and fielding new antisatellite weapons to hold U.S. and allied space services at risk. . . . Both countries recognize the world's growing reliance on space and view the capability to attack space services as a part of their broader effort to deter an adversary from or defeat one in combat."[13]

CHINESE MILITARY AND CIVIL SPACE PROGRAMS

China has embarked on a major expansion of its national security space programs. The most concerning of these programs has been its development of a robust set of ASAT capabilities designed to target satellites and disrupt the flow of space-derived information. According to several U.S. government and other open source reports, China is developing and deploying a full spectrum of ASAT capabilities.[14] These include a network of space situational awareness sensors "capable of searching, tracking, and characterizing satellites in all Earth orbits"; electronic warfare capabilities designed to jam satellite transmissions; laser weapons to "disrupt, degrade, or damage satellites and their sensors"; offensive cyber capabilities to target computer networks; sophisticated on-orbit satellite attack capabilities; and ground-based missiles designed to destroy satellites kinetically.[15]

In addition to its ASAT capabilities, China is improving and expanding its other national security space-related capabilities. For example, China possesses a robust constellation of intelligence, reconnaissance, and surveillance satellites that allow it to monitor political and military developments around the world.[16] It is also continuing to expand its BeiDou precision, navigation, and timing system, which is similar to the U.S. Global Positioning System (GPS), and is on track to achieve global coverage with the system later this year.[17] The expansion of BeiDou will likely improve its ability to target precision-guided munitions, and lessen China's dependence on GPS, which the Chinese government fears the United States might deny access to during a crisis.[18]

China has simultaneously emerged as a major international actor in the civil space arena. For example, last year, China became the first country to land a space probe on the far side of the moon. China's civil space activities are certain to grow in the coming years. According to a December 2018 report by the National Air and Space Intelligence Center, "China plans to become an international leader in lunar research and exploration with goals to assemble a lunar research station beginning in 2025, perform a crewed Moon landing mission in 2036, and establish a Lunar Research and Development Base around 2050."[19] China also deployed a rover to Mars in July 2020 and plans to probe asteroids around 2022 and send a mission to Jupiter around 2029.[20] It has also deployed several deep space ground stations around the world, including in Argentina,[21] and is developing its own space station, the Tiangong, which is scheduled to become fully operationally around 2022.

China's civil space activities are certainly impressive and present multiple opportunities for collaboration with international partners, including the United States. However, one of the key challenges faced when cooperating with China in more robust civil space cooperation is the fact that the Chinese civil space program, led by the China National Space Administration, is controlled by the Chinese military. As a result, there is a real possibility that any bilateral cooperation could contribute to China's military space programs.

RECOMMENDATIONS

The United States faces a fundamental dilemma as it attempts to effectively manage China's rise as a major actor in outer space. On the one hand, China's development of ASAT weapons represents a direct threat to U.S. and allied space systems. On the other hand, it is difficult to see how the United States and the international community will be able to address the key challenges facing the outer space environment—that is, the growth of orbital debris and the rise of mega constellations—without engaging with China. Recognizing this dilemma, what follows are several recommendations that could serve as an outline for a potential U.S. strategy for managing China's rise in outer space.

- *Enhance deterrence and increase resiliency against Chinese ASAT threats.* The threat to U.S. and allied satellites from Chinese ASAT weapons is growing. In response, the United States, under both the Obama and Trump administrations, has taken actions to expand deterrence in space and increase the resiliency of U.S. space systems. China and other nations are developing ASAT weapons because they believe that the current vulnerability of satellites is an "asymmetric vulnerability" or "Achilles' heel" for the United States. Therefore, it is imperative that the United States continue to take the necessary operational and technical actions to close these vulnerabilities.

- *Reinvigorate the U.S.-China diplomatic dialogue on outer space issues.* While this author largely supports many of the military-focused space security initiatives the Trump administration proposed, such as the creation of U.S. Space Command,[22] military solutions alone will not be enough to address the pressing challenges China presents to space security. Bilateral diplomatic engagements with China also need to be part of the strategy. Therefore, it is critical that the United States and China reinvigorate civil and security space dialogues, which have been largely dormant during the Trump administration.

- *Develop bilateral and multilateral norms of behavior for outer space.* The United States should develop bilateral norms of behavior or confidence-building measures with China, focused on reducing the risks of misperception and miscalculation in outer space. One area where the two countries might work together is on developing mechanisms to further reduce the growth of orbital debris. In addition to developing bilateral norms, the United States should also work to develop multilateral norms. One option could be for the United States to propose some type of ban or limitation on further debris-generating events in outer space.[23]

- *Identify ways to cooperate with China on pragmatic civil space projects.* The United States will need both carrots and sticks if it is to find a way to effectively manage China's rise in outer space. The prospect of increasing bilateral civil space cooperation is a potential carrot that the United States could deploy. But since the Chinese civil space program is controlled by the military, any cooperation will need to be carefully calibrated to ensure that bilateral cooperation does not contribute to China's military space programs. Any serious cooperative efforts with China will likely require Congress to modify or remove existing restrictions.

CONCLUSION

As the 2017 U.S. National Security Strategy notes,[24] the United States has returned to an era of renewed great power competition with Russia and China. But as my Brookings Institution colleague Thomas Wright has argued, "As the United States competes with Russia and China it cannot lose sight of the many areas in which the United States must cooperate with its rivals out of shared interest. . . . The issue is whether it is possible to cooperate on these problems while competing on others."[25] This is the essential balance that the United States will need to strike regarding outer space: finding a way to work with states like Russia and China on space sustainability and safety issues, while at the same time pushing back on security issues when necessary.

NOTES

1. "Challenges to Security in Space" (Washington, DC: U.S. Defense Intelligence Agency, January 2019), 13, www.dia.mil/Portals/27/Documents/News/Military%20Power%20Publications/Space_Threat_V14_020119_sm.pdf.

2. "UCS Satellite Database," Union of Concerned Scientists, www.ucsusa.org/resources/satellite-database.

3. "18th Space Control Squadron," Peterson Air Force Base, August 6, 2018, www.peterson.af.mil/About/Fact-Sheets/Display/Article/1060346/18th-space-control-squadron/.

4. John E. Hyten, "Statement Before the Joint Hearing of the House Strategic Forces Subcommittee and House Space Subcommittee" (Washington, DC, U.S. House of Representatives, June 22, 2018), https://science.house.gov/imo/media/doc/Hyten%20Testimony.pdf.

5. Ibid.

6. "FCC Boosts Satellite Broadband Connectivity and Competition in the United States," U.S. Federal Communications Commission, November 15, 2018, www.fcc.gov/document/fcc-boosts-satellite-broadband-connectivity-competition.

7. Caleb Henry, "SpaceX Submits Paperwork for 30,000 More Starlink Satellites," Space News, October 15, 2019, https://spacenews.com/spacex-submits-paperwork -for-30000-more-starlink-satellites/.

8. Caleb Henry, "OneWeb's First Large Batch of Satellites Launch on Arianespace Soyuz Rocket," Space News, February 6, 2020, https://spacenews.com/arianespace -launches-first-large-batch-of-oneweb-satellites-on-soyuz-rocket/.

9. Deyana Goh, "China Launches First Hongyan LEO Comms Satellites," Space Tech Asia, December 22, 2018, www.spacetechasia.com/china-launches-first -hongyan-leo-comms-satellite/.

10. John Sheldon, "China's New Space Race: First Satellite of CASC's Hongyan LEO SATCOM Constellation to Launch by End of 2018," Spacewatch Asia Pacific, November 23, 2018, https://spacewatch.global/2018/11/chinas-new-space-race-first -satellite-of-cascs-hongyan-leo-satcom-constellation-to-launch-by-end-of-2018/.

11. For a good discussion of the history of space security issues, see James Clay Moltz, *The Politics of Space Security: Strategic Restraint and the Pursuit of National Interests* (Stanford, CA: Stanford University Press, 2008).

12. Brian Weeden, "Anti-satellite Tests in Space—the Case of China," Secure World Foundation, May 18, 2015, https://swfound.org/media/115643/china_asat_ fact_sheet_may2015.pdf.

13. Daniel R. Coats, "Statement for the Record: Worldwide Threat Assessment of the U.S. Intelligence Community" (Washington, DC, Office of the Director of National Intelligence, January 29, 2019), 17, www.dni.gov/files/ODNI/documents/ 2019-ATA-SFR---SSCI.pdf.

14. In addition to the government reports on the threat to outer space systems cited in this chapter, the Center for Strategic and International Studies and the Secure World Foundation have both published excellent reports on the counterspace threat. See Todd Harrison, Kaitlyn Johnson, and Thomas G. Roberts, "Space Threat Assessment 2019" (Washington, DC: Center for Strategic and International Studies, April 4, 2019), www.csis.org/analysis/space-threat-assessment-2019; Brian Weeden and Victoria Samson, eds., "Global Counterspace Capabilities: An Open Source Assessment" (Broomfield, CO: Secure World Foundation, April 2019), https:// swfound.org/counterspace/.

15. "Challenges to Security in Space," U.S. Defense Intelligence Agency, 20–21.

16. Ibid., 19.

17. Pratik Jakhar, "How China's GPS 'Rival' Beidou Is Plotting to Go Global," *BBC News*, September 20, 2018, www.bbc.com/news/technology-45471959.

18. Ibid.

19. "Competing in Space" (Wright-Patterson AFB, OH: National Air and Space Intelligence Center, December 2018), https://media.defense.gov/2019/Jan/16/ 2002080386/-1/-1/1/190115-F-NV711-0002.PDF.

20. Mike Ives, "As America Looks Inward, China Looks to Outer Space," *New York Times*, May 23, 2018, www.nytimes.com/2018/05/23/world/asia/china-space-moon.html.

21. Lara Seligman, "U.S. Military Warns of Threat from Chinese-Run Space Station in Argentina," *Foreign Policy*, February 9, 2019, https://foreignpolicy.com/2019/02/08/us-military-warns-of-threat-from-chinese-run-space-station-in-argentina/#.

22. Frank A. Rose, "Re-establishing U.S. Space Command Is a Great Idea," The Brookings Institution, *Order from Chaos* (blog), January 7, 2019, www.brookings.edu/blog/order-from-chaos/2019/01/07/re-establishing-u-s-space-command-is-a-great-idea/.

23. For a greater discussion of potential options, see Frank A. Rose, "India's Anti-satellite Test Presents a Window of Opportunity for the Trump Administration. Will It Take Advantage?," The Brookings Institution, May 10, 2019, www.brookings.edu/blog/order-from-chaos/2019/05/10/indias-anti-satellite-test-presents-a-window-of-opportunity-for-the-trump-administration/.

24. "National Security Strategy of the United States of America" (Washington, DC: The White House, December 2017), www.whitehouse.gov/wp-content/uploads/2017/12/NSS-Final-12-18-2017-0905.pdf.

25. Thomas J. Wright, *All Measures Short of War: The Contest for the 21st Century and the Future of American Power* (New Haven, CT: Yale University Press, 2017), 218.

18

Dealing with Global Demand for China's Surveillance Exports

SHEENA CHESTNUT GREITENS

Countries and cities worldwide now employ public security and surveillance technology platforms from the People's Republic of China (PRC). The drivers of this trend are complex, stemming from the expansion of China's geopolitical interests, the increasing market power of its technology companies, and conditions in recipient states that make Chinese technology an attractive choice despite security and privacy concerns. Both "push" and "pull" factors contribute to the growing use of Chinese surveillance technology: countries that are strategically important to the PRC are comparatively more likely to adopt it, but so are countries with high crime rates.

Major questions remain about the implications and advantages that China could derive from these developments, including how dominance in this sector and access to data could shape the contours of strategic competition between China and the United States. Questions also remain about what impact these technologies will have on data privacy/security, human rights, and democracy.[1] There is relatively little correlation between the level of democracy in a country and the likelihood that it will adopt Chinese surveillance technology, but advocates fear that introduction of these technologies will subsequently corrode democratic institutions and civil liberties. While leaders in adopting countries share some concerns about data security, civil liberties, and democracy, many also focus on these platforms' potential to solve urgent public problems, such as violent crime. Understanding the true impacts of these technologies will be important for crafting effective policy.

This evidence also suggests that the current one-size-fits-all message from U.S. policymakers about the risks of Chinese technology needs to be differentiated and adapted to each country in which such concerns are raised. These messages need to be paired with nuanced understanding of the priorities and incentives of the officials making adoption decisions—often subnational officials rather than foreign policy or national security experts. The United States must also address Chinese technology companies' ongoing efforts to shape the global regulatory environment; to do so, policymakers need to articulate and execute a comprehensive strategy to promulgate standards compatible with American values and interests.

CHARTING EXPORTS OF CHINA'S SURVEILLANCE AND SECURITY PLATFORMS

Despite a high degree of concern about Chinese surveillance technology, policy discussions in the United States and abroad may have underestimated its spread: think tank reports discuss anywhere from 18 to ~50 countries,[2] but Huawei reports that it has provided "'Safe City' solutions" in well over 100 countries.[3] Our dataset, based on corporate, government, and media reporting in English, French, Spanish, and Chinese,[4] shows that Chinese surveillance and public security technology platforms have been adopted in at least 80 countries since 2008, the majority in the last several years. Figures 18-1 and 18-2 show the temporal trend in adoption and geographic location of countries that have adopted these platforms.

These estimates focus on surveillance technology platforms used specifically for policing and public security, not just on broader surveillance or artificial intelligence exports.[5] The projects—such as Huawei's "Safe City" solutions[6]—involve a data integration platform that collects, integrates, and analyzes data from a wide range of sources, from existing government records to facial-recognition-enabled or license-plate-recognition-enabled cameras. The projects are often multilayered, meaning that one company provides the core platform, while others can be involved in inputs or extensions.[7] Projects sometimes include technical consulting in addition to technology sales. Companies such as Huawei, Hikvision, ZTE, Dahua, and China National Electronics Import and Export Corporation (CEIEC), among others, are common providers.

Figure 18-1. **Growth in Adoption of Chinese Surveillance and Public Security Technology Platforms, 2008–2019**

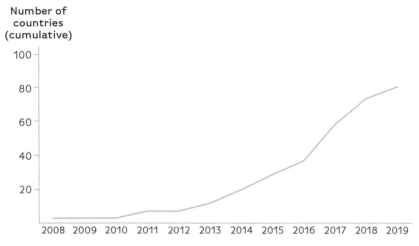

Source: Author's dataset.

Figure 18-2. **Presence of Chinese Surveillance and Public Security Technology Platforms (2008–2019)**

Source: Author's dataset.

The identity of the companies involved has raised concerns in the U.S. foreign policy community. At least some are linked to the PRC defense-industrial complex; CEIEC, for example, is a state-owned enterprise under China Electronics Corporation that concentrates on defense electronics, and was previously sanctioned by the United States for nonproliferation violations.[8] Others, such as Hikvision and Dahua, have been implicated in and sanctioned for human rights violations in Xinjiang.[9]

DRIVERS OF CHINA'S GLOBAL EXPORTS: PUSH AND PULL FACTORS

What is driving the increased global adoption of Chinese surveillance and public security technologies? Critics in the United States and elsewhere tend to see Chinese geopolitical strategy and authoritarian interests at work: a supply-side or "push factor" explanation.[10] One report, for example, emphasizes "[technology exports'] value to Chinese foreign policy and strategy . . . exporting its information technology is not only about securing important new sources of revenue and data, but also generating greater strategic leverage vis-à-vis the West."[11] Another suggests that PRC government loans subsidize countries' acquisition of repressive technologies to further Beijing's foreign policy interests.[12] In this view, global adoption is China-driven, as Beijing pushes their use for its own geopolitical strategic objectives.

Chinese tech companies and adopters, however, tend to focus on demand or "pull" factors: technology's capacity to address recipient governance challenges. Huawei's marketing materials, for example, emphasize their relevance for extremist threats in the Middle East, crime in Latin America, and environmental sustainability in Europe.[13] Officials whose jurisdictions have pursued such projects also typically emphasize the value of crime control technologies for public safety and inbound investment.[14] Thus, in this view, recipient countries "pull" technology from China to solve local challenges, whether or not their interests overlap with Beijing's.

Debate over Huawei's Safe City projects in the Philippines illustrates how demand for crime-control, Chinese statecraft, and concerns about Chinese technology intersect. Huawei, which already has a major telecommunications presence in the Philippines, significantly expanded its role during Xi Jinping's state visit in 2018.[15] The visit launched the Safe Philippines Project partnership, established between the Department of the Interior and Local Government (DILG), Huawei, and China International Telecommunication and Construction Corporation, financed primarily by a loan from China Eximbank (19.11 billion Philippine pesos [PHP] of the PHP 20.31 billion project, close to US$400 million). The centerpiece of the project is a 12,000-camera surveillance system with an integrated command and control center for video monitoring, critical communication, and information management/analytics, linking the Philippine National Police, DILG, the national 911 system, and fire/prison agencies. It set a target of 15 percent crime reduction, as well as faster response time, and was scheduled to be a fully operational system by 2022.[16] Philippine legislators subsequently raised concerns about cybersecurity and data privacy, prompting Interior Secretary Eduardo Año to clarify that all data and project management would be handled by Filipinos. This example shows how recipient government interest in reducing crime and Chinese willingness to provide development funding helped to move the platform toward reality, while concerns about security and privacy generated opposition within the Philippine legislature.

This contestation is not limited to the Indo-Pacific. In Malta, the government established a company to engage in a public-private Safe City Malta partnership with Huawei. Citizens objected to facial recognition, however, and U.S. officials expressed concern that the data "could end up back in Beijing . . . exploited for authoritarian purposes." The director subsequently stated that Huawei would not operate or have direct access to equipment, even for technical support, saying that "data will be stored in Malta and will stay in Malta, governed by a security and data retention policy."[17] Similarly, Huawei's Safe City project in Belgrade has created contention between the Serbian Ministry of Internal Affairs and civil society watchdogs, who raised concerns about the compatibility of video surveillance with Serbian laws on data protection/privacy.[18]

What this suggests is that both China-centered push factors and recipient-centered demand factors matter. Countries with high crime rates are comparatively more likely to adopt these technologies—but so are countries that are strategically important to the PRC.[19] Moreover, a country's level of democracy or freedom is not particularly strongly correlated with the likelihood of platform adoption: Safe City-type projects have appeared in free/democratic countries like France and Germany, "partly free"/anocratic countries like Uganda and Pakistan, and unfree authoritarian states like Laos and Saudi Arabia.[20]

CHALLENGES FOR U.S. AND INTERNATIONAL POLICY

Concerns for U.S. foreign policy can be grouped into three clusters: data security and privacy; technology's role in U.S.-China strategic competition; and facilitation of authoritarian backsliding or human rights infringement.

The first concern centers on whether Chinese dominance of the global surveillance technology industry could create vulnerabilities among U.S. allies and other countries in terms of privacy, data protection, and other cybersecurity risks. Trump administration officials asserted that Huawei can covertly access mobile communications through "back doors" for law enforcement; and that these access points weren't disclosed to local customers or "host nation national-security agencies."[21] Huawei has rejected these allegations; some recipient countries claim that data are managed by their own nationals and stored locally—but there is no systematic, publicly available information on how common it is to include such measures in the project agreements. Should a Chinese company have access to user information, however, that information would be available to the government under provisions in the 2017 National Intelligence Law.[22]

Second, these technologies may facilitate autocratization and human rights violations.[23] At present, however, little is known about their actual global impact. Corporate marketing materials tout crime-reduction success stories, while critics point to cases of tech-enabled surveillance and repression. The effects are not mutually exclusive: improved surveillance may enhance general public safety, while also contributing to targeted repression of political opposition or marginalized groups. The question du jour—of whether China is "exporting digital authoritarianism" or "making the world safe for autocracy"—is less a matter of divining Beijing's intent in providing the technology, and more an empirical question of the scale and direction of its impact in different political environments. These vital questions require careful thinking and analytical precision going forward.

A third cluster of concerns revolves around technology's perceived importance in U.S.-China strategic competition.[24] China's activities could increase tech companies' "access to foreign talent and data" in ways detrimental to the United States or its partners[25]—presumably through partnerships with foreign data scientists, recruitment programs like Huawei's Seeds for the Future, or international offices and agreements that allow Chinese companies to use overseas data to improve their products. Access to global data may also enable Chinese researchers and government bodies to improve algorithms and machine learning processes, with implications for security and military competition with the United States.[26] Although there is technical debate over these claims, widespread surveillance could also allow PRC actors to generate intelligence insights on countries and populations, with secondary strategic effects on U.S.-China competition. Finally, growing use of Chinese surveillance technology around the world, combined with American pushback, could bifurcate the world into adopters and nonadopters, with implications that are as yet incompletely understood.[27]

IMPLICATIONS FOR POLICY

How should the United States respond? First, current discussions in Washington focus, understandably, on Chinese intent, but the importance of recipient interests (noted earlier) suggests that a tailored, country-specific approach is likely necessary, rather than one-size-fits-all rhetoric centered on American concerns about China. U.S. policy initiatives and messaging need to engage in dialogue with recipient-country counterparts based on a nuanced and accurate view of the trade-offs that leaders in each of these countries face, many of which have little to do with China at all. Here, it is especially important to note that the decisionmakers on platform adoption are often subnational officials—mayors and governors—who are more focused on crime control and local employment than national security, and who may feel pressure to deliver results on specific electoral timetables, which can heighten the appeal of China's "turnkey" platforms.[28] The United States will also need to account for its own competing policy priorities in different regions: for example, the potential tension between encouraging countries in Latin America to avoid using Chinese policing technology while also pressing them to decrease criminal activity that leads to migration pressure on the U.S. border.

The United States and international community must also consider what norms and mechanisms should govern the marketing and use of surveillance platforms, where regulation is currently minimal.[29] The PRC has pursued a strategic approach to global standard-setting, both domestically and internationally, and Chinese companies have been outpacing others in setting global standards.[30] If this trend continues, China's leadership in shaping the global regulatory environment will assist PRC-owned companies in increasing market access and market share in a self-reinforcing feedback loop. In response, the United States must articulate a comprehensive strategy:[31] which forums should set standards for which technologies; what those standards and safeguards should be; how U.S. interagency efforts should be organized; and how the United States should work with allies, partners, and international organizations to collaboratively and assertively shape a global regulatory environment compatible with liberal democracy and American interests.[32] Tools such as export controls, sanctions, and restrictions on foreign investment in surveillance technology companies should also be incorporated, preferably in partnership with the private sector and also coordinated multilaterally. Finally, American foreign assistance partners and programs should work with emerging, weak, or backsliding democracies to craft technical and regulatory safeguards to protect citizen rights and democratic institutions.

This is an urgent task, as the expanded use of health surveillance technology following the outbreak of COVID-19 has the potential to accelerate the export and adoption of Chinese surveillance technology.[33] China's management of public health is closely entwined with its broader approach to policing, social control, and internal stability; for example, information gathered through health apps (e.g., on citizen movements) is now shared with local police.[34] China has already begun to promote its model of coronavirus management around the world, and other countries may not know where else to turn, especially if American and other democratic countries' leadership appears ineffective. If Chinese firms, bolstered by aid and propaganda from Beijing, can make a good case that their approach to health surveillance is best-in-class, then COVID-19 is likely to accelerate global reliance on Chinese technology, as well as acceptance of the political norms that govern its use. Moreover, tools that gain credibility for public health purposes will become difficult to roll back, even if subsequently used for less benign and more repressive purposes.[35] Alternatively, if the United States is able to join with like-minded partners around the world to provide an alternative—such as the approaches followed by South Korea and Taiwan—it is less likely that the world will default to Chinese surveillance technology simply due to a lack of alternatives. These factors heighten the urgency and importance of developing a coordinated and robust American strategy.

NOTES

1. "Hearing: China's Digital Authoritarianism: Surveillance, Influence, and Social Control (Open)," Permanent Select Committee on Intelligence, U.S. House of Representatives, May 16, 2019, https://intelligence.house.gov/calendar/eventsingle .aspx?EventID=632; Richard Fontaine and Kara Frederick, "The Autocrat's New Tool Kit," *Wall Street Journal*, March 15, 2019, www.wsj.com/articles/the-autocrats -new-tool-kit-11552662637; Louise Lucas and Emily Feng, "Inside China's Surveillance State," *Financial Times*, July 19, 2018, www.ft.com/content/2182eebe-8a17 -11e8-bf9e-8771d5404543; Paul Mozur, "Inside China's Dystopian Dreams," *New*

York Times, July 8, 2018, www.nytimes.com/2018/07/08/business/china-surveillance
-technology.html; Paul Mozur, "Made in China, Exported to the World: The
Surveillance State," *New York Times*, April 24, 2019, www.nytimes.com/2019/04/24
/technology/ecuador-surveillance-cameras-police-government.html; Chris
Buckley, Paul Mozur, and Austin Ramzy, "How China Turned a City Into a Prison,"
New York Times, April 4, 2019, www.nytimes.com/interactive/2019/04/04/world/
asia/xinjiang-china-surveillance-prison.html; Josh Chin and Clement Burge,
"Twelve Days in Xinjiang," *Wall Street Journal*, December 19, 2017, www.wsj.com/
articles/twelve-days-in-xinjiang-how-chinas-surveillance-state-overwhelms-daily
-life-1513700355; Maya Wang, *China's Algorithms of Repression: Reverse Engineering
a Xinjiang Police Mass Surveillance App* (New York: Human Rights Watch, May
2019), www.hrw.org/report/2019/05/01/chinas-algorithms-repression/reverse
-engineering-xinjiang-police-mass-surveillance; Joe Parkinson, Nicholas Bariyo,
and Josh Chin, "Huawei Technicians Helped African Governments Spy on Political
Opponents," *Wall Street Journal*, August 14, 2019, www.wsj.com/articles/huawei
-technicians-helped-african-governments-spy-on-political-opponents
-11565793017.

2. Danielle Cave, Samantha Hoffman, Alex Joske, Fergus Ryan, and Elise Thomas,
Mapping China's Tech Giants (Barton, Australia: Australian Strategic Policy Institute,
April 18, 2019), www.aspi.org.au/report/mapping-chinas-tech-giants; Adrian
Shahbaz, *Freedom on the Net 2018: The Rise of Digital Authoritarianism* (Washington,
DC: Freedom House, October 2018), https://freedomhouse.org/report/freedom-net/
2018/rise-digital-authoritarianism; Jonathan E. Hillman and Maesea McCalpin,
"Watching Huawei's 'Safe Cities'" (Washington, DC: Center for Strategic and
International Studies, November 4, 2019), www.csis.org/analysis/watching-huaweis
-safe-cities; Steven Feldstein, "The Global Expansion of AI Surveillance" (Washington,
DC: Carnegie Endowment, September 2019), https://carnegieendowment.org/2019/
09/17/global-expansion-of-ai-surveillance-pub-79847.

3. *2018 Annual Report* (Shenzhen: Huawei, 2019), 30, www-file.huawei.com/-/
media/corporate/pdf/annual-report/annual_report2018_en_v2.pdf?la=zh.

4. Dataset developed as part of a broader research project; details available from
the author.

5. For example, a recent Carnegie paper discusses hardware usage (rather than
full "platforms" that integrate data) and examines both Chinese and non-Chinese
tech. Steven Feldstein, "The Global Expansion of AI Surveillance."

6. Huawei describes its Smart City projects as providing a city's "nervous system."
Safe City platforms are a subcomponent specifically focused on public safety.
"Huawei Creates a Smart City Nervous System for More Than 100 Cities with Leading New ICT," Huawei, November 14, 2017, www.huawei.com/en/press-events/
news/2017/11/Huawei-Smart-City-Nervous-System-SCEWC2017.

7. There are often multiple Chinese tech companies involved, and anecdotal
reports of cities incorporating both Chinese and Western products into different
layers of the tech stack. Systematic, fine-grained data on which companies provide
which layers of a particular city-project's tech stack are not yet available.

8. "Iran, North Korea, and Syria Nonproliferation Act: Imposed Sanctions," U.S. Department of State, May 23, 2013, https://2009-2017.state.gov/t/isn/inksna/c28836.htm; Fan Feifei, "Transforming Public Security," *China Daily*, January 9, 2017, www.chinadaily.com.cn/business/2017-01/09/content_27896419.htm.

9. "Addition of Certain Entities to the Entity List," *Federal Register*, October 9, 2019, www.federalregister.gov/documents/2019/10/09/2019-22210/addition-of-certain-entities-to-the-entity-list.

10. This is consistent with how historians understand public security training and technology transfer during the Cold War, when national security played a major role. Jeremy Kuzmarov, *Modernizing Repression: Police Training and Nation-Building in the American Century* (Amherst: University of Massachusetts Press, 2012).

11. Alina Polyakova and Chris Meserole, *Exporting Digital Authoritarianism: Russian and Chinese Models* (Washington, DC: The Brookings Institution, August 2019), www.brookings.edu/research/exporting-digital-authoritarianism/.

12. Steven Feldstein, "The Global Expansion of AI Surveillance."

13. "Safe Cities: A Revolution Driven by New ICT," Huawei, https://e.huawei.com/us/publications/global/ict_insights/201608271037/ecosystem/201608271557; Koh Hong-Eng, "How Video Cameras Can Make Cities Safer and Contribute to Economic Growth," *South China Morning Post*, June 3, 2018, www.scmp.com/comment/insight-opinion/article/2148860/big-brother-surveillance-how-video-cameras-can-make-cities.

14. Myat Pyae Pho, "Huawei to Supply Mandalay's Safe City Project with Security Cameras, Equipment," *The Irrawaddy*, May 9, 2019, www.irrawaddy.com/news/burma/huawei-supply-mandalays-safe-city-project-cameras-security-equipment.html; Cassandra Garrison, "Safe Like China: In Argentina, ZTE Finds Eager Buyer for Surveillance Tech," Reuters, July 5, 2019, www.reuters.com/article/us-argentina-china-zte-insight-idUSKCN1U00ZG; "Chinese Technology Brings Falling Crime Rate to Ecuador," Xinhua, January 19, 2018, www.xinhuanet.com/english/2018-01/19/c_136908255.htm.

15. Huawei had an existing Safe City project in Metro Manila (Bonifacio). "Transforming Bonifacio Global City into a Safe City with Huawei," Huawei, https://e.huawei.com/topic/leading-new-ict-en/safe-city-case.html.

16. Loreben Tuquero, "Año Says China-Funded Safe Philippines Project Will Be 'All-Filipino'" Rappler, November 22, 2019, www.rappler.com/nation/245529-ano-china-funded-safe-philippines-project-all-filipino; Camille Elemia, "Senators Sound Alarm over China-Funded DILG Surveillance Project," Rappler, December 13, 2018, www.rappler.com/nation/218831-dilg-china-telecom-affiliate-partnership-video-surveillance-system-philippines.

17. Jacob Borg, "Huawei Project Similar to That Considered in Malta Had Security Issues," *Times of Malta*, April 19, 2019, https://timesofmalta.com/articles/view/security-vulnerabilities-found-in-huawei-project-considered-in-malta.707260; Yannick Pace, "Huawei Not Operating Safe City Equipment, as Concerns Mount over Chinese Tech Giant," *Malta Today*, January 30, 2019, www.maltatoday

.com.mt/news/national/92556/huawei_not_operating_safe_city_equipment_as_concerns_mount_over_chinese_tech_giant#.XpouNOu1vOQ; Matthew Vella, "Huawei Link to China Carries Risk in Safe City Malta Project, Says US Official," *Malta Today*, May 13, 2019, www.maltatoday.com.mt/news/national/94927/huawei_link_in_safe_city_carries_risk#.XposwuulvOQ.

18. Bojan Stojkovski, "Huawei's Surveillance System in Serbia Threatens Citizens' Rights, Watchdog Warns," ZDNet, April 10, 2019, www.zdnet.com/article/huaweis-surveillance-system-in-serbia-threatens-citizens-rights-watchdog-warns/; "New Surveillance Cameras in Belgrade: Location and Human Rights Impact Analysis—'Withheld,'" SHARE Foundation, March 29, 2019, www.sharefoundation.info/en/new-surveillance-cameras-in-belgrade-location-and-human-rights-impact-analysis-withheld/.

19. A systematic quantitative exploration of these associations is available from the author.

20. Jonathan E. Hillman and Maesea McCalpin use Freedom House ratings. Similar variation exists across Polity scores; "The Polity Project," Center for Systemic Peace, www.systemicpeace.org/polityproject.html.

21. Bojan Pancevski, "U.S. Officials Say Huawei Can Covertly Access Telecom Networks," *Wall Street Journal*, February 12, 2020, www.wsj.com/articles/u-s-officials-say-huawei-can-covertly-access-telecom-networks-11581452256.

22. Sheena Chestnut Greitens, "Domestic Security in China under Xi Jinping," *China Leadership Monitor*, March 1, 2019, www.prcleader.org/greitens; Murray Scot Tanner, "Beijing's New National Intelligence Law: From Defense to Offense," *Lawfare*, July 20, 2017, www.lawfareblog.com/beijings-new-national-intelligence-law-defense-offense.

23. Andrea Kendall-Taylor, Erica Frantz, and Joseph Wright, "The Digital Dictators: How Technology Strengthens Autocracy," *Foreign Affairs* 99, no. 2 (March/April 2020), www.foreignaffairs.com/articles/china/2020-02-06/digital-dictators.

24. Ryan Hass and Mira Rapp-Hooper, "Responsible Competition and the Future of U.S.-China Relations: Seven Critical Questions for Strategy," The Brookings Institution, *Order from Chaos* (blog), February 6, 2019, www.brookings.edu/blog/order-from-chaos/2019/02/06/responsible-competition-and-the-future-of-u-s-china-relations/.

25. *Annual Report to Congress: Military and Security Developments Involving the People's Republic of China 2019* (Arlington, VA: U.S. Department of Defense, May 2, 2019), 101, https://media.defense.gov/2019/May/02/2002127082/-1/-1/1/2019_CHINA_MILITARY_POWER_REPORT.pdf.

26. "Hearing on Technology, Trade, and Military-Civil Fusion: China's Pursuit of Artificial Intelligence, New Materials, and New Energy" (Washington, DC: U.S.-China Economic and Security Review Commission, June 7, 2019), www.uscc.gov/sites/default/files/2019-10/June%207,%202019%20Hearing%20Transcript.pdf.

27. Kelly Hammond, "Reconfiguring Geopolitics in the Era of the Surveillance

State: Uyghurs, the Chinese Party-State, and the Reshaping of Middle Eastern Politics," Hoover Institution, June 27, 2019, www.hoover.org/research/reconfiguring -geopolitics-era-surveillance-state-uyghurs-chinese-party-state-and-reshaping.

28. Sokwoo Rhee, Associate Director of Cyber-Physical Systems Program at the National Institute of Standards and Technology (NIST), in remarks at Cities of Tomorrow: Safety, Smarts, and Surveillance, CSIS Event, Center for Strategic and International Security, Washington, DC, January 23, 2020, https://reconnectingasia .csis.org/analysis/entries/cities-tomorrow-safety-smarts-and-surveillance/.

29. "Moratorium Call on Surveillance Technology to End 'Free-for-All' Abuses: UN Expert," United Nations, June 25, 2019, https://news.un.org/en/story/2019/06/ 1041231.

30. During 2016–2019, for example, Chinese tech companies made the only submissions to the UN's International Telecommunications Union (ITU) for standards on facial recognition; at least half have been approved. Anna Gross and Madhumita Murgia, "China Shows Its Dominance in Surveillance Technology," *Financial Times*, December 26, 2019, www.ft.com/content/b34d8ff8-21b4-11ea-92 da-f0c92e957a96; Elsa Kania, "China's Play for Global 5G Dominance—Standards and the 'Digital Silk Road,'" Australian Strategic Policy Institute, June 27, 2018, www.aspistrategist.org.au/chinas-play-for-global-5g-dominance-standards-and -the-digital-silk-road/.

31. Sheena Chestnut Greitens, Testimony to the U.S. Commission on International Religious Freedom, Hearing on Technological Surveillance of Religion in China (virtual hearing, July 2020).

32. The European Union's role in regulatory norms and standard-setting make it a prime candidate for this kind of mutually beneficial partnership. Anu Bradford, *The Brussels Effect: How the European Union Rules the World* (New York: Oxford University Press, 2020).

33. Sheena Chestnut Greitens and Julian Gewirtz, "China's Troubling Vision for the Future of Public Health," *Foreign Affairs*, July 10, 2020, www.foreignaffairs.com /articles/china/2020-07-10/chinas-troubling-vision-future-public-health.

34. On other ways in which domestic security tools are being used to enforce quarantines, etc., in China, see Paul Mozur, Raymond Zhong, and Aaron Krolik, "In Coronavirus Fight, China Gives Citizens a Color Code, with Red Flags," *New York Times*, March 1, 2020, www.nytimes.com/2020/03/01/business/china-corona virus-surveillance.html; Raymond Zhong and Paul Mozur, "To Tame Coronavirus, Mao-Style Social Controls Blanket China," *New York Times*, February 15, 2020, www.nytimes.com/2020/02/15/business/china-coronavirus-lockdown.html.

35. Carrie Cordero and Richard Fontaine, "Health Surveillance Is Here to Stay," *Wall Street Journal*, March 27, 2020, www.wsj.com/articles/health-surveillance-is -here-to-stay-11585339451; Nicholas Wright, "Coronavirus and the Future of Surveillance," *Foreign Affairs*, April 6, 2020, www.foreignaffairs.com/articles/2020 -04-06/coronavirus-and-future-surveillance.

19

Maintaining China's Dependence on Democracies for Advanced Computer Chips

SAIF M. KHAN
CARRICK FLYNN

The Chinese government is investing tens of billions of dollars in its computer chip factories and may eventually achieve global state-of-the-art manufacturing capabilities. But China can succeed only if the United States, Japan, and the Netherlands continue to sell it the manufacturing equipment necessary to operate its chip factories. If denied access to this specialized equipment, China would find it nearly impossible to develop or maintain advanced chip factories for the foreseeable future.

It is in the security interests of democratic states, including the United States, for China to remain reliant on democracies for state-of-the-art chips. Advanced weapons systems and many emerging technologies for surveillance and oppression depend on state-of-the-art chips—currently produced only by firms in the United States, Taiwan, and South Korea. Maintaining exclusive control of these chips will let democracies implement targeted end-use and end-user export controls on them, preempting China's development and use of many dangerous or destabilizing technologies.

THE VALUE OF STATE-OF-THE-ART CHIPS

State-of-the-art computer chips underpin many of today's strategically important emerging technologies, including artificial intelligence, 5G, autonomous drones, and surveillance tools. They also power the supercomputers essential to design hypersonic weapons and the latest generation of nuclear weapons.

Chips with the smallest transistors—state-of-the-art chips—are critical for computer systems requiring cost-effective operation. The state of the art advances with a shrinking of transistors that approximately doubles their number per chip every two years.[1] Figure 19-1 demonstrates that competi-

Figure 19-1. **Chip Costs at Different Transistor Sizes**

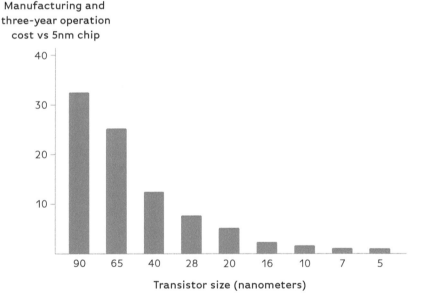

Manufacturing and three-year operation cost vs 5nm chip

Transistor size (nanometers)

Source: Data based on Center for Security and Emerging Technology (CSET) chip economics model and CSET analysis of TSMC's reported node-by-node speed improvements. Saif M. Khan and Alexander Mann, "AI Chips: What They Are and Why They Matter" (Washington, DC: Center for Security and Emerging Technology, April 2020), https://cset.georgetown.edu/wp-content/uploads/AI-Chips%E2%80%94What-They-Are-and-Why-They-Matter.pdf. The model uses the chip specifications of an Nvidia P100 graphics processing unit. The model also assumes that at each transistor size, the same number of transistors are manufactured. This means that larger transistor sizes require larger (or more) chips.

tiveness in computationally intensive technologies requires chips at or near the state of the art. Only a small number of leading chip factories and equipment companies can exist at the state of the art.

Given the expense of fabricating state-of-the-art chips, only a few chip fabrication factories ("fabs") can profitably operate at or near the state of the art. Table 19-1 and figure 19-2 show the number of fabs at or below various chip transistor sizes. The trend is clear: for decades, firms producing state-of-the-art chips have dropped out as production costs demand much larger economies of scale to be profitable.[2] State-of-the-art fabs now cost more than $10 billion to build.[3] If only a small number of fabs can profitably exist, the question becomes whether they will be based in democracies or in China.

China currently lacks fabs at the state of the art. However, its top chipmaker,[4] Semiconductor Manufacturing International Corporation (SMIC), recently introduced the ability to manufacture a small number of 14 nm chips—half a decade behind the state of the art.

Semiconductor manufacturing equipment (SME) accounts for as much as 80 percent of fab construction costs.[5] Three countries control over 90 per-

Table 19-1. Number of Chipmakers with Current or Planned Capacity to Make Chips of Certain Transistor Sizes and Below, as of 2019, by Location of Headquarters

≤ Transistor size (nm)	180	130	90	65	45	32	22	16	10	7	5
Total Chipmakers	94	72	48	36	26	20	16	12	5	3	3
United States	24	18	11	8	4	4	4	4	1	1	1
Taiwan	9	9	6	6	6	6	5	3	2	1	1
South Korea	4	4	3	2	2	2	2	2	2	1	1
China	19	18	16	13	8	6	3	1			
Japan	18	10	7	6	5	1	1	1			
Other	20	13	5	1	1	1	1	1			
Year this size reached mass production	1999	2001	2003	2005	2007	2009	2012	2014	2016	2018	2020

Note: Data from "World Fab Forecast," (Milpitas, CA: SEMI, May 2019 edition), https://www.semi.org/en/news-resources/market-data/world-fab-forecast.

Figure 19-2. **Number of Chipmakers with Current or Planned Capacity to Make Chips of Certain Transistor Sizes and Below, as of 2019, by Location of Headquarters**

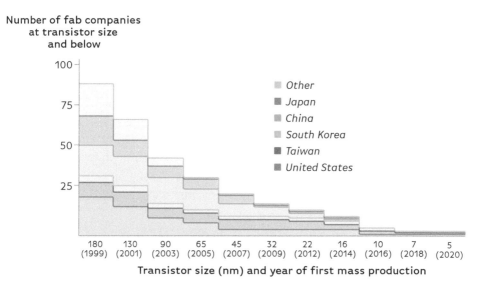

Source: Data from "World Fab Forecast," SEMI, May 2019 edition.

cent of global SME market share: the United States, the Netherlands, and Japan.[6] Consolidation trends are even more dramatic among firms supplying SME than firms operating fabs. Only two companies—Netherlands-based ASML and Japan-based Nikon—sell essential photolithography equipment capable of manufacturing ≤ 90 nm chips at scale.[7] ASML alone produces extreme ultraviolet (EUV) photolithography equipment. This equipment is necessary to mass produce state-of-the-art chips and can cost more than a billion dollars per fab.[8] Meanwhile, China produces only about 2 percent of worldwide SME,[9] and cannot replace imports of essential SME if it is controlled by the United States and its allies.

CHINA LAGS, BUT IS BECOMING MORE
SOPHISTICATED AT PRODUCING CHIPS

Chinese firms cannot produce state-of-the-art chips at present, and almost all of their chip-making capacity is over a decade behind the state of the art. However, they are aggressively building up their domestic chip industry.

As shown in figure 19-3, adjusting for the quality of chip fab capacity—

Figure 19-3. **Global Chip Fab Capacity by Fab Headquarters**

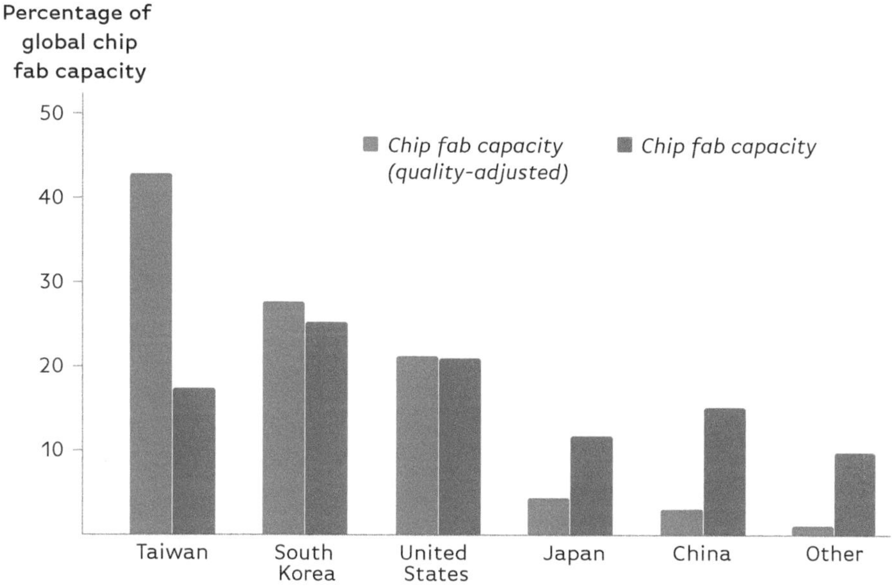

Source: Data from "World Fab Forecast," SEMI, May 2019 edition. Chip fab capacity refers to the total number of wafers (the raw input from which chips are manufactured) processed per month. Quality-adjusted chip fab capacity is equal to the number of transistors manufactured on wafers per month. This measure captures quality because companies with the capacity to manufacture smaller transistors can pack transistors more densely on their chips, therefore manufacturing more transistors at a given level of chip production. However, there are several acknowledged limitations in the way we estimate the number of transistors manufactured. First, many fab sites process different transistor sizes, so not all of their capacity is at the smallest transistor size they support. Because it is difficult to get the specific breakdown of capacity by transistor size, we used the simplifying assumption that 100% of capacity of each site is at the smallest supported transistor size. Second, the data includes the smallest transistor size planned for any given fab site, even if fabrication at that size has not begun. Third, in cases where a fab site is owned by two companies headquartered in different countries, we allocate its fab capacity equally between the co-owners.

that is, giving greater weight to the production of more advanced chips—
reduces China's share from 15 to 3 percent of global capacity and increases
the global lead of Taiwan, South Korea, and the United States from 63.7 to
91.7 percent.[10]

However, figure 19-4 shows that China's share of global fab capacity has
risen from 8 percent in 2007 to 15 percent today and is projected to increase
if the United States and its allies continue to export critical SME and China
continues to dramatically subsidize its chip fabs. This will displace U.S. fabs.

FIGURE 19-4. Change In Chip Fab Capacity Share by Country/
Region from 2007–2021

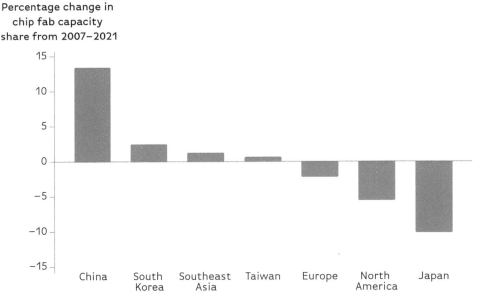

Source: Data from "World Fab Forecast," SEMI, August 2018 edition. Data for 2018 to 2021
are projections.

CHINA FACES CHALLENGES IN ACHIEVING STATE-OF-THE-ART FABRICATION EVEN WITHOUT EQUIPMENT EXPORT CONTROLS

China's success has resulted from an industrial policy by the Chinese Communist Party (CCP) of advancing chip fab capacity to the state of the art using imported SME. Although Chinese firms today produce a minority of chips consumed in China,[11] the CCP seeks to move toward chip independence by 2030.[12] China has so far managed growth rates in excess of market demand.[13] It might succeed in developing state-of-the-art fabs if the United States, the Netherlands, and Japan continue to supply Chinese fabs with SME. Yet China will rely on imports for SME because it has little chance of indigenizing its SME industry in the foreseeable future, despite ambitions to do so.[14] SME export controls imposed by the United States, the Netherlands, and Japan could decisively maintain China's chip dependence on democracies.

Driven by the Made in China 2025 plan,[15] China's industrial policy evidently aims to achieve the preceding goals through state subsidies, industrial espionage, forced technology transfer, and protectionism. China's industrial policy departs from international norms, both in the degree of market distortions produced by its state subsidies and in its ambition to localize its entire chip supply chain and achieve chip independence.[16]

The Chinese government plans to spend $150 billion on its chip industry over a span of 10 years.[17] Of the initial $12.7 billion spent by one of the state funds as of 2017, 65 percent went to fabs ($8.3 billion) and 8 percent to SME and materials ($1 billion).[18] SMIC alone received nearly $6 billion between 2014 and 2018.[19] Heavy state support is why China was the second-largest importer of U.S. SME by late 2018, ahead of Taiwan and slightly behind South Korea—both of which have more chip fab capacity than China.[20] Figure 19-5 shows that SMIC receives a subsidy equivalent to as much as 40 percent of its revenue, as compared to between about 1 to 3 percent for the state-of-the-art chipmakers.

China's crown jewel is SMIC's development of a small amount of 14 nm capacity. In addition to massive subsidies, SMIC's limited success required billions of dollars of intellectual property theft from Taiwan,[21] and the poaching of perhaps a thousand engineers from Taiwan's chip industry.[22] For SMIC to displace state-of-the-art chipmakers Intel, TSMC, and Samsung, China must greatly increase SMIC's subsidies. Intel, TSMC, and Sam-

Figure 19-5. **State Subsidies as a Percentage of Revenue for Chip Fabs between 2014–2018**

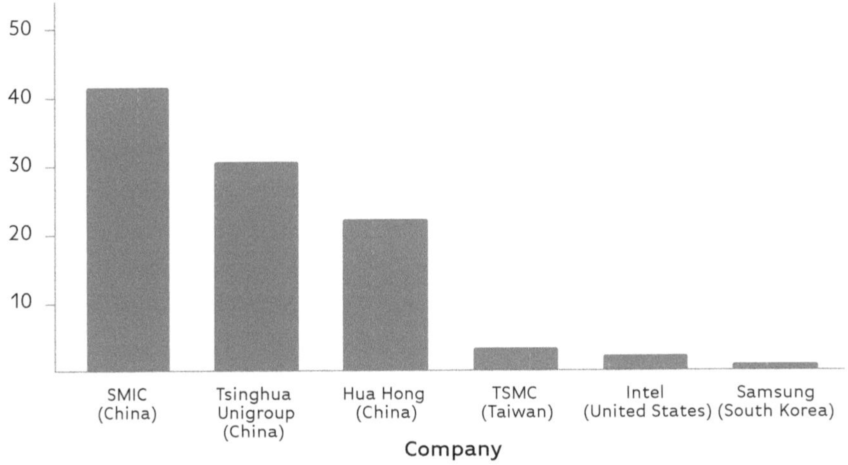

Source: Data from "Measuring distortions in international markets," OECD, 84. For the non-Chinese companies, not all state-subsidies are from the companies' home countries. Additionally, the true subsidy percentage for Tsinghua Unigroup's chip fabs may be even higher than shown in Figure 19-6; while the firm's revenue reflects many businesses besides chip fabs, China's subsidies have focused on its chip fabs.

sung all have much larger revenues than SMIC and depend far less on state support, even though each receives subsidies similar, in absolute terms, to those received by SMIC.[23] The outsized scale of the chip industry challenges even China's appetite for industrial subsidies.

China could dramatically increase its chip subsidies, but these interventions may fail to create market-disciplined, internationally competitive fabs. China's chipmaker subsidies have focused almost entirely on below-market-rate loans and equity for established companies.[24] But historically, Chinese state-owned chip firms relying on below-market financing have struggled with profitability.[25]

Subsidized Chinese chip fabs are only about three generations behind the state of the art, and the slowing of Moore's law—given increasing difficulty in shrinking transistors—could allow them to catch up.[26] In this scenario, the current Dutch export ban on EUV photolithography equipment becomes more critical, preventing Chinese chip fabs from progressing beyond 7 nm transistors for the foreseeable future.[27]

The news is even worse for China's ambitions to develop an indigenous advanced SME industry. Chinese companies produce some SME types essential to chip production, but their SME is too outdated for state-of-the-art fabs. Even with massive subsidies, China will face steep barriers in building a fully localized advanced SME industry for five reasons: (1) poor resource allocation due to central planning, (2) lack of engineers with the necessary know-how, (3) the complexity of SME, (4) the first-mover advantages of top SME companies, and (5) export controls on SME. China will especially struggle if SME becomes export controlled.[28] Moreover, as of 2017, China's national-level chip fund spent, at most, $1 billion on SME and materials, focusing instead on other parts of the chip supply chain,[29] although China's state funds are now increasing their focus on SME.

THE UNITED STATES AND ITS ALLIES SHOULD ENSURE CHINESE DEPENDENCE ON IMPORTS FOR STATE-OF-THE-ART CHIPS

If China succeeds in increasing its state-of-the-art chip fab capacity through subsidies, it will displace the chip fab capacity of democratic states. Chinese independence in global state-of-the-art chip fab capacity would allow China to freely manufacture advanced security-relevant technologies and significantly reduce U.S. and allied leverage over the CCP's conduct relating to human rights or global stability.

The United States, Japan, the Netherlands, and other allies should apply more stringent export controls on SME to prevent China from capturing state-of-the-art global chip fab capacity.[30] The highest priority should be photolithography equipment capable of manufacturing ≤ 45 nm transistors.[31] In a commendable start to our suggested approach, the Dutch government recently decided not to renew an export license for ASML to ship EUV photolithography equipment to China.[32] Additional priorities include the United States, Japan, and their allies applying more stringent export controls on other types of SME dominated by these countries. For SME supply chain chokepoints, these countries should presumptively deny licenses to export to China.[33] Foreign-owned fabs capable of manufacturing ≤ 45 nm transistors in China should also be subject to export scrutiny.[34]

As shown in figure 19-6, SME export controls could dramatically reduce China's advanced chip fab capacity. Under the proposed export controls, China's current stock of already-imported ≤ 45-nm-capable SME would

Figure 19-6. **China's Chip Fab Capacity with and without SME Export Controls**

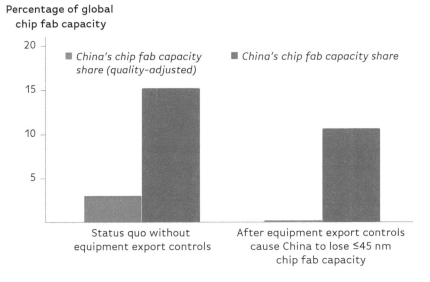

Percentage of global
chip fab capacity

■ *China's chip fab capacity*
  share (quality-adjusted)   ■ *China's chip fab capacity share*

Status quo without
equipment export controls

After equipment export controls
cause China to lose ≤45 nm
chip fab capacity

Source: Data from "World Fab Forecast," SEMI, May 2019 Edition.

gradually reach end of life,[35] and China's chip fabs capable of manufacturing chips with ≤ 45 nm transistors would face the prospect of shutting down.[36]

Because global chip demand is independent of where chips are produced, export controls on SME would, in the long term, shift China's lost chip fab capacity to the United States, Taiwan, and South Korea.[37] Although SME companies may lose out on lucrative Chinese subsidies in the near term,[38] they would experience little revenue harm in the long term. They would instead benefit from more reliable partners and a weakened Chinese SME industry.[39]

If SME export controls reduce China's fab capacity, the United States, Taiwan, and South Korea—the only remaining economies with significant near-state-of-the-art fab capacity[40]—could coordinate on further, targeted end-use and end-user controls on advanced chips[41] to advance global stability and human rights while continuing to export chips to China for peaceful commercial purposes.[42]

ACKNOWLEDGMENTS: For helpful discussions, comments, and input, great thanks go to Jeff Alstott, Tarun Chhabra, Douglas Fuller, Alexander

Mann, Kathryn Mecrow-Flynn, Igor Mikolic-Torreira, Dahlia Peterson, and Helen Toner. Daniel Hague, Ted Reinert, Alexandra Vreeman, and Lynne Weil edited this chapter. The authors are solely responsible for all mistakes.

NOTES

1. This is known as Moore's law.

2. Neil Thompson and Svenja Spanuth, "The Decline of Computers as a General Purpose Technology: Why Deep Learning and the End of Moore's Law Are Fragmenting Computing," SSRN, December 12, 2018, 32–35, https://papers.ssrn.com/sol3/papers.cfm?abstract_id=3287769.

3. "A Look Inside the Factory around Which the Modern World Turns," *The Economist*, December 18, 2019, www.economist.com/christmas-specials/2019/12/18/a-look-inside-the-factory-around-which-the-modern-world-turns.

4. In this chapter, "chipmaker" refers to a company that operates chip fabs.

5. The 80 percent estimate comes from "World Fab Forecast," SEMI, May 2019 edition. The Semiconductor Industry Association estimates that SME accounts for 57 percent of fab capital expenses. John Neuffer, "U.S. Standing in Key S&T Fields: Computing Devices Panel," slides for presentation at National Academy of Sciences meeting, February 11, 2020, 15.

6. *2016 Top Markets Report Semiconductors and Related Equipment* (Washington, DC: U.S. International Trade Administration, July 2016), 5, https://legacy.trade.gov/topmarkets/pdf/Semiconductors_Top_Markets_Report.pdf.

7. Saif M. Khan and Alexander W. Mann, "AI Chips: What They Are and Why They Matter" (Washington, DC: Center for Security and Emerging Technology, April 2020), https://cset.georgetown.edu/wp-content/uploads/AI-Chips—What-They-Are-and-Why-They-Matter.pdf.

8. "TSMC Purchases Lithography Machines with $2.2 Billion for the Second Generation 7nm Mass Production Making Apple and Huawei Being Overjoyed!" ELINFOR, February 21, 2019, www.elinfor.com/news/tsmc-purchases-lithography-machines-with-22-billion-for-the-second-generation-7nm-mass-production-making-apple-and-huawei-being-overjoyed-p-11016.

9. Based on analysis of Chinese SME company financial reports.

10. When organizing the data by fab location rather than fab headquarters, China's chip fab capacity share is 22.6 percent, its quality-adjusted chip fab capacity share is 6.1 percent, its near-state-of-the-art (≤ 16 nm) chip fab capacity share is 3.2 percent, and its quality-adjusted near-state-of-the-art chip fab capacity share is 1.2 percent. The non-Chinese-headquartered chip fabs in China with ≤ 45 nm capacity are owned by U.S., Taiwanese, and South Korean chipmakers: TSMC (16 nm), SK Hynix (18 nm), Intel (20 nm), Samsung (21 nm), and UMC (28 nm).

11. There are methodological challenges in determining the exact percentage. Typically, the percentage is estimated by dividing revenues of China's semiconductor industry by China's semiconductor market size. In 2018, the Chinese semiconductor

industry produced $24 billion in revenue. This number excludes the operations of non-Chinese semiconductor companies in China. "2019 Factbook," Semiconductor Industry Association, May 20, 2019, 2–3, www.semiconductors.org/resources/2019 -sia-factbook/. By comparison, in 2018, China consumed $155 billion worth of chips. "Can We Believe the Hype about China's Domestic IC Production Plans?" IC Insights, June 13, 2019, www.icinsights.com/news/bulletins/Can-We-Believe-The -Hype-About-Chinas-Domestic-IC-Production-Plans/. With these numbers, we obtain an estimate of 15 percent. However, the $155 billion market size includes chips packaged into other devices that were later exported. When excluding these exports, China's chip consumption is much lower. Dan Kim and John VerWey, "The Potential Impacts of the Made in China 2025 Roadmap on the Integrated Circuit Industries in the U.S., EU and Japan" (Washington, DC: U.S. International Trade Commission, August 2019), 22–23, www.usitc.gov/publications/332/working_ papers/id_19_061_china_integrated_circuits_technology_roadmap_final_080519 _kim_verwey-508_compliant.pdf.

12. Dan Kim and John VerWey, "The Potential Impacts of the Made in China 2025 Roadmap," 2.

13. OECD, "Measuring Distortions in International Markets: The Semiconductor Value Chain," OECD Trade Policy Papers, no. 234 (Paris: Organisation for Economic Cooperation and Development, December 12, 2019), 91–94, http://dx.doi .org/10.1787/8fe4491d-en.

14. "Guideline for the Promotion of the Development of the National Integrated Circuit Industry," State Council of the People's Republic of China, 2014, https:// members.wto.org/CRNAttachments/2014/SCMQ2/law47.pdf.

15. "Made in China 2025," State Council of the People's Republic of China, July 7, 2015, www.cittadellascienza.it/cina/wp-content/uploads/2017/02/IoT-ONE -Made-in-China-2025.pdf.

16. Samuel M. Goodman, Dan Kim, and John VerWey, "The South Korea–Japan Trade Dispute in Context: Semiconductor Manufacturing, Chemicals, and Concentrated Supply Chains" (Washington, DC: U.S. International Trade Commission, October 2019), 2–3, https://usitc.gov/publications/332/working_papers/the_ south_korea-japan_trade_dispute_in_context_semiconductor_manufacturing_ chemicals_and_concentrated_supply_chains.pdf.

17. Yuan Gao, "China Is Raising up to $31.5 Billion to Fuel Chip Vision," Bloomberg, March 1, 2018, www.bloomberg.com/news/articles/2018-03-01/china -is-said-raising-up-to-31-5-billion-to-fuel-chip-vision. The $150 billion includes funding from two rounds of funding totaling more than $50 billion by China's National Integrated Circuit (IC) Investment Fund. "China IC Ecosystem Report" (Milpitas, CA: SEMI, 2018 edition), 7, www.semi.org/en/news-resources/market -data/china-ic-ecosystem; Sarah Dai, "China Completes Second Round of US$29 Billion Big Fund Aimed at Investing in Domestic Chip Industry," *South China Morning Post*, July 26, 2019, www.scmp.com/tech/science-research/article/3020172 /china-said-complete-second-round-us29-billion-fund-will. As of 2018, $18.8 billion (86 percent) of the National IC Fund had been allocated. Alan Patterson,

"Semiconductors: China Goes Its Own Way," EE Times Asia, April 3, 2018, www .eetasia.com/news/article/18040301-semiconductors-china-goes-its-own-way. The $150 billion also includes even more funding from provincial and municipal funds. See "China IC Ecosystem Report," SEMI, 10.

18. "China IC Ecosystem Report," SEMI, 7. Another analysis suggests that the first round of China's National IC Fund allocated only about $500 million to SME companies. "[We have totaled the recipients from the first investment phase of the Big Fund]," 雪球 [Xueqiu], December 25, 2019, https://xueqiu.com/8186228019/ 137965308.

19. OECD, "Measuring Distortions in International Markets," 84.

20. "Economics and Trade Bulletin" (Washington, DC: U.S.-China Economic and Security Review Commission, January 11, 2019), 9, www.uscc.gov/sites/default /files/Research/January%202019%20Trade%20Bulletin.pdf. China has also spared U.S. SME imports from tariffs. Ibid.

21. Douglas B. Fuller, *Paper Tigers, Hidden Dragons: Firms and the Political Economy of China's Technological Development* (Oxford: Oxford University Press, 2016), 137.

22. Ibid., 135; Yimou Lee, "China Lures Chip Talent from Taiwan with Fat Salaries Perks," Reuters, September 4, 2018, www.reuters.com/article/us-china -semiconductors-taiwan-insight/china-lures-chip-talent-from-taiwan-with-fat -salaries-perks-idUSKCN1LK0H1.

23. Because Intel, TSMC, and Samsung have such large revenues compared to SMIC, even small state subsidies as a percentage of their revenue result in absolute subsidies over 2014–2018 that are similar to SMIC's $6 billion state subsidy over the same time period. OECD, "Measuring Distortions in International Markets," 84. For a further sense of scale, China's national-level chip subsidies of $18.8 billion by 2018 are dwarfed by just TSMC's $34 billion investment on new fabs. China's national-level chip subsidies allocated as of 2018 are from Alan Patterson, "Semiconductors." TSMC's spending is accurate as of mid-2019. "World Fab Forecast," SEMI, May 2019 edition.

24. Ibid., 84, 93.

25. Ibid., 97, 98; Douglas B. Fuller, *Paper Tigers*, 118, 156; Douglas B. Fuller, "Growth, Upgrading, and Limited Catch-up in China's Semiconductor Industry," in *Policy, Regulation and Innovation in China's Electricity and Telecom Industries*, eds. Loren Brandt and Thomas G. Rawski (Cambridge: Cambridge University Press, 2019), 262–303, https://doi.org/10.1017/9781108645997.007. By contrast, subsidies to Intel, TSMC, and Samsung—which focus on tax breaks for R&D, capital investment, and corporate income—are relatively more efficient than China's SMIC subsidies. Industry-specific tax breaks for capital investment and corporate income risk capital misallocation. Yet R&D tax breaks can correct for market failures by producing foundational research breakthroughs that can have massive positive spillovers to the broader economy. OECD, "Measuring Distortions in International Markets," 62, 90–92.

26. For discussion on the importance of and the difficulty of acquiring know-

how for complex technologies, see Andrea Gilli and Mauro Gilli, "Why China Has Not Caught Up Yet: Military-Technological Superiority and the Limits of Imitation, Reverse Engineering, and Cyber Espionage," *International Security* 43, no. 3 (February 15, 2019): 141–189, www.mitpressjournals.org/doi/full/10.1162/isec_a _00337.

27. Even if Chinese chip fabs do later obtain access to EUV tools, they would need time to tinker before reaching low enough manufacturing error rates to enable mass production. TSMC, which is now introducing 5 nm chip fabs, experimented considerably before they could use EUV-based manufacturing techniques at scale. For discussion on TSMC's efforts to reduce error rates for EUV-based 5 nm manufacturing, see Ian Cuttress, "Early TSMC 5nm Test Chip Yields 80%, HVM Coming in H1 2020," AnandTech, December 11, 2019, www.anandtech.com/show/ 15219/early-tsmc-5nm-test-chip-yields-80-hvm-coming-in-h1-2020.

28. China's development of its chip industry has relied heavily on importing Taiwanese experts. However, Taiwan, like China, does not have a significant SME industry. If SME is export-controlled by the United States, Japan, and the Netherlands, it will be illegal for experts from these countries to provide their expertise in China. While China has been able to attract Taiwanese experts with high salaries and no legal consequences, it seems unlikely it will be able to attract as many Americans, Japanese, and Dutch.

29. See note 18.

30. To promote cooperation on export controls and to compensate for near-term revenue shortfalls, the United States and its allies could partner on semiconductor R&D to maintain their technological advantages.

31. This equipment includes EUV photolithography equipment supplied by the Netherlands and argon fluoride (ArF) immersion photolithography equipment supplied by the Netherlands and Japan. Saif M. Khan, "Maintaining the AI Chip Competitive Advantage of the United States and Its Allies" (Washington, DC: Center for Security and Emerging Technology, December 2019), 4, https://cset. georgetown.edu/wp-content/uploads/CSET-Maintaining-the-AI-Chip-Competi tive-Advantage-of-the-United-States-and-its-Allies-20191206.pdf. EUV photolithography equipment, used to fabricate chips with state-of-the-art 5 nm transistors, is already controlled. ArF photolithography equipment, used to fabricate chips with transistors between 45 nm and 7 nm, is not controlled. "U.S. Commerce Control List, Supplement No. 1 to Part 774, Category 3" (Washington, DC: Bureau of Industry and Security, May 23, 2019), 38–39, www.bis.doc.gov/index .php/documents/regulations-docs/2334-ccl3-8/file.

32. Alexandra Alper, Toby Sterling, and Stephen Nellis, "Trump Administration Pressed Dutch Hard to Cancel China Chip-Equipment Sale: Sources," Reuters, January 6, 2020, www.reuters.com/article/us-asml-holding-usa-china-insight -idUSKBN1Z50HN.

33. Saif M. Khan, "Maintaining the AI Chip Competitive Advantage," 5.

34. U.S., Taiwanese, and South Korean chipmakers with ≤ 45 nm chip fab capacity also operate in China. See note 12. The choice of whether to permit SME

exports to these chip fabs is difficult. One option is to approve licenses for existing foreign-owned chip fabs—so long as they comply with end-use and end-user export controls—but deny licenses that would facilitate upgrades or new construction of foreign-owned chip fabs. Export controls on ≤ 45-nm-capable SME that spare U.S., Taiwanese, and South Korean chip fabs in China would reduce the capacity share of chip fabs in China (including foreign-owned fabs) from 22.6 percent to 18.0 percent and the quality-adjusted capacity share from 6.1 percent to 3.3 percent.

35. SME companies offer repair services for the equipment they sell. However, export controls could prevent these companies from offering these repair services to Chinese chipmakers. Our scenario assumes Chinese companies are unable to perform adequate upkeep on their own over the long term. We believe this assumption is reasonable, as the scale of refurbished SME sales—which account for a large percentage of all SME sales—speaks to the expense and technical difficulty of repair. John VerWey, "What's Causing U.S. Semiconductor Equipment Production and Exports to Grow?" (Washington, DC: U.S. International Trade Commission, January 2019), 2, www.usitc.gov/publications/332/executive_briefings/ebot_john_verwey_semi_manufacturing_equipment_pdf.pdf.

36. There is recent precedent for the inability of Chinese chip fabs to import-substitute in response to export controls. In 2018, the United States applied strict export controls on the Chinese chipmaker Fujian Jinhua as it was receiving and bringing online SME in its new $6 billion fab. In response, U.S. and Dutch SME companies immediately withdrew support staff. As a result, Fujian Jinhua halted operations. "The Chipmaker Caught in U.S. Assault on China's Tech Ambitions," Bloomberg, November 25, 2018, www.bloomberg.com/news/articles/2018-11-25/the-chipmaker-caught-in-u-s-assault-on-china-s-tech-ambitions; Kathrin Hille, "Trade War Forces Chinese Chipmaker Fujian Jinhua to Halt Output," *Financial Times*, January 28, 2019, www.ft.com/content/87b5580c-22bf-11e9-8ce6-5db454 3da632.

37. In response to the Dutch denial of an export license for ASML's EUV photolithography equipment exports to China, ASML's CEO Peter Wennink said, "If we cannot ship to customer A or country B, we'll ship it to customer C and country D" to meet growing global chip demand, including from China. Toby Sterling, "ASML Sees No Impact from China Trade War, Good Growth in 2020," Yahoo News, January 22, 2020, www.yahoo.com/news/asml-sees-no-impact-china-144103 191.html.

38. For SME company revenue exposure to China, see Saif M. Khan, "Maintaining the AI Chip Competitive Advantage," 4.

39. See note 33.

40. Leading chipmakers headquartered in the United States, Taiwan, and South Korea have fabs in foreign countries. For example, U.S.-based Intel and Global-Foundries own ≤ 22 nm fabs in Israel, Ireland, Germany, and even one fab in China. The United States, Taiwan, and South Korea would therefore have to carefully craft export controls to cover sales by these foreign-located fabs.

41. An example end-user export control would be a ban on exports of chips to

the Chinese military. An example end-use export control would be a ban on exports to any Chinese entity using chips in weapons.

42. To avoid import substitution by China's domestic chip fabs, expanded export controls on chips may be inadvisable until strict SME export controls ensure China's advanced chip fab capacity remains limited. Carrick Flynn, "Recommendations on Export Controls for Artificial Intelligence" (Washington, DC: Center for Security and Emerging Technology, 2020), https://cset.georgetown.edu/wp-content/uploads/Recommendations-on-Export-Controls-for-Artificial-Intelligence.pdf.

20

Artificial Intelligence and Autonomy in China's Drive for Military Innovation

ELSA B. KANIA

As the Chinese People's Liberation Army (PLA) seeks to become a "world-class military," its progress in advanced weapons systems continues to provoke intense concern from its neighbors and competitors.[1] The Chinese military and China's defense industry have been pursuing significant investments in robotics, swarming, and other applications of artificial intelligence (AI) and machine learning (ML) across multiple services and multiple domains of warfare.[2] Thus far, advances in weapons systems described or advertised as "autonomous" (自主) or "intelligentized" (智能化) have built on existing strengths in the research and development of unmanned systems and missile technology.[3] As military technological competition emerges as an ever more prominent component of great power rivalries, the Chinese military and defense industry have been pursuing active initiatives in research, development, and experimentation. Ultimately, China's progress will remain contingent upon the capacity to operationalize emerging weapons systems, which requires overcoming current technological and organizational challenges, including in data, talent, testing, training, and concepts of operations.[4] The future impact of AI on in military affairs remains contingent on the capacity to operationalize "intelligentization" as a component of military modernization and innovation.

China's advances in autonomy and AI-enabled weapons systems could impact the military balance, while potentially exacerbating threats to global security and strategic stability as great power rivalry intensifies.[5] In striving to achieve technological advantage, there is a risk that the PLA could deploy weapons systems that are unsafe, untested, or unreliable under actual operational conditions. The PLA's strategic choices about which capabilities could prove advantageous will influence the direction of Chinese military innovation. However, it is encouraging that Chinese military scientists and researchers have been starting to debate and engage with safety issues and technical concerns, as well as legal and ethical considerations.[6] Going forward, the United States should monitor these trends and pursue measures to mitigate such risks.

The current advances in autonomy and AI-enabled weapons systems promise to increase the speed, reach, precision, and lethality of future operations.[7] Today, militaries worldwide, including in the United States and Russia,[8] are exploring and pursuing these capabilities.[9] Current definitions of autonomy and understanding of the characteristics of "lethal autonomous weapons systems" (LAWS) vary.[10] The use of AI/ML techniques, while not required to achieve autonomy, can enable these capabilities.[11] In an era of high-tech warfare, the boundary between a "smart weapon" that is capable of great precision relative to a weapons system that is considered partly or fully autonomous can be complex and contingent.[12] No clear consensus exists on how to manage issues of law, ethics, and arms control that arise with the development of such capabilities, other than emergent agreement that existing elements of international law do apply, including the law of armed conflict.[13] To date, major militaries have remained unwilling to accept any serious constraints on development due to the potential for future operational advantage.[14]

China's military initiatives in AI are motivated by concern with global trends in military technology and operations[15]; anxieties about falling behind the U.S. military, which is perceived and often characterized as the "powerful adversary" (强敌)[16]; and recognition of the opportunities in this ongoing military and technological transformation.[17] "China's military security is confronted by risks from technology surprise and a growing technological generation gap," according to the official white paper on "China's National Defense in the New Era," released in July 2019.[18] "Intelligent(ized) warfare is on the horizon," the assessment finds; the ongoing "Revolution in Military Affairs" will change the very mechanisms for victory in future warfare.[19] Chinese military scientists and strategists, including from lead-ing and authoritative institutions, such as the PLA's Academy of Military Science, National Defense University, and National University of Defense Technology, envision AI systems and intelligent weapons becoming increas-ingly important, even decisive, in future warfare. Their research closely ex-amines antecedents in U.S. strategy and capabilities to inform their own assessments.[20]

The PLA's quest for innovation is an element of China's national strat-egy to leverage science and technology to enhance national capabilities as a rising power.[21] In the process, the Chinese military is developing not only more traditional but also emerging capabilities, often concentrating on asymmetric approaches against the U.S. military. The efforts of Chinese military scientists and strategists have been impelled by guidance at the highest levels. Xi Jinping, in his capacity as Chairman of China's Central Military Competition, has emphasized that "under a situation of increas-ingly fierce international military competition, only the innovators win."[22] Moreover, on the importance of contesting new frontiers of global military scientific and technological developments, he urged, "We must attach great importance to the development of strategic frontier technologies, striving to surpass the predecessor as latecomers, turning sharply to surpass."[23] To some extent, the PLA could be regarded as unduly sanguine, even enthused, about the opportunities for disruption that may arise with emerging tech-nologies, while still recognizing the challenges and uncertainties about their prospects on the future battlefield.

While the military applications of AI are hardly limited to weapons sys-tems, the use of AI to enable more precise strikes and achieve kinetic initiative could prove significant. The PLA's official dictionary included a definition of an "AI weapon" (人工智能武器) as early as 2011, characterized as "a weapon that utilizes AI to pursue, distinguish, and destroy enemy targets automati-cally; often composed of information collection and management systems, knowledge base systems, decision assistance systems, mission implementa-tion systems, etc."[24] Typically, Chinese military strategists and scientists tend to discuss "AI weapons" or "intelligent(ized) weapons" (智能化武器) more often than "autonomous weapons" (自主武器) in academic and technical writings.[25] This terminological difference is subtle but potentially significant, implying a focus on the "smartness" or "intelligence" of weapons systems in selecting and engaging targets.[26] For instance, techniques for adaptive or autonomous control can leverage a range of algorithms, including neural networks.[27] Even as the function of certain weapons systems becomes "unmanned" (无人化) or "dronified" and to some degree automatic (自动化), greater degrees of autonomy or "intelligence" in function may remain challenging to implement or evaluate with high confidence.

While Chinese leaders have prioritized advances in AI as an important direction for military modernization, China's Central Military Commission has yet to release any policy or official strategy that formally clarifies such plans and priorities. However, in July 2017, the New Generation Artificial Intelligence Development Plan called for China to "strengthen the use of AI in military applications that include command decision-making, military deductions,[28] and defense equipment."[29] Concurrently, China's strategy on military-civil fusion highlighted AI as a priority and important frontier for dual-use development. In fall 2017, Xi Jinping, in his address to the 19th Party Congress of the Chinese Communist Party (CCP), urged, "Accelerate the development of military intelligentization, and improve joint operations capabilities and all-domain combat capabilities based on network information systems."[30] His remarks provided authoritative guidance to pursue military applications of AI that could be integrated across the whole system of systems for future operations.[31] This emerging emphasis on "military intelligentization" (军事智能化), or the "development of an intelligent military,"[32] extends beyond AI-enabled weapons systems and autonomy to involve prioritizing as an integral element of China's military strategy and modernization going forward.[33]

The PLA has been actively pursuing AI-enabled systems and autonomous capabilities in its military modernization.[34] Across services and for all domains of warfare, it has fielded a growing number of robotic and unmanned systems, as well as advanced missiles with precision guidance, certain of which may possess at least limited degrees of autonomy. For instance, the PLA Army (PLAA) has concentrated on military robotics and unmanned ground vehicles, which could be used for logistics and urban combat.[35] The PLA Navy (PLAN) is experimenting with unmanned surface vessels that may operate with some autonomy and is reportedly developing autonomous submarines.[36] The PLA Air Force (PLAAF) operates advanced unmanned systems with limited autonomy, which could be upgraded to include greater autonomy, while exploring options for manned-unmanned teaming.[37] The PLA Rocket Force (PLARF) may leverage use cases in remote sensing, targeting, and decision support,[38] and its missiles may be augmented to become more "intelligentized" in their capabilities, incorporating higher levels of automation to facilitate operations.[39] There are indications that the PLA Strategic Support Force (PLASSF) could apply advances in AI to its missions of space, cyber, electronic, and psychological operations.[40] PLA capabilities and advancements very likely extend well beyond what is known and knowable from open sources and there is extensive research underway across academia, the defense industry, and military institutions.

The Chinese defense industry can build on its apparent strengths in armed drones and advanced missiles to introduce greater autonomy into operations.[41] In particular, certain advanced unmanned aerial vehicles could be modified to operate with greater autonomy instead of under remote control.[42] Currently, China leads in export of medium-altitude long endurance unmanned aerial vehicles (UAVs).[43] Made in China UAVs, such as the Wing Loong platform, from the Aviation Industry Corporation of China (AVIC), and the CH-4, developed by China Aerospace Science and Technology Corporation (CASC), are actively marketed for export.[44] Within the PLAAF, the GJ-1 and its successor GJ-2 are used for integrated reconnaissance and precision strike, including in support of joint operations.[45] According to the systems' designer, the GJ-2 is "highly intelligent" and capable of operating autonomously in certain circumstances.[46]

While there is no direct evidence that the PLA has formally fielded a weapons system that fully meets the definition of "AI weapon," certain systems are analogous or comparable in their functionality. The Chinese defense industry's attempts to make cruise and ballistic missiles more "intelligent" build upon work on automatic target recognition that predates the recent concern with autonomous weapons.[47] The Chinese military has reportedly converted older models of tanks to operate via remote control or with some degree of autonomy.[48] There are also reports of ongoing developments in and the procurement and potential deployment of "suicide drones," such as the CH-901 and WS-43, based on loitering munitions, as well as ongoing experimentation with swarming.[49] The PLAN has tested and operated a range of undersea gliders and unmanned underwater vehicle (UUVs) for scientific or military missions,[50] including the HN-1 glider used in exercises in the South China Sea.[51] Often, limited technical information is available, rendering the disclosure of capabilities and signaling—including the potential for misdirection or disinformation—important to evaluate carefully.[52]

Such advances in Chinese military capabilities are taking shape through the efforts of Chinese military research institutes, the Chinese defense industry, and the emerging ecosystem of commercial enterprises supporting military-civil fusion.[53] For instance, the Key Laboratory of Precision Guidance and Automatic Target Recognition at the PLA's National University of Defense Technology has concentrated on a range of automatic target recognition techniques. The available technical literature also points to interest in applying neural networks to the guidance of hypersonic glide vehicles, enabling adaptive control and greater autonomy.[54] For new directions in research, the Tianjin Binhai Artificial Intelligence Military-Civil Fusion Center was established in partnership with the PLA's Academy of Military Science, and pursues developments in autonomy and the capacity for coordination of unmanned systems, such as for undersea drones.[55]

Future Chinese aerospace capabilities will be enabled and enhanced by research currently underway within the major state-owned defense conglomerates. For instance, starting in 2015, the China Aerospace Science and Industry Corporation (CASIC) 3rd Academy 35th Research Institute began pursuing breakthroughs in core technologies that include target detection and recognition techniques based on deep learning.[56] Notably, in 2016, this CASIC team organized an innovation competition on AI-Based Radar Target Classification and Recognition,[57] which was the Chinese defense industry's first major event of this kind, involving companies and universities with AI research proficiency applying that expertise to finding intelligent processing solutions for targeting.[58] According to a senior missile designer from CASIC, "Our future cruise missiles will have a very high level of AI and autonomy," such that commanders will be able "to control them in a real-time manner, or to use a fire-and-forget mode, or even to add more tasks to in-flight missiles."[59] Future missiles might have increasingly sophisticated capabilities in sensing, decisionmaking, and implementation—even potentially gaining a degree of "cognition" and continual learning capability.[60] Significantly, the PLA's development of hypersonic weapons systems has also incorporated advances in techniques for greater autonomy.[61]

Absent official policy or guidance from Chinese military leaders, it is difficult to anticipate how the PLA will approach issues of human control over autonomous systems, particularly as these capabilities progress and evolve. Historically, Chinese leaders have prized centralized, consolidated control over the military. They may therefore be generally disinclined to relinquish control to individual humans, let alone machines, fearing loss of the Party's "absolute command."[62] At the same time, Chinese military scholars and scientists appear to be relatively pragmatic in discussing the nuances of having a human in, on, or out of the loop. Given technical constraints and uncertainties, there are reasons to expect that in the near term the Chinese military will keep humans "in the loop," or at least "on the loop," but it is harder to anticipate whether the PLA or any military will maintain that position if conditions and technical considerations change.[63] However, discussion of meaningful human control appears to be less established in Chinese writings than in U.S. debates on these topics to date.[64]

There is no clear evidence indicating that the Chinese military is more inclined to pursue autonomy and/or automation in a manner that removes humans from decisionmaking relative to other militaries. In the near term, human involvement in command and control appears to be deemed necessary for technical reasons, and the Chinese military is actively exploring concepts that leverage synergies between human and artificial intelligence, such as that of human-machine intelligent integration (人机智能融合).[65] In the future, concerns of operational expediency could supersede safety if having a human in the loop became a liability, as greater involvement of AI systems in command decisionmaking is considered potentially advantageous.[66] Yet, at the level of strategic decisionmaking, including for decisions that involve the employment of nuclear weapons, it is all but certain that one human will remain in the loop for the foreseeable future: Xi Jinping.[67]

Going forward, U.S.-China military competition is oriented upon on the fight to innovate in emerging technologies critical to the future of warfare. China's future progress in developing AI-enabled and autonomous weapons systems must be contextualized by the uncertain trajectory of its military modernization, as well as that of AI/ML research and development. The eventual realization of such capabilities will depend on the PLA's capacity to test, integrate new capabilities into existing concepts of operations, and create new theories of victory that recognize the ongoing changes in the character of conflict.[68] Such advances could constitute an important component of the PLA's emergence as a world-class military aspiring to achieve an advantage in future warfare.

NOTES

1. For further context on the notion of the PLA as a world-class military, see M. Taylor Fravel, Testimony before the U.S.-China Economic and Security Review Commission—Hearing on "A 'World-Class' Military: Assessing China's Global Military Ambitions," U.S.-China Economic and Security Review Commission, June 20, 2019, www.uscc.gov/sites/default/files/Fravel_USCC%20Testimony_FINAL.pdf.

2. For the author's prior research and writing on the topic, see, for instance, Elsa B. Kania, "Chinese Military Innovation in Artificial Intelligence: Hearing of the U.S.-China Economic and Security Review Commission," June 7, 2019, www.cnas .org/publications/congressional-testimony/chinese-military-innovation-in-artifi cial-intelligence.

3. Although the term "uninhabited" is generally preferable to "unmanned" as a more accurate characterization, the Chinese terminology is literally "un-(hu) manned" (无人), which is the phrasing that this chapter chooses to use. Certain unmanned systems that can be optionally operated as remotely controlled or autonomous. See, for instance, "天下谁人能识"机" [Who in the world can know the "machine"], *PLA Daily*, April 7, 2017, www.81.cn/jfjbmap/content/2017-04/07/ content_174361.htm; Zheng Yufu, "武器装备机械化、信息化、智能化怎么融" [How to integrate mechanization, informatization, and intelligentization of weapons and equipment], *PLA Daily*, October 10, 2019, https://web.archive.org/web /20200215014553/www.xinhuanet.com/mil/2019-10/10/c_1210306210.htm.

4. Zhang Jie, Zhang Chi, and Zhao Xinghua, "军事人才培养与战争形态演 进"[Military personnel cultivation and the evolution of patterns of warfare], 光明 日报 [*Guangming Daily*], December 21, 2019,
https://web.archive.org/web/20200215012903/https://news.gmw.cn/2019-12/21/ content_33419288.htm.

5. For an early and insightful academic perspective on the topic, see Michael C. Horowitz, "Artificial Intelligence, International Competition, and the Balance of Power," *Texas National Security Review* 1, no. 3 (May 2018), https://tnsr.org/2018/05 /artificial-intelligence-international-competition-and-the-balance-of-power/. However, there are also reasons to be skeptical about the actual impact that AI may have on the future balance of power, which will depend on the progress in overcoming issues of safety and reliability that arise in its operationalization.

6. See, for instance, Liang Jie, "智能化作战法律问题漫谈"[Discussing the legal issues of intelligentized operations], 光明日报 [*Guangming Daily*], July 20, 2019, https://web.archive.org/web/20200215011803/http://news.gmw.cn/2019-07/20/ content_33013497.htm.

7. See, for instance, research that is forthcoming from Dr. Margarita Konaev at the Center for Security and Emerging Technology at Georgetown.

8. See, for comparison, Margarita Konaev and Samuel Bendett, "Russian AI -Enabled Combat: Coming to a City Near You?" War on the Rocks, July 31, 2019, https://warontherocks.com/2019/07/russian-ai-enabled-combat-coming-to-a-city -near-you/. See also Samuel Bendett, "The Development of Artificial Intelligence in Russia," in *AI, China, Russia, and the Global Order: Technological, Political, Global, and Creative Perspectives* (Boston: NSI, January 2019), https://nsiteam.com/ai-china -russia-and-the-global-order-technological-political-global-and-creative-perspec tives/.

9. See, for instance, Michael C. Horowitz, Gregory C. Allen, Elsa B. Kania, and Paul Scharre, *Strategic Competition in an Era of Artificial Intelligence* (Washington,

DC: Center for New American Security, July 25, 2018), www.cnas.org/publications/reports/strategic-competition-in-an-era-of-artificial-intelligence.

10. For reference, see that of the U.S. military in this position paper: "Characteristics of Lethal Autonomous Weapons Systems: Submitted by the United States of America," United Nations, November 10, 2017, www.unog.ch/80256EDD006B89 54/(httpAssets)/A4466587B0DABE6CC12581D400660157/$file/2017_GGEon LAWS_WP7_USA.pdf. An estimated 154 or more weapons systems already exist around the world that incorporate some degree of autonomy. Thanks to Margarita Konaev for sharing her insights on this point. See also Vincent Boulanin and Maaike Verbruggen, *Mapping the Development of Autonomy in Unmanned Systems* (Stockholm: Stockholm International Peace Research Institute, November 2017), 24, 26, www.sipri.org/sites/default/files/2017-11/siprireport_mapping_the_develop ment_of_autonomy_in_weapon_systems_1117_1.pdf.

11. Thank you so much to Lindsey Sheppard for highlighting the importance of this distinction.

12. See, for context, Paul G. Gillespie, *Weapons of Choice: The Development of Precision Guided Munitions* (Tuscaloosa: The University of Alabama Press, 2006).

13. For American legal academic perspective on the topic, see for instance, Marco Sassoli, "Autonomous Weapons and International Humanitarian Law: Advantages, Open Technical Questions and Legal Issues to Be Clarified," *International Law Studies/Naval War College* 90 (2014): 308–340, https://digital-commons.usnwc .edu/cgi/viewcontent.cgi?article=1017&context=ils; Kenneth Anderson and Matthew C. Waxman, "Law and Ethics for Autonomous Weapons Systems: Why a Ban Won't Work and How the Laws of War Can," SSRN, April 14, 2013, https:// papers.ssrn.com/sol3/papers.cfm?abstract_id=2250126.

14. However, the U.S. Department of Defense has created and is starting to institutionalize ethical principles that will guide the use of AI in defense. See Patrick Tucker, "Pentagon to Adopt Detailed Principles for Using AI," Defense One, February 18, 2020, www.defenseone.com/technology/2020/02/pentagon-adopt -detailed-principles-using-ai/163185/; "AI Principles: Recommendations on the Ethical Use of Artificial Intelligence by the Department of Defense," Defense Innovation Board, https://media.defense.gov/2019/Oct/31/2002204459/-1/-1/0/ DIB_AI_PRINCIPLES_SUPPORTING_DOCUMENT.PDF.

15. "习近平:准确把握世界军事发展新趋势 与时俱进大力推进军事创新" [Xi Jinping: Accurately Grasp the New Trend in Global Military Developments and Keep Pace with the Times, Forcefully Advancing Military Innovation], Xinhua, August 30, 2014, http://news.xinhuanet.com/politics/2014-08/30/c_1112294869. htm.

16. Zheng Lianjie, "战斗力发展"弯道超车", 需要何种方略" [What strategies are needed for the development of combat effectiveness "overtaking around the curve"], China Military Network, January 19, 2017, www.xinhuanet.com/mil/2017 -01/19/c_129453510.htm.

17. Not unlike the U.S. military, the PLA's interest in AI is not a recent phenom-

enon and can be traced back to the mid-1980s to projects that involved robotics, intelligent computing, and applying expert systems to military operations research. These early antecedents are beyond the scope of this chapter.

18. "China's National Defense in the New Era," Xinhua, July 24, 2019, www.xinhuanet.com/english/2019-07/24/c_138253389.htm.

19. Ibid.

20. See, for instance, Zhu Feng, Hu Xiaofeng, Wu Lin, He Xiaoyuan, and Guo Shengming, "Inspiration for Battlefield Situation Cognition from AI Military Programs Launched by DARPA of USA and Development of AI Technology," in *Theory, Methodology, Tools and Applications for Modeling and Simulation of Complex Systems*, eds. Zhang Lin, Song Xiao, and Wu Yunjie (Singapore: Springer, 2016), 566–577.

21. For instance, the national strategy for innovation-driven development. See the official strategy released on innovation-driven development, "中共中央 国务院印发《国家创新驱动发展战略纲要"" [The CCP Central Commission and State Council Release the National Innovation-Driven Development Strategy Outline], Xinhua, May 19, 2016, http://news.xinhuanet.com/politics/2016-05/19/c_1118898033.htm. See also Xi Jinping's remarks on this approach in the context of military modernization: "习近平: 全面实施创新驱动发展战略 推动国防和军队建设实现新跨越" [Xi Jinping: Comprehensively advance an innovation-driven development strategy, promote new leaps in national defense and military construction], Xinhua, March 13, 2016, http://news.xinhuanet.com/politics/2016lh/2016-03/13/c_1118316426.htm.

22. See, for instance, Xi Jinping's remarks as quoted in this article: "科技创新, 迈向世界一流军队的强大引擎" [S&T innovation, a powerful engine for the world-class military], Xinhua, September 15, 2017, www.gov.cn/xinwen/2017-09/15/content_5225216.htm.

23. Ibid.

24. 全军军事术语管理委员会 [All-Military Military Terminology Management Committee], 中国人民解放军军语 [People's Liberation Army military terminology] (Beijing: 军事科学出版社 [Military Science Press], 2011).

25. By contrast, references to autonomous weapons are more prominent in Chinese writings on the global debate on LAWS. See, for instance, "主武器: 技术与伦理的边缘" [Autonomous weapons: The edge of technology and ethics] 自中国科学报 [China Science Report], April 20, 2018, http://news.sciencenet.cn/.

26. Yin Junsong, Li Minghai, Li Shijiang, and Gao Kaize, "积极应对战争形态智能化挑战"[Actively addressing the challenges of the intelligentization of the form of warfare], *PLA Daily*, February 6, 2020, www.mod.gov.cn/education/2020-02/06/content_4859784.htm.

27. There is extensive technical literature on the topic, including in the journal Tactical Missile Technology (战术导弹技术), and further references are available upon request.

28. This term (*bingqi tuiyan*, 兵棋推演) is often used in reference to Chinese military wargaming and simulations.

29. "国务院关于印发新一代人工智能发展规划的通知" [State Council notice on the issuance of the new generation AI development plan], State Council, People's Republic of China, August 20, 2017, www.gov.cn/zhengce/content/2017-07/20/content_5211996.htm.

30. "习近平在中国共产党第十九次全国代表大会上的报告" [Xi Jinping's report at the Chinese Communist Party 19th National Congress], Xinhua, October 27, 2017, www.china.com.cn/19da/2017-10/27/content_41805113_3.htm.

31. "专家: 军事智能化绝不仅仅是人工智能" [Experts: Military intelligentization is not merely artificial intelligence], *People's Daily*, December 6, 2017, http://military.people.com.cn/n1/2017/1206/c1011-29689750.html.

32. This latter translation is from the official English translation of China's national defense white paper, but the former is the more literal and consistent rendering of the phrase.

33. Elsa B. Kania, "Chinese Military Innovation in Artificial Intelligence."

34. Of course, many of the AI systems in question are not weapons systems per se, but this chapter is scoped to concentrate primarily on weapons systems.

35. "陆军对照十九大要求完善陆军"十三五"装备建设规划" [Army to improve the Army's "13th Five-Year" Equipment Construction Plan in accordance with the requirements of the 19th Party Congress], People's Daily Network, January 9, 2018, https://xw.qq.com/cmsid/20180109C04CYW/20180109C04CYW00. See also "陆军加快推动无人化智能化运用发展" [Army accelerates the development of unmanned [systems and] intelligentization], *PLA Daily*, August 5, 2019, www.xinhuanet.com/mil/2019-08/05/c_1210228994.htm; "陆军举办无人化智能化建设运用论坛"[PLA Army hosts unmanned intelligent construction application forum], *PLA Daily*, August 5, 2019, www.81.cn/lj/2019-08/05/content_9578823.htm.

36. "中国首个实海况智能船艇竞赛在上海交大" [China's first real sea state intelligent boat competition convened at Shanghai Jiaotong University], Shanghai Jiaotong University, October 14, 2019, https://news.sjtu.edu.cn/jdyw/20191014/112627.html.

37. "访"翼龙"总设计师: 平时工兵战时尖兵" [Interview with chief designer of Pterosaur: Peacetime engineers and the wartime vanguard], Xinhua, April 14, 2017, http://news.xinhuanet.com/politics/2017-04/14/c_1120807914_2.htm.

38. On relevant research from PLARF scientists, see, for instance, "证据推理与人工智能高峰论坛宣传册" [Evidential Reasoning and Artificial Intelligence Summit Forum], Tencent Cloud, December 26, 2017, https://new.qq.com/omn/20171226/20171226G0DFLD.html.

39. "火箭军导弹武器装备信息化程度大幅提升" [The Rocket Force's missile weaponry and equipment has greatly improved the degree of informatization], *PLA Daily*, February 8, 2020, www.xinhuanet.com/2020-02/08/c_1210465719.htm.

40. For related research, see, "顶级科研院所齐聚"眼神杯", 探索AI+遥感影像科研应用新风向" [Top research institutes gather for the "Eye Cup," exploring new trends in AI+ remote sensing image research and applications], 36 kr, June 5, 2018, https://xw.qq.com/cmsid/20180605A0B3AL/20180605A0B3AL00. For context on the potential of AI in cyber security, see "一只章鱼改变了网络安全游戏规则"[An

octopus has changed the rules of the cyber security game], 科技日报 [*S&T Daily*], May 28, 2019, www.cac.gov.cn/2019-05/28/c_1124549858.htm.

41. Thank you to Margarita Konaev for discussion and assistance on this point, and see her forthcoming research on policy concerns for the U.S. military. At present, three Chinese companies, the Aviation Industry Corporation of China (AVIC), China North Industries Group Corporation Ltd. (NORINCO), and China Electronics Technology Group (CETC), are ranked among the top 10 largest arms-producing and military services companies globally. See Nan Tian and Fei Su, "Estimating the Arms Sales of Chinese Companies," Stockholm International Peace Research Institute, January 2020, www.sipri.org/sites/default/files/2020-01/sipriinsight2002_1.pdf.

42. On the trajectory of UAV developments at one prominent research institution, see "北航无人机六十年" [Sixty years of Beihang's UAVs], Beihang UAS Technology Co. Ltd., April 29, 2019, www.buaauas.com/news/dynic/159.html.

43. See "SIPRI Arms Transfers Database," Stockholm International Peace Research Institute, www.sipri.org/databases/armstransfers. Notably, 60 percent of medium-altitude long-endurance (MALE) platforms have weapons capabilities; of these, 96 percent include precision and anti-armor strikes. Thanks to Margarita Konaev for highlighting this point. See also Norine MacDonald and George Howell, "Killing Me Softly: Competition in Artificial Intelligence and Unmanned Aerial Vehicles," *PRISM* 8, no. 3 (2020): 103–126, https://ndupress.ndu.edu/Portals/68/Documents/prism/prism_8-3/prism_8-3_MacDonald-Howell_102-126.pdf.

44. For a recent example, see Sophia Yan, "China Sells Armed Drones to Serbia amid Concerns Arms Deal Could Destabilise Region," *The Telegraph*, December 2019, www.telegraph.co.uk/news/2019/09/11/china-sells-armed-drones-serbia-amid-concerns-arms-deal-could/.

45. "等你来战! 空军第二届"无人争锋"挑战赛赛事发布" [Waiting for you to fight! The Air Force's Second "Unmanned Warrior" Challenge Event Released], Air Force News, November 7, 2019, http://kj.81.cn/content/2019-11/07/content_9670776.htm.

46. "访"翼龙"总设计师: 平时工兵战时尖兵" [Interview with chief designer of Pterosaur]; "翼龙Ⅱ无人机首露真容" [Pterodactyl II drone first revealed], *Science Times*, September 30, 2017, http://news.sciencenet.cn/htmlnews/2017/9/390010.shtm; "翼龙"无人机是如何制造的? 听听总设计师怎么说" [How is the "Pterosaur" drone made? Listen to how the chief designer speaks], Southern Network, November 11, 2019, http://kb.southcn.com/content/2019-11/11/content_189485801.htm. For initial developments in Chinese military research institutes and the Chinese defense industry on this front, see "人的使命在于追求完美" [The human mission is to pursue perfection], Xidian University, https://mobile.xidian.edu.cn/info/1439/31879.htm.

47. For initial developments in Chinese military research institutes and the Chinese defense industry on this front, see "人的使命在于追求完美" [The human mission is to pursue perfection].

48. Jeffrey Lin and P. W. Singer, "China Is Converting Old Soviet Tanks into

Autonomous Vehicles," *Popular Science*, June 8, 2018, www.popsci.com/robot
-tanks-china/; 中国无人坦克亮相备受关注" [Chinese unmanned tank debut
attracts much attention], March 20, 2018, https://mil.huanqiu.com/article/9CaKrn
K6ZRn; "中国陆军已列装无人战车"[The Chinese Army has fielded unmanned
combat vehicles that can be operated remotely by a 99A tank], Sina, August 20,
2019, https://mil.news.sina.com.cn/jssd/2019-08-20/doc-ihytcitn0494109.shtml.

49. "Chinese military to procure suicide drones," *Global Times*, March 11, 2020,
www.globaltimes.cn/content/1182330.shtml.

50. For context on another glider, see "科院自主研发"海翼号"水下滑翔机正式
亮相" [Chinese Academy of Sciences' independently developed "Sea Wing" glider
officially unveiled], Xinhua, November 19, 2016, www.xinhuanet.com//tech/2016
-11/19/c_1119946415.htm.

51. "美媒炒作中国"机器鱼"威胁 渲染中美海底竞争"[US media speculates on
"robot fish" threatening undersea competition between China and the United
States], *People's Daily*, July 17, 2018, http://military.people.com.cn/n1/2018/0717/
c1011-30152078.html.

52. For relevant academic literature on these considerations, see Brendan
Rittenhouse Green and Austin Long, "Conceal or Reveal? Managing Clandestine
Military Capabilities in Peacetime Competition," *International Security* 44, no. 3
(2020): 48–83, www.mitpressjournals.org/doi/abs/10.1162/isec_a_00367; Evan
Braden Montgomery, "Signals of Strength: Capability Demonstrations and Perceptions of Military Power," *Journal of Strategic Studies* 43, no. 2 (2020): 309–330, www
.tandfonline.com/doi/abs/10.1080/01402390.2019.1626724?journalCode=fjss20.

53. For reference on military-civil fusion, see "习近平谈军民融合: 关乎国家安
全和发展全局" [Xi Jinping's remarks on military-civil fusion: Regarding the whole
outlook for national security and development], *Qiushi*, October 16, 2018, www.
qstheory.cn/zhuanqu/rdjj/2018-10/16/c_1123565364.htm; Jin Zhuanglong, "开创新
时代军民融合深度发展新局面" [Opening an era of innovation in the deepening
development of military-civil fusion a new era of in-depth development], 求是
[Seeking Truth], July 16, 2018, https://web.archive.org/save/www.xinhuanet.com/
politics/2018-07/16/c_1123133733.htm. The author is the deputy director of the
Office of the Central Committee for the Development of Military-Civil Fusion (中
央军民融合发展委员会办公室).

54. For an authoritative assessment, see Lora Saalman, "China's Integration of
Neural Networks into Hypersonic Glide Vehicles," in *AI, China, Russia, and the
Global Order: Technological, Political, Global, and Creative Perspectives* (Boston:
NSI, January 2019), https://nsiteam.com/ai-china-russia-and-the-global-order
-technological-political-global-and-creative-perspectives/.

55. See, for instance, "天津人工智能军民融合创新中心项目签约仪式在开发
区举行" [The Tianjin Artificial Intelligence Military-Civil Fusion Innovation
Center project signing ceremony was convened in the development zone], Tianjin
Economic-Technological Development Area, February 11, 2018, https://teda.gov.cn
/contents/3976/4407.html. See also "深之蓝与天津（滨海）人工智能军民融合创
新中心签订战略合作协议" [Deep Blue Signs Strategic Cooperation Agreement

with Tianjin (Binhai) Artificial Intelligence Military-Civil Fusion Innovation Center], Tianjin Economic-Technological Development Area, February 22, 2019, www.tedaonline.com/news/memberinfo/2019-02-22/10968.html.

56. For an interview with the director of the laboratory describing its activities, see "当导弹遇上人工智能" [When the missile encounters artificial intelligence], *China Youth Daily*, April 23, 2018, www.xinhuanet.com/mil/2018-04/23/c_129856 863.htm.

57. "三年前的航天人已开始"破局"人工智能" [Aerospace personnel three years ago started to "break into" artificial intelligence], CASIC, May 30, 2018, http://old .sasac.gov.cn/n2588025/n2641616/c8942859/content.html.

58. Ibid.

59. "Nation's Next Generation of Missiles to Be Highly Flexible," *China Daily*, August 19, 2016, www.chinadaily.com.cn/china/2016-08/19/content_26530461. htm. That this information appeared in English seems to indicate this was intended to reach a Western audience.

60. Ibid.

61. For a more detailed and technical assessment, see Lora Saalman, "China's Integration of Neural Networks into Hypersonic Glide Vehicles."

62. Wang Zhaobing and Chang Sheng, "塑造人工智能军事应用的政治属性" [Shaping the political attributes of military applications of artificial intelligence], *Study Times*, November 14, 2018, www.qstheory.cn/defense/2018-11/14/c_11237130 07.htm.

63. "围棋人机大战与军事指挥决策智能化研讨会观点综述" [A summary of the Workshop on the Game between AlphaGo and Lee Sedol and the Intelligentization of Military Command and Decisionmaking], 中国军事科学 [*China Military Science*], April 2016.

64. Heather M. Roff and Richard Moyes, "Meaningful Human Control, Artificial Intelligence and Autonomous Weapons—Briefing Paper for Delegates at the Convention on Certain Conventional Weapons (CCW) Meeting of Experts on Lethal Autonomous Weapons Systems (LAWS)," Article 36, April 2016, www. article36.org/wp-content/uploads/2016/04/MHC-AI-and-AWS-FINAL.pdf; Heather M. Roff and David Danks, "'Trust but Verify': The Difficulty of Trusting Autonomous Weapons Systems," *Journal of Military Ethics* 17, no. 1 (2018): 2–20, www.tandfonline.com/doi/full/10.1080/15027570.2018.1481907.

65. Zhao Xiaozhe, "指挥控制系统中的自然智能和人工智能" [Natural intelligence and artificial intelligence in command and control systems], Sohu, April 23, 2017, http://wemedia.ifeng.com/13425965/wemedia.shtml; "认知域下智能化战争制胜机理" [The winning mechanisms of intelligentized warfare in the cognitive domain], *PLA Daily*, December 24, 2019, https://m.chinanews.com/wap/detail/zw/mil/2019/12-24/9041718.shtml.

66. For one example from this more extensive debate in the literature, see, for instance, Dong Wei and Gao Kai, "智能化战争呼唤指挥智能化" [Intelligentized warfare calls for command intelligentization], Ministry of National Defense,

People's Republic of China, June 26, 2019, www.mod.gov.cn/jmsd/2019-06/26/content_4844369.htm.

67. See Fiona S. Cunningham, "Nuclear Command, Control, and Communications Systems of the People's Republic of China," San Francisco, Technology for Global Security, July 18, 2019, www.tech4gs.org/fiona-s-cunningham.html. See also Elsa B. Kania, *Emerging Technologies, Emerging Challenges—the Potential Employment of New Technologies in Future PLA NC3* (San Francisco: Technology for Global Security, September 5, 2019), www.tech4gs.org/elsa-b-kania-nc3report.html.

68. This topic is beyond the scope of this chapter but will be addressed in the author's ongoing research on these issues. For the PLA's approach to integrating theoretical and technological expertise in its creation of new concepts, see, for instance, "理技融合创新"新春座谈会在京成功召开" ["Theory-Technology Fusion Innovation" New Year Seminar Successfully Convened in Beijing], China Association for Artificial Intelligence, February 9, 2018, https://chaoshao.com/w/CAAI-1981/0.

21

China's Role in the Global Biotechnology Sector and Implications for U.S. Policy

SCOTT MOORE

This chapter assesses the implications of China's growing role in biotechnology for the United States, which span national security, data security, and economic competitiveness. On current trends the United States is likely to remain the world leader in most biotechnology areas. Nonetheless, U.S. policymakers must pursue reforms to ensure that America remains competitive. At the same time, areas like regulation of synthetic biology present important opportunities for Sino-U.S. cooperation.

CHINA'S POLICIES AND ACTIONS IN BIOTECHNOLOGY

The policy framework for biotechnology industry development in China is set by the 13th Five-Year Plan (13th FYP), which covers the period 2016–2020.[1] Ambitious goals include that biotechnology should account for 4 percent of China's GDP by 2020.[2] Chinese policymakers view biotechnology industry development as important not only for future economic development but also for objectives like food security and environmental protection.[3] China's biotechnology policy increasingly prioritizes indigenous capacity-building,[4] transformational research,[5] and the use of protectionist economic policies to support the sector's development.[6] Supplementary guidance to the 13th FYP issued by the State Council on development of "Strategic Emerging Industries" calls for China to "form a group of new internationally competitive biotechnology enterprises and biotech economy clusters." The guidance further calls for new initiatives to support drug creation, especially vaccines and recombinant protein drugs; development of "beneficial biotechnology," such as biotherapeutics and biodegradable materials; and expansion of research-support infrastructure, including gene banks, high-specification research laboratories, and stem cell banks.[7]

These policies have translated into substantial investment. Some estimates claim that collectively, China's central, local, and provincial governments have invested over $100 billion in life sciences research and development over the past decade. In just the two-year period from 2015 to 2017, venture capital and private equity investment in the sector totaled some $45 billion.[8] Annual research and development expenditures by Chinese pharmaceutical firms, the foundation of the biotechnology sector, rose from RMB 39 billion in 2014 (US$5.5 billion) to over RMB 53 billion (US$7.5 billion) by 2017.[9] Even so, by Western standards, some of these figures are still low. Swiss drugmaker Roche, the world leader in biotechnology research and development, spent some $11 billion in 2018 alone.[10]

This investment has produced notable results in certain subsegments of the biotechnology industry. Perhaps the most notable of these is CAR T-cell therapy, a cancer treatment approach that involves modifying T cells. Use of this approach appears to be as or more advanced than in the United States thanks to a combination of lower-cost manufacturing and favorable regulations that classify CAR-T as a medical device rather than a drug, accelerating government approvals.[11] In addition, China's breakneck efforts to produce a vaccine for the COVID-19 virus have resulted in a sharp increase in resources available for its biopharmaceutical subsector, and likely portend growing global competitiveness in this segment of the biotechnology industry.[12] Going forward, areas that promise technological and commercialization breakthroughs like precision medicine, synthetic biotechnology, big data, and biomimetic materials are likely to drive future industry growth and development.[13]

BARRIERS TO FUTURE DEVELOPMENT

China's biotechnology sector possesses several shortcomings when it comes to research, development, and innovation. Chinese official sources are forthcoming about the relative weaknesses of China's biotechnology industry. An official statement regarding the biotechnology provisions of the 13th FYP, for example, conceded that "China lacks original scientific discoveries and disruptive technologies, has a weak research base in areas like biological big data, and lacks independent intellectual property rights" to support advanced drug development.[14] An independent analysis from market consultancy Foresight Industry Research Institute similarly concluded that "the lack of independent innovation capabilities of China's biotechnology sector restricts the sector's development."[15]

These frank assessments of the Chinese biotechnology sector's relatively limited research and development capabilities are moreover reflected in international scientific publication and patent data. A Chinese Academy of Sciences report concluded that while China produced nearly half the world's patent applications in the subsector of industrial biotechnology from 2012 to 2014, the number of overseas patent applications was very low—just 112—suggesting a dearth of breakthrough innovations.[16] Moreover, while the life sciences have been a significant focus of Chinese talent-recruitment schemes like the Thousand Talents (accounting for over 40 percent of the 2018 cohort, according to one estimate), the United States remains, by most measures, the preferred destination for most highly skilled biotechnology researchers.[17]

Apart from innovation capacity, China's biotechnology industry also faces financial constraints. Despite the large capital inflows into the sector, the precommercial state of many biotechnologies and their high-risk, capital-intensive nature restricts financing availability for small- and medium-sized biotech enterprises.[18] As a result, China's biotechnology sector remains some distance from being truly globally competitive. Even the Ministry of Science and Technology concedes that the industry's international "market competitiveness is not strong."[19] Nonetheless, though not presently as advanced as that of the United States or other Western countries, the Chinese market can be counted on to increasingly shape biotechnology research, development, and commercialization. The Chinese state, meanwhile,can be counted on to become a critical player in policy and governance issues related to biotechnology.

POLICY IMPLICATIONS AND RESPONSES

This reality poses several issues for U.S. policymakers. National security issues include growing Chinese military interest in biotechnology applications,[20] concentration of pharmaceutical precursor supply chains in China,[21] and proliferating risks related to bioterrorism.[22] Other concerns include intellectual property theft of biotechnology,[23] biomedical surveillance of vulnerable groups like the Uighur minority,[24] and covert biomedical data collection abroad.[25] Moreover, the fact that Chinese biotechnology firms are likely to have access to larger quantities of such data than their competitors elsewhere given the size of China's population and relatively weak rules governing data collection and sharing creates economic competitiveness concerns,[26] though there are reasons to believe these advantages may be limited.[27] On the other hand, biotechnology holds considerable promise to help address shared global challenges like infectious disease prevention and biodiversity protection.[28]

Potential U.S. policy responses to the growth of China's biotechnology industry generally fall into two categories. The first involves providing greater and more effective support to U.S. biotechnology researchers and firms. Beyond increasing funding, the U.S. government should consider adopting more flexible regulatory provisions in biotechnology subsegments like CAR T-cell therapy where Chinese firms are highly competitive.[29] A second priority for policy support should be human capital enhancement, including maintaining openness to foreign biotechnology talent and new approaches to translational life sciences work that bridge basic research and potential commercial applications.[30]

The second category of policy responses involves cultivating biotechnology as an area for U.S.-China bilateral cooperation. Initially, this might build on existing Track II efforts and take the form of an intergovernmental dialogue on biosafety and biosecurity.[31] The COVID-19 pandemic has underscored the importance of jointly securing the use of gene templates, exotic microbes, and other biological threats and hazards. At the same time, the growing threat of synthetic bioterrorism presents an enormous shared security threat for the United States, China, and other major powers. Cooperation to strengthen biosafety and biosecurity protocols worldwide might open a significant new frontier for U.S.-China cooperation, analogous to cooperation on nuclear security and nonproliferation in previous decades.[32]

ACKNOWLEDGMENTS: The author would like to thank several colleagues at Penn who provided valuable guidance and feedback, especially Mahlet Mesfin, Zeke Emanuel, Steven Joffe, and Amy Gadsden, and two anonymous reviewers whose comments greatly improved this chapter. Ted Reinert edited this chapter.

NOTES

1. Wang Yinghu, "2018年生物技术产业发展趋势分析; 生物科技产业布局初步形成; 技术突破将推动产业进一步变革" [2018 Biotechnology Industry Development Trend Analysis; Bioscience Industry Initial Structure and Layout; technological breakthroughs will promote reform of the sector].

2. "'十三五'生物产业发展规划" [13th Five Year Plan Biotechnology Industry Development Plan], 国务院 [State Council, People's Republic of China], January 12, 2017, www.gov.cn/xinwen/2017-01/12/5159179/files/516df96cc5254eb4976d1470 8e14056f.pdf.

3. See, for example, Dong Jun, "发展生物技术是保障国家粮食安全的战略选择" [Development of biotechnology is a strategic option for ensuring national food security], 新华社 [Xinhua], February 10, 2010, www.gov.cn/jrzg/2010-02/10/content_1532893.htm.

4. Zhou Runjian, "中国采取五项措施推动生物技术研究和产业化发展" [China adopts five measures to promote biotechnology research and industrial development], 新华社 [Xinhua], June 26, 2011, www.gov.cn/jrzg/2011-06/26/content_1893192.htm.

5. Hu Zhe, "科技部: 2020年我国生物技术产业GDP比重将超" [Ministry of Science and Technology: Biotechnology Sector will account for more than 4% of GDP by 2020], 新华社 [Xinhua News Agency], April 28, 2017, available at www.gov.cn/xinwen/2017-04/28/content_5189628.htm .

6. Mark Kazmierczak, Thilo Hanemann, Ryan Ritterson, Daniel Rosen, Danielle Gardner, and Rocco Casagrande, "China's Biotechnology Development: The Role of US and Other Foreign Engagement: A report prepared for the U.S.-China Economic and Security Review Commission," Gryphon Scientific, February 14, 2019, www.uscc.gov/sites/default/files/Research/US-China%20Biotech%20Report.pdf.

7. See "Circular of the State Council on Issuing the National 13th Five-Year Plan for the Development of Strategic Emerging Industries," State Council, People's Republic of China, November 29, 2016, republished in translation by Center for Security and Emerging Technologies, https://cset.georgetown.edu/wp-content/uploads/Circular-of-the-State-Council-on-Issuing-the-National-13th-Five-Year-Plan-for-the-Development-of-Strategic-Emerging-Industries.pdf.

8. Shannon Ellis, "Biotech Booms in China," *Nature*, January 17, 2018, www.nature.com/articles/d41586-018-00542-3.

9. See Tables 20-6 and 20-9, "Annual Data," China National Bureau of Statistics, www.stats.gov.cn/english/statisticaldata/annualdata/.

10. Sasha Mortimer, "Investing into R&D Pays Off for Some of Biotech's Biggest Companies," Biospace, January 2, 2019, www.biospace.com/article/investing-into-r -and-d-pays-off-for-some-of-biotech-s-biggest-companies/.

11. Mark Kazmierczak et al., "China's Biotechnology Development."

12. See Jon Cohen, "Vaccine Designers Take First Shots at COVID-19," *Science* 368, no. 6486 (April 2020): 14–16, https://science.sciencemag.org/content/368/6486 /14.

13. Wang Yinghu, "2018年生物技术产业发展趋势分析；生物科技产业布局初步形成；技术突破将推动产业进一步变革" [2018 Biotechnology Industry Development Trend Analysis].

14. See Hu Zhe, "科技部: 2020年我国生物技术产业GDP比重将超" [Ministry of Science and Technology: Biotechnology sector will account for more than 4% of GDP by 2020].

15. Wang Yinghu, "2018年生物技术产业发展趋势分析；生物科技产业布局初步形成；技术突破将推动产业进一步变革" [2018 Biotechnology Industry Development Trend Analysis].

16. Zhou Runjian, "中国采取五项措施推动生物技术研究和产业化发展" [China adopts five measures to promote biotechnology research and industrial development], 新华社 [Xinhua News Agency], June 26, 2011, available at www.gov .cn/jrzg/2011-06/26/content_1893192.htm.

17. Mark Kazmierczak et al., "China's Biotechnology Development."

18. Wang Yinghu, "2018年生物技术产业发展趋势分析；生物科技产业布局初步形成；技术突破将推动产业进一步变革" [2018 Biotechnology Industry Development Trend Analysis].

19. See Hu Zhe, "科技部: 2020年我国生物技术产业GDP比重将超" [Ministry of Science and Technology: Biotechnology sector will account for more than 4% of GDP by 2020].

20. See Elsa Kania and Wilson Vorndik, "Weaponizing Biotech: How China's Military Is Preparing for a 'New Domain of Warfare,'" Defense One, August 14, 2019, www.defenseone.com/ideas/2019/08/chinas-military-pursuing-biotech/159 167/.

21. Anna Eshoo and Adam Schiff, "China's Grip on Pharmaceutical Drugs Is a National Security Issue," *Washington Post*, September 10, 2019, www.washington post.com/opinions/we-rely-on-china-for-pharmaceutical-drugs-thats-a-security -threat/2019/09/10/5f35e1ce-d3ec-11e9-9343-40db57cf6abd_story.html.

22. See Scott Moore, "China's Biotech Boom Could Transform Lives—Or Destroy Them," *Foreign Policy*, November 8, 2019, https://foreignpolicy.com/2019/ 11/08/cloning-crispr-he-jiankui-china-biotech-boom-could-transform-lives -destroy-them/.

23. Ibid.

24. Sui-Lee Wee, "China Uses DNA to Track Its People, with the Help of American Expertise," *New York Times*, February 21, 2019, www.nytimes.com/2019/02/21/ business/china-xinjiang-uighur-dna-thermo-fisher.html.

25. Mark Kazmierczak et al., "China's Biotechnology Development."

26. Luxia Zhang, Haibo Wang, Quanzheng Li, Ming-Hui Zhao, and Qi-Min Zhan, "Big Data and Medical Research in China," *British Medical Journal* 360 (February 5, 2018), https://doi.org/10.1136/bmj.j5910.

27. Author's personal communications. Author is especially grateful to Mahlet Mesfin, Penn Biden Center for Diplomacy and Global Engagement, for input on this point.

28. Scott Moore, "China's Biotech Boom Could Transform Lives."

29. These proposals echo those made in Mark Kazmierczak et al., "China's Biotechnology Development."

30. This idea is described in "University of Pennsylvania Input to National Security Commission on Artificial Intelligence" (Philadelphia: Perry World House, February 2020), https://global.upenn.edu/perryworldhouse/news/penn-input-national-security-commission-artificial-intelligence.

31. Scott Moore, "China's Biotech Boom Could Transform Lives."

32. Ibid.

REGIONAL INFLUENCE AND STRATEGY

China Now Touches Virtually Every Region in the World—How Is China's Increasing Involvement Impacting South Asia, the Middle East, Latin America, and Elsewhere?

22

China and Latin America

A Pragmatic Embrace

TED PICCONE

Since it burst onto the scene over a decade ago, China's budding relationship with the countries of Latin America and the Caribbean (LAC) has entered a more complicated stage as both sides test the costs and benefits of a tighter embrace. In economic terms, China has risen in the region from a near nonentity in 2000 to a clear heavyweight in terms of trade and investment. China's self-proclaimed "win-win" economic statecraft offers the LAC region an important route to expand its reach into global supply chains, finance new infrastructure and energy systems, and spur greater demand for its natural resources.

As LAC's dependency on China grows, however, tensions and contradictions are mounting, forcing both sides to navigate more troubled domestic and international waters. The United States, in particular, has ramped up a campaign to compete more directly with Beijing on several fronts, including in its hemisphere. The COVID-19 pandemic has further complicated these tensions, as China's quicker economic recovery may give it more flexibility to exploit an increasingly desperate economic situation in the hemisphere.

For Washington, China's expanding influence in its southern neighborhood has presented a substantial dilemma: should it try to match China's new activism by offering improved policies that would tie the region's most important countries to its model of democratic capitalism? Or should the

United States accept China's new role as an important economic partner for the LAC's thirty-two countries and look for other ways to regain influence?

CHINA'S AFFAIR WITH LATIN AMERICA AND THE CARIBBEAN

As part of a wider international strategy, Beijing's leaders began targeting the LAC region in the 2000s as a natural window of opportunity for advancing their global ambitions. China's core interests in the region are straightforward: it seeks primarily to secure the energy, metals, and food inputs it needs to fuel its robust economy and growing middle class, and to expand export markets for its excess capacity in both heavy and retail manufactured goods. Secondarily, it sees the region as a zone of competition with its diplomatic rival, Taiwan (Republic of China), which retains recognition and support from some sympathetic LAC governments.[1] Third, it looks to compete with the United States in its own neighborhood. And finally, Beijing wants to support ideological and other friendly fellow travelers in Venezuela and Cuba. The overarching goal driving these interests is the Chinese Communist Party's obsession with preserving power, reducing poverty, and building a "Chinese dream" of middle-class security.

To advance these core interests, China's top leaders issued a comprehensive LAC policy in 2008, packaged under the banner of peaceful coexistence, mutual respect, South-South solidarity, and protection of national sovereignty, along with huge increases in trade, loans, and investment.[2] Not surprisingly, this approach was well received throughout the region.[3] An updated version of the regional policy, released in November 2016, builds on these themes of "equality, mutual benefit and common development."[4] A new "1+3+6" formula for building closer trade, investment, and financial ties emphasized such priorities as energy, agriculture, infrastructure, and information technology[5] and building new partnerships with political parties, youth, think tanks, and legal experts.

Such a broad range of relationships between communist China and Latin America represents a stunning sea change in the regional landscape, where the United States, with Europe a distant second, was the dominant player for decades. The main driver, however, is economic. It was not so long ago when China was literally absent from economic life in Latin America and the Caribbean. In 2000, China's volume of trade with the region amounted to $12 billion; by 2019, it had reached almost $315 billion.[6] Chinese state policy loans to LAC governments exceeded $140 billion since 2005[7]; prior to 2008, they had never reached $1 billion a year.

While Chinese policy banks have slowed down their investment over the last four years, the overall economic relationship remains strong when taking into account other measures. Chinese greenfield investments, for example, in which Chinese state-owned and private enterprises establish their own commercial entities in the region with greater control over hiring, capital investment, and business strategy, reached a record $12 billion in 2019 alone.[8] Chinese companies have shifted from investing solely in extractive sectors to service and infrastructure as well (e.g., in electricity, internet, railway, and port projects). A growing number of LAC countries have signed up to China's signature Belt and Road Initiative (BRI)[9] and joined the Asian Infrastructure Investment Bank.

Despite some diversification, at the heart of this intensifying relationship is the same traditional model followed by most LAC countries for decades: LAC sells China raw materials like oil, metals, and foodstuffs, while China sells LAC manufactured goods and technical services like engineering and information technology. For this arrangement to prosper, China is shifting more resources toward overcoming Latin America's major transportation challenges and logistics gaps, for example, by underwriting bridges, railroads, ports, and energy-generation projects.[10]

As China has expanded and shifted its economic activities in the region, it has continued to find partners who, for the most part, are eager to diversify their trade and financial dependence away from the United States and the International Monetary Fund. As these countries have struggled to maintain creditworthiness to borrow on international markets, they have been more willing to turn to China, even as Beijing's terms have hardened. Concerns are growing of debt traps in which Chinese banks are extending unsustainable credit to low-income states as a way to gain control of important strategic assets upon default.[11] On the trade front, as cheap Chinese exports flood LAC markets, manufacturers are increasingly complaining that China has not fulfilled its promise to open its own domestic markets to LAC goods and services.[12]

FROM HAPPY HONEYMOON TO BUMPY MARRIAGE

The positive effects of China's amped-up economic activity in the LAC region—booming exports of iron ore from Brazil, soy crops from Argentina, and metals from Chile, and new bridges, tunnels, and football stadiums sprinkled from Dominica to Bolivia—are substantial. Nonetheless, tensions over China's role are growing at different levels of LAC societies. Elites are divided between those who have benefited from the relationship, and those, like Brazilian manufacturers, who have been hit hard by cheap Chinese imports. China's commercial behavior—stipulations to use Chinese companies, labor, or equipment as a condition of financing, and a general lack of transparency—has sparked significant controversies with labor unions, local communities, and environmental movements.

Public opinion is also split: some complain that China's deep pockets have enriched the upper class, further worsening inequality, while others see Beijing as a positive counterweight to the United States. In a recent Pew Research Center poll taken in Brazil, Argentina, and Mexico, favorable views of China easily prevailed over negative views, particularly when it came to the positive effects of Chinese economic growth on their countries, where ratings improved markedly since 2014.[13] Layered through this dynamic is the unmistakable impact of Chinese propaganda, training of journalists and foreign officials, professional and student exchanges and language courses, and use of sophisticated technology to convey a more positive impression of Chinese influence.[14]

Not surprisingly, the outsized role China has assumed in the region's economic development has spilled over into its politics. As candidates on the campaign trail, political leaders such as Jair Bolsonaro of Brazil, Nayib Bukele of El Salvador, and Mauricio Macri of Argentina exploited populist anger and skepticism toward China and promised a tougher approach toward Beijing.[15] Once in power, all three leaders reversed course and found ways to accommodate China and its own domestic powerbrokers.[16] Although the COVID-19 pandemic has scrambled this calculus at the rhetorical level, for example in Brazil,[17] most governments in the region recognize that they cannot climb out of the severe pandemic-induced recession without China's largesse.

When it comes to marshaling a regional or subregional response to China's increasingly assertive diplomacy in the LAC region, there are few signs of any coherent strategy. Over the last decade, the region has largely fragmented along heterodox political lines and no regional hegemon has emerged to unify its parts for or against China. Brazil, Mexico, and Venezuela have largely collapsed as power brokers or turned inward. The Pacific Alliance, a loose grouping of four Latin American democratic states (Chile, Colombia, Mexico, and Peru) committed to more open trading regimes and stronger rules for transparency, labor, and environmental protection, offers some limited promise as a counterweight to China's state-led model, but its influence remains to be seen. The European Union has stepped up its regional activities through a trade accord with Mercosur; diplomatic activism in Venezuela, Colombia, and Cuba; and on a few priority items like climate change. Russia remains a player, mainly on energy and security matters with its closest partners (Venezuela and Cuba), and acts in a complementary if more explicitly anti-U.S. fashion to China. The bottom line, however, is that the strategic field is mainly clear for more direct U.S.-China competition.

IMPLICATIONS FOR THE UNITED STATES

After decades of interventionist and hegemonic behavior in the region, the United States after the Cold War shifted to playing a more benign, pro-reform role, supporting civilian democratic control of once dominant Latin American militaries, opening space for a more diverse civil society, and investing in environmentally friendly development. The Bush administration, after the 9/11 attacks, adopted a more onerous national security and counterterrorism approach to the region but also kept faith with robust funding for development assistance.

The Obama administration, saddled with a major migration crisis from the Northern Triangle, nonetheless made important progress toward a middle course, notably on rapprochement with Cuba and facilitating a major peace agreement in Colombia. This included negotiation of the Trans-Pacific Partnership (TPP), an upgraded trade arrangement incorporating several Latin American countries and designed to rival China's rise in the region. In sum, the United States in late 2016 retained outsized, if declining, influence in what was becoming a more multipolar world.

More recently, comparatively speaking, the state of U.S.-LAC relations looks bleak. After four years of the Trump administration, the United States is practically displaced, largely absent, or has reverted to type as the threatening hegemon, prompting major declines in LAC favorable opinions toward Washington. Trump dramatically reversed course on a host of well-established policies from trade (e.g., withdrawal from TPP) and migration to climate change and development assistance. The administration reclaimed and expanded strong-arm tactics and punitive sanctions against leftist regimes in Venezuela, Bolivia, and Cuba. In the face of China's assertive commercial and soft power diplomacy, these hardball tactics played directly into the hands of Beijing and anti-U.S. constituencies in the LAC region. In the COVID-19 response, China seems to have done a better job in rushing medical supplies to more states in showy displays of solidarity and friendship (except, of course, to countries that still recognize Taiwan).[18]

The Democrats, on the other hand, appear determined to restore or build upon many of the Obama-era policies that most affect the region, including softer treatment of migrants and refugees, support for clean energy, constructive engagement toward Cuba and Venezuela, and new funding for anticorruption, judicial reform, and other rule of law challenges that plague the region.[19] As for taking on China's rise in the region more directly, Joe Biden as candidate laid more blame on Washington than Beijing: "It is the current absence of American leadership in the Western Hemisphere that is the primary threat to U.S. national security. Russia and China can't match our extraordinary ties and common history with the people of Latin America and the Caribbean."[20]

This more pragmatic approach by a future Biden administration to challenging China's rise in the hemisphere implicitly acknowledges that even pro-U.S. governments in the region have come to depend on Beijing for important trade and investment deals. While Washington can help rally private sector engagement and development aid to the region, it is unlikely on its own to match Beijing's level of economic statecraft, with or without a pandemic-induced recession.

That said, the United States does have natural geographic, cultural, familial, security, educational, and historical ties to its neighbors that give it a distinct advantage over China. Now is the time to raise its ambitions with a high-level and comprehensive strategy toward the region. The trick will be to offer positive alternatives to a China-centric political and economic model without cornering LAC governments into an "us or them" proposition. Either way, it will take many years of sustained investment and deft diplomacy to move current trends in favor of the United States.

NOTES

1. Nine of the fifteen governments that still officially recognize Taiwan instead of the People's Republic of China (PRC) are in the LAC region: Belize, Guatemala, Haiti, Honduras, Nicaragua, Paraguay, St. Kitts and Nevis, St. Lucia, and St. Vincent and the Grenadines. Recent converts from Taiwan to the PRC include Panama, Dominican Republic, and El Salvador.

2. China's Policy Paper on Latin America and the Caribbean, USC US-China

Institute, November 5, 2008, https://china.usc.edu/chinas-policy-paper-latin
-america-and-caribbean.

3. Ted Piccone, *The Geopolitics of China's Rise in Latin America* (Washington, DC: The Brookings Institution, November 2016), www.brookings.edu/research/the
-geopolitics-of-chinas-rise-in-latin-america/.

4. "Full text of China's Policy Paper on Latin America and the Caribbean," State Council, People's Republic of China, November 24, 2016, http://english.www.gov.cn
/archive/white_paper/2016/11/24/content_281475499069158.htm

5. According to Chinese state media, the "1" refers to the China-LAC Countries Cooperation Plan 2015–2019 to guide specific cooperation projects. The "3" identi-fies three driving forces for cooperation, namely trade, investment, and finance. The "6" prioritizes six fields of cooperation: energy and resources; infrastructure construction; agriculture; manufacturing; scientific and technological innovation; and information technology. "2nd Ministerial Meeting of China-CELAC Forum Opens Up New Cooperation Areas," Xinhua, January 23, 2018, www.xinhuanet.com/english/2018-01/23/c_136918217.htm.

6. Mark P. Sullivan and Thomas Lum, "China's Engagement with Latin America and the Caribbean," Congressional Research Service, June 1, 2020, https://fas.org/sgp/crs/row/IF10982.pdf.

7. "China-Latin America Finance Database 2019," Boston University Global Development Policy Center, www.bu.edu/gdp/2019/02/21/china-latin-america-fi
nance-database-2019/#:~:text=The%20year%202018%20was%20among,govern
ments%20and%20state%2Downed%20enterprises.

8. Margaret Myers and Kevin P. Gallagher, *Scaling Back: Chinese Development Finance in LAC, 2019* (Washington, DC: Inter-American Dialogue, March 18, 2020), www.thedialogue.org/analysis/scaling-back-chinese-development-finance
-in-lac-2019/.

9. As of 2019, eighteen of thirty-three countries in the region have joined the BRI, although the region's four largest—Brazil, Mexico, Colombia, and Argentina—have not. Pepe Zhang, "Belt and Road in Latin America: A Regional Game Changer?" (Washington, DC: Atlantic Council, October 8, 2019), www.atlantic
council.org/in-depth-research-reports/issue-brief/belt-and-road-in-latin-america
-a-regional-game-changer/.

10. Recent examples include a $2.3 billion investment by China Ocean Shipping Company, a Chinese state-owned enterprise, in a shipping port in Peru; $3.9 billion in construction contracts to build a major highway and modernize railroads in Argentina; and a $3.45 billion deal by China's State Grid Corporation to buy a controlling stake in Brazil's third-largest electric utility. "China Global Investment Tracker," American Enterprise Institute and the Heritage Foundation, www.aei.org
/china-global-investment-tracker/.

11. Nicholas Casey and Clifford Krauss, "It Doesn't Matter If Ecuador Can Afford This Dam. China Still Gets Paid," *New York Times*, December 24, 2018, www
.nytimes.com/2018/12/24/world/americas/ecuador-china-dam.html; Zhang Chun, "Latin America's Oil-Dependent States Struggle to Repay Chinese Debts," *The*

Diplomat, April 15, 2017, https://thediplomat.com/2017/04/latin-americas-oil
-dependent-states-struggle-to-repay-chinese-debts/; "Chinese Bank Loans Cripple
Latin America and Africa, Says NGO," Al Jazeera, February 27, 2020, www.aljazeera
.com/ajimpact/chinese-bank-loans-cripple-latin-america-africa-ngo-2002270408
00972.html?xif=.

12. Anabel Gonzalez, *Latin America-China Trade and Investment amid Global
Tensions* (Washington, DC: Atlantic Council, March 17, 2020), www.atlanticcouncil
.org/in-depth-research-reports/report/latin-america-china-trade-and-investment
-amid-global-tensions/.

13. Laura Silvers and Kat Devlin, "Around the World, More See the US Positively
Than China, but Little Confidence in Trump or Xi," Pew Research Center, January
10, 2020. www.pewresearch.org/fact-tank/2020/01/10/around-the-world-more-see
-the-u-s-positively-than-china-but-little-confidence-in-trump-or-xi/.

14. David Shulman, "Protect the Party: China's Growing Influence in the
Developing World" (Washington, DC: The Brookings Institution, January 22,
2019), www.brookings.edu/articles/protect-the-party-chinas-growing-influence-in
-the-developing-world/.

15. Nelson Renteria, "Responding to El Salvador President-Elect, China Denies
It's Meddling," Reuters, March 14, 2019, www.reuters.com/article/us-el-salvador
-diplomacy-china/responding-to-el-salvador-president-elect-china-denies-it
-meddles-idUSKCN1QV3AI.

16. Nelson Renteria, "China Signs on for 'Gigantic' Investment in El Salvador
Infrastructure," Reuters, December 3, 2019, www.reuters.com/article/us-el-salva
dor-china/china-signs-on-for-gigantic-investment-in-el-salvador-infrastructure
-idUSKBN1Y7266.

17. Oliver Stuenkel, "China's Diplomats Are Going on the Offensive in Brazil,"
Foreign Policy, May 15, 2020, https://foreignpolicy.com/2020/05/15/chinas
-diplomats-are-going-on-the-offensive-in-brazil/.

18. For more details on the distribution of COVID-19 medical relief supplies
and assistance from China and the United States, see "Aid from China and the U.S
. to Latin America amid the COVID-19 Crisis," Wilson Center, www.wilsoncenter
.org/aid-china-and-us-latin-america-amid-covid-19-crisis. Note that countries
that recognize Taiwan instead of the PRC have no recorded assistance from Beijing.

19. For a comparative assessment of rule-of-law performance of twenty-nine
countries from Latin America and the Caribbean, see "World Justice Project Rule
of Law Index 2020," World Justice Project, March 2020, https://worldjusticeproject
.org/our-work/research-and-data/wjp-rule-law-index-2020.

20. "2020 Candidates Answer 10 Questions on Latin America," *Americas
Quarterly*, March 4, 2020, www.americasquarterly.org/article/updated-2020
-candidates-answer-10-questions-on-latin-america/.

23

The Middle East and a Global China

Israel amid U.S.-China Competition

NATAN SACHS
KEVIN HUGGARD

In May 2020, U.S. secretary of state Mike Pompeo flew to Israel. His extraordinary visit—made at the height of the COVID-19 pandemic despite severe restrictions on U.S. travel to Israel—reportedly sought to pressure Prime Minister Benjamin Netanyahu and his cabinet to reject a Chinese bid to run Israel's largest desalination plant.[1] Pompeo succeeded. Not nearly for the first time, the United States had intervened in a major Israeli economic interest to limit Chinese engagement.

American policymakers and experts across much of the political spectrum expect partners around the world to make stark choices between the United States and China should their competition deepen. This leaves Israel to play a difficult balancing act: contending with the rising clout of China and the economic opportunity it provides, while safeguarding its core national security interest in the U.S.-Israeli partnership.

China's presence in the region has broadened and deepened over the last decade, and its regional importance will likely continue to rise. Already, as shown in figure 23-1, China is the largest importer of Middle Eastern energy, with regional commercial and financial ties growing as part of the Belt and Road Initiative.[2] Still, despite its increasing centrality to Middle

Eastern economic affairs and its intensifying diplomatic presence, Beijing hesitates to involve itself in regional security issues. Even if Beijing does not now intend to take on such a role, potential American retrenchment in the region could change its calculations in the long term.

Meanwhile, for many in the United States, the Middle East seems like yesterday's problem. The American public and many policymakers consistently express weariness of U.S. involvement in Middle Eastern affairs, especially military conflicts.[3] This can be overstated at times: The United States does remain heavily involved in the region and few policymakers support simply cutting ties, but its focus is clearly trending elsewhere.

Both major powers would therefore prefer less security involvement in the region, not more, but the broader global competition between them may cause them to try and exploit any fissures they can find. In other words, their global rivalry could draw both the United States and China to greater involvement in Middle Eastern affairs, pursuing local alliances to counter the other's, with each increasing their investments and commitments to counter the other's regional influence.

Such heightened competition would only make U.S. concerns regarding

Figure 23-1. **Chinese Fuel Imports from the MENA Region**

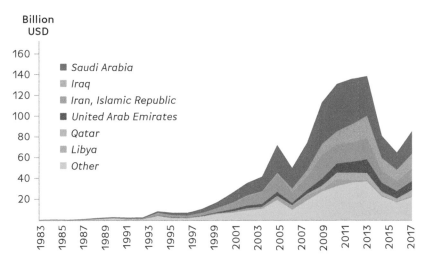

Source: "China Fuel Imports from 1992–2017 by Country and Region," World Integrated Trade Solution, The World Bank, https://wits.worldbank.org/CountryProfile/en/Country/ CHN/StartYear/1992/EndYear/2017/TradeFlow/Import/Indicator/MPRT-TRD-VL/Partner/ ALL/Product/27-27_Fuels#.

Israeli-Chinese arms deals more urgent. In 1999, Israel and China signed a deal for the sale of three Israeli Phalcon early warning aircraft to China. Strenuous U.S. objection led to the canceling of the deal even after a Chinese advance had been paid.[4] Needless to say, the case caused a great deal of strain in Israeli-Chinese relations. In 2004, China sent Israeli-made Harpy unmanned aircraft for upgrades in Israel. The United States demanded that the unmanned aerial vehicles—already Chinese state property—be confiscated. Israel eventually returned the aircraft to China without repair, causing both serious stress between Israel and the United States, and a second crisis between Israel and China.[5]

U.S.-Chinese competition would place significant pressures on the countries of the region, especially those that have traditionally partnered with the United States. Israel would likely find greater pressure placed on its task of managing relations with the United States while seeking to pursue opportunities with China, and greater costs for failure.[6] China's need for the secure flow of Middle Eastern energy means that its primary regional interests lie with parties other than Israel, notably Saudi Arabia and Iran.[7] Even if Beijing does not now intend to take on a more central role in regional security or politics, potential American retrenchment in the region could change its calculations in the long term. From an Israeli perspective, this prospect raises the specter of an external power with influence over regional security affairs that is far less attuned to Israel's core interests than the United States. For Israel, more than for other regional actors, the choice is clear: Beijing cannot replace Washington.

Saudi Arabia's Relations with China

BRUCE RIEDEL

As with most issues concerning the kingdom, Saudi Arabia's relations with China are all about oil. China is Saudi Arabia's top economic trading partner because China is the biggest importer of Saudi oil. There is little strategic cooperation between the two. Saudi Arabia's strategic partner remains the United States, and almost all of its arms supply comes from the United States, the United Kingdom, and other Western states.

Saudi Arabia was a strong opponent of communism in the Cold War and did not have any diplomatic relations with China until the late 1980s. It was a firm supporter of the nationalist government in Taiwan. The impulse to open relations flowed from a clandestine arms deal between the two. In the mid-1980s Saudi Arabia felt threatened from two sources: Iran and Israel. The Saudis were eager to acquire medium-range ballistic missiles to deter both Iran and Israel, but their traditional arms suppliers in the West would not sell them.

Fahd and his defense minister Prince Sultan decided to reach out to China. Sultan turned to two of his sons to open a dialogue with Beijing and then bring and install missiles to the kingdom covertly: Saudi ambassador to the United States Prince Bandar and his brother, who commanded Saudi Arabia's air defense, Prince Khalid. Bandar privately approached his Chinese counterpart in Washington, Han Xu, and asked if Beijing would provide missiles, then Bandar traveled to Pakistan where he met secretly with Chinese officials. In July 1985 Bandar made the first of three secret visits to Beijing to work out the details

The Chinese then sent a secret team to Riyadh to meet with Prince Khalid to engage military to military. The deal was finalized in December 1986; approximately fifty Chinese CSS2 missiles, code named East Wind, would be shipped to Saudi Arabia, installed in hidden in-ground installations, and the Chinese would train Saudi crews to operate them. Khalid made four trips to China to finalize all the details and oversee the transfer. Khalid later wrote that the missiles "[gave] us the capability to counterattack in event of an attack on us by either Israel or Iran."[8]

The Central Intelligence Agency detected the missile base in Saudi Arabia in early 1988, prompting an immediate crisis between Washington and Riyadh. President Reagan wanted the missiles removed immediately, but Fahd refused. The story leaked into the *Washington Post* on March 18, 1988.[9] The Saudis worried that Israel would attack the installation. Bandar asked Colin Powell, Reagan's national security advisor, to assure the Israelis that the missiles were for defensive use only. Powell later recalled that the situation was very tense. Had Israel attacked the missile base, Chinese technicians would have been killed along with Saudis, but Israel demurred under intense pressure from Reagan.

The missile deal led to the opening of diplomatic relations with China after another Bandar trip to Beijing in July 1990. But it did not lead to additional large sales of military equipment.

China has not joined in Saudi Arabia's conflicts with Iran, its regional rival. Saudi Arabia and Iran back hostile proxy forces from Lebanon to Yemen, and China remains a supporter of the Joint Comprehensive Plan of Action, or the Iran nuclear deal. There is no indication that the Saudis have sought to press China to violate the JCPOA as the United States has done.

China rapidly became a major consumer of Saudi oil exports. As trade grew so did Saudi interest in developing high-level dialogue with Beijing. As a reflection of the importance of China for Saudi Arabia, it was a stop on King Abdallah's first trip abroad after he ascended to the throne in 2005. Riyadh was looking east, not west.

The most important recent exchange between Saudi Arabia and China was in February 2019 when the crown prince Muhammad bin Salman visited as part of an Asian tour. It was the crown prince's first big foreign trip since the murder of the Saudi journalist Jamal Khashoggi in Istanbul, Turkey, at the Saudi consulate in October 2018.

The global pandemic and the drop in demand for oil have had serious consequences for the kingdom. The pilgrimage of Muslims to Mecca and Medina has been suspended indefinitely. Oil prices have crashed, and the Saudi economy is in depression. Saudi Arabia has turned to China to purchase 9 million test kits to fight the virus, and 500 Chinese medical experts have come to the kingdom to run six laboratories. Until global demand for oil returns to pre-virus levels, Saudi finances will have to draw down on the kingdom's reserves. Trade with China will go down.

NOTES

1. Itamar Eichner, "China Loses Bid to Run Israel's Biggest Desalination Plant after U.S. Pressure," ynetnews, May 26, 2020, www.ynetnews.com/article/HkBaQN co8.

2. For background regarding the Belt and Road Initiative, see Nadège Rolland, "A Concise Guide to the Belt and Road Initiative," The National Bureau of Asian Research, April 11, 2019, www.nbr.org/publication/a-guide-to-the-belt-and-road -initiative/.

3. Shibley Telhami, "American Attitudes toward the Middle East: A Survey of the Critical Issues Poll" (College Park: The University of Maryland, 2019), https:// criticalissues.umd.edu/sites/criticalissues.umd.edu/files/UMCIP%20Middle%20 East%20PowerPoint.pdf.

4. Lior Kodner, "China Irked at U.S. Interference in Phalcon Deal," *Haaretz*, June 8, 2005, www.haaretz.com/1.4929020.

5. Conal Urquhart, "US Acts over Israeli Arms Sales to China," *The Guardian*, June 12, 2005, www.theguardian.com/world/2005/jun/13/usa.israel.

6. Sheera Efron et al., *The Evolving Israel-China Relationship* (Santa Monica, CA: RAND Corporation, 2019), www.rand.org/pubs/research_reports/RR2641.html.

7. Jeremy Garlick and Radka Havlová, "China's 'Belt and Road' Economic Diplomacy in the Persian Gulf: Strategic Hedging amidst Saudi-Iranian Regional Rivalry," *Journal of Current Chinese Affairs* (January 30, 2020), https://doi.org/10.11 77%2F1868102619898706.

8. Bruce Riedel, *Kings and Presidents Saudi Arabia and the United States since FDR* (Washington, DC: Brookings Institution Press, 2017), 94.

9. John M. Goshko and Don Oberdorfer, "Chinese Sell Saudis Missiles Capable of Covering Mideast," *Washington Post*, March 18, 1988, www.washingtonpost.com/archive/politics/1988/03/18/chinese-sell-saudis-missiles-capable-of-covering-mideast/c9dfdf67-3697-42a8-9164-e0239a0b3154/.

24

Great Expectations

The Unraveling of the Australia-China Relationship

NATASHA KASSAM

In November 2014, China's president Xi Jinping told the Australian Parliament: "It is the steady streams of mutual understanding and friendship between our two peoples that have created the vast ocean of goodwill between China and Australia. I am greatly heartened by the immense support for China-Australia relations in both countries."[1]

In 2021, these words are almost impossible to believe: China's leader on a state visit to Australia, announcing the conclusion of a free trade agreement and elevation of the relationship to a comprehensive strategic partnership.[2] Canberra's streets were lined with twirling dancers and students waving Chinese flags. Yet, amid the pomp and ceremony, signs of deep-seated structural tensions were already on display: flag wavers obscured a Falun Gong protest from view,[3] and it was later alleged that the student supporters had been bussed in by the Chinese Embassy.[4]

Seven years later, those tensions now define the relationship. Since Australia called for an independent inquiry into the origins of COVID-19 prior to the World Health Assembly in May, the bilateral relationship has been in a downward spiral.[5]

China's Foreign Ministry spokesperson is detailing the many risks of racist attacks against Chinese people if they travel to Australia.[6] Australia is spiriting journalists at risk of detention out of China and warning its citizens of the risk of arbitrary detention in China.[7] An Australian journalist, Cheng Lei, working for state broadcaster CGTN, has been arrested on national security grounds. China has banned exports from a number of Australian beef facilities, started investigating wine exports, and placed a dramatic 80 percent tariff on Australian barley after an eighteen-month-long anti-dumping investigation.[8]

Why have political and trade tensions between Australia and China escalated so quickly? How is Australia responding? And why should the rest of the world care about the state of play between Australia and China?

"THE AUSTRALIAN PEOPLE STAND UP"

"There has been foreign interference in Australian politics," said then prime minister Malcolm Turnbull in December 2017, "and so we say—the Australian people stand up."[9] New legislation was introduced, in part as a response to a nationwide scandal in which it was discovered that an Australian senator had warned a Chinese political donor and businessman that he may have been under surveillance.[10] Months later, Australia announced that it would exclude Huawei from the development of its 5G network—one of the first countries in the world to do so.[11]

Australia quickly found itself in the diplomatic freezer. High-level visits were paused, state media lashed out, and ministerial exchanges were deferred.[12] The deterioration in bilateral relations seemed hugely consequential for Australia's national interests: not only is China Australia's largest trading partner, it is also a major player in almost every issue of Australian foreign policy. But while Beijing's ire affected ministerial and official contact, the political friction had little discernible effect on two-way trade: in the same period, Australian exports to China grew by 26 percent.[13]

Beijing has expressed dissatisfaction with Australia's behavior before—when it has spoken out about the South China Sea,[14] or allowed Uighur dissidents to travel to Australia.[15] But the situation in 2021 is unprecedented in terms of the breadth of economic measures, real and threatened, as well as Beijing's seeming lack of concern about both the economic costs and the political fallout of its behavior.

WHY AUSTRALIA, AND WHY NOW?

China has long sought to divide and isolate U.S. allies—and in Beijing's eyes, Australia's identity has always been defined by its relationship with the United States. What has changed of late is twofold: China is increasingly assertive in achieving its goals, and, contrary to Beijing's intent, Australia has become increasingly assertive in pushing back. The clash of China's expanding interests and Australia's unwillingness to defer illustrates the structural challenge for Australia that will characterize future relations with the People's Republic of China.

Even as Australia has distanced itself from White House conspiracy theories about the origin of the virus,[16] China continues to view Australia as loyal and deferential to the United States. Beijing's official statements will often refer to Australia "dancing to the tune of a certain country,"[17] and state media goes so far as to describe Australia as "a close collaborator of the U.S. in its anti-China strategy at the expense of China-Australia relations."[18]

Beijing does see Australia as a force multiplier for the United States in the western Pacific, with an unhelpful interest in the sea lines of communication and the South China Sea.[19] And Australia also forms an important element of the U.S. alliance networks in East Asia, including through U.S. Marines stationed in Darwin.[20] As such, Beijing has looked for opportunities to pry Australia away from the embrace of the United States.

To the contrary, successive governments in Canberra have taken a series of policy decisions that the Chinese Communist Party (CCP) leadership has interpreted as directly challenging the critical interests of not just their country but also their party. Previous examples of China leveraging economic coercion have generally focused on Taiwan, Tibet, and maritime sovereignty.[21] But recent treatment of Australia and other countries points to an expanding remit of interests over which China is willing to coerce, even at a cost to itself. Early estimates suggest that China's barley tariffs on Australia will cost Australian farmers AUD 330 million, but as much as AUD 3.6 billion for China.[22]

Many in Australia thought that the level of interdependence between the economies of Australia and China would insulate Australia from the kind of economic coercion that other countries have experienced.[23] While China purchases over a third of Australia's exports, more than 70 percent are resource commodities. These are vital inputs for China's steel, construction, and other industrial sectors, which are still central to its economy (and employment), especially so in recovering from COVID-19. Australia supplies over 60 percent of China's iron ore imports, almost half its liquefied natural gas imports, and around 40 percent of its coal imports.[24] Half of Australia's goods exports to China are of iron ore, for which it is especially difficult to find sizable alternative sources of supply.[25]

This interdependence was always seen as in Australia's favor, and likely to deter forcible decoupling from either side. But recent behavior suggests that China sees such interdependence as a vulnerability, as it does with the United States.[26]

The current raft of economic and political sanctions is an example of the CCP testing Australia's resolve. Beijing may hope to force deference from Canberra through fear, but even in the absence of capitulation on specific decisions, China has a history of using economic punishments to teach wayward partners a lesson and defend both the Chinese system and the pride of the Chinese people. For example, Seoul did not reverse its decision to deploy the Terminal High Altitude Area Defense (THAAD) U.S. antimissile system, despite the campaign of coercive measures against South Korean economic interests. But it is possible that China hopes this response will encourage policymakers to think twice about future decisions that could similarly antagonize China.[27]

Even where Beijing realizes that it cannot or will not change decisions of the Australian government, this behavior could prompt preemptive deference from other capitals through the painful Australian experience. Rather than attempt to change Australia's mind about Huawei and 5G, Beijing sought to isolate Australia in the decision, and telegraph to the United Kingdom and Germany, among others, that there would be consequences for making similar decisions.[28]

THE AUSTRALIAN DEBATE

In many eyes, China's efforts in Australia have backfired. Australia has not retreated in the face of Beijing's ire. If anything, the bullying tactics have hardened attitudes. The growing public awareness of China's willingness to use economic coercion has created a powerful imperative in Australia—on both the left and right ends of the political spectrum as well as among the public and business leaders alike.[29] The great unraveling coincides with a grim appreciation in the minds of the Australian public of the true nature of the Leninist party-state that rules China.

Trust in China has halved in the past two years, according to successive Lowy Institute polls. Only 23 percent of Australians now trust China to act responsibly in the world. One in five say they have confidence in President Xi Jinping to do the right thing regarding world affairs, a 21-point fall from 2018. And an overwhelming 94 percent of Australians say the government should find other markets to reduce Australia's economic dependence on China.[30] Criticism of Beijing from business leaders that just a few months ago were calling for calm diplomacy are testament to the shifting winds.[31] Backbenchers on both sides of politics are regularly critical of China's behavior in public.[32]

The calls to discuss so-called sensitive issues with Beijing on Beijing's terms are falling silent.[33] A public souring on China will no longer accept discussions behind closed doors, and especially when Australian citizens like Yang Hengjun remain detained for no particular reason or others are sentenced to death,[34] Canberra can no longer remain quiet. Beijing's behavior has made Australian politics more resilient to its criticism and given strength to the most hawkish voices. In Australia now, the idea of meeting China halfway, or trying to improve the relationship, is seen as a version of acquiescence or compliance.

Having said that, despite China's view of Australia as a loyal U.S. ally, Australians are not necessarily turning toward the United States. The presidency of Donald Trump has shaken some Australians' belief about the future of the United States.[35] And Australia is not necessarily waiting for the United States to reclaim its position as the leader of the rules-based order. Without ignoring the importance of Australia's alliance with the United States, Australia's Defence Strategic Update 2020 places a renewed emphasis on Australia's need to develop independent capabilities, as well as partnerships with other countries, including Japan, India, and Indonesia.[36]

SO WHY DOES IT MATTER?

Although Australia looks like a strategic target for Beijing's ire, it is hardly an outlier. China is a rising power with expanding interests that will increasingly clash with others. As internal pressures place the CCP leadership under growing strain, more disputes will arise with more countries.

Australia may be unique as a Five Eyes member with a particularly high level of economic interdependence with China.[37] And it may be seen by Beijing as a necessary target given Canberra's willingness to play a critical role in supporting the U.S.-led alliance system and leading the global charge on scrutiny of Beijing's interference in the affairs of other countries.

But the struggles facing Canberra are structural and cannot be fixed simply with better diplomacy.[38] More countries in the region will find that Beijing's strategic and territorial goals are mutually exclusive with their own interests. Whether seizing disputed tracts of territory on China's borders, snuffing out Taiwan's liberal democracy, or achieving military overmatch against the United States and its allies and partners on the East Asian littoral, Beijing's goals are an existential challenge to the status quo.

Where once China had neither the means nor the inclination to achieve its goals, China has now emerged as a great economic and military power. Perhaps unsurprisingly, Beijing's policy planners are keen to use the full spectrum of state power to get on with the unfinished business of China's statecraft. Australia has felt the rough touch of this coercion of late. And perhaps Australia's resilience in the face of this pressure is an opportunity to demonstrate regional leadership.

But it is neither an aberration nor a discomfort that only close U.S. alliance partners and bold critics of China's foreign interference will feel. In the coming years, any state that makes policy choices adverse to what Beijing judges are in its interest risks taking blows from China's coercive statecraft. This pain can be avoided, but only at the cost of deference to Beijing's goals.

Hard questions will be asked in national capitals across the region, not just in Canberra. Beijing is testing Australia, with different sources of leverage. The long arm of the CCP is reaching even farther. More tests, for more countries, are coming in the future.

NOTES

1. Xi Jinping, "Address to the Parliament of Australia" (speech, Australian Parliament, November 17, 2014), https://parlinfo.aph.gov.au/parlInfo/search/display/display.w3p;query=Id%3A%22chamber%2Fhansardr%2F35c9c2cf-9347-4a82-be89-20df5f76529b%2F0005%22;src1=sm1.

2. Xinhua, "Feature: Chinese President Wins Hearts, Minds in Australia," *People's Daily*, November 25, 2014, http://en.people.cn/n/2014/1125/c90883-8813852.html.

3. Megan Gorrey, "Chinese Protestors Mix with Supporters as President Xi Jinping Visits Parliament House," *Canberra Times*, November 17, 2014, www.canberratimes.com.au/story/6075732/chinese-protesters-mix-with-supporters-as-president-xi-jinping-visits-parliament-house/digital-subscription/#gsc.tab=0.

4. Nick McKenzie and Sarah Ferguson, "Power and Influence," ABC, June 5, 2017, www.abc.net.au/4corners/power-and-influence-promo/8579844.

5. Stephen Dziedzic, "Australia Started a Fight with China over an Investigation into COVID-19—Did It Go Too Hard?" ABC, May 20, 2020, www.abc.net.au/news /2020-05-20/wha-passes-coronavirus-investigation-australia-what-cost/12265896.

6. Hua Chunying, "Regular Press Conference" (press conference, China, June 8, 2020), www.fmprc.gov.cn/mfa_eng/xwfw_665399/s2510_665401/2511_665403/ t1787042.shtml.

7. Matthew Doran and Stephen Dziedzic, "Australian Correspondents Bill Birtles and Mike Smith Pulled Out of China after Five-Day Diplomatic Standoff over National Security Case," ABC, September 8, 2020, www.abc.net.au/news/2020-09 -08/bill-birtles-mike-smith-evacuated-china-safety-concerns/12638786.

8. Bill Birtles and staff, "China denies Australian minister's request to talk about barley amid coronavirus investigation tension," ABC, May 17, 2020, www.abc.net. au/news/2020-05-18/coronavirus-trade-troubles-david-littleproud-china-call/ 12258274.www

9. Caitlyn Gribbin, "Malcolm Turnbull Declares He Will 'Stand Up' for Australia in Response to China's Criticism," ABC, December 9, 2017, www.abc.net.au/news/ 2017-12-09/malcolm-turnbull-says-he-will-stand-up-for-australia/9243274.

10. Nick McKenzie, James Massola, and Richard Baker, "Labor Senator Sam Dastyari Warned Wealthy Chinese Donor Huang Xiangmo His Phone Was Bugged," *Sydney Morning Herald*, November 29, 2017, www.smh.com.au/politics/ federal/labor-senator-sam-dastyari-warned-wealthy-chinese-donor-huang -xiangmo-his-phone-was-bugged-20171128-gzu14c.html.

11. The Hon. Scott Morrison MP and Senator the Hon. Mitch Fifeld, "Government Provides 5G Security Guidance to Australian Carriers," August 23, 2018, https://parlinfo.aph.gov.au/parlInfo/search/display/display.w3p;query=Id:%22 media/pressrel/6164495%22.

12. Kirsty Needham, "Chinese Media Calls for Turnbull Visit to Be Called Off," *Sydney Morning Herald,* May 23, 2018, www.smh.com.au/world/asia/chinese -media-calls-for-turnbull-visit-to-be-called-off-20180523-p4zgzb.html.

13. "China Fact Sheet," Australian Department of Foreign Affairs and Trade, August 2019, www.dfat.gov.au/sites/default/files/chin-cef.pdf.

14. John Kehoe, "Why Australia and Julie Bishop Are in Beijing's Crosshairs," *Australian Financial Review*, May 28, 2018, www.afr.com/opinion/why-australia -and-julie-bishop-are-in-beijings-crosshairs-20180527-h10l7p.

15. Rowan Callick and Michael Sainsbury, "Uighur Rebiya Kadeer Gets Visa Despite China Protest," News.com.au, August 16, 2009, www.news.com.au/news/ uighur-rebiya-kadeer-gets-visa-despite-china-protest/news-story/e794d66a5e532d 57400d0018f8f76170?sv=7aeab0df742b38b80777bf9fb11a6785.

16. Stephen Dziedzic, "Scott Morrison distances himself from Donald Trump's claim coronavirus started in a Wuhan lab," ABC, May 1, 2020, www.abc.net.au/ news/2020-05-01/scott-morrison-donald-trump-coronavirus-wuhan-lab-claim/ 12207322.

17. "Chinese Foreign Ministry Spokesperson's Remarks," Embassy of the People's Republic of China in the Commonwealth of Australia, April 20, 2020, www.fmprc.gov.cn/mfa_eng/xwfw_665399/s2510_665401/2511_665403/t1771576.shtml .

18. Zhang Han, "China's Travel Warning a Result of Australian Animosity, Rocky Bilateral Ties," *Global Times*, June 7, 2020, www.globaltimes.cn/content/1190827.shtml.

19. Lu Kang, "Foreign Ministry Spokesperson Lu Kang's Regular Press Conference on November 23, 2017" (press conference, November 23, 2017), www.fmprc.gov.cn/mfa_eng/xwfw_665399/s2510_665401/2511_665403/t1513437.shtml.

20. Tom Westbrook, "U.S. Marines Arrive in Darwin for Australia, China Exercises," Reuters, April 18, 2017, www.reuters.com/article/us-australia-usa-defence-idUSKBN17K09N.

21. Peter Harrell, Elizabeth Rosenberg, and Edoardo Saravalle, *China's Use of Coercive Economic Measures* (Washington, DC: Center for a New American Security, June 11, 2018), www.cnas.org/publications/reports/chinas-use-of-coercive-economic-measures.

22. Andrew Tillett, "Barley Backfire: Tariffs to Cost China $3.6b, Birmingham Reveals," *Australian Financial Review*, June 7, 2020, www.afr.com/politics/federal/barley-backfire-tariffs-to-cost-china-3-6b-birmingham-reveals-20200617-p553ej.

23. Richard McGregor, "China Dependence," *Australian Foreign Affairs*, October 2019, www.australianforeignaffairs.com/essay/2019/10/china-dependence.

24. "China Fact Sheet," Australian Department of Foreign Affairs and Trade.

25. Natasha Kassam, Richard McGregor, and Roland Rajah, "Changing Australia's Conversation about Chinese Economic Coercion," Lowy Institute, June 30, 2020, https://interactives.lowyinstitute.org/features/covid-recovery/issues/china/; Darren Lim and Victor Ferguson, "China's 'Boycott Diplomacy' over Calls for Coronavirus Inquiry Could Harm Australian Exporters," ABC, April 29, 2020, www.abc.net.au/news/2020-04-29/china-boycott-diplomacy--coronavirus-comes-more-government/12194482.

26. Julian Gewirtz, "The Chinese Reassessment of Interdependence," China Leadership Monitor, June 1, 2020, www.prcleader.org/gewirtz.

27. Darren Lim and Victor Ferguson, "Chinese Economic Coercion during the THAAD Dispute," The Asan Forum, December 28, 2019, www.theasanforum.org/chinese-economic-coercion-during-the-thaad-dispute/,

28. Li Qingqing, "Australia to Pay for 5G Restrictions on Huawei", *Global Times*, 15 April 2019, www.globaltimes.cn/content/1146018.shtml; Li Xuanmin, "China Will Not Sit Idle if Huawei Is Excluded from Germany's 5G Rollout," *Global Times*, January 5, 2020, www.globaltimes.cn/content/1175723.shtml.

29. Elizabeth Rosenberg, Peter Harrell, and Ashley Feng, *A New Arsenal for Competition* (Washington, DC: Center for a New American Security, April 24, 2020), www.cnas.org/publications/reports/a-new-arsenal-for-competition.

30. Natasha Kassam, *Lowy Institute Poll 2020* (Sydney: Lowy Institute, June 24, 2020), https://poll.lowyinstitute.org/report.

31. Alexander Downer, "China Must Be Held to Account for Unleashing a Global Catastrophe," *Australian Financial Review*, April 19, 2020, www.afr.com/policy/foreign-affairs/china-must-be-held-to-account-for-unleashing-a-global-catastrophe-20200419-p54l3o; Geoff Raby, "Why the Bell Must Toll for WHO Chief Tedros," Australian Financial Review, April 17, 2020, www.afr.com/policy/foreign-affairs/why-the-bell-must-toll-for-who-chief-tedros-20200417-p54kpe.

32. Ben Packham, "Andrew Hastie, Kimberley Kitching to Co-chair New Inter-Parliamentary Alliance on China," *The Australian*, June 5, 2020, www.theaustralian.com.au/nation/politics/andrew-hastie-kimberley-kitching-to-cochair-new-inter parliamentary-alliance-on-china/news-story/cb0fc2a277fa3059a0f791e02f67b1af.

33. John Power, "As China Tensions Mount, Australia's Dovish Voices Calling for Engagement Are Fading Away," *South China Morning Post*, June 12, 2020, www.scmp.com/week-asia/politics/article/3088611/china-tensions-mount-australias-dovish-voices-calling-engagement.

34. Will Glasgow, "Australian Drug Smuggler Sentenced to Death in China," *The Australian*, June 17, 2020, www.theaustralian.com.au/nation/australian-drug-smuggler-sentenced-to-death-in-china-report/news-story/00349f30dbd82e8091bc531a2af11424.

35. Daniel Flitton, "Australia: Is the United States Still a Reliable Ally?" Council on Foreign Relations, May 11, 2020, www.cfr.org/blog/australia-united-states-still-reliable-ally.

36. James Goldrick, "Defence Strategic Update 2020: A First Assessment," Lowy Institute, July 2, 2020, www.lowyinstitute.org/the-interpreter/defence-strategic-update-2020-first-assessment.

37. "Asia Power Index 2019," Lowy Institute, May 29, 2019, https://power.lowyinstitute.org/.

38. Natasha Kassam and Darren Lim, "Australia Can Expect China to Lash Out More Often," *The Guardian*, June 10, 2020, www.theguardian.com/commentisfree/2020/jun/10/australia-can-expect-china-to-lash-out-more-often-we-must-foster-resilience-and-sangfroid.

25

The Risks of China's Ambitions in the South Pacific

JONATHAN PRYKE

This century China has been steadily building its influence in the South Pacific. The intensity and scale has set off alarm bells and led many analysts in the West to ask what China's ambitions are in the South Pacific, and what risks they might create.

THE STRATEGIC SIGNIFICANCE OF THE PACIFIC ISLANDS

The South Pacific is known for its pristine beaches, geographic and cultural diversity, and unique development challenges. With a cumulative population of under 13 million people, these fourteen sovereign nations and seven territories span over 15 percent of the world's surface.

The dual tyrannies of small size and remoteness make conventional economic pathways in most of these countries nearly impossible. South Pacific nations are also among the most exposed to natural disasters in the world,[1] a threat being further exacerbated by climate change. All these factors, along with some of the highest population growth rates in the world, combine to make the Pacific one of the most fragile regions in the world, and the most aid dependent.[2]

The geostrategic significance of these islands is clear. In World War II, control over them was critical, both for maintaining logistical supply lines and for military force projection. Since the war, the Pacific has largely enjoyed a benign status on the geopolitical stage.

CHINA'S GROWING FOOTPRINT

China has always had a presence in the South Pacific. Ethnic Chinese have resided in the region for centuries, running some of the regions oldest trading houses. The China-Taiwan rivalry for diplomatic allies in the region has seen some degree of jockeying through briefcase diplomacy in the region for decades.

Since 2006 China's trade, aid, diplomatic, and commercial activity in the Pacific region has been steadily and significantly scaling up. Excluding Papua New Guinea, two-way trade with China has overtaken that of Australia since 2013.[3] For the Solomon Islands, two-way trade with China now makes up 46 percent of all trade.[4]

China has also dramatically scaled up its aid activities. According to Lowy Institute research, between 2006 and 2017 China provided close to US$1.5 billion in foreign aid to the Pacific Islands region through a mixture of grants and loans.[5] As of 2017, China was the third-largest donor to the Pacific, contributing 8 percent of all foreign aid to the region between 2011 and 2017.[6] While China is by no means the dominant donor in the Pacific, the way in which it delivers its aid—large infrastructure projects funded by concessional loans—makes these projects stand out. Chinese lending has also been used as a vehicle to get into the region Chinese state-owned enterprises that are now competing in commercial activity across the board. According to China's own investment statistics, Chinese construction activity in the region was $958 million in 2017, almost six times greater than its foreign aid activities.[7]

RISKS OF CHINA'S RISE

So why does all of this matter? You could argue that this is a good thing for the Pacific, a region facing significant development challenges. China gives them options, and in turn greater influence over, and attention from, traditional development partners who have often treated them with benign neglect.

There is no depth of scholarly Chinese works on the Pacific Islands region, nor does it factor heavily in official statements, speeches, or strategic documents from Beijing. While this may be illustrative on where the Pacific sits in China's strategic priorities, it creates a great deal of ambiguity around how China plans to wield its newfound influence in the Pacific region.

Whatever the ambition of China may be in the region, opinions have crystallized for analysts in Canberra and other like-minded countries that China's growing footprint and influence in the Pacific presents two serious risks to their national interest.

The first risk, which has a low probability of occurring but would have profound impact, is that China is trying to use its leverage through diplomacy, debt, trade, or elite capture to establish a military base somewhere in the South Pacific.

This is a high-impact risk because such a development would completely change the way Australia looks at its national defense and security settings. Australia's armed forces are built to complement and plug in to U.S.-led coalitions. A Chinese military base as little as 2,000 kilometers (1,243 miles) from Australia's eastern coast would force a wedge between Australia and its traditional strategic anchor, the United States. While the strategic benefit and size of such a facility for China are questionable—the logistics of maintaining supply routes alone would be challenging—it would have a profound psychological impact on Australia. It would accelerate a military buildup, confirm all the most extreme prejudice around China's strategic intent in the region, and force Australia to "go it alone." Some analysts argue that Australia should be doing this anyway.[8] A Chinese base or outpost of only moderate size would rapidly accelerate this discussion.

There is, however, a low probability that this would occur. Pacific governments are not simply pawns sitting between Australia and China. They are fiercely protective of their sovereignty, have agency that they wield liberally, and have no interest in a further militarized region. While they may be willing to align themselves with China in certain United Nations votes, it is a long stretch to handing over a military base or outpost that would so rapidly undermine the sovereignty that they so viscerally protect. The West is also now paying attention. Australia, in particular, is forcing China to be more than just opportunistic in their ambitions because of the scaling up of its own efforts—both in money and in attention—devoted to the South Pacific.

Despite these factors, because of the acute vulnerability and size of these nations, and the potentially large strategic benefits to China for relatively minimal potential investments, this is not a risk to be taken lightly. There have been a number of recent incidences that have fueled anxiety on the prospects of a Chinese military base. The prospects of a Chinese-financed major wharf on Vanuatu's larger but less populated Santo Island being converted into a "dual use" facility were shot down by China and Vanuatu after plans were leaked to the press. Australia and the United States quickly partnered with Papua New Guinea to rehabilitate naval facilities on Manus Island to enhance illegal fishing enforcement operations and also to prevent China getting a foothold on the island. A mooted leasing of the entire island of Tulagi in the Solomon Islands—ridiculous to anyone with a basic understanding of landowner rights in the Solomon Islands—caught global attention. Examples like these are likely to arise with increasing frequency in the years to come.

The second risk, which is of a lower impact but has a higher probability of occurring, is that China and Chinese businesses, through elite capture and corruption, are rapidly undermining institutions of governance, which Western donors spend considerable money trying to support. This has become so acute in recent years that one of these nations may be pushed toward a scenario of state failure.

This is a lower-impact risk for Australia, which aspires to be "partner of choice" for the Pacific in all areas. Australia would be at the forefront of any intervention to restore stability. This would be a costly exercise, particularly in one of the larger Pacific nations, but it would not fundamentally shift Australia's security settings. Australia has intervened in the region before, in Timor-Leste in 1999 and again in the Solomon Islands in 2003, and will do so again if called upon.

This risk has a higher probability of occurring, particularly in light of the economic devastation facing the region as a result of COVID-19. While China did not introduce corruption into the Pacific, it is contributing to entrenching systems of corruption and patronage in the Pacific, particularly in Melanesia.

For Australia and other traditional partners in the Pacific, the stakes of China's potential ambitions in the South Pacific are significant. The opportunity, if it ever truly existed, to keep China out of the region has long passed. Greater and more consistent resolve from the West will be necessary to mitigate these risks.

China has, however, found it harder to maintain its momentum in the South Pacific as it becomes a more familiar development partner to Pacific governments, and as traditional partners have started stepping up their own engagement in response. Chinese debt in particular is being further scrutinized by Pacific leaders. This has been driven by a number of factors, including a recognition of subpar quality and inflated pricing, access to cheaper financing options, a desire for greater spillover benefits from infrastructure projects, limited debt space remaining in a number of Pacific countries, and a desire for budget support not project earmarked lending.[9]

Australia has also worked hard in revitalizing its self-proclaimed leadership position in the Pacific. The Australian government is the biggest donor with the largest diplomatic footprint in the region. The Australian market is one of the largest investors and sources of tourism for the region. The government is leveraging these significant advantages with even more diplomats and aid, and more political attention.

Finding it more difficult to build its influence in the countries in the Pacific it retains relations with, China instead focused its attention in 2019 on broadening the playing field. In the same week in September 2019 both the Solomon Islands, the third most populous Pacific nation, and Kiribati, an atoll nation with an exclusive economic zone the width of Australia, swapped their diplomatic recognition from Taipei to Beijing.

THE POST-COVID-19 LANDSCAPE

This year, COVID-19 introduces a completely new challenge for China, already facing greater headwinds in the Pacific. Facing a potential 10 percent economic contraction this year, the needs of the Pacific will be far greater. While China has been opportunistic in supporting the Pacific in responding to COVID-19,[10] its support pales in comparison to that provided by traditional partners.[11] The pandemic has reminded the region of its economic reliance on Australia and New Zealand, in particular for tourism-dependent economies. A mooted travel bubble between Australia, New Zealand, and the Pacific will be a critical economic lifeline for the region.

China has rapidly built its profile and influence in the South Pacific. While the COVID-19 pandemic does provide China an opportunity to further grow its influence in the Pacific, the cost will be much higher. Greater resolve from the West, greater awareness within the Pacific, and growing financial demands at home and abroad may all make the price of China's aspiring influence in the Pacific too high for the country to bear. The year ahead will reveal just how much further China is willing to go and how much it is willing to spend to build its influence in the South Pacific.

NOTES

1. Dongyeol Lee, Huan Zhang, and Chau Nguyen, "The Economic Impact of Natural Disasters in Pacific Island Countries: Adaptation and Preparedness" (Washington, DC: International Monetary Fund, May 10, 2018),www.imf.org/en/Publications/WP/Issues/2018/05/10/The-Economic-Impact-of-Natural-Disasters-in-Pacific-Island-Countries-Adaptation-and-45826.

2. Matthew Dornan and Jonathan Pryke, "Foreign Aid to the Pacific: Trends and Developments in the Twenty-First Century," *Asia and the Pacific Policy Studies* 4, no. 3 (March 25, 2017): 386–404, https://apo.org.au/sites/default/files/resource-files/2017-05/apo-nid189541.pdf.

3. Matthew Dornan and Sachini Muller, "The China Shift in Pacific Trade," *Devpolicy Blog*, November 15, 2018, https://devpolicy.org/china-in-the-pacific-australias-trade-challenge-20181115/.

4. "Direction of Trade Statistics," International Monetary Fund, https://data.imf.org/?sk=9D6028D4-F14A-464C-A2F2-59B2CD424B85.

5. "Pacific Aid Map," Lowy Institute, https://pacificaidmap.lowyinstitute.org/.

6. Ibid.

7. "Statistic—Monthly FDI Absorption," Ministry of Commerce, People's Republic of China, http://english.mofcom.gov.cn/statistic/charts.shtml.

8. Hugh White, "Our Sphere of Influence: Rivalry in the Pacific," *Australian Foreign Affairs*, July 2019, www.australianforeignaffairs.com/essay/2019/07/our-sphere-of-influence.

9. Roland Rajah, Alexandre Dayant, and Jonathan Pryke, "Ocean of Debt? Belt and Road and Debt Diplomacy in the Pacific," Lowy Institute, October 21, 2019, www.lowyinstitute.org/publications/ocean-debt-belt-and-road-and-debt-diplomacy-pacific.

10. Denghua Zhang, "China's COVID-19 Pacific Diplomacy," *Devpolicy Blog*, May 27, 2020, https://devpolicy.org/chinas-coronavirus-covid-19-diplomacy-in-the-pacific-20200527-1/.

11. Alexandre Dayant and Roland Rajah, "Aiding the Pacific during Covid—a Stock-Take and Further Steps," Lowy Institute, June 4, 2020, www.lowyinstitute.org/the-interpreter/aiding-pacific-during-covid-stock-take-and-further-steps.

26

China, the Gray Zone, and Contingency Planning at the Department of Defense and Beyond

MICHAEL O'HANLON

The 2018 National Defense Strategy restored great power competition to the top tier of U.S. defense strategy and planning priorities. Deterring China and Russia through preparation for possible war against them has become the preeminent concern of military planners. But where and how could war really erupt in a way that would pit nuclear-armed nations against each other in lethal combat? The stakes seem too high for leaders in Beijing, Moscow, Washington, or other key capitals to risk war over the kinds of matters that great powers have historically contested, like conquest of an entire nation. Surely, we do not expect to see Chinese tanks disembarking on one of Japan's four main islands or moving southward on the Korean Peninsula toward Seoul.

Indeed, the dangers of great-power war do seem greatest in regard to a different category of problem altogether, one that is often captured by the term gray-zone conflict. In this space, small skirmishes over small stakes, perhaps carried out by paramilitaries rather than national armed forces, could lead to exchanges of fire. Then, great uncertainty about what would happen next might prevail. Such a situation could be very dangerous, given the escalatory risks that are inherent in most wars and the ways in which many military establishments seem to plan for rapid escalation in the event of war. (Such planning does not heed the lessons of conflicts like World War I, when dependence on rapid mobilization and escalation through concepts like the Schlieffen Plan plunged the world into unspeakable horrors.) Indeed, even nuclear escalation could result. For example, a country that saw itself losing a conventional conflict that could have larger ramifications for its future role in the western Pacific might be highly tempted to use a nuclear weapon against large ships in the adversary's navy or large but isolated bases on Pacific islands in an attempt to change the momentum of battle and favorably influence the ultimate outcome of the war. Once such nuclear use began, however, it might not remain so "surgical" or limited, given the proclivities of many human leaders for risk-prone behavior, combined with their deep aversions to accepting defeat.

Washington needs better answers to this challenge than it now has. The United States and allies, I argue here and in my recent book *The Senkaku Paradox*, from which some of this chapter is drawn, need a more comprehensive and integrated toolkit for the gray-area problem.[1]

To cope with China's gray-zone challenge, economic warfare needs to play at least as large a role as direct use of force, and generally a larger role in an overall approach I term asymmetric defense. Although I focus here, as in the book, on the "Senkaku challenge"—the dispute between Japan and China over islands administered by the former and claimed by the latter—the logic of asymmetric and integrated defense is widely applicable to the broader problem of gray-zone conflict.

CHINA AND THE GRAY ZONE

Gray-zone conflicts could take a number of forms in the case of China, particularly in the East and South China Seas. Indeed, they are not matters of conjecture; they are already incipient, and evident. In the East China Sea, Chinese ships—generally not naval vessels but law enforcement or paramilitary hulls—routinely operate in the territorial waters of the Senkaku Islands; in 2018, China routinely had four Coast Guard ships in those waters.[2] The islands, called Diaoyu by Beijing, are claimed by both Japan and China. Because they are administered by Japan, the U.S.-Japan Mutual Security Treaty covers them even though the United States takes no position on whose islands they should rightfully be. China also declared an Air Defense Identification Zone in the region in 2013 that includes the Senkakus.

As a result of ensuing changes in Chinese military aircraft behavior, Japanese Air Self-Defense Forces planes have dramatically increased their rate of "scrambles" against Chinese aircraft, from less than 100 per year through 2010 to at least 500 annually since 2015.

Outside the East China Sea, China has built up and militarized seven artificial islands in the South China Sea, creating 3,000-meter military runways on three of them: Fiery Cross Reef, Subi Reef, and Mischief Reef. It has used cunning, deceit, and force to establish its claims to the Scarborough Shoal in that same area, at the expense of the Philippines and in violation of a 2016 ruling by the Permanent Court of Arbitration at The Hague. It even lays claim, through its so-called nine-dash line, to the waters of virtually the entire South China Sea and seeks to back up that claim through occasional harassment of U.S. Navy ships exercising their freedom of navigation rights in these important international waters. Indeed, on this latter point, the issue may rise above the gray zone to a first-order international security problem, if China ups the ante.[3]

China's exact goals in behaving in this fashion remain conjectural—and perhaps even uncertain or undetermined in the minds of the country's top leaders. They probably include historical motives, such as settling scores with Japan over past wrongs. They also may include more offensive motivations, akin to how rising powers have often conducted themselves historically, with their ambitions expanding as their power grows. To paraphrase Robert Kagan, wondering why China is behaving assertively now may be like asking why a baby tiger grows teeth.[4] There may be economic interests involved, as with seabed and fishing resources in the South China Sea and East China Sea. Finally, there may exist defensive military motives. American military forces now often operate close to China in the region. Beijing may wish to push such potentially hostile capabilities beyond the region's so-called first and second island chains at some future point. It may also hope to guarantee its access to crucial resources, such as oil coming from the Persian Gulf region and Africa.

To some extent, President Xi Jinping and cohorts may be opportunistic, seeing what they can get away with short of war. However, the danger of miscalculation leading to violence and then escalation remains real regardless. And one thing seems certain: assertive Chinese behavior is overdetermined by the foregoing list of motivations. China may not want war, but Beijing certainly seems to want *more*—however that is ultimately defined. Gray-area competition provides a means for pursuing it, without necessarily or consciously pulling the trigger on direct conflict against a major country. Given traditional American commitment to allies and to defense of today's global order—not to mention the motives and uncertain future behavior of key countries like Japan, the Philippines, Vietnam, and Australia—the dye may be set for ongoing rivalry in the western Pacific region, with a constant risk of war.

Washington needs better, less escalatory, and thus more credible options for limited but serious gray-zone scenarios involving China. The general concept could be described as asymmetric defense. It should not formally displace existing policy, under which there is a strong implication of prompt U.S.-led military action to defend or liberate any allied territory that might be attacked by an aggressor. This current policy may have deterrence benefits, as well as reassurance benefits for allies, so it should not be formally scrapped. But it may also prove inadequate for deterrence. It may not give U.S. and allied policymakers sufficient options in the event of deterrence failure. And it may be quite dangerous. Thus the new strategy of asymmetric defense that I propose here is intended to complement rather than replace existing concepts and plans. Under the new paradigm, the United States and its allies would not be obliged to fire the first shot or to quickly escalate after a hypothetical Russian or Chinese aggression. They would have indirect and asymmetric options that avoided rapid escalation to serious hostilities.

SPECIFIC RECOMMENDATIONS

The specific policy changes that a strategy of asymmetric defense should feature include the following. Some of them, by their very nature, should be implemented right away, *before* any crisis might occur. That is because they are designed to deter potential adversaries from creating such crises in the first place, and to ensure that Western nations are ready and capable should a crisis erupt nonetheless. Other policy recommendations are more conceptual and need to be understood now but invoked only if and when a scenario of the type addressed here actually occurs.

- *Strengthen economic warfare education.* The United States needs multiagency education and doctrine on how to think about economic warfare, and the U.S. military needs to emphasize these matters to a much greater extent in its war colleges and other key internal intellectual institutions. Already today, defense colleges tend to recognize the importance of "whole-of-government" approaches to security problems, but the language of many texts and manuals is hortatory, not specific or technical. Taxonomies of different types of economic sanctions should be developed. Basic knowledge of the workings and interdependencies of the modern global economy should be expanded throughout military and other government ranks. Recent experience with the use of U.S. and multilateral sanctions as applied to Iran, North Korea, Russia, and other countries should be widely studied. War-games should imagine various applications of sanctions and then play out possible adversarial retaliatory responses. Allies should undertake similar efforts, of course.

- *Secure energy and critical mineral/material stockpiles and minimize over-reliance on any one supplier in complex global supply chains.* Among the necessary steps that can be identified without further study to remediate existing American economic vulnerabilities is the restoration of the size and scale of the American strategic mineral reserve to Cold War–like levels, roughly ten times greater in dollar value than is the case today ($15 billion versus $1.5 billion). In light of trends in North American energy production, increases in the size of the national petroleum stockpile may be less crucial. However, key U.S. allies and friends, including especially South Korea and Japan (and Taiwan), may need to take steps to ensure adequate fuel stocks for themselves.

- Similarly, European allies should continue their ongoing efforts to further integrate European pipeline networks and to import liquid natural gas as a hedge against possible energy showdowns with Russia in the future. Indeed, because of the importance of such energy resilience and adaptability for alliance security, it might be worth considering subsidizing an increase in the number of liquid natural gas terminals and other related capabilities through an expanded NATO Infrastructure Program.

- *Prioritize long-range strike platforms.* American military investments need to prioritize, among other assets, long-range strike platforms that could be relevant to protracted sanctions-reinforcing operations in places such as the broader Indian Ocean region, and various kinds of long-range stealthy sensor platforms and other backups to satellites. The U.S. military needs to be serious about defense against high-altitude nuclear-induced electromagnetic pulse (HEMP). It needs much better cyber defenses, and backups to undersea fiber-optic cables for core military functions. Such systems are likely to be attacked earlier rather than later in any future wars against other great powers. That the paradigm of asymmetric defense I propose is designed to avoid and limit conflict rather than to wage an all-out war does not lessen the importance of preserving U.S. military superiority when and where possible. America and its allies need to preserve escalation dominance in both economic and military realms for the strategy proposed here to be most effective.

- *Innovate nonlethal weapons.* The U.S. armed forces also need to innovate much more seriously in the area of nonlethal weapons, with a particular eye toward weapons that could interrupt maritime shipping in some conflict scenarios. Smart mines and unmanned underwater systems that could also deliver such nonlethal weaponry are also important as complements to a robust attack submarine fleet. The guiding principle should be that, while explosive and kinetic attacks against ships cannot be ruled out, they should be avoided to the extent possible, to control escalation.

- *Retain traditional military capabilities.* The American military also needs to retain or even expand certain types of traditional military capabilities. Ample amounts of airlift and sealift, with an attrition reserve for each, are needed for the forward defense parts of an asymmetric defense strategy. NATO as a whole needs better logistics and transportation capabilities for deploying forces to the Baltic region and sustaining them there, along the lines suggested by Lieutenant General Ben Hodges (retired). Hardened, resilient airfields at multiple locations abroad (in the western Pacific, Indian Ocean, Persian Gulf, and Europe) are required as well. A blend of shorter-range systems with long-range assets operating from the homeland or other effective sanctuaries is the right goal; adding more of the latter should not lead to inattention to the former.

- Allied improvements in such military capabilities would be welcome as well, including in the realms of long-range transport, sustainable logistics, and interoperable high-end weaponry. However, it is probably even more important that key allies prepare for protracted and painful economic warfare by implementing a combination of offensive and defensive measures that collectively improve their resilience.

- *Reexamine economic tools and economic vulnerabilities.* Many of the Trump administration's tougher policies against Chinese actors who are seeking access to American and allied technology, while often debatable in their specifics, are generally sound. Indeed, they should become more systematic, with agencies such as the Committee on Foreign Investment in the United States (CFIUS) going beyond traditional mandates on foreign investment (and now joint ventures) to include assessments of such matters as supply-chain vulnerabilities. Indeed, CFIUS might even be renamed the Committee on Foreign Investment and Economic Resilience in the United States, with an expanded mandate to accompany the name change. It could be given the authorities to incentivize, or even mandate, a degree of supply-chain diversification for key products with national security significance as a hedge against excessive reliance on Russia or China.[5]

- As suggested by Ely Ratner of the Center for a New American Security, Congress might also mandate that the executive branch produce a national economic security strategy that, in addition to diagnosing the nation's economic vulnerabilities, would include recommendations to mitigate those vulnerabilities and track progress toward achieving those objectives.[6]

- The United States needs to be careful about overusing sanctions on financial transactions, such as prohibitions on access to the SWIFT (Society for Worldwide Interbank Financial Telecommunications) bank communications system, for lower-grade problems. Otherwise countries will have incentives to create alternatives to SWIFT that could weaken American financial leverage and reduce U.S. options in a major crisis.

This strategy will work only if it is prepared in advance; it is time we got on with it.

NOTES

1. For related ideas, see CSIS Working Group on the South China Sea, *Defusing the South China Sea Disputes: A Regional Blueprint* (Washington, DC: Center for Strategic and International Studies, October 11, 2018), www.csis.org/analysis/defusing-south-china-sea-disputes; and Melissa Dalton, Kathleen Hicks, et al., *By Other Means Part II: Adapting to Compete in the Gray Zone* (Washington, DC: Center for Strategic and International Studies, August 13, 2019), www.csis.org/analysis/other-means-part-ii-adapting-compete-gray-zone.

2. *Annual Report to Congress: Military and Security Developments Involving the People's Republic of China 2019* (Washington, DC: Office of the Secretary of Defense,

May 2, 2019), 71, https://media.defense.gov/2019/May/02/2002127082/-1/-1/1/2019_CHINA_MILITARY_POWER_REPORT.pdf.

3. National Institute for Defense Studies, *NIDS China Security Report 2019* (Tokyo: The National Institute for Defense Studies, 2019), 12–19, http:///www.nids .mod.go.jp; and Michael Macarthur Bosack, "China's Senkaku Islands Ambition," *Japan Times*, June 12, 2019, www.japantimes.co.jp/opinion/2019/06/12/commentary /japan-commentary/chinas-senkaku-islands-ambition/#.XRzdwpNKiUk.

4. Robert Kagan, *The World America Made* (New York: Alfred A. Knopf, 2012), 87.

5. *Blunting China's Economic Coercion, Hearing on the China Challenge, Part 1: Economic Coercion as Statecraft, Before Senate Foreign Relations Committee Subcommittee on East Asia, the Pacific, and International Cybersecurity Policy*, 115th Cong. 8 (July 24, 2018) (statement of Ely Ratner, Vice President and Director of Studies, Center for a New American Security), www.foreign.senate.gov/imo/ media/doc/072418_Ratner_Testimony.pdf.

6. Ibid., 5.

27

All That Xi Wants

China Attempts to Ace Bases Overseas

LEAH DREYFUSS
MARA KARLIN

The People's Republic of China and the United States have taken remarkably different approaches to military bases overseas. In its post–World War II superpower glow, and throughout the Cold War facing a Soviet rival, the United States developed a robust architecture of military bases to project power. It fostered security and economic growth that benefited U.S. national security interests—and often those of other states as well.

In contrast, Beijing is developing its international network of bases to maintain stability that will foster its own economic growth and interests. So far, its model does not meaningfully benefit other countries. It does not have the political opportunity that would allow it to do so, nor does it face the existential threat the United States did. Simply put, China is not yet building up a global network of bases to massively project power abroad or to attack the United States. Nonetheless, it is building a global footprint to protect its growing interests in a unique way—one that can still threaten U.S. interests.

China's initial forays into military basing abroad reflect its strategic priorities: continued economic growth and development, and stability that fosters such growth. China's approach to foreign bases has been gradual, so as not to provoke others (namely the United States). Chinese debates regarding overseas bases date back at least twenty years, yet—setting aside the question of artificial islands in the South China Sea—China possesses only one foreign base.

Western debates focus on whether China's plans for foreign bases, the Belt and Road Initiative (BRI), and military modernization amount to a long-term strategy to encircle China's competitors. To be sure, such an outcome is not inconceivable. Should China face real threats or find its flexibility severely hampered, it will likely retaliate. China's actions do not suggest intentions to "spring a trap" on an unsuspecting world, but that world would do well to monitor those actions closely lest it tumble into dangerous complacency.

OVERSEAS BASING: THE U.S. APPROACH

The U.S. military's global posture, an intricate system of forces, footprint, and agreements, took hold a century after the country's founding. Competitors and adversaries throughout the Western Hemisphere triggered fears—about territorial security and U.S. interests overseas—and U.S. military posture grew accordingly.[1] Much of that early posture, particularly in Latin America, was mercantilist in emphasis and direction.

By the early twentieth century, the military was increasingly operating worldwide. Despite fits and starts in subsequent decades, World War II prompted a fundamental reevaluation of military posture. Within a few years of its cessation, the U.S. military had bases or access to bases in fifteen countries.[2] Throughout the Cold War, its bases extended across Europe, Asia, and the Middle East. Some posture focused on ensuring access to oil and open waterways, while elsewhere it aimed to foster stability. The Cold War's end prompted decreased overseas posture and somewhat of a return to garrison. The post-9/11 era has seen enhancements across the Middle East, Asia, and Africa, and a slow return to Europe.

Today, the U.S. military's global posture includes bases in nearly 100 different countries. It helps reassure allies and partners; deter adversaries and frenemies; and is operationally crucial to the American way of war, which seeks "away" games far from the homeland.[3] In Asia and Europe, this approach is growing trickier even as a global posture remains important, since China and Russia invested in capabilities designed to target U.S. military advantages.[4]

In Asia, the U.S. military has sought to increase its posture since

2012: "*We will of necessity rebalance toward the Asia-Pacific region.*"[5] It has expanded its forces, footprint, and agreements across Asia to create a "more geographically distributed, operationally resilient, and politically sustainable"[6] posture, while sending the most sophisticated military capabilities there and updating theater-relevant operational concepts.[7] The June 2019 Defense Department's Asia strategy redoubled this focus, declaring it "the single most consequential region for America's future."[8]

OVERSEAS BASING: THE CHINESE APPROACH

China has deliberately avoided an expansionist presence abroad since the Chinese Communist Party (CCP) came to power. In keeping with its military strategy of "active defense"[9] and concerns about major war on its territory, China has focused military planning around homeland defense, prioritizing the People's Liberation Army (PLA) and land capabilities—a legacy of 200 years of wars there.

Only in recent decades has China focused on broadening capabilities across its services. Current reorganization and modernization efforts—aimed at what China calls "informationized warfare"[10]—emphasize maritime forces, with major investments in the People's Liberation Army Navy (PLAN) and Marine Corps (PLANMC).[11] Notably, the latest Chinese defense white paper makes this explicit, underscoring for the first time "far seas protection," thereby describing a strategic rationale for a Chinese blue-water navy.[12] China's military reorganization into "theater commands"[13] reveals its prioritization of a joint force capable of power projection and organized command and control over a growing set of challenges. While focus has continued on China's near-periphery, coverage is expanding toward the Middle East, China's largest source of crude oil.[14]

Combined with the strategically defensive, operationally offensive concept of "active defense," the principle of noninterference—one of Five Principles of Peaceful Coexistence characterizing Chinese foreign policy—has historically restricted Chinese pursuit of overseas bases.[15] Chinese military leaders and scholars highlight China's lack of overseas bases as indicative of its respect for other states' sovereignty and its peaceful—not revanchist or imperialist—ambitions.[16] Official white papers through 2000 affirmed China's policy not to "station any troops or set up any military bases in any foreign country" nor "seek military expansion."[17]

As Chinese interests overseas expanded, discourse around noninterference and overseas bases in Chinese circles shifted.[18] The past two decades witnessed more voices calling for reinterpretations of the principles to reflect current circumstances.[19] With significant investments, personnel, and energy imports abroad, China recognized the need to reimagine overseas options to protect its growing interests.[20] Even the Chinese public supports expansion: nearly 90 percent of respondents in a 2009 poll answered "yes" when asked whether China should establish overseas military bases.[21]

Short of formal basing, over the last decade China increased its out-of-area operations abilities. Following hiccups in evacuating citizens from Afghanistan and Pakistan in 2004 and Libya in 2011, China improved this capability, as demonstrated by its swift evacuations from Yemen in 2015.[22] It participated in the Gulf of Aden counter-piracy coalition, increasing the military's experience in extraregional operations.[23]

President Xi Jinping's Belt and Road Initiative only accelerated the acceptance of overseas bases as a necessity: China's 2015 Military Strategy white paper confirmed that "the security of overseas interests . . . has become an imminent issue."[24] It stopped short of suggesting a complete policy reversal, but the opening of China's first overseas base in Djibouti confirmed the transition. So far, China shows no signs of regret. The Ministry of Defense's 2019 white paper cemented its commitment to overseas interests and basing, and its transformation from regional to global power.[25] The paper highlights China's overseas interests more than previous versions, and, perhaps inadvertently, refers to Djibouti as a base in the official English translation.[26]

CHINA'S BASES: RUMORED AND REAL

After much speculation, the PLA Djibouti Support Base opened in 2017. China calls it a logistics facility, intended solely to support peacekeeping, counter-piracy, and humanitarian missions,[27] yet satellite imagery and unofficial reports indicate that it has more fulsome infrastructure.[28] Its location near a strategic oil chokepoint, the Bab al Mandab Strait, and the only U.S. base in Africa, Camp Lemonnier, suggest dual purposes of ensuring free-flowing oil while gathering intelligence on U.S. forces.[29] Equally as critical is the base's role in protecting China's economic expansion into Africa, in both human and financial capital.[30] China invested $34.7 billion across the continent, which hosts over 260,000 Chinese citizens.[31] The Djibouti base is "a concrete manifestation of China's new naval strategy of near seas defense, far seas protection."[32]

These developments spurred conjecture about PLA plans for future bases. In 2017, Sri Lanka handed China a controlling stake in the Hambantota Port, plus a ninety-nine-year lease and 15,000 acres of land, in exchange for $1.1 billion in debt relief from BRI-related loans.[33] Though the agreement bars foreign military use of the port, it provides an exception should Colombo grant permission. China repeatedly claims its interests are exclusively commercial, but experts note that "the economic rationale for Hambantota is weak."[34]

The most developed Chinese precursor base, the China-Pakistan Economic Corridor, is more than its name suggests. A Chinese state-owned enterprise operates Gwadar port, and China invested in a robust transportation system facilitating access. Paired with deepening Chinese-Pakistani military cooperation, this access could pay military dividends like refueling rights and landing access.[35] Given the strategic corridor Gwadar and the roadway system exemplify—facilitating access to India, Iran, and Afghanistan—China's actions may reveal crasser aims.

Rumored potential "bases" in Haifa, Israel and Ream, Cambodia reflect similar priorities: protecting BRI investments and ensuring free-flowing energy transports. By 2022, a Chinese state-owned enterprise will operate part of Haifa port near an Israeli naval base used by the U.S. Navy's Sixth Fleet.[36] Haifa could be a foothold for protecting investments and collecting intelligence on the United States and Israeli militaries and espionage on high-technology Israeli industry.[37]

Buzz surrounding Ream indicates that China might acquire exclusive rights to part of a Cambodian naval installation, allowing base use for thirty years in exchange for building two new piers. Though the nearby airport is supposedly commercial, the sparsely populated surroundings and two-mile bomber-friendly runway hint otherwise.[38] A facility in Cambodia furthers China's ability to manipulate neighboring economic partners, which it views as within its rightful sphere of influence.[39]

Rumors about other facilities reinforce China's emphasis on "near seas defense, far seas protection" and protecting mainland territory.[40] Further bases may mitigate its vulnerability to strangulation attempts in key waterways like the Strait of Malacca. The past decade witnessed the development and militarization of South China Sea islands, extending its defensive periphery and bolstering natural resource claims.[41] In 2018, Vanuatu denied it would allow China a foothold, let alone a military base, which would extend China's eastern defensive periphery and complicate U.S. military movements.[42] Reports in 2019 indicated an "initial presence" in Tajikistan, in addition to BRI investments across Central Asia. Both countries deny the presence—or talk—of Chinese bases, but evidence and Tajikistan's strategic BRI location suggest otherwise.[43]

(PLA)NS FOR THE FUTURE

In keeping with its noninterference and nonalignment policies, China will continue forgoing military alliances and bases in the traditional U.S. sense, instead seeking to develop partnerships that allow access to protect its interests. Partnerships rooted in economic relations enable China to establish soft footholds in investment-hungry countries, gradually building leverage to assert a stronger presence. They can then expand; as China's defense minister told a group of foreign military leaders, the "BRI would provide a 'framework' for greater military cooperation."[44]

This alternative to the U.S. basing approach capitalizes on lessons learned from the U.S. experience. China's light-touch facilities and leasing agreements are quicker to build, easier to operationalize, drastically less expensive to establish and maintain, and effectively Chinese-owned. Should a host country consider reneging on an agreement, China has financial leverage to enforce compliance. Given the success thus far, it is unsurprising that Xi instructed the PLA to "steadily advance overseas base construction."[45] Nevertheless, as tiffs over BRI projects in Malaysia demonstrated, compliance may not be as total as China wants.[46]

The priorities driving site selection for potential Chinese bases remain constant for now. Sustaining growth and development through energy imports and protecting investments and citizens abroad will explain new facilities, despite more internationally palatable claims. According to China's Naval Research Institute, future sites may include Myanmar, Tanzania, and the Seychelles.[47] With military diplomacy activities surging, China's overseas basing approach may become a cost-efficient model for other countries seeking to protect expanding interests.[48]

Nevertheless, observers should focus on a few considerations to assess China's overseas basing trajectory. It may prop up sympathetic regimes through investment. It could face extraterritorial terrorists and respond with expansion. Its desire for access to distant locales like the Arctic may grow. The resource-ascendant PLAN may take advantage of its growth to push into new arenas. Potential U.S. efforts to limit the efficacy of Chinese anti-access/area-denial capabilities may make out-of-area operations more appealing. And, as its basing infrastructure grows, it may suffer the self-licking ice cream cone fate, insofar as forward-deployed bases are vulnerable and require other bases (or assets) for support.

POTENTIAL FLASH POINTS

Traditionally, the most worrisome flash point for the United States and China is Taiwan; however, the list is growing. South and East China Seas scenarios pose varied challenges based on geography, topography, and distance. Moreover, concern exists over what circumstances might ignite a conflict, how the parties might respond, and where the rungs on their escalation ladders lie.[49]

This list is not exhaustive as China's presence burgeons beyond Asia. Personnel at its Djibouti base could intentionally or accidentally engage U.S. assets at Camp Lemonnier, or constrain U.S. access across the Horn of Africa.[50] Increasing cooperation with Israel, and Chinese investment in key dual-use institutions like the Haifa port, could lead to interference in U.S. Middle East operations.[51] China could use its presence in Tajikistan to hinder or harm U.S. personnel or facilities in Afghanistan.[52] Worryingly for U.S. military planners, this enhanced Chinese posture will make monitoring U.S. military movements cheaper and easier. Operationally, this means China will be better able to surveil U.S. assets; track U.S. ships, aircraft, and personnel; and interfere with these movements. Plainly, as the Chinese military gradually expands its global posture and hence its global reach, the number and nature of potential flash points increases.

LOOKING FORWARD

China's evolving global military posture requires serious study. Regular assessments are critical to understanding the strategic and operational implications, particularly vis-à-vis regions or partners where the United States has been the primary external actor. While the Defense Department's China military power report outlines the challenges an increasingly capable and active military presents, it would benefit from a retrospective on when, where, and how it has accurately—and inaccurately—assessed Chinese progress and intentions.[53]

Many steps that the U.S. military can take to enhance its Asia posture's efficacy are well known, including the following:

- Establishing more access agreements

- Increasing bilateral and multilateral military exercises with allies and partners in the region (and including extraregional allies)

- Building new and informal security frameworks when and where possible, such as facilitating military cooperation among various combinations of Japan, South Korea, India, and Australia

- Deepening investments in and exercising and testing new operational concepts for a more distributed, capable, and resilient posture

- Doubling down on key U.S. military advantages, such as undersea capabilities

Congress's $6.9 billion Pacific Deterrence Initiative will catapult these efforts, as will continued close collaboration with allies and partners—absent pressure on them to publicly take sides.[54]

China's approach to date merits serious monitoring, but it does not yet merit hysteria. Yes, China is expanding its military presence abroad concurrently with its broadening economic interests, but—as its leadership reiterates ad infinitum—it follows its own path of "peaceful" development. With an unofficial pact between the Chinese people and the CCP promising continued growth in exchange for one-party rule, forecasts of decelerating economic growth require China to look abroad for opportunities.[55] Xi recognizes this, throwing his full weight behind BRI proliferation, which provides not only growth opportunities but also the soft power benefit of positively predisposing other less-developed countries toward China.

With such projects comes the need to protect human and financial investments, plus China's international image. Building traditional bases would be expensive, time consuming, and a maintenance hassle—not to mention potentially at odds with Chinese principles; devising more agile arrangements that afford China the access and ability to protect its interests is not. China is leapfrogging the United States in its strategy, cutting straight to dual-use and public-private setups that are more economically and logistically efficient than America's global network of military bases. Nonetheless, as Chinese influence and power grow, China's approach will be tested by cold geopolitical realities. Though Beijing seems intent on avoiding the challenges faced by the U.S. global network of bases, it may find itself facing similar—or even more difficult—challenges in the twenty-first century.

NOTES

1. Stacie L. Pettyjohn, *U.S. Global Defense Posture, 1783–2011* (Santa Monica, CA: The RAND Corporation, 2012), 25–29. www.rand.org/pubs/monographs/MG1244.html.

2. Ibid., 50–59.

3. For more detail, see U.S. Department of Defense, "Summary of the 2018 National Defense Strategy of the United States of America" (Washington, DC: January 2018), https://dod.defense.gov/Portals/1/Documents/pubs/2018-National-Defense-Strategy-Summary.pdf. For an overview of the National Defense Strategy, see Mara Karlin, "How to Read the National Defense Strategy," The Brookings Institution, *Order from Chaos* (blog), January 21, 2018, www.brookings.edu/blog/order-from-chaos/2018/01/21/how-to-read-the-2018-national-defense-strategy/. For more detail on the American way of war, Chris Dougherty has published a superb overview—including why it is under serious threat. Christopher M. Dougherty, *Why America Needs a New Way of War* (Washington, DC: Center for a New American Security, June 2019). https://s3.amazonaws.com/files.cnas.org/CNAS+Report+-+ANAWOW+-+FINAL2.pdf.

4. These advantages include its ability to knit together a sophisticated system of stealth capabilities, precision-guided munitions, and intelligence, surveillance, and reconnaissance. RAND has done rigorous research on this topic: Scott Boston et al., *Assessing the Conventional Force Imbalance in Europe: Implications for Countering Russian Local Superiority* (Santa Monica, CA: The RAND Corporation, 2018), www.rand.org/pubs/research_reports/RR2402.html. Eric Heginbotham et al., *The U.S.-China Military Scorecard: Forces, Geography, and the Evolving Balance of Power, 1996–2017* (Santa Monica, CA: The RAND Corporation, 2015), www.rand.org/pubs/research_reports/RR392.html. The 2018 National Defense Strategy Commission warned that the military "now faces far graver challenges in projecting power and operating effectively in the Western Pacific and Eastern Europe." Eric Edelman and Gary Roughead et al., *Providing For the Common Defense: The Assessment and Recommendations of the National Defense Strategy Commission* (Washington, DC: U.S. Institute of Peace, November 2018), 25, www.usip.org/sites/default/files/2018-11/providing-for-the-common-defense.pdf. NB: one of the authors worked on the Commission.

5. Italics in original. U.S. Department of Defense, *Sustaining U.S. Global Leadership: Priorities for 21st Century Defense* (Washington, DC: January 2012), http://nssarchive.us/national-defense-strategy/defense_strategic_guidance/

6. Ash Carter, "The Rebalance and Asia-Pacific Security," *Foreign Affairs,*

October 17, 2016, www.foreignaffairs.com/articles/united-states/2016-10-17/rebalance-and-asia-pacific-security.

7. Although progress has been plodding, examples include: basing Marines in Australia; rotating littoral combat ships and P-8s out of Singapore; adding new capabilities to Guam; enhancing forces and capabilities across Japan; increasing pre-positioned equipment in Korea; augmenting base access in the Philippines; inaugurating new exercises with India; an aircraft carrier strike group visiting Sri Lanka and Vietnam; and deepening collaboration with the Pacific Islands. And of course, the most controversial aspect of U.S. partnership in Asia—military cooperation with Taiwan—continues to grow.

8. U.S. Department of Defense, Indo-Pacific Strategy Report (Washington, DC: June 2019): 1.

9. The State Council Information Office of the People's Republic of China, *China's National Defense in the New Era* (Beijing, China: Foreign Languages Press Co. Ltd., July 2019), http://eng.mod.gov.cn/news/2019-07/24/content_4846443.htm.

10. "Xi Jinping Wants China's Armed Forces to Be "World-Class" by 2050," *The Economist*, June 27, 2019, www.economist.com/china/2019/06/27/xi-jinping-wants-chinas-armed-forces-to-be-world-class-by-2050.

11. Office of the Secretary of Defense, *Annual Report to Congress: Military and Security Developments Involving the People's Republic of China 2019* (Washington, DC: Department of Defense, May 2, 2019), https://media.defense.gov/2019/May/02/2002127082/-1/-1/1/2019_CHINA_MILITARY_POWER_REPORT.pdf.

12. *China's National Defense in the New Era*, 12, 19, 21.

13. Many have written about how closely China's 2015 reorganization mirrored that of the United States following the Goldwater-Nichols Department of Defense Reorganization Act of 1986. See Phillip C. Saunders and Joel Wuthnow, "China's Goldwater-Nichols? Assessing PLA Organizational Reforms," *Joint Force Quarterly* 82 (3rd Quarter, July 2016), https://ndupress.ndu.edu/JFQ/Joint-Force-Quarterly-82/Article/793267/chinas-goldwater-nichols-assessing-pla-organizational-reforms/; also see James Mulvenon "China's 'Goldwater-Nichols'? The Long-Awaited PLA Reorganization Has Finally Arrived," *China Leadership Monitor* 49 (Winter 2016), www.hoover.org/research/chinas-goldwater-nichols-long-awaited-pla-reorganization-has-finally-arrived.

14. Office of the Secretary of Defense, *Annual Report to Congress: Military and Security Developments Involving the People's Republic of China 2019*, 120.

15. Ibid.

16. Michael S. Chase and Andrew S. Erickson, "Changes in Beijing's Approach to Overseas Basing?" *China Brief* 9, no. 19 (September 24, 2009), https://jamestown.org/program/changes-in-beijings-approach-to-overseas-basing/.

17. The State Council Information Office of the People's Republic of China, "China's National Defense in 2000" (Beijing, China: September 2000), http://eng.mod.gov.cn/news/2019-07/24/content_4846443.htm.

18. For examples of the increasing variety in opinion, see Timothy R. Heath,

China's Pursuit of Overseas Security (Santa Monica, CA: RAND Corporation, 2018), 17, www.rand.org/pubs/research_reports/RR2271.html; Shen Dingli, "Don't Shun the Idea of Setting Up Overseas Military Bases," China.org.cn, January 28, 2010, www.china.org.cn/opinion/2010-01/28/content_19324522.htm; and Dai Xu, "China Should Establish Overseas Base," *Huanqiu Shibao*, February 3, 2009, http://mil.huanqiu.com/top/2009-02/363027.html.

19. Chen Zheng, "China Debates the Non-Interference Principle," *Chinese Journal of International Politics* 9, no. 3 (Autumn 2016): 349–374, https://doi.org/10.1093/cjip/pow010.

20. Mathieu Duchâtel, Oliver Bräuner, and Zhou Hang, "Protecting China's Overseas Interests: The Slow Shift away from Non-interference," SIPRI Policy Paper 41 (Solna, Sweden: Stockholm International Peace Research Institute, 2014), 13–20, www.sipri.org/sites/default/files/files/PP/SIPRIPP41.pdf.

21. Christopher D. Yung and Ross Rustici, *"Not an Idea We Have to Shun": Chinese Overseas Basing Requirements in the 21st Century*, China Strategic Perspectives 7 (Washington, DC: National Defense University, 2014), 53, https://ndupress.ndu.edu/Portals/68/Documents/stratperspective/china/ChinaPerspectives-7.pdf.

22. Peter Connolly, "Chinese Evacuations and Power Projection (Part 1): Overseas Citizen Protection," Barton, Australia, Australian Strategic Policy Institute, 2018, www.aspistrategist.org.au/chinese-evacuations-and-power-projection-part-1-overseas-citizen-protection/. See also Gabe Collins and Andrew S. Erickson, "Implications of China's Military Evacuation of Citizens from Libya," *China Brief* 11, no. 4 (March 11, 2011), https://jamestown.org/program/implications-of-chinas-military-evacuation-of-citizens-from-libya/.

23. Ankit Panda, "China Dispatches New Naval Fleet for Gulf of Aden Escort Mission," *The Diplomat*, December 11, 2018, https://thediplomat.com/2018/12/china-dispatches-new-naval-fleet-for-gulf-of-aden-escort-mission/. While China did not ultimately join the Strait of Hormuz coalition, it publicly considered it. See Alexander Cornwell, "China Might Escort Ships in Gulf under U.S. Proposal: Envoy," Reuters, August 6, 2019, www.reuters.com/article/us-mideast-iran-tanker-china/china-might-escort-ships-in-gulf-under-u-s-proposal-envoy-idUSKCN1UW1DR.

24. The State Council Information Office of the People's Republic of China, "China's Military Strategy (2015)" (Beijing, China: May 2015), https://jamestown.org/wp-content/uploads/2016/07/China%E2%80%99s-Military-Strategy-2015.pdf.

25. *China's National Defense in the New Era*.

26. Ibid., 14–15.

27. John Fei, "China's Overseas Military Base in Djibouti: Features, Motivations, and Policy Implications," *China Brief* 17, no. 17 (December 22, 2017), https://jamestown.org/program/chinas-overseas-military-base-djibouti-features-motivations-policy-implications/.

28. Sarah Zheng, "China's Djibouti Military Base: 'Logistics Facility,' or Platform

for Geopolitical Ambitions Overseas?" *South China Morning Post*, October 1, 2017, www.scmp.com/news/china/diplomacy-defence/article/2113300/chinas-djibouti -military-base-logistics-facility-or.

29. Kathy Gilsinan, "The U.S. Is Worried about China's Investments—This Time in Israel," *The Atlantic*, July 11, 2019, www.theatlantic.com/politics/archive/2019/07 /us-concerned-about-chinese-investments-israel/593794/.

30. Erica Downs, Jeffrey Becker, and Patrick deGategno, "China's Military Support Facility in Djibouti: The Economic and Security Dimensions of China's First Overseas Base" (Arlington, VA: CNA, July 2017), www.cna.org/cna_files/pdf/ DIM-2017-U-015308-Final3.pdf.

31. Ibid., 41.

32. Ibid., 41.

33. Shihar Aneez, "Exclusive: Sri Lanka's Cabinet 'Clears Port Deal' with China Firm after Concerns Addressed," Reuters, July 25, 2017, www.reuters.com/article/ us-sri-lanka-china-port/exclusive-sri-lankas-cabinet-clears-port-deal-with-china -firm-after-concerns-addressed-idUSKBN1AA0PI.

34. Jonathan E. Hillman, "Game of Loans: How China Bought Hambantota" (Washington, DC, CSIS, April 2, 2018), www.csis.org/analysis/game-loans-how -china-bought-hambantota. For additional background, see Maria Abi-Habib, "How China Got Sri Lanka to Cough Up a Port," *New York Times*, June 25, 2018, www.nytimes.com/2018/06/25/world/asia/china-sri-lanka-port.html.

35. Maria Abi-Habib, "China's 'Belt and Road' Plan in Pakistan Takes a Military Turn," *New York Times*, December 19, 2018, www.nytimes.com/2018/12/19/world/ asia/pakistan-china-belt-road-military.html.

36. Kathy Gilsinan, "The U.S. Is Worried About China's Investments —This Time in Israel." More broadly, Chinese state-owned enterprises also control or operate ports in places like Piraeus, Greece, and Valencia, Spain; both are used by the U.S. Navy for operations.

37. Jack Detsch, "Pentagon Repeats Warning to Israel on Chinese Port Deal," *Al -Monitor*, August 7, 2019, www.al-monitor.com/pulse/originals/2019/08/pentagon -repeat-warning-israel-china-port-deal.html.

38. Jeremy Page, Gordon Lubold, and Rob Taylor, "Deal for Naval Outpost in Cambodia Furthers China's Quest for Military Network," *Wall Street Journal*, July 22, 2019, www.wsj.com/articles/secret-deal-for-chinese-naval-outpost-in -cambodia-raises-u-s-fears-of-beijings-ambitions-11563732482.

39. The Chinese Ministry of Defense's 2019 white paper asserts that "no matter how it might develop, China will never threaten any other country or seek any sphere of influence," yet it also states that "China holds it a priority to manage differences and enhance mutual trust in maintaining the stability of its neighborhood." The State Council Information Office of the People's Republic of China, *China's National Defense in the New Era*.

40. Erica Downs et al., "China's Military Support Facility in Djibouti."

41. "China Builds New Military Facilities on South China Sea Islands: Think

Tank," *Reuters*, June 29, 2017, https://reuters.com/article/us-southchinasea-china
-islands/china-builds-new-military-facilities-on-south-china-sea-islands-think
-tank-idUSKBN19L02J.

42. "Vanuatu and China Deny Holding Military Base Talks," *Reuters*, April 20,
2018, https://af.reuters.com/article/worldNews/idAFKBN1HH0MJ. Australia has
also decried Chinese efforts to militarize the region. David Crow, "'Great Concern':
Malcolm Turnbull Draws a Line in the Sand on Military Bases Near Australia,"
Sydney Morning Herald, April 10, 2018, www.smh.com.au/politics/federal/great
-concern-malcolm-turnbull-draws-a-line-in-the-sand-on-military-bases-near
-australia-20180410-p4z8t3.html. In response to China's moves in the region, the
Republic of Palau has asked the United States to build ports, bases, and airfields on
its territory, and to bolster its relationship for the long term. Gordon Lubold, "U.S.
Military Is Offered New Bases in the Pacific," *Wall Street Journal*, September 8,
2020, www.wsj.com/artiles/u-s-military-is-offered-new-bases-in-the-pacific-115
99557401.

43. Elsa B. Kania, "Testimony before the House Permanent Select Committee
on Intelligence: China's Threat to American Government and Private Sector
Research and Innovation Leadership," July 19, 2018, www.cnas.org/publications/
congressional-testimony/testimony-before-the-house-permanent-select-commit
tee-on-intelligence. Gerry Shih, "In Central Asia's Forbidding Highlands, a Quiet
Newcomer: Chinese Troops," *Washington Post*, February 18, 2019, www.washing
tonpost.com/world/asia_pacific/in-central-asias-forbidding-highlands-a-quiet
-newcomer-chinese-troops/2019/02/18/78d4a8d0-1e62-11e9-a759-2b8541bbbe20_
story.html.

44. Andrew Tillett, "China to Raise Military Presence in the Pacific," *Australian
Financial Review*, July 10, 2019, www.afr.com/politics/federal/china-to-boost
-pacific-military-presence-20190709-p525h5.

45. Erica Downs et al., "China's Military Support Facility in Djibouti," 40.

46. Amanda Erickson, "Malaysia Cancels Two Big Chinese Projects, Fearing
They Will Bankrupt the Country," *Washington Post*, August 21, 2018, www.wash
ingtonpost.com/world/asia_pacific/malaysia-cancels-two-massive-chinese
-projects-fearing-they-will-bankrupt-the-country/2018/08/21/2bd150e0-a515-11e8
-b76b-d513a40042f6_story.html.

47. Erica Downs et al., "China's Military Support Facility in Djibouti."

48. "How Is China Bolstering Its Military Diplomatic Relations?" China Power
Project, October 27, 2017, https://chinapower.csis.org/china-military-diplomacy/.

49. Michael O'Hanlon, *The Senkaku Paradox: Risking Great Power War over
Small Stakes* (Washington, DC: Brookings Institution Press, 2019).

50. Patrick Martin, "Could China Squeeze the U.S. Out of Its Only Permanent
Military Base in Africa?" *Washington Post*, December 14, 2018. www.washingtonpost
.com/national-security/2018/12/14/could-china-squeeze-us-out-its-only
-permanent-military-base-africa/.

51. Shira Efron, Howard J. Shatz, Arthur Chan, Emily Haskel, Lyle J. Morris,
and Andrew Scobell, *The Evolving Israel-China Relationship* (Santa Monica, CA:

The RAND Corporation, 2019), 107, www.rand.org/pubs/research_reports/RR2641
.html.

52. Gerry Shih, "In Central Asia's Forbidding Highlands, a Quiet Newcomer."

53. Office of the Secretary of Defense, *Annual Report to Congress: Military and Security Developments Involving the People's Republic of China 2019.* It is also worth noting the United States' inability to marshal the attention and resources to address concerns about China's growing global footprint over the past decade—see the predictions since proven accurate in Michael Chase and Andrew S. Erickson, "Changes in Beijing's Approach to Overseas Basing?"—due to Washington's preoccupations with engagements in the Middle East and terrorism.

54. Jim Inhofe and Jack Reed, "The Pacific Deterrence Initiative: Peace through Strength in the Indo-Pacific," War on the Rocks, May 28, 2020. https://warontherocks .com/2020/05/the-pacific-deterrence-initiative-peace-through-strength-in-the -indo-pacific/. Also Michael S. Chase and Mara Karlin, "Navigating Asia's Stormy Seas: Regional Perspectives on U.S.-China Competition," *The Diplomat,* August 7, 2018. https://thediplomat.com/2018/08/navigating-asias-stormy-seas-regional -perspectives-on-us-china-competition/.

55. Christopher Balding, "What's Causing China's Economic Slowdown," *Foreign Affairs*, March 11, 2019. www.foreignaffairs.com/articles/china/2019-03-11 /whats-causing-chinas-economic-slowdown.

THE GLOBAL ECONOMY

*How Is China's Rise Reshaping
Global Economic Institutions
and Affecting Progress on Goals
Like Poverty and Climate?*

28

Reluctant Player

China's Approach to International Economic Institutions

DAVID DOLLAR

China has been an active participant in the international economic institutions, namely the World Trade Organization (WTO), the International Monetary Fund (IMF), and the World Bank. China has generally lived up to its commitments in these institutions, but it has been reluctant to take on the stronger responsibilities that fall on developed countries. China's insistence on being treated as a developing country is a main source of tension in its economic relations with the advanced economies. A further area of tension is that China's bilateral economic relations with other developing countries do not always meet global standards and norms. From an institutional point of view, it is a problem that China is not a member of the Government Procurement Arrangement within the WTO, the Paris Club of official creditors, or the Development Assistance Committee.

Much of America's concern with China's role in the world is related to this *partial integration* of the country into the global economic institutions. To change China's behavior and bring its practices into line with advanced-country norms would require recognition that China deserves greater say in the international economic institutions in return for greater responsibility.

CHINA HAS BEEN AN ACTIVE PARTICIPANT IN
INTERNATIONAL ECONOMIC INSTITUTIONS . . .

In the case of the WTO, China has become a very active member since joining in 2001. Between 2006 and 2015, more than a quarter of the WTO case-
load involved China as a complainant or as a respondent.[1] Only the United
States and the European Union had more active cases over the period. Furthermore, in general, when China has lost cases it has changed the necessary
laws and regulations and complied with the ruling, though not always as
expeditiously as complainants had hoped.

However, China presents a number of unique challenges for the trading
regime. Since the Great Recession, WTO litigation has increasingly taken
on a dynamic of the United States, the EU, and Japan versus China. Between
2009 and 2015, China-related cases accounted for 90 percent of the cases
brought by the four big economies vis-à-vis each other. Increasingly, the
United States, EU, and Japan join together against China.[2]

The problems arise from the dualistic nature of the Chinese economy.
While the economy is often characterized as state dominated, private enterprises are at the heart of China's dynamic growth. Traditionally, most
exports have come from foreign-invested firms. Recently most of the value
added in China's exports has come from the domestic private sector as value
chains have lengthened in China. State enterprises dominate in fields such
as heavy industry and especially services—finance, telecom, and logistics.
These characteristics make it difficult to determine certain legal issues under
WTO rules—such as whether a firm is associated with the state, or how to
characterize the overall form of China's economy. These elements also pose
issues for certain activities that fall outside the scope of the WTO's present
disciplines. It is difficult, for example, for the WTO to deal with investment
restrictions, forced technology transfer, and intellectual property theft.

China's relationship with the IMF has changed remarkably in recent
years. In the mid-2000s, China allowed its currency to become undervalued
and its current account surplus to balloon above 10 percent of gross domestic product. The U.S. Department of the Treasury put pressure on the IMF to
highlight the issue of global imbalances and currency misalignment. China
had very large trade surpluses and an undervalued currency for four years,
from 2005 to 2008, after which the authorities allowed the yuan to appreciate and made other policy changes that eliminated the large surpluses.[3] This
is a good example of China adapting to global norms.

Since that time, the China-IMF relationship has evolved into a close partnership. As attention shifted away from the exchange rate, starting around 2009, the IMF focused its China program more on financial supervision with a series of welcome technical interventions and policy advice.[4] Quota reform in the IMF, pushed by the United States, shifted shares toward emerging markets, especially China. While China has gained quota share in the IMF, its share still lags far behind its weight in the world economy.

Turning to the multilateral development banks, China has had a long and positive relationship with the World Bank, starting with a famous meeting between Deng Xiaoping and (former president of the World Bank Group) Robert McNamara in 1980. Deng told McNamara that China would modernize with or without World Bank assistance, but it would do so more rapidly with the assistance.[5] For many years China was the largest borrower.

More recently, China has become an important donor to the concessional window of the World Bank, which finances the poorest countries, mostly in Africa. At the most recent replenishment in December 2019, China was the sixth-largest donor behind the United Kingdom, Japan, United States, Germany, and France and ahead of G7 members Canada and Italy.[6] While China's relationship with the World Bank has largely been positive, it does have criticisms of the Bank's shift away from infrastructure and growth and of its slow preparation times and costly bureaucracy. China established the Asian Infrastructure Investment Bank (AIIB) as a new multilateral development bank, one that has attracted over 100 members and is off to a good start, working closely with the existing development banks.

. . . BUT CHINA HAS BEEN RELUCTANT TO TAKE ON THE SAME RESPONSIBILITIES OF RICH COUNTRIES

While China is an active player in global economic institutions, it has been careful to define itself as a developing country and to avoid taking on the responsibilities of rich countries. This approach is somewhat understandable as China has a GDP per capita around one-sixth of the U.S. level.[7] However, given the size of its population, China has the second-largest economy in the world and is likely to overtake the United States in 15–20 years. It is hard to imagine solving global economic problems without China taking on more responsibility.

Examples of China's reluctance to take on new responsibilities abound in every domain. In the IMF, for example, China has resisted capital account convertibility so that it can manage capital inflows and outflows and the level of its exchange rate. The IMF in 2016 made a forward-looking decision to include China's yuan in its basket currency, the Special Drawing Right, but it is odd to have a reserve currency that is not freely convertible.

In the WTO, China has dragged its feet on its commitment years ago to join the Government Procurement Arrangement, a club of countries that have opened up government procurement markets to each other. China is also reluctant to see the WTO take on new issues such as cross-border data flows, intellectual property rights (IPR) protection, subsidies, and investment.

The previous section noted that China is the sixth-largest donor to the World Bank's concessional window. But it has positioned itself carefully; for this replenishment it gave $1.2 billion, compared to the U.S. contribution of $3 billion.[8] China's economy is two-thirds of the U.S. economy, so a proportionate contribution would have been $2 billion. China is by far the most generous of developing countries, but it does not want to be expected to meet the obligations of rich countries. (Russia, incidentally, gave nothing.) China has similarly been reluctant to join the Development Assistance Committee (DAC), which sets standards for transparency of foreign aid, or the Paris Club, which coordinates official debt reschedulings. One issue is that the Paris Club and the DAC are linked to the Organization for Economic Co-operation and Development (OECD), which defines itself as a club of democracies. The solution seems straightforward: delink the Paris Club and the DAC from the OECD because the issues they address now involve other important countries beyond the advanced democracies.

CHINA'S BILATERAL RELATIONS UNDERMINE ITS GLOBAL CONTRIBUTIONS

In addition to China's reluctance to take on greater responsibilities, its extensive bilateral economic relations often undermine its global contributions. The clearest example is in development finance. It is a major contributor to the World Bank's concessional window, has started the AIIB, and supports the IMF's debt sustainability approach. At the same time, through its Belt and Road Initiative, it is lending $40–$50 billion per year to developing countries for projects in transport and power infrastructure. While the financing amount is large, the terms are largely commercial. The whole effort lacks transparency in terms of selection of contractors, amounts lent, detailed terms, and environmental and social sustainability.

The Center for Global Development (CGD) ranks donor countries along various dimensions in terms of their policies contributing to development. On development finance, CGD ranks China last of forty countries because its finance is opaque and nonconcessional.[9] The implication of nonconcessionality is hitting home during the coronavirus pandemic: half of China's big clients in Africa are in debt distress or at high risk of debt distress, according to the IMF.[10] On the positive side, China joined the G-20 plan for a moratorium on debt payments by the poorest countries during 2020.[11] This is just a small first step, however, as a lingering global recession will probably require debt relief beyond this initial moratorium.

CONCLUSIONS AND RECOMMENDATIONS

The current situation is characterized by China deeply imbedded in the global economic system as a developing country, reluctant to take on the responsibilities of a rich country, and conducting bilateral relations that often run counter to global norms. This situation is unsustainable, as the United States demands more of China and, at the same time, is reluctant to cede it any influence on the global stage.

The long-run solution is clear: China and other developing countries should receive more weight in global economic decisionmaking in return for greater consistency of their policies with global rules and norms. With greater influence, China and others will have more say on what those global rules and norms are. Concretely, this would involve changes such as increasing the voting share for these countries in the IMF and World Bank; reconfiguring (and renaming) the Paris Club as a global group of official creditors rather than a club of rich countries; de-linking the DAC from the OECD; and refocusing a new WTO round on the modern issues of cross-border data flows, IPR protection, investment, and subsidies.

Right now it is hard to imagine the United States leading such an initiative. The United States is engaged in trade wars in all directions. Washington needs to repair relations with allies, starting with the removal of self-destructive tariffs. The harder negotiation will be with China, starting from the worst relations that the two countries have had in forty years. The United States should negotiate to eliminate the tariffs aimed at China in return for specific market-opening moves, as well as put on the table an increase in China's voting shares in the Bretton Woods institutions in return for reforms of the Belt and Road Initiative. Both sides will have to be willing to compromise in order to have any chance of success. Without forward progress on China's integration into the global economic system, it is hard to see how the two sides will avoid a spiral into increased economic conflict.

NOTES

1. Mark Wu, "The 'China, Inc.' Challenge to Global Trade Governance," *Harvard International Law Journal* 57, no. 2 (Spring 2016): 264, https://harvardilj.org/wp-content/uploads/sites/15/HLI210_crop.pdf.

2. Ibid.

3. David Dollar, "China's Evolving Role in the International Economic Institutions," in *China 2049: Economic Challenges of a Rising Global Power*, eds. David Dollar, Yiping Huang, and Yang Yao (Washington, DC: Brookings Institution Press, 2020), 388–389.

4. David Dollar, "Chapter 2—IMF Financial Surveillance of China," in *IMF Financial Surveillance in Action: Country Case Studies from Asia and the Western Hemisphere* (Washington, DC: Independent Evaluation Office, International Monetary Fund, December 14, 2018), 15–34, https://ieo.imf.org/en/our-work/Evaluations/Completed/2019-0115-fis-evaluation/.

5. Pieter Bottelier, "China and the World Bank: How a Partnership Was Built," *Journal of Contemporary China* 16, no. 51 (April 18, 2007), 239–258, www.tandfonline.com/doi/abs/10.1080/10670560701194475.

6. "Contributor Countries," International Development Association, The World Bank, https://ida.worldbank.org/about/contributor-countries.

7. "GDP Per Capita (Current US$)," Data, The World Bank, https://data.worldbank.org/indicator/NY.GDP.PCAP.CD.

8. "Contributor Countries," International Development Association, The World Bank.

9. Ian Mitchell and Evan Ritchie, "CDI 2020: China's Commitment to Development," Center for Global Development, June 25, 2020, www.cgdev.org/blog/chinas-commitment-development.

10. In an earlier report for the Global China project, the author identifies the ten largest borrowers from China on the continent: Angola, South Africa, Egypt, Uganda, Nigeria, Kenya, Ethiopia, Zambia, Cameroon, and the Republic of the Congo. David Dollar, *Understanding China's Belt and Road Infrastructure Projects in Africa* (Washington, DC: The Brookings Institution, September 2019), www.brookings.edu/research/understanding-chinas-belt-and-road-infrastructure-projects-in-africa/). The last five countries on the list are in debt distress or at high risk of debt distress according to the most recent IMF debt sustainability analysis, contained in each country's Article IV report on the IMF's website, www.imf.org/external/index.htm.

11. "Communiqué, G20 Finance Ministers and Central Bank Governors Meeting [Virtual]," G-20, April 15, 2020, https://g20.org/en/media/Documents/G20_FMCBG_Communiqué_EN%20(2).pdf.

29

The Renminbi's Prospects as an International Currency

ESWAR PRASAD

China's economy is now the second largest in the world and a key driver of global growth. But the prominence of its currency, the renminbi, is not commensurate with its weight in the world economy. As a result of measures taken by the Chinese government, the renminbi has certainly made some progress as an international currency over the last decade, although this progress has leveled off in the latter half of the decade. It is likely that the renminbi will gradually become a more significant player in international financial markets, yet its full potential will remain unrealized unless the Chinese government undertakes a broad range of economic and financial system reforms. In the long run, what the renminbi's ascendance means for the global financial system depends, to a large extent, on how China's economy itself changes in the process of elevating its currency.

Around the year 2010, the Chinese government began to promote the international use of the renminbi. This put the currency on a path to what seemed to be an inexorable rise to global dominance. The renminbi quickly became the fifth most important currency in international payments (behind the U.S. dollar, the euro, the Japanese yen, and the British pound sterling).[1] In 2016, the International Monetary Fund (IMF) included the renminbi in an elite basket of currencies that represent the institution's Special Drawing Rights (SDR), making it an official reserve currency.[2] Since then, however, the renminbi's progress has stalled. The renminbi's share of international payments has fallen below 2 percent,[3] and the share of global foreign exchange reserves held in renminbi-denominated assets has plateaued at about 2 percent.[4] Other quantitative indicators of the currency's use in international finance, including trade settlement in the currency and issuance of renminbi-denominated bonds offshore, all point to signs of a stalling of the currency's advance as an international currency.

After a hiatus during the mid-2010s, when a surge of capital outflows put the renminbi under severe depreciation pressures, the government has recently resumed progress on policies to promote the currency's international use. It has resumed removing restrictions on capital inflows and outflows in a controlled and gradual manner. Chinese stock and bond markets are now largely open to foreign investors. At the same time, there are now many channels available for Chinese households, corporations, and institutional investors that wish to invest some portion of their investments in foreign markets. China has promoted renminbi availability outside its borders, including approving more than 15 offshore trading centers where transactions between renminbi and other currencies can be conducted. The government has also set up a payment system to facilitate commercial transactions between domestic and foreign companies using renminbi rather than more widely used currencies, such as the dollar and the euro. These measures have helped the internationalization of the currency. This term signifies its greater use in denominating and settling cross-border trade and financial transactions—that is, its use as an international medium of exchange.

A different aspect of a currency's role in international finance is its status as a reserve currency, one that is held by foreign central banks as protection against balance of payments crises. Even though the IMF has officially anointed the renminbi as a reserve currency, financial market participants' views are more important in determining a currency's status. The renminbi's status as a reserve currency has been impeded by the Chinese government's unwillingness to free up its exchange rate, allowing the currency's external value to be determined by market forces, and to fully open the capital account. Moreover, China's financial markets remain limited and underdeveloped, with a number of constraints, such as a rigid interest rate structure.

China is now in the process of rolling out its central bank digital currency—the Digital Currency/Electronic Payment (DCEP).[5] The DCEP by itself will not be a game changer for the renminbi's role in global finance. For all the hype about DCEP, China's Cross-border Interbank Payments

System is a more important innovation that makes it easier to use the currency for international transactions. This payments system also has the ability to bypass the Western-dominated SWIFT (Society for Worldwide Interbank Financial Telecommunications) messaging system for international payments. As the renminbi becomes more widely used, other smaller and developing countries that have strong trade and financial links with China might start to invoice and settle their trade transactions directly in that currency. The DCEP could eventually be linked to the cross-border payments system, further digitizing international payments.

However, the DCEP by itself will make little difference to whether foreign investors see the renminbi as a reserve currency. That will require significant reforms on a variety of fronts, including financial market development and openness. The required reforms are very much in China's own interests as it tries to create a foundation for sustained and balanced growth. For instance, China's government and corporate debt securities markets are quite large but still seen as having limited trading volume and weak regulatory frameworks. Strengthening its financial markets is important both for China's own economic development and for promoting the international role of its currency. A more comprehensive and robust regulatory framework would also help build confidence in China's financial markets.

Finally, there is the question about whether the renminbi can realistically aspire to the status of a "safe haven" currency. Such a currency is one that investors turn to for safety during times of global turmoil, rather than for diversifying their stores of assets denominated in foreign currencies or seeking higher yields on their investments. History suggests that a country seeking this status for its currency must have a sound institutional framework—including an independent judiciary, an open and transparent government with institutionalized checks and balances, and robust public institutions (especially a credible central bank). These elements have traditionally been seen as vital for earning the trust of foreign investors, both private as well as official, including central banks and sovereign wealth funds.

Although the Chinese leadership is pursuing financial liberalization and limited market-oriented economic reforms, it appears to have repudiated political, legal, and institutional reforms. In short, while the renminbi has the potential to become a significant reserve currency, it is unlikely to attain safe haven status in the absence of far-reaching reforms to China's institutional and political structures. Under the present regime, the prospects of such changes are dim.

What implications does the renminbi's rise have for the configuration of the international monetary system, especially the dollar's dominance? Any gains the renminbi has made in recent years, both as a payment currency and as a reserve currency, have come mostly at the expense of currencies such as the euro and the British pound sterling. Even when the IMF inducted the renminbi into the SDR basket of currencies, its weight of 10.9 percent came largely at the expense of the other currencies in the basket—the euro, the pound sterling, and the Japanese yen—rather than the dollar. There seems little prospect of the renminbi's growing prominence having a significant impact on the dollar's status as the dominant payment and reserve currency.

To sum up, the renminbi is on its way to eventually becoming a more widely used currency in international trade and finance. So long as China continues to make progress on financial sector and other market-oriented reforms, it is likely that the renminbi will become a more important reserve currency within the next decade. For the renminbi to become a safe haven currency, however, would require not just economic and financial reforms but also significant institutional reforms.

NOTES

1. "RMB Tracker: Monthly Reporting and Statistics on Renminbi (RMB) Progress towards Becoming an International Currency," SWIFT, August 2020, www.swift.com/sites/default/files/files/SWIFT_RMB_Tracker_August_2020_Slides.pdf.

2. "IMF Launches New SDR Basket Including Chinese Renminbi, Determines New Currency Amounts," International Monetary Fund, September 30, 2016, www.imf.org/en/News/Articles/2016/09/30/AM16-PR16440-IMF-Launches-New-SDR-Basket-Including-Chinese-Renminbi.

3. "RMB Tracker: Monthly Reporting and Statistics on Renminbi (RMB) Progress towards Becoming an International Currency," SWIFT.

4. "Currency Composition of Official Foreign Exchange Reserves (COFER)," International Monetary Fund, https://data.imf.org/?sk=E6A5F467-C14B-4AA8-9F6D-5A09EC4E62A4.

5. Eswar Prasad, "China's Digital Currency Will Rise but Not Rule," Project Syndicate, August 25, 2020, www.project-syndicate.org/commentary/china-digital-currency-will-not-threaten-dollar-by-eswar-prasad-2020-08.

30

China's Digital Services Trade and Data Governance

How Should the United States Respond?

JOSHUA P. MELTZER

China is the world's second-largest digital economy, second only to the United States, and leads the world in the value of many digital applications, including e-commerce and mobile payments. This extensive online activity by Chinese netizens also provides huge amounts of data that can be used to train artificial intelligence (AI) algorithms. China's digital economy and the importance of data and digital services are also intertwined with its manufacturing activity and the centrality of China in global value chains (GVCs), providing enormous scope to export digital services as inputs in manufactured products.

Yet China remains largely closed to foreign competition, with restrictions on digital services imports, a heavily restricted and regulated internet that requires data to be localized, and limited access to online information. These limits to foreign competition stand in contrast to China's outward-focused efforts to shape the international environment and the development of norms and rules affecting data governance consistent with its domestic approach. This includes in international standard-setting bodies, through its support for broadband connectivity and smart cities as part of its Digital Silk Road (DSR) and broader Belt and Road Initiative (BRI).

These Chinese efforts abroad and restrictions domestically are harmful to U.S. interests. The United States has been leading efforts supporting an open internet, particularly through its development of digital trade commitments and support for similar efforts in the G20 and Organization for Economic Cooperation and Development (OECD). However, more is needed to effectively counter China's efforts globally, including as part of its DSR, or risk an internet bifurcated between the United States and China, with security and economic consequences for the United States and its allies.

HOW BIG IS CHINA'S DIGITAL ECONOMY?

China's digital economy is large and growing. Based on an OECD taxonomy, figure 30-1 shows that China's digital economy was around 6 percent of gross domestic product in 2018, compared to around 7 percent in the United States, 8 percent in Japan, and 10 percent in Korea.

However, in absolute terms China has the world's second-largest digital economy, second only to the United States. Moreover, China has particular digital strengths. For example, China accounts for 40 percent of global e-

Figure 30-1. **China's Digital Economy**

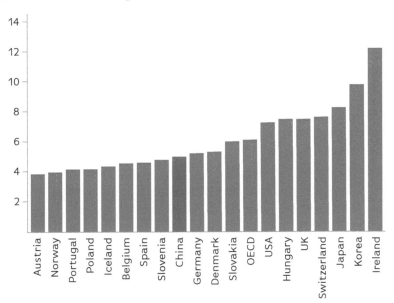

Sources: OECD, Natixis.

commerce transactions, larger than the value of France, Germany, Japan, the United Kingdom, and the United States combined.[1] The transaction value of China's mobile payments in 2016 was $790 billion, eleven times that of the United States, the next largest market. When it comes to AI, China overall trails the United States but leads in specific applications, such as facial recognition.[2] This range of digital activity drives extensive online activity that generates enormous quantities of data which can be used to train AI algorithms.

DIGITAL SERVICES, DATA, AND MANUFACTURING

Much of what drives China's digital economy—the data and key digital technologies—are digital services. In fact, the digital economy is largely about digital services and includes cloud computing, AI, blockchain, and data analytics to derive better business insights, manage supply chains, and enable digital payment, as well as the online delivery of professional services, retail, education, and health care.

Understanding the scope of China's digital services exports needs to account for the role of digital services as important inputs into manufacturing exports. In some areas of manufacturing, such as automobiles, the digital services component (including software, sensors, and AI) provides much of the value-add and is where competition is most fierce. In fact, McKinsey estimates that by 2030 up to 30 percent of automotive manufacturers' revenues will come from services offering.[3] China's growth in using digital services in manufacturing is part of a broader push by China into advanced manufacturing, which includes leading the world in its use of robots, where China holds one-third of global stock, over twice that of the United States.[4]

Chinese companies are also dominant in the supply of 5G hardware, which will also affect growth in data-driven services. By one measure, Huawei owns the largest share of standard essential patents on 5G.[5] 5G will bring high speed connectivity to the edge of the network, reducing latency and increasing speed.[6] This will enable the Internet of Things (IoT) and edge computing, and support a range of new applications, content, and businesses, such as augmented reality and autonomous delivery systems. Cisco estimates that the number of devices connected to the internet will be 30 billion by 2023, half of these being machine-to-machine connections, including connected factories, home devices, and cars.[7] 5G will also impact the development of global value chains and the role of digital services as 5G and associated technologies expand the capacity of business to collect data from things in real time, analyze the data, and develop business solutions along supply chains.[8] 5G will affect Chinese growth in digital services. In part as China rapidly installs 5G domestically, Chinese entrepreneurs will have a head start over their Western competitors developing new data-driven business models that 5G will enable with opportunities to get to market first. And where network effects create winner-take-all outcomes, potentially new and dominant tech companies.

CHINA'S DIGITAL SERVICES IN GVCs

China is also expanding its digital services exports and data governance more generally through its role as a central hub in GVCs and the BRI.

China is a central player when it comes to information and communication technology (ICT) goods exports as part of global supply chains. For instance, China accounts for 32 percent of global ICT goods exports (11 percent in value-added terms—reflecting China's position in GVCs), and around 6 percent of ICT services exports. However, these figures understate the importance of China's digital services exports because they fail to account for services as value-added inputs into manufacturing and export—often in the context of GVCs.[9] This growth of services in manufacturing GVCs has contributed to services exports growing faster than goods exports.[10] The World Trade Organization (WTO) estimates that services account for 30 percent of the value of China manufactured exports in 2015, which is a 19 percent growth in services value added since 2005.[11] The trends toward using services and data in GVC point to the broader servicification of manufacturing, another development that China is driving and is well positioned to take advantage of.[12]

THE DIGITAL DIMENSION TO BRI

China is also expanding its digital services and approach to data governance through the development of a Digital Silk Road (DSR), which aims to expand internet infrastructure, promote e-commerce, and develop common internet technology standards among participating countries.[13] China's March 2015 white paper made digital connectivity a top priority. As of 2019, China had invested over $80 billion in digital DSR projects, including fiber-optic cables. China is also building data centers, which Beijing has called a "fundamental strategic resource."[14] These developments are integrated with other BRI initiatives, including smart cities, ports, and space systems.[15] Each of these developments creates new opportunities for China to expand access to data and integrate DSR countries into a broader digital ecosystem centered around China.[16]

CHINA'S GOVERNANCE OF DIGITAL SERVICES AND DATA

China's regime for governing digital services and data is based around a relatively closed domestic market for digital services alongside restrictions on cross-border data flows, including access to information. This closed market helps underpin Chinese support for national champions, including by preventing access by Chinese citizens to their U.S. competitors. The extent of Chinese control over data and access to information led former Google CEO Eric Schmidt to foresee the single global internet bifurcating into a U.S.- and China-led internet.[17] This could also include different standards and frequencies for 5G. Indeed, both the United States and China have identified leadership in 5G standards as a key element to securing their version of 5G.[18] The risk for the United States of a bifurcated internet is further heightened by China's efforts to shape the international environment to support its vision of data governance and digital services exports.

Restricted Domestic Market for Digital Services

China maintains a relatively restricted market for digital services. The OECD digital services trade index in figure 30-2 shows barriers affecting trade in digitally enabled services categorized into five policy areas: infrastructure and connectivity, electronic transactions, payment systems, intellectual property rights, and other barriers. The higher the score, the greater the restrictions. As can be seen, among the countries listed, China is most restrictive when it comes to digital service across all metrics. China is also most restrictive when it comes to telecommunications services.[19]

These restrictions are paired with domestic policy aimed at dominating emerging technologies. This includes industrial policies, such as the National Medium and Long-Term Science and Technology Development Plan Outline (2006–2020), which calls for China to become an innovation-oriented society by the year 2020 and a world leader in science and technology by 2050, based on developing capabilities for indigenous innovation. The Made in China 2025 initiative launched in 2015 is a ten-year plan for China to achieve 70 percent self-sufficiency in strategic technologies, such

Figure 30-2. China's Digital Services Trade Regulation Are the Most Restrictive

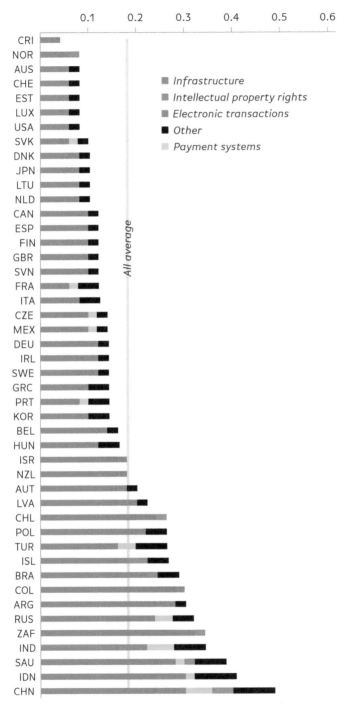

Legend:
- Infrastructure
- Intellectual property rights
- Electronic transactions
- Other
- Payment systems

Note: The indices take values between zero and one, one being the most restrictive. Scale adjusted to 0.6.

Source: OECD Digital STRI database (http://oe.cd/stri-db).

as advance information technology, robotics, aircraft, new energy vehicles, new material, and biotechnology. Similar industrial policies are also being implemented at the sub–central government level.[20]

Restrictions on Cross-Border Data Flows

China also employs the most extensive restriction on access to and use of data, including data localization requirements and restrictions on movement of data across borders, further restricting opportunities for digital services trade. Figure 30-3 shows the number of data flow restrictions and compares that with other economies within the Asia-Pacific Economic Cooperation (APEC).

Figure 30-3. China Has the Largest Number of and the Most Data Flow Restrictions in Asia-Pacific Economic Cooperation

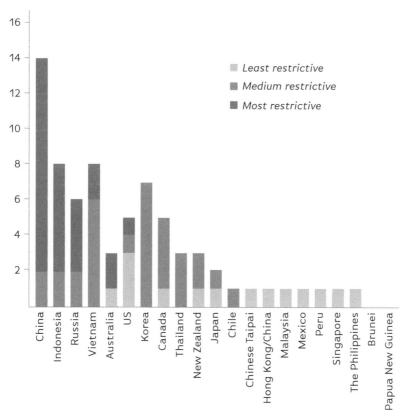

Source: Joshua P. Meltzer, 2020, "How APEC can address restrictions on cross-border data flows," https://ab46bb92-a539-4d61-9a28-f77eb5f41c00.usrfiles.com/ugd/ab46bb_830a70b4 f8dc4508a38d3e480ffa9cb2.pdf.

China's most restrictive cross-border data flow regulations are around security, internet access, and control and financial flows and services. Such data flow restrictions include China requiring banks and insurers to localize data and China's data localization requirements under its cybersecurity law. In addition to restricting data flows, which affects access for digital services, these regulations could be used to require access to companies' source codes and intellectual property under the guise of national security, which could be used by Chinese companies to compete against U.S. and other companies.[21]

Shaping the International Environment to Suit Chinese Interests
China is affecting the market for digital services and the uptake globally of Chinese data governance practices by influencing international norms and rules and by creating facts on the ground, such as by leveraging the DSR and access to China's internal market.

A key area where China is working to develop rules and norms that will affect growth for China's digital services trade is by shaping international standards to suit Chinese companies and technologies.[22] Chinese companies and officials engage across standards-setting organizations and forums, including the 3GPP (3rd Generation Partnership Project), which is responsible for 5G standards, and in the International Telecommunication Union (ITU), where China is working to develop standards that suit its technological ambitions, such as in areas of facial recognition and IoT.[23] This includes placing Chinese officials in senior positions in the ITU and supporting participation of Chinese engineers in technical working groups.[24] Chinese-specific standards are also being normalized through the DSR as investments in connectivity, smart cities, and data centers, which come with Chinese standards.[25]

HOW SHOULD THE UNITED STATES RESPOND?

The United States has already responded in part. It is developing new digital trade rules in free trade agreements supporting the free flow of data and further services trade liberalization. The United States is also pushing for data flow commitments in the WTO e-commerce negotiations.[26] In the G20, the United States has worked with leaders on statements regarding data flows and digital trade, yet these G20 outcomes have been limited by G20 members China, India, and Russia.[27]

The United States continues to work on developing international standards. As noted, however, China's strategic engagement with international standards bodies, including the resources China brings to bear, suggests that the United States needs to revisit its approach to standard setting, including allocating increased resources and political capital to ensure that international standards are technically optimal and support open and competitive markets.

U.S. efforts to address Huawei's engagement in 5G are well documented. Tom Wheeler has suggested that another way of addressing Huawei's proprietary edge in 5G equipment is to support open standards for 5G.[28]

The United States is also working with allies on broader data governance issues around specific technologies, such as through the Global Partnership on Artificial Intelligence and developing OECD principles on AI. These efforts strengthen normative expectations that markets remain open and competitive.

However, more is needed from the United States. Any approach to addressing the challenges China presents on digital services trade and data governance will require a coordinated approach with allies as well as more attention domestically to the regulatory issues that drive data flow restrictions.[29] On the international front, the United States should work with likeminded countries on a comprehensive approach to data governance that could also draw in market access issues around data flows and access to digital services. This could involve some combination of more robust common international standards and development of interoperability mechanisms that support data flows and achieving domestic regulatory objectives, such as privacy and cybersecurity.[30]

In parallel, the United States needs more comprehensive domestic regulation on various data and tech issues, particularly federal privacy regulation. This is needed to address concerns among allies, especially the EU with respect to online privacy. Progress here could lead to better alignment and ambition among U.S. allies on other U.S. data governance priorities. More broadly, the traditional reliance of the United States on industry self-regulation has left the U.S. government with an absence of robust regulatory models around data governance that can serve as a guide to other countries looking to understand how to shore up trust in online activity while also benefiting from the economic and trade opportunities of cross-border data flows. The lack of any such U.S. regulatory models has provided space for China's approach to gain traction, pulling these countries closer into the digital sphere that China is carving out for itself, including all the concomitant emphasis on data restrictions and data localization that act as barriers to trade in digital services.

NOTES

1. Jonathan Woetzel, Jeongmin Seong, Kevin Wei Wang, James Manyika, Michael Chui, and Wendy Wong, *China's Digital Economy a Leading Global Force* (New York: McKinsey Global Institute, August 3, 2017), www.mckinsey.com/featured-insights/china/chinas-digital-economy-a-leading-global-force#.

2. Daniel Castro, Michael McLaughlin, and Eline Chivot, "Who Is Winning the AI Race: China, the EU or the United States?" Center for Data Innovation, August 19, 2019, www.datainnovation.org/2019/08/who-is-winning-the-ai-race-china-the-eu-or-the-united-states/.

3. Susan Lund, James Manyika, Jonathan Woetzel, Jacques Bughin, Mekala Krishnan, Jeongmin Seong, and Mac Muir, *Globalization in Transition: The Future of Trade and Value Chains* (New York: McKinsey Global Institute, January 16, 2019), www.mckinsey.com/featured-insights/innovation-and-growth/globalization-in-transition-the-future-of-trade-and-value-chains.

4. International Federation of Robotics, China forecast 2020. https://ifr.org/news/robots-china-breaks-historic-records-in-automation/.

5. Robert Clark, "Who Rules 5G Patents? It Depends How You Ask," Light-Reading, January 14, 2020, www.lightreading.com/asia-pacific/who-rules-5g-patents-it-depends-how-you-ask/d/d-id/756790.

6. Tom Wheeler, *5G in Five (not so) Easy Pieces* (Washington, DC: The Brookings Institution, July 2019), www.brookings.edu/research/5g-in-five-not-so-easy-pieces/.

7. "Cisco Annual Internet Report (20182–023)," San Jose, CA: Cisco, March 9, 2020, www.cisco.com/c/en/us/solutions/collateral/executive-perspectives/annual-internet-report/white-paper-c11-741490.html.

8. Yun Chao Hu, Milan Patel, Dario Sabella, Nurit Sprecher, and Valerie Young, *Mobile Edge Computing: A Key Technology Towards 5G* (Sophia Antipolis, France: European Telecommunications Standards Institute, September 2015), https://infotech.report/Resources/Whitepapers/f205849d-0109-4de3-8c47-be52f4e4fb27_etsi_wp11_mec_a_key_technology_towards_5g.pdf.

9. Sébastien Miroudot and Charles Cadestin, "Services in Global Value Chains: From Inputs to Value-Creating Activities" OECD Trade Policy Papers 197 (Paris: Organisation for Economic Co-operation and Development, March 15, 2017), https://doi.org/10.1787/465f0d8b-en.

10. *World Development Report 2020: Trading for Development in the Age of Global Value Chains* (Washington, DC: World Bank, 2020), file:///C:/Users/Owner/Downloads/9781464814570.pdf.

11. "China: Trade in Value Added and Global Value Chains," World Trade Organization, www.wto.org/english/res_e/statis_e/miwi_e/CN_e.pdf.

12. Rainer Lanz and Andreas Maurer, "Services and Global Value Chains: Some Evidence on Servicification of Manufacturing and Services Networks" (Geneva: World Trade Organization, 2015), https://ideas.repec.org/p/zbw/wtowps/ersd2015 03.html; Sébastien Miroudot and Charles Cadestin, "Services in Global Value Chains."

13. "Full Text of the Vision for Maritime Cooperation under the Belt and Road Initiative," State Council of the People's Republic of China, June 20, 2017, http://english.www.gov.cn/archive/publications/2017/06/20/content_281475691873460.htm.

14. "The 13th Five-Year Plan for Economic and Social Development of the People's Republic of China (2016–2020)," National Development and Reform Commission, 2016, https://en.ndrc.gov.cn/policyrelease_8233/201612/P02019110148 2242850325.pdf.

15. Daniel R. Russell and Blake H. Berger, *Weaponizing the Belt and Road Initiative* (Washington, DC: Asia Policy Society Institute, September 2020), https://asiasociety.org/sites/default/files/2020-09/Weaponizing%20the%20Belt%20 and%20Road%20Initiative_0.pdf.

16. Ibid.; Melanie Hart, *Mapping China's Global Governance Ambitions* (Washington, DC: Center for American Progress, February 28, 2019), www.americanprog ress.org/issues/security/reports/2019/02/28/466768/mapping-chinas-global-gover nance-ambitions/.

17. Laura Kolodny, "Former Google CEO Predicts the Internet Will Split in Two—and One Part Will Be Led by China," CNBC, September 20, 2018, www.cnbc .com/2018/09/20/eric-schmidt-ex-google-ceo-predicts-internet-split-china.html.

18. "National Strategy to Secure 5G of the United States of America" (Washington, DC: The White House, March 2020), www.whitehouse.gov/wp-content/up loads/2020/03/National-Strategy-5G-Final.pdf.

19. *OECD Services Trade Restrictiveness Index: Policy Trends up to 2020* (Paris: Organisation for Economic Co-operation and Development, January 2020,) www .oecd.org/trade/topics/services-trade/documents/oecd-stri-policy-trends-up-to -2020.pdf.

20. *Priority Recommendations for U.S.-China Trade Negotiations* (Washington, DC: American Chamber of Commerce and American Chamber of Commerce in China, 2019),www.wsj.com/public/resources/documents/tradereport.pdf?mod= article_inline

21. Aruna Viswanatha, Kate O'Keeffe, and Dustin Volz, "U.S. Accuses Chinese Firm, Partner of Stealing Trade Secrets from Micron," *Wall Street Journal*, November 1, 2018, www.wsj.com/articles/u-s-accuses-two-firms-of-stealing-trade-secrets -from-micron-technology-1541093537.

22. John Chen, Emily Walz, Brian Lafferty, Joe McReynolds, Kieran Green, Jonathan Ray, and James Mulvenon, *China's Internet of Things* (Vienna, VA: SOS International LLC, October 2018,) www.uscc.gov/sites/default/files/Research/ SOSi_China%27s%20Internet%20of%20Things.pdf.

23. Anna Gross, Madhumita Murgia, and Yuan Yang, "Chinese Tech Groups

Shaping UN Facial Recognition Standards," *Financial Times*, December 1, 2019, www.ft.com/content/c3555a3c-0d3e-11ea-b2d6-9bf4d1957a67. John Chen et al., *China's Internet of Things*.

24. Alan Weissberger, "Strategic Analytics: Huawei 1st among Top 5 Contributors to 3GPP 5G Specs," *IEEE ComSoc Technology Blog*, March 17, 2020, https://techblog.comsoc.org/2020/03/17/strategy-analytics-huawei-1st-among-top-5-contributors-to-3gpp-5g-specs/.

25. John Chen et al., *China's Internet of Things*.

26. Joshua P. Meltzer, "The United States-Mexico-Canada Agreement: Developing Trade Policy for Digital Trade," *Trade Law and Development* 11, no. 2 (Winter 2019), www.tradelawdevelopment.com/index.php/tld/article/view/11%282%29%20TL%26D%20239%20%282019%29/365.

27. "2019 G20 Osaka Leaders' Declaration," G20, 2019, https://g20.org/en/g20/Documents/2019-Japan-G20%20Osaka%20Leaders%20Declaration.pdf.

28. Tom Wheeler, "Moving from 'Secret Sauce' to Open Standards for 5G," The Brookings Institution, *Techtank* (blog), February 18, 2020, www.brookings.edu/blog/techtank/2020/02/18/moving-from-secret-sauce-to-open-standards-for-5g/.

29. Joshua P. Meltzer, "Governing Digital Trade," *World Trade Review* 18, no. S1 (April 12, 2019), www.cambridge.org/core/journals/world-trade-review/article/governing-digital-trade/6FFC3F6D33D0887663F72FA0101FCBDC.

30. Joshua P. Meltzer and Abdelhamid Mamdouh, "Trade Policy and Data Flows—Progress to Data and Future Innovations," in *Exploring International Data Flow Governance: Platform for Shaping the Future of Trade and Global Economic Interdependence*, ed. Richard Samans and Kimberly Botwright (Geneva: World Economic Forum, December 2019), www3.weforum.org/docs/WEF_Trade_Policy_Data_Flows_Report.pdf.

31

China's Influence on the Global Middle Class

HOMI KHARAS
MEAGAN DOOLEY

Around 1950, over 90 percent of the global middle class resided in Europe and North America; the United States alone was home to almost 40 percent of the middle class. So it is not surprising that a middle-class lifestyle became synonymous with achieving the American Dream. The middle class consisted of those with the aspirations and means to own a home and a car, take an annual vacation, send their kids to college, and achieve reasonable health and retirement security. The middle class valued hard work, education, thrift, and determination as pathways to this lifestyle—individualistic attributes that could flourish in a democracy.

This American model was so successfully developed in Western economies and Japan that by 1978 about 1 billion people in the world had become middle class, according to at least one definition.[1] Coincidentally, 1978 also marked the year when Deng Xiaoping visited Malaysia, Thailand, and Singapore and then announced that China would henceforth pursue an "Open Door" policy to encourage foreign investment to help transform China's economy—the start of the development of China's middle class.

Since that time, China has impacted the global middle class through its size and numbers, its increasing ability to set new middle-class trends, and its challenge to the values and attributes of what belonging to the middle class really means.

THE NUMBERS GAME

As is true on so many economic issues, the immediate impact of China on the middle class has been in terms of numbers. We measure the size of the middle class here following the methodology laid out in a 2010 working paper by one of us, Kharas, as those individuals spending $11 to $110 per person per day in 2011 purchasing power parity (PPP) terms.[2] This metric, an absolute definition, allows us to compare numbers across countries and over time in a consistent way.[3] The Chinese are relative latecomers to the global middle class. Although China's economy has grown rapidly for many years now, Chinese households receive a very low share of national income and so did not have the income to achieve a middle-class lifestyle until quite recently—around 2010, household consumption was just 36 percent of GDP, compared to 68 percent in the United States. So the absolute number of Chinese middle-class consumers was quite small. In fact, in 2006, when the Chinese middle class started to explode, less than 10 percent of China's population was probably middle class—perhaps 90 million people compared to well over 200 million in the United States.

In the ensuing years, however, China has been adding an average of 60 million people to its middle class every year. By 2016, most Chinese could be classified as middle class—some 730 million of them. This mirrors findings in a recent McKinsey report, which estimates that 730 million people in urban areas in China in 2018 fell into the income categories of "aspirants" and "affluents" (roughly corresponding to our definition of middle class).[4] (Rural China is still largely poor.) Part of the growth in China's middle class comes from job creation—an estimated 7.7 million per year, according to the Chinese Academy of Social Sciences.[5] But the vast majority of the growth is driven by higher wages as workers shift to more productive jobs.

There are other indicators of China's rapidly growing middle class. China has become the world's largest car producer, accounting for one-third to one-half of all global sales.[6] China is the world's largest smartphone market, accounting for 20 percent of Apple's iPhone sales as well as providing a large home market for domestic Chinese brands. Chinese citizens took 300 million vacation and business trips in 2019; 166 million of these trips were abroad and 140 million were within China.[7]

Already, China has the largest middle-class consumption market segment in the world (table 31-1). The global middle-class market is massive—over $41 trillion in 2020 measured in PPP terms. Of this total, Chinese middle-class consumers were on track to spend $7.3 trillion in 2020. Of course, each individual middle-class consumer in the United States spends more than the Chinese counterpart on average, but the sheer numbers of the Chinese middle class make its market size larger. And the gap between China's middle-class market size and that of other countries is only set to expand as China continues to enjoy more rapid economic growth than any other major economy, a gap accentuated by the seemingly limited impact of COVID-19 on the Chinese economy compared with that of other countries.

The growth in China's middle-class consumption on a global scale is exceptional by historical standards. Other countries have also increased their share of the global middle-class market, starting with the United Kingdom, where the middle class was launched by the Industrial Revolution, followed by the United States, and later on, Europe and Japan. However, none of these episodes has been as dramatic as China's rise. As figure 31-1 shows, China is still in its most expansionary phase, and by the time it is over in 2027 it will have raised its share of global middle-class consumption by almost 20 percentage points. At this point, an estimated 1.2 billion Chinese will be in the middle class, one-quarter of the global total.

Table 31-1. **Top 10 Countires by Total Middle-Class Expenditures in 2020 (Trillions, 2011 PPP)**

Country	Middle class expenditures
China	$7.30
United States	$4.70
India	$2.90
Japan	$2.00
Russian Federation	$1.60
Germany	$1.50
Indonesia	$1.20
United Kingdom	$1.10
Brazil	$1.10
France	$1.00

Source: Authors' calculations based on methodology in Kharas 2010 and using International Monetary Fund June 2020 GDP estimates.

Figure 31-1. **Biggest Change over 20 Years in Share of Middle-Class Consumption Expenditures, PPP**

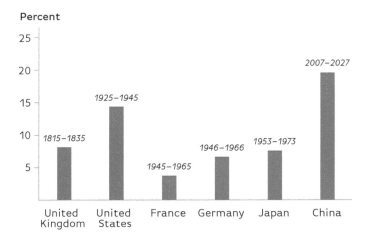

Source: Maddison Historical Statistics; International Monetary Fund; author calculations.

FROM COPYING TO TREND-SETTING

The initial phase of China's middle-class expansion copied Western trends in many ways. It was defined by increased spending on consumer durables like cars and appliances, preferences for upgraded quality, and expanded homeownership.

However, China has moved beyond copying the model of middle-class growth in other countries and is now setting global trends. China has emerged as a leader in e-commerce, fintech, and social networking platforms, driven by tech giants like Alibaba and Tencent. Fintech innovations have transformed the way consumers make purchases and interact with vendors.

China now accounts for 40 percent of global e-commerce transactions and is seeing exponential growth (figure 31-2). Online sales account for 15 percent of total retail sales in China, compared with 10 percent in the United States.[8] The Chinese middle class has leapfrogged from using cash as a dominant form of payment to using mobile money on platforms like Alibaba and WeChat. There are now over 1 billion users on each of these platforms, and 90 percent of Chinese consumers rely on mobile money as their primary form of payment.[9]

Figure 31-2. **Mobile Payment Transaction Volume**

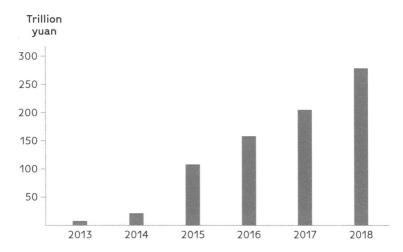

Source: The Brookings Institution, reprinted from Aaron Klein, "China's digital payments revolution." Data from People's Bank of China, Caixin Data, CEIC.

In addition, fintech is changing the ecosystem of small and medium-sized enterprise (SME) finance in China. Credit card processing fees cost American small businesses an average of 2 percent of gross sales.[10] Alipay and WeChat Pay, on the other hand, have no transaction fees on purchases made within their digital commerce platform, and a 0.1 percent fee on outside transfers.[11] Fintech is also opening credit and financing options for SMEs. Only 20 percent of SMEs in China have borrowed from a formal financial institution. Banks have traditionally not lent to SMEs due to perceived credit risk, though the government is working to incentivize greater SME lending.[12] E-commerce and fintech players are entering the lending space and using new digital tools to improve risk assessments. MYbank (backed by Alibaba) and WeBank (backed by Tencent) are using real-time transaction data, social network and behavioral data from social media, and machine learning to come up with their own credit scores to assess loan eligibility. Fintech players are thus able to offer loans almost instantly to firms that may have been unable to access credit before, due to limited or poor credit history. These platforms have now lent to over 10 million SMEs, with a nonperformance rate of just 1 percent. Fintech credit reached $543 billion globally in 2017, $170 billion of which came from tech players like Alibaba and Tencent.[13]

Based on the changing nature of the economy that these platforms have enabled, the Chinese leadership is trying to encourage mass entrepreneurship and innovation as a driver of economic growth, jobs for graduates, and quality upgrading.[14] If successful, this will change the nature of the middle class, from "salaryman" to "small businesswoman," from a risk-averse worker to a risk-taking, creative, independent gig contractor.

THE CHALLENGES AND COSTS OF CHINESE MIDDLE-CLASS EXPANSION

As China's middle class grows, it poses three challenges and costs for others around the world. First, can the world sustain such a large consumer class within the boundaries set by the planet's natural resources? Second, does China's middle class pose a competitive threat to the middle class elsewhere, or is it a positive force promoting global growth? Third, how will the politics of China's new middle class play out?

Planetary Boundaries

Consumerism across the world is damaging our planet. Climate change, zoonotic disease, species extinction, plastic contamination of marine areas, overfishing and collapsing fish stocks, and excess use of phosphorus and nitrogen are all by-products of the unsustainable consumption and production structures that try to satisfy the middle and rich classes' demand for more, and cheaper, goods, services, and food.

China is a contributor to this problem—China is the world's largest builder of new coal plants and the largest carbon emitter in absolute terms.[15] But the problem has not been caused by China alone. Pollution damage is cumulative—the impact of two centuries of growth since the Industrial Revolution. With the entry of China, India, and the rest of developing Asia into middle-class powerhouses, there is now a new sense of urgency to tackle these issues on a global scale. China's recent announcement to reach carbon neutrality by 2060,[16] its efforts to develop smart cities,[17] and its leadership in various green technologies including solar, rail, and batteries,[18] suggest it is mindful of commercial opportunities in sustainable development. But the problems are global and need global collective action involving all large economies if planetary sustainability and global prosperity are to coexist.

Does China's Middle Class Help or Hurt Others?

Traditionally, international trade has been seen as beneficial to the middle class. If a trading partner grows, everyone benefits in the new equilibrium. The new middle classes of China and the rest of Asia have provided cheap consumer goods (and a greater variety of consumer goods) to the middle-class markets of America and Europe. At the same time, Chinese middle-class consumers provide a large and growing market for American firms—the top twenty U.S. firms alone had sales in China of $158 billion last year. These are classic gains from trade.

Because of China's size, however, and the failure to preadjust to the global decision to terminate the Agreement on Textiles and Clothing in 2005, there have been significant adjustment costs to workers in specific sectors and places in developed countries. For these workers, job losses and depressed wages have damaged their middle-class standing.[19] Indeed, the whole issue of whether the middle class gains or loses from trade and globalization is being reevaluated. Most academic studies show a mixed pattern of some winners and some losers, but an aggregate net gain. The better the ability of governments to compensate losers from the gains of winners, the greater the likelihood the middle class supports free trade.

The Politics Challenge

In America and the West, becoming middle class is no longer synonymous with being happy. The General Social Survey in the United States shows a steep decline in perceived happiness since the late 1980s.[20] Mortality from suicide, opioids, and alcohol in the United States and deaths of exhaustion in the case of Japan suggest a large disconnect between people's lived experiences in middle-class households and the theory that the middle class is the ticket to a good life.

In China, by contrast, middle-class households are seemingly more content with the way things are going. China leads the world in the Edelman Trust Barometer in terms of the general population's trust that the system is working for them.[21] Chinese households are far more likely to reply affirmatively to a question about whether they and their families are likely to be better off in five years' time than their Western counterparts.

Among the Chinese middle class, administrative efficiency and performance seem to be valued above, or as much as, participation in political affairs.[22] This "authoritarian bargain,"[23] however, can lead to a toxic mix of politics and economics. Just as the middle class lent its support to fascism in

Germany and Italy, a middle class in China could support nationalism and expansionism if it believes these to be necessary to safeguard their economic interests. This is not inevitable—indeed there is almost no correlation across countries or over time between the size of the middle class and the degree of liberalism in domestic politics—but equally not a scenario to be ignored.

CONCLUSION

The global middle class is evolving fast. The sheer size of the Chinese middle class suggests that its power and influence are here to stay—as young Chinese professionals move to second- and third-tier cities so that they are able to afford a middle-class lifestyle, their preferences will increasingly shape global consumption. Hopefully, they will be steered toward a more sustainable consumption footprint than current middle-class consumers in the West. Whether these new middle-class citizens push for more openness and liberalism, or opt for the current nationalist model that provides predictability and stable growth, remains to be seen.

NOTES

1. Homi Kharas, "The Emerging Middle Class in Developing Countries," Working Paper 285 (Paris: OECD Development Centre, 2010), www.oecd.org/development/pgd/44457738.pdf.

2. Ibid.

3. There are many alternative definitions of the middle class. None of these measures are right or wrong. Generally speaking, the thresholds used fall into two categories; relative thresholds (xx% to yy% of median income, for example), and absolute thresholds. Absolute thresholds, including ours, are more appropriate for looking at comparisons over time and across countries. However, absolute numbers and growth rates of the middle class will vary according to the definition used. Richard V. Reeves, Katherine Guyot, and Eleanor Krause, "A Dozen Ways to Be Middle Class," The Brookings Institution, May 8, 2018, www.brookings.edu/interactives/a-dozen-ways-to-be-middle-class/.

4. Johnny Ho, Felix Poh, Jia Zhou, and Daniel Zipster, *China Consumer Report 2020: The Many Faces of the Chinese Consumer* (New York: McKinsey and Company, December 18, 2019), www.mckinsey.com/featured-insights/china/china-consumer-report-2020-the-many-faces-of-the-chinese-consumer#.

5. Lu Xueyi, "现在是中国中产阶层发展的黄金时期" [It's the "golden age" of Chinese middle-class development], 中国青年报 [China youth daily], February 11, 2010, http://zqb.cyol.com/content/2010-02/11/content_3088401.htm.

6. Tom Hancock, "Carmakers Face Cuts and Gloom as China Sales Shift into

Reverse," *Financial Times*, January 15, 2019, www.ft.com/content/bcb902e4-1895 -11e9-9e64-d150b3105d21.

7. "2019 China Tourism Facts & Figures," Travel China Guide, 2019, www. travelchinaguide.com/tourism/2019statistics/.

8. Longmei Zhang and Sally Chen, "China's Digital Economy: Opportunities and Risks," Working Paper 19/16 (Washington, DC: International Monetary Fund, January 17, 2019), www.imf.org/en/Publications/WP/Issues/2019/01/17/Chinas -Digital-Economy-Opportunities-and-Risks-46459.

9. Aaron Klein, *China's Digital Payments Revolution* (Washington, DC: The Brookings Institution, April 2020), www.brookings.edu/research/chinas-digital -payments-revolution/.

10. Chris Kissell, "How Small Businesses Can Save on Credit Card Processing Fees," *U.S. News & World Report*, October 24, 2018, https://creditcards.usnews.com /articles/how-small-businesses-can-save-on-credit-card-processing-fees.

11. "Alipay to Charge Bank Transfer Free from Oct 12," *China Daily*, September 13, 2016, www.chinadaily.com.cn/bizchina/2016-09/13/content_26778445.htm; Zen Soo, "Tencent to Charge Users in China for Transferring Money from WeChat Wallet to Bank Accounts," *South China Morning Post*, February 16, 2016, www. scmp.com/tech/apps-gaming/article/1913503/tencent-charge-users-china -transferring-money-wechat-wallet-bank.

12. Huang Yiping, "This Is How Digital Banking Could Boost China's Economy," World Economic Forum, February 17, 2020, www.weforum.org/agenda/2020/02/ china-digital-revolution-bank-lending-finance-economy.

13. Giulio Cornelli, Vukile Davidson, Jon Frost, Leonardo Gambacorta, and Kyoko Oishi, "SME Finance in Asia: Recent Innovations in Fintech Credit, Trade Finance, and Beyond," ADBI Working Paper Series 1027 (Tokyo: Asian Development Bank Institute, October 2019), www.adb.org/sites/default/files/publication/535836/ adbi-wp1027.pdf.

14. "China to Upgrade Mass Entrepreneurship and Innovation," Xinhua, September 6, 2018, www.xinhuanet.com/english/2018-09/06/c_137450275.htm.

15. Thomas Hale and Leslie Hook, "China Expands Coal Plant Capacity to Boost Post-virus Economy," *Financial Times*, June 24, 2020, www.ft.com/content/ cdcd8a02-81b5-48f1-a4a5-60a93a6ffa1e; Steve Inskeep and Ashley Westerman, "Why Is China Placing a Global Bet on Coal?" NPR, April 29, 2019, www.npr.org/ 2019/04/29/716347646/why-is-china-placing-a-global-bet-on-coal.

16. Somini Sengupta, "China, in Pointed Message to U.S., Tightens Its Climate Targets," *New York Times*, September 22, 2020, www.nytimes.com/2020/09/22/ climate/china-emissions.html.

17. Katherine Atha, Jason Callahan, John Chen, Jessica Drun, Ed Francis, Kieran Green, Dr. Brian Lafferty, Joe McReynolds, Dr. James Mulvenon, Benjamin Rosen, and Emily Walz, *China's Smart Cities Development* (Vienna, VA: SOS International LLC, January 2020), www.uscc.gov/sites/default/files/China_Smart_ Cities_Development.pdf.

18. Scott Malcomson, "How China Became the World's Leader in Green Energy,"

Foreign Affairs, February 28, 2020, www.foreignaffairs.com/articles/china/2020-02 -28/how-china-became-worlds-leader-green-energy.

19. David Autor, David Dorn, and Gordon Hanson, "The China Shock: Learning from Labor Market Adjustment to Large Changes in Trade," *Annual Review of Economics* 8, no. 1 (October 2016): 205–240, www.annualreviews.org/doi/10.1146/ annurev-economics-080315-015041.

20. "The General Social Survey," NORC at University of Chicago, https://gss. norc.org/.

21. *2019 Edelman Trust Barometer Global Report* (Chicago: Edelman, 2019), www.edelman.com/sites/g/files/aatuss191/files/2019-02/2019_Edelman_Trust_ Barometer_Global_Report_2.pdf.

22. Michael Swaine and Ryan DeVries, "Chinese State-Society Relations: Why Beijing Isn't Trembling and Containment Won't Work," Carnegie Endowment for International Peace, March 14, 2019, https://carnegieendowment.org/2019/03/14/ chinese-state-society-relations-why-beijing-isn-t-trembling-and-containment-won -t-work-pub-78596.

23. Raj M. Desai, Anders Olofsgård, and Tarik Yousef, "The Logic of Authoritarian Bargains," *Economics & Politics* 21, no. 1 (March 2009): 93–125, www .brookings.edu/articles/the-logic-of-authoritarian-bargains/.

32

The Global Energy Trade's New Center of Gravity

SAMANTHA GROSS

China has become the center of gravity for global energy markets. While energy demand growth has slowed or stopped in the Organization for Economic Co-operation and Development (OECD) countries, China's primary energy demand increased by more than 45 percent over the last decade.[1] The question is whether such growth will continue and how China's energy system will change in response to the dual challenges of climate change and local pollution.

China depends on fossil fuel imports; it is the world's largest importer of oil and natural gas[2] and an important coal importer as well. At the same time, China strives to lead in wind and solar electricity generation and electric vehicles. To understand how China fits into energy markets and how energy shapes its policy, examining the electricity and oil and gas industries separately is illustrative. China is more in charge of its own fate in electricity, while it remains highly vulnerable to market conditions and supply shocks in oil and gas.

ELECTRICITY

As a result of rapid economic growth, demand for electricity in China in 2019 was more than five times its level in 2000. Thus China has added vast generation capacity of every type.

Coal dominates the Chinese power sector, although its share of generation dropped from its high point of 81 percent in 2007 to 66 percent in 2019.[3]
From 2000 to 2019, China added 493 gigawatts of coal-fired generation capacity.[4] Natural gas generation has also grown rapidly since 2014, but from
a much smaller base, and reached 3.2 percent of Chinese power generation
in 2019.[5]

Coal additions were particularly rapid during the 12th Five-Year Plan,
from 2011 through 2015, as China encouraged the construction of coal-fired
power plants to stimulate growth as the economy recovered from the global
financial crisis. However, this situation led to overcapacity, and the subsequent 13th Five-Year Plan, for 2016 through 2020, aimed to contain growth
in coal-fired power.[6] Nonetheless, China is still experiencing overcapacity
of coal-fired generation, with its plants running at less than 50 percent of
capacity on average in 2019.[7]

The upcoming 14th Five-Year Plan, for 2021 through 2025, will be a key
document in mapping the future of China's electricity system. China's Nationally Determined Contribution (NDC) under the Paris Agreement calls
for its greenhouse gas emissions to peak no later than 2030. However, the
behemoth State Grid Corporation and the China Electricity Council are
both pushing for inclusion of more coal-fired power in the new plan, in part
to encourage economic recovery from the COVID-19 pandemic.[8] Building
more coal, even the most efficient ultra-supercritical plants, is not consistent
with China meeting its NDC nor with the world's overall climate goals.

As demand for coal-fired power plants declines in China, the country is
financing and building capacity abroad through the Belt and Road Initiative
(BRI). As of 2017, China had committed to or offered financing for more
than one-quarter of the coal-fired capacity being built outside China, often
with Chinese companies as the engineering, procurement, and construction contractors.[9] China is becoming the lender of last resort for coal-fired
generation, as many international banks are no longer financing coal-fired
power projects.[10]

Rapid growth in China's renewable energy sector gets a lot of attention,
and rightly so. Over the last decade, China added 36 percent of the world's
total new wind and solar capacity. In 2017, wind and solar capacity additions
in China were 45 percent of the global total. Despite these additions, in 2019
wind and solar together still made up less than 10 percent of China's power
generation, with wind at 5.5 percent and solar at 3.0 percent (figure 32-1).[11]

China faces challenges in integrating that new wind and solar power

Figure 32-1. **Chinese Electricity Generation, by Fuel**

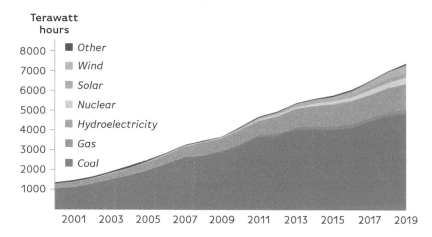

Source: "BP Statistical Review of World Energy 2020."

into its grid. The lack of long-distance, high-voltage transmission capacity results in significant amounts of wind and solar power being curtailed, meaning that it is generated without being used. Excessive curtailment led China's National Energy Agency in 2019 to halt new solar development in Gansu, Xinjiang, and Tibet provinces.[12] Many large renewable projects are located in these remote regions, where there is less competition for land.

Additionally, subsidies for renewable energy are being phased out. China is halving its feed-in-tariff for solar power and eliminating subsidies for off-shore wind in 2020, and plans to end subsidies for onshore wind in 2021.[13] Falling costs mean that new wind and solar installations can compete with coal- and gas-fired power.

China is a world leader in solar equipment manufacturing, with seven of the top ten solar manufacturers globally in 2019.[14] China is less dominant in wind turbine manufacturing; top-ten manufacturers are in Europe, the United States, India, and China.[15] China also leads the world in renewable energy patents since 2000. Renewable energy is an industrial priority for President Xi Jinping and is included in the 13th Five-Year Plan as a "Strategic Emerging Industry."[16]

OIL AND GAS

Unlike in electricity, where China is a technology leader, China depends on imports for its oil and gas supply. China has been a net oil importer since 1993 and became the world's largest oil importer in 2017. Most of China's oil production takes place in aging fields with high production costs. Although production increased by about 100,000 barrels per day in 2019,[17] this production rise, and Chinese production in general, is unlikely to be profitable in today's low oil price environment.

From the early 2000s until about 2015, China's oil companies focused on acquiring production assets abroad to meet the country's insatiable demand. However, more recent years have brought lower prices, well-supplied markets, and less concern about scarcity in light of the production boom in the United States. Today, China's oil companies are more comfortable buying oil on the market, rather than buying oil-producing assets abroad.

More than half of China's oil imports come from countries that are members of the Organization of the Petroleum Exporting Countries (OPEC), and China has been the focus of global oil demand growth in the past decade. The Middle East dominates Chinese oil supply, as a region, but Russia is the country's single largest supplier.[18] As demand is flat-to-declining in the OECD countries and oil production in the United States has taken off, China and the rest of developing Asia have become the market of choice for oil producers around the world (figure 32-2).

China's appetite for natural gas grew rapidly over the last decade, much faster than its domestic production capacity. China has thus become an important importer of gas, with imports making up 45 percent of China's natural gas supply in 2018, an increase from 15 percent in 2010.[19] China is now the world's largest importer of natural gas,[20] with 36 percent of that gas coming through pipelines and 64 percent imported as liquefied natural gas (LNG) in 2019.[21] China's pipeline gas has historically come almost entirely from Central Asia. However, the balance in China's natural gas market is changing fast, as the Power of Siberia pipeline from Russia delivered its first gas at the end of 2019.[22] This pipeline will deliver 38 billion cubic meters of gas annually, an 80 percent increase in pipeline gas supply.

Figure 32-2. **Sources of China's Oil Imports**

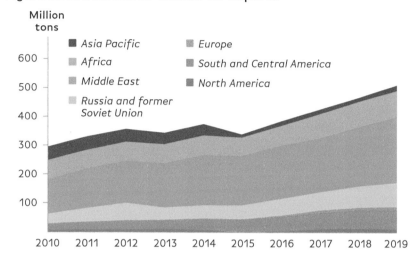

Source: "Statistical Review of World Energy," BP, www.bp.com/en/global/corporate/energy-economics/statistical-review-of-world-energy.html. Series gleaned by looking back on BP Statistical Reviews from 2011 to 2020.

ENERGY CONCERNS INFLUENCE CHINESE GEOPOLITICS

Securing its oil and gas supply is a key goal of China's trade relationships. This has recently become a two-way street, as oil and gas producers become concerned about security of demand for their products, in a world of growing concern about climate change and flattening OECD demand. As a result, China's relationships with key energy producers have become broader and deeper in recent years.

At the Third High-level Meeting of the OPEC-China Energy Dialogue in October 2019, the parties agreed to strengthen cooperation and to collaborate on future market outlooks.[23] Saudi Arabia, in particular, has been investing in Chinese refining and petrochemical complexes to ensure a market for its oil.[24] The Abu Dhabi National Oil Company and the China National Offshore Oil Corporation signed an agreement in 2019 to explore opportunities and share expertise in upstream and downstream oil and LNG.[25] In return, China is investing in the Gulf States, in oil and gas projects[26] and in infrastructure through BRI.[27] China has also pledged $23 billion in loans and development aid to the region through the China-Arab States Cooperation Forum.[28]

China's focus on renewable energy also has geopolitical implications.

China is aware of its vulnerability as a significant energy importer, but its focus on renewable energy and electric vehicles aims to make it a supplier of the energy forms of the future, rather than an importer. Additionally, China's focus on electric vehicles can allow it to rely on local renewable and coal-fired electricity to fuel its transportation sector, rather than imported oil, potentially improving its balance of trade and better insulating its economy from fuel price fluctuations. Unlike its current energy partners in the Gulf States and Russia, China stands to gain from the transition to greener, low-carbon forms of energy. However, the Chinese economy has a long way to go to reduce its dependence on imported oil, and thus will continue its quest to ensure supply security.

NOTES

1. *Statistical Review of World Energy 2020* (London: BP, 2020), www.bp.com/content/dam/bp/business-sites/en/global/corporate/pdfs/energy-economics/statistical-review/bp-stats-review-2020-full-report.pdf.

2. Jude Clement, "China Is The World's Largest Oil & Gas Importer," *Forbes*, October 17, 2019, www.forbes.com/sites/judeclemente/2019/10/17/china-is-the-worlds-largest-oil--gas-importer/.

3. *Statistical Review of World Energy 2020*, BP.

4. Lauri Myllyvirta, Shuwei Zhang, and Xinyi Shen, "Analysis: Will China Build Hundreds of New Coal Plants in the 2020s?" Carbon Brief, March 24, 2020, www.carbonbrief.org/analysis-will-china-build-hundreds-of-new-coal-plants-in-the-2020s.

5. *Statistical Review of World Energy 2020*, BP.

6. Jorrit Gosens, Tomas Kaberger, and Yufei Wang, "China's Next Renewable Energy Revolution: Goals and Mechanisms in the 13th Five Year Plan for Energy," *Energy Science & Engineering* 5, no. 3 (May 2017): 141–155, https://onlinelibrary.wiley.com/doi/epdf/10.1002/ese3.161.

7. Lauri Myllyvirta, Shuwei Zhang, and Xinyi Shen, "Analysis: Will China Build Hundreds of New Coal Plants in the 2020s?"

8. Ibid.

9. Christine Shearer, Melissa Brown, and Tim Buckley, "China at a Crossroads: Continued Support for Coal Power Erodes Country's Clean Energy Leadership" (Lakewood, OH: Institute for Energy Economics and Financial Analysis, January 2019), https://ieefa.org/wp-content/uploads/2019/01/China-at-a-Crossroads_January-2019.pdf.

10. Tim Buckley, "Over 100 Global Financial Institutions Are Exiting Coal, with More to Come" (Lakewood, OH: Institute for Energy Economics and Financial Analysis, February 27, 2019), http://ieefa.org/wp-content/uploads/2019/02/IEEFA-Report_100-and-counting_Coal-Exit_Feb-2019.pdf.

11. *Statistical Review of World Energy 2020*, BP.

12. David Stanway, "China Blocks New Solar in 3 NW Regions amid Overcapacity Fears," Reuters, February 14, 2019, www.reuters.com/article/us-china-solarpower/china-blocks-new-solar-in-3-nw-regions-amid-overcapacity-fears-idUSKCN1Q404G.

13. Chen Xuewan and Lu Yutong, "China to Slash Subsidies for Renewable Energy," Sixth Tone, May 12, 2020, www.sixthtone.com/news/1005309/china-to-slash-subsidies-for-renewable-energy.

14. "Top 10 Solar Energy Companies in the World 2019," *Technavio* (blog), May 9, 2019, https://blog.technavio.com/blog/top-10-solar-energy-companies.

15. "Top Ten Wind Turbine Suppliers," Energy Digital, April 10, 2015, www.energydigital.com/top-10/top-10-wind-turbine-suppliers.

16. *The 13th Five-Year Plan for Economic and Social Development of the People's Republic of China* (Beijing: Central Committee of the Communist Party of China, 2016), https://en.ndrc.gov.cn/policyrelease_8233/201612/P020191101482242850325.pdf.

17. Jeff Barron, "China's Crude Oil Imports Surpassed 10 Million Barrels per Day in 2019," U.S. Energy Information Administration, March 23, 2020, www.eia.gov/todayinenergy/detail.php?id=43216.

18. *Statistical Review of World Energy 2020*, BP.

19. Faouzi Aloulou and Victoria Zaretskaya, "China Adds Incentives for Domestic Natural Gas Production as Imports Increase," U.S. Energy Information Administration, October 23, 2019, www.eia.gov/todayinenergy/detail.php?id=41773.

20. *Natural Gas Information 2019* (Paris: International Energy Administration, September 17, 2019), https://webstore.iea.org/natural-gas-information-2019.

21. *Statistical Review of World Energy 2020*, BP.

22. Anna Galtsova and Jenny Yang, "The Era of Russian Pipeline Gas Supply to China Begins," IHS Markit, December 2, 2019, https://ihsmarkit.com/research-analysis/the-era-of-russian-pipeline-gas-supply-to-china-begins.html.

23. "Third High-Level Meeting of the OPEC-China Energy Dialogue," Organization of the Petroleum Importing Countries, October 21, 2019, www.opec.org/opec_web/en/press_room/5720.htm.

24. "Saudi Aramco Boosts Ties with China," The Economist Intelligence Unit, November 12, 2018, www.eiu.com/industry/article/1718678555/saudi-aramco-boosts-ties-with-china/2019-11-12.

25. Varun Godinho, "UAE and China Sign Strategic Oil and Gas Agreement," Gulf Business, July 22, 2019, https://gulfbusiness.com/uae-china-sign-strategic-oil-agreement/.

26. James Murray, "China Leads Investment for Middle East Oil and Gas Projects Worth $75bn," NS Energy, November 21, 2019, www.nsenergybusiness.com/features/china-oil-and-gas-investment/.

27. Jonathan Fulton, "China's Gulf Investments Reveal Regional Strategy," The Arab Gulf States Institute in Washington, July 29, 2020, https://agsiw.org/chinas-gulf-investments-reveal-regional-strategy/.

28. James Murray, "China Leads Investment for Middle East Oil and Gas Projects Worth $75bn."

33

Can the United States and China Reboot Their Climate Cooperation?

TODD STERN

During the Obama administration, the U.S.-China climate relationship was central to the global progress that culminated in the Paris climate agreement. The administration started developing that relationship right away: from Secretary of State Hillary Clinton's first trip to China in February 2009; to my first meeting in March 2009 with my Chinese counterpart, Minister Xie Zenhua, where I proposed trying to make climate a positive pillar in an often-fraught relationship; to Secretary of State John Kerry's establishment of a new U.S.-China Climate Change Working Group; to the historic joint announcement by Presidents Barack Obama and Xi Jinping in Beijing in November 2014. The nature of our cooperation was never easy; Xie and I were still battling down to the last two days of negotiations in Paris in 2015. But the two sides came to understand that at the end of the day we would find a way to agree.

Of course, President Donald Trump pulled the plug on U.S.-China climate engagement. A new Biden administration, fully committed to ambitious action on climate change, will surely want to work again with China on this issue. Given China's footprint—it accounted for 27 percent of global greenhouse emissions in 2019, the United States for 13 percent—as well as its influence, there is no way to contain climate change worldwide without

China's full-throttle engagement. And yet reviving our climate cooperation will be no mean feat in light of both the deterioration of our overall relationship and the evolving landscape of the climate challenge.

THE BROADER BILATERAL RELATIONSHIP

The U.S.-China bilateral relationship has deteriorated significantly in recent years. Across the U.S. political spectrum, people are distressed about a range of Chinese behaviors: from Hong Kong, to the South China Sea, the persecution of the Uyghurs, Xi's authoritarian crackdown and elimination of term limits, continued unfair trade practices, and more. But the call by some for a new Cold War is a mistake. Working with allies, we will need to compete with China in many areas and confront unacceptable Chinese behavior, while also seeking to collaborate where we can, especially on global challenges like climate change.

Unless we can get this mix of competition and collaboration right, renewed climate cooperation won't get off the ground. And that would have grave consequences in the United States and around the world. You have only to look at the authoritative reports on the enormity of the climate risk, such as the "1.5°C Report" of the U.N.'s Intergovernmental Panel on Climate Change (IPCC) in 2018,[1] or the crescendo of climate disasters around the world to see that what many once regarded as an environmental concern is in fact a full-fledged national security threat.

A DIFFERENT CLIMATE LANDSCAPE

Reviving our climate cooperation will also depend on the extent to which our two countries are prepared to dramatically ramp up our climate action. The challenge of rapidly decarbonizing the global economy has grown even more urgent since the Paris Agreement was reached in 2015, with a growing consensus of scientists and experts persuaded that the Paris best-efforts goal of holding the increase to 1.5°C[2] must now be our actual, working goal. Biden has made clear his commitment to reaching net-zero emissions by 2050, in line with the 1.5°C target. Executing on that commitment will require concerted executive and legislative action and a broad mobilization of national will. Some may be tempted to dismiss this as impractical, but the question is: Compared to what? We know what to do in terms of technology, innovation, and policy and we can afford it—indeed, failing to act will cost much more. Knowing all this, will we look at this metastasizing threat and go all out to conquer it? Or will we look away?

But what about China? To date, China's record on the transition to clean energy is mixed. It is the world leader in renewable energy, sold more electric vehicles in 2019 than the rest of the world combined, and has put in place a wide range of policies to propel clean energy further.[3] At the same time, China can't seem to quit coal. Its coal consumption in 2019 fell as a percentage of primary energy (down to around 58 percent), but it is still actively building coal plants at home and abroad. With a current coal capacity of around 1,040 gigawatts (GW)—about equivalent to the entire U.S. electricity system—China has roughly 100 GW under construction and a further 150 GW on the drawing board.[4] Moreover, China supports (through development, construction, and/or financing) more than 100 GW of coal plants under construction as part of its massive Belt and Road Initiative.[5] And Premier Li Keqiang called for increased development of China's coal resources at an October 2019 meeting of the National Energy Commission and at the May 2020 National People's Congress.[6]

The magnitude of China's coal infrastructure might suggest that change at the speed and scale required is undoable, but that is not so. Two expert analyses in the past year suggest that it would be technically and economically feasible for China to largely phase out its coal infrastructure by 2050.[7] This would require tremendous effort, to be sure, but of course that is the point. To take a global energy system that relies on fossil fuels for 80 percent of primary energy down to net-zero by approximately 2050, a fundamental transformation at speed and scale will be required, including by China, the United States, Europe, and others.[8] A more gradual path threatens grave danger to our economy, national security, and overall well-being, if not outright catastrophe.

China's leadership will need to understand that there is no way for China to maintain and enhance its standing in the world, with rich and poor countries alike, if climate change starts to wreak widespread havoc and China stands out as the leading polluter who refused to do enough. If we get to that dangerous place, the conventional rhetoric of UN climate negotiations—where developed countries as listed in 1992 were blamed and all others held harmless—will be unavailing. The audience, at that point, will be the world, not UN negotiators. China, by that time the world's largest economy, will have no place to hide.

President Xi Jinping's September 2020 pledge at the UN that China would reach "carbon neutrality" "before 2060," was a very welcome surprise, and may bode well. At the same time, he gave little indication that China planned to take aggressive action now, in the 2020s, to start China on the path to steep emission cuts, and without such steps, the 1.5°C global goal will not stay within reach.

RESTARTING CLIMATE COOPERATION

The new Biden administration will need to send the right signals regarding climate cooperation with China. It is off to a good start. First, Biden has put in place a best-in-class climate team led by former secretary of state John Kerry abroad and former EPA administrator Gina McCarthy at home, buttressed by committed climate actors in the other key national security and domestic leadership posts. And the Biden team has made clear that climate change will be a true organizing principle of his national security strategy. The administration will also surely and promptly develop a set of strong climate policies at home demonstrating its commitment to transformational change. The Chinese know Biden has made big promises and will want to see whether he is going to deliver. And, at the right time, the Biden team will need to convey its interest in making climate change a renewed area of active cooperation, in the context of U.S. expectations for bold, decisive, and early action by both countries.

Biden will also doubtless plan a summit with Xi in his first year, and climate change will need to be a featured topic, both to convey that Biden is serious and to provide the time they'll need for meaningful discussion. Biden should explain how seriously he views the issue, the transformational goals he embraces, the benefits he sees economically and politically in taking this path, and the win-win opportunity for the United States and China if they can cooperate. When Presidents Xi and Obama made their joint announcement in 2014, it paved the way for the Paris Agreement. The challenge now is even greater—to deliver on the promise of Paris.

We have a solid foundation on which to build expanded cooperation, starting with the U.S.-China Climate Change Working Group. With our global focus on economic transformation, the working group could become a useful venue for collaborating on low- or no-carbon technologies and policies. We could also work together to revive the Major Economies Forum, meeting at the leader level every year and at the ministerial level in between. And we could collaborate on ongoing issues related to the Paris regime.

ADDITIONAL TOOLS

The new Biden administration will also need to deploy a broader range of tools to influence China's approach on clean energy and climate change. The administration should conduct an active climate diplomacy aimed at spurring global action for transformational change at speed and scale. Europe has long been a climate ally of the United States, and now, with the drive to transform the global economy taking center stage, our alliance should become even closer, including in working with China. The Biden administration should also rekindle our traditional climate alliance with Canada, Mexico, Japan, Australia, and New Zealand, as well as pick up the torch with crucial international players, such as India, Brazil, South Africa, and Indonesia. And the administration, with its allies, should work on a diplomatic initiative with progressive developing countries that inspired the important High Ambition Coalition at the Paris conference in 2015. Such an initiative, outside of but supporting the UN Framework Convention on Climate Change, could be launched at the leader level and focus on building political support and moral authority for the transformational change we need.

The administration should also work with the European Union to design border adjustment measures on high-carbon goods to prevent countries that lack adequate carbon controls from gaining an unfair trade advantage.

CONCLUSION

As the Biden administration gets going, a lot will be riding on the renewal of the U.S.-China climate relationship. The complications are plain to see: the tense state of the overall relationship, the challenges Biden will face in achieving necessary domestic progress on climate, and the scale of what China needs to do to meet this moment. But the dangers of failing to revive an effective working relationship on climate are unacceptably high. We have to get this right.

NOTES

1. Valérie Masson-Delmotte, Panmao Zhai, Hans-Otto Pörtner, Debra Roberts, Jim Skea, Priyadarshi R. Shukla, Anna Pirani, Wilfran Moufouma-Okia, Clotilde Péan, Roz Pidcock, Sarah Connors, J. B. Robin Matthews, Yang Chen, Xiao Zhou, Melissa I. Gomis, Elisabeth Lonnoy, Tom Maycock, Melinda Tignor, and Tim Waterfield (eds.), *Global Warming of 1.5°C: An IPCC Special Report on the impacts*

of global warming of 1.5°C above pre-industrial levels and related global greenhouse gas emission pathways, in the context of strengthening the global response to the threat of climate change, sustainable development, and efforts to eradicate poverty (New York: United Nations Intergovernmental Panel on Climate Change, 2018), www.ipcc.ch/sr15/download/#full.

2. The Paris Agreement calls for holding the increase in global average temperature to "well below 2°C above pre-industrial levels" and pursuing best efforts to hold that increase to 1.5°C.

3. David Sandalow, "China's Response to Climate Change: A Study in Contrasts and a Policy at a Crossroads," The Asia Society, July 30, 2020, https://asiasociety.org /policy-institute/chinas-response-climate-change-study-contrasts-and-policy -crossroads.

4. "A New Coal Boom in China: New Coal Plant Permitting and Proposals Accelerate," Center for Research on Energy and Clean Air, June 2020, https://global energymonitor.org/wp-content/uploads/2020/06/A-New-Coal-Boom-in-China_ English.pdf.

5. David Sandalow, "China's Response to Climate Change."

6. Ibid.

7. Ibid.; Fredrich Kahrl, Jiang Lin, Xu Liu, and Junfeng Hu, "Sunsetting Coal Power in China," Working Paper 007 (Berkeley, CA: Energy Technologies Area, Berkeley Lab, September 2019), https://eta.lbl.gov/publications/working-paper-007 -sunsetting-coal.

8. The "net" in the net-zero formula is important. Some amount of carbon emissions, yet to be determined, can be captured and either used or stored, so net-zero would allow for some ongoing emissions. But, for a number of reasons, the safe assumption is not very much.

GLOBAL GOVERNANCE

*How Is China Reshaping Global
Governance, Human Rights Norms,
and International Institutions?*

34

International Law with Chinese Characteristics

Assessing China's Role in the "Rules-Based" Global Order

ROBERT D. WILLIAMS

China presents a paradigmatic case of the limits and value of international law in shaping and constraining the behavior of powerful nation-states. On some questions that generate international conflict, international law simply does not provide norms or institutions to effectively govern those conflicts. Even where norms exist, many countries—China and the United States included—display selectively "revisionist" ambitions to adjust the system of international law and make it more compatible with their own preferences.[1] Major powers are occasionally willing to defy international law when it conflicts with their fundamental interests.[2]

China exhibits a pragmatic and flexible attitude toward international law that enables it to benefit from and exploit the international legal order without the need to advocate major changes to the letter of the law in most areas.[3] Even as China exerts increasing influence over the norms and interpretive

This chapter is a condensed version of a paper written for the Brookings Institution's Global China series. For helpful comments, I am indebted to Paul Gewirtz, Maggie Lewis, and two anonymous Brookings Institution reviewers. Emilie Kimball and Ted Reinert edited this chapter.

meanings of international law, policymakers should consider the extent to which international law also influences China. Law creates legitimation incentives and can help to shape the context in which Chinese leaders make decisions.[4] Thus a central question for U.S. strategists is not simply how to preserve a "rules-based" international order as such, but instead how to reinforce and reshape international law in ways that account for the complex challenges that China presents.

BACKGROUND ON CHINA'S ENGAGEMENT WITH INTERNATIONAL LAW

In the two decades following the founding of the People's Republic of China (PRC) in 1949, China's limited engagement with international law was heavily influenced by Soviet practice and Marxist theories of proletarian internationalism.[5] Although generally accepting of international law and institutions in principle,[6] Chinese officials criticized international law for "primarily protect[ing] the interests of the colonial and imperialist powers to the detriment of most undeveloped nations and peoples."[7]

During the "opening and reform" period after 1978, as China emerged from the devastation of the Cultural Revolution, Beijing gradually joined more than 300 multilateral treaties and 130 international organizations.[8] China incorporated a variety of international commercial legal regimes into its domestic legal system to promote economic development. Beijing also enacted a range of domestic legal reforms in the lead-up to its accession to the World Trade Organization (WTO) in 2001.[9]

Under the Chinese system, like many other jurisdictions, substantive treaty obligations generally become applicable in domestic law only through specific provisions of national legislation.[10] During the post-1978 period, China ratified a number of international human rights treaties that, unlike the commercial treaties already noted, were not incorporated into its domestic legal system in a way that could be applied by Chinese courts to constrain state power.[11] Thus China's functional approach has tended to incorporate international law into its domestic legal system when doing so supports economic growth or other objectives without posing a direct threat to the authority of the ruling Chinese Communist Party.[12]

China, today, is an active participant in the major international institutions—the United Nations, the WTO, the International Monetary Fund, and various specialized bodies. Chinese representatives now lead four of the UN's fifteen specialized agencies.[13] China is a signatory to hundreds of multilateral treaties and thousands of bilateral treaties, covering everything from arms control to trade and commerce.[14]

Chinese leaders retain a degree of skepticism about the prospect that international law will be manipulated to undermine China's sovereign interests.[15] At the same time, however, Chinese officials regularly invoke the importance of international law and seek to portray China as a "staunch defender and builder" of international rule of law.[16]

CURRENT AND FUTURE ISSUES

Trade

The area of international trade aptly illustrates the extent to which China has benefited from existing international rules and institutions, including the ambiguity and gaps that allow China to exploit those rules, while also being shaped by those rules and seeking to adapt and shape them in turn.

China undertook a broad range of liberalizing reforms to bring its economy in line with its 2001 WTO accession protocol. Many of those reforms, however, have stalled in recent years.[17] There is increasing consensus among the United States, the European Union, and Japan that existing WTO rules are simply outdated and inadequate to address concerns regarding certain Chinese practices, including market-distortive industrial subsidies and forced technology transfer.[18] This conclusion has been bolstered by analyses indicating that existing WTO disciplines and dispute resolution mechanisms, although effective in addressing a range of trade disputes, do not adequately account for complex features of China's economic model that blur the lines between state and private sectors.[19]

China has grown increasingly comfortable with the WTO's dispute resolution system and generally complies with adverse rulings of the WTO's Dispute Settlement Body (DSB).[20] To a considerable extent, the DSB has provided an effective legal forum for channeling trade tensions.[21] Some analysts point out, however, that China's "compliance" with DSB decisions is often carried out through superficial reforms that enable circumvention of the spirit of WTO rules.[22] Others note that even when it faithfully implements adverse WTO judgments, Beijing sometimes gets a "free pass" for trade violations because the DSB's rulings do not afford retrospective remedies, and its judgments are issued after long processes during which the distortions caused by Chinese trade practices can become entrenched.[23]

At the rhetorical level, China has consistently reaffirmed the country's commitment to the multilateral rules-based trading system with the WTO at its core.[24] This rhetoric reveals the importance of international trade law in defining China's perception of its interests. As the United States and other countries seek major updates in global trade rules to counter Chinese mercantilism,[25] China retains an enormous stake in the status quo.[26]

Maritime and Territorial Disputes

China's long-standing disputes with neighboring Asian countries concerning rights and jurisdiction over the waters in the South China Sea are partly defined by law. The disputes involve manipulation and argumentation to promote self-interested interpretations of legal norms, but law also creates incentives that influence China's actions.

Under the compulsory dispute settlement mechanisms of the United Nations Convention on the Law of the Sea (UNCLOS), which China has ratified,[27] in 2013 the Philippines brought a landmark arbitration in response to increasing Chinese artificial-island construction and occupation of disputed features within China's so-called nine-dash line that covers most of the South China Sea.[28] China refused to participate in the proceedings and rejected the final award issued in July 2016 that resolved nearly every claim in the Philippines' favor.[29] China's refusal to recognize the outcome directly contravenes UNCLOS, which stipulates that even nonparticipating parties are bound by the decisions of UNCLOS dispute resolution bodies.[30]

Despite its apparent dismissiveness toward the Philippines arbitration, Beijing's behavior implicitly recognizes the legitimating function of international law. To illustrate, consider that the law of the sea gives nations control over an "exclusive economic zone" (EEZ) of up to 200 nautical miles of ocean and seabed resources surrounding island features—as compared with mere "rocks" that do not generate such rights.[31] The South China Sea is rich in fish and petroleum resources.[32] International law thus creates the strategic context that renders the disputed features of the South China Sea meaningful in the first place.[33] China also advocates a position that coastal states have the right to regulate the activities of foreign military vessels in the coastal state's EEZ—a legal interpretation that could support China's strategy to exclude hostile naval powers from the waters in its region.[34] In sum, although law has its limits—for example, the law of the sea cannot resolve sovereignty disputes[35]—it is also a constitutive element of China's interests in the maritime domain.

Hong Kong

China recently enacted a sweeping law to "safeguard national security" in the Hong Kong Special Administrative Region, institutionalizing broad powers for PRC authorities to enforce vaguely defined political crimes in and beyond the territory.[36] China regained the exercise of sovereignty over Hong Kong in a 1997 handover from the United Kingdom pursuant to the Sino-British Joint Declaration.[37] That bilateral treaty underpins the "one country, two systems" governing framework codified in the Basic Law of the Hong Kong Special Administrative Region, according to which Hong Kong was granted a "high degree of autonomy" for 50 years following the handover.[38]

Foreign commentators pronounced the new security law an effective "takeover" of Hong Kong, which is renowned for its dynamic economy underpinned by the rule of law, freedom of expression, and an independent judiciary.[39] That critique was borne out in the early implementation of the security law through arrests of pro-democracy protesters, officials, and activists and the promulgation of broadly permissive regulations codifying special police powers, including with respect to online expression.[40]

Numerous observers have argued that China's Hong Kong national security legislation violates the Sino-British Joint Declaration and the International Covenant on Civil and Political Rights (ICCPR), which the Joint Declaration and Basic Law specify shall remain in force in Hong Kong following the handover.[41] In recent years, China has argued that the Joint Declaration expired in 1997, a proposition that finds no basis in international law.[42] On the other hand, both the Joint Declaration and Basic Law explicitly provide that Hong Kong's autonomy does not extend to foreign affairs and defense.[43] There is a colorable argument that this carve-out, combined with Hong Kong's failure thus far to "enact laws on its own" regarding treason and subversion in accordance with the Basic Law, renders Beijing's new security legislation consistent with the letter (if not the spirit) of international law and the Basic Law.[44]

The abuses in implementation of the security law violate the spirit of the rights to association, expression, and personal liberty as enunciated in the ICCPR.[45] As a textual matter, however, one could argue that these actions fall within the ICCPR's general allowance for limits on the protection of civil rights where required by the interests of "national security" and "public order."[46] The Chinese government notoriously interprets and applies these concepts expansively to suit the objectives of the party-state.[47] Thus international law appears to offer little that would compel Beijing to pursue a different course in Hong Kong.

Human Rights

China's approach to multilateral human rights regimes follows a similar pattern: China rhetorically endorses many human rights norms while advocating self-serving interpretations of their meaning and future development.[48] China has joined a number of major human rights conventions, including the Convention Against Torture and the International Covenant on Economic, Social, and Cultural Rights. The PRC has also signed but not ratified the ICCPR.[49] Where China has adopted legislation to implement these human rights protections in its domestic legal system, those rules "frequently prove difficult to enforce and are sometimes even illusory in practice."[50] More broadly, law and legal institutions have little power to protect human rights in areas that are "politically sensitive" for the Chinese party-state.[51]

Against this backdrop, China's government has perpetrated massive human rights abuses even as its domestic legal reforms have smoothed the path for hundreds of millions of Chinese citizens to rise out of poverty and stimulated improvements in the transparency and responsiveness of Chinese governance across a range of issues.[52] Among the most egregious of China's human rights violations is the ongoing campaign against Uyghurs and Turkic Muslims in Xinjiang—reportedly ranging from arbitrary detention of hundreds of thousands of Chinese citizens in indoctrination and forced-labor camps[53] to population-reduction measures, such as forced sterilization, forced abortion, and coercive family planning policies.[54]

Such practices meet the definition of genocide under the UN Convention on the Prevention and Punishment of the Crime of Genocide, which China has ratified.[55] Beijing has denied the reports of forced birth control as "baseless" and released a white paper in September 2020 seeking to defend the Xinjiang internment camps as "vocational training centers."[56] Because China has not accepted international judicial mechanisms for individual complaints over human rights abuses, international legal oversight is limited to "periodic reviews" by treaty bodies and other means of public pressure—work which can be made difficult by Beijing's lack of transparency and retaliation against critics.[57]

In their public statements on human rights, Chinese officials often emphasize "the sovereign independence of each country; the differing economic circumstances, values, traditions, and priorities of different countries; and the relativity of various human rights."[58] In the realm of civil and political rights, this does not necessarily require rewriting international human rights law, but instead promoting interpretations that render those norms hollow.[59] At the UN Security Council, General Assembly, Human Rights Council, and elsewhere, Chinese diplomats have found various ways to insulate China against criticism for its human rights record and to promote its "statist, development-as-top-priority view" of human rights—in some cases through "distorting procedures, undercutting institutional strength, and diluting conventional human rights norms."[60]

Climate Change

On climate change, as the United States has pulled back from a leadership role, other countries have begun looking to China to set the terms of global debate.[61] Following years of insistence that developed countries such as the United States should face more onerous obligations in addressing climate change than developing countries,[62] China played an important role in the negotiations leading to the 2016 Paris Agreement on climate change.[63]

The Paris treaty introduces the concept of "nationally determined contributions" for emissions targets to be set voluntarily by each country.[64] Some analysts have argued that China's core Paris commitments—to reach peak carbon emissions by 2030 and to increase the proportion of renewables in its energy mix to about 20 percent by then—are simply a reflection of what China's energy policies were already on track to deliver due to domestic imperatives.[65] Xi Jinping has attempted to cast China as a "torchbearer" in global climate change efforts,[66] and even announced in a recent speech that China would go beyond its Paris targets to achieve "carbon neutrality before 2060."[67] It remains to be seen, however, whether China will live up to its open-ended pledges.[68] Meanwhile, China is financing a host of low-efficiency, coal-fired power plants under its Belt and Road Initiative, setting a path toward increased global emissions that could undercut broader climate change efforts.[69]

The pliability of the Paris regime highlights the limits of existing international law in shaping China's (and other states') behavior. Even though many elements of the Paris Agreement are "binding" under international law, countries' respective emissions reduction pledges are entirely voluntary.[70] In this context, the U.S. withdrawal from the Paris accord has left the door open for China to claim the rhetorical mantle of climate leadership under a regime that affords China enormous flexibility in whether and how to adhere to its voluntary commitments.[71]

Emerging Issues: Cybersecurity and New Weapons Technology
China has begun to play an increasingly active role in areas where there is no consensus on how existing law applies to nations' use of technologies or whether new binding legal instruments are needed. China's approach in forums aiming to create "soft law" norms has been characterized by qualified endorsement of the applicability of international law to cyberspace and emerging technologies, but resistance to specification of the law's applicability beyond general terms that leave open large questions of interpretation and flexibility for state action.[72]

The UN Group of Governmental Experts on Advancing Responsible State Behavior in Cyberspace in the Context of International Security (Cyber GGE)[73] made slow progress for several years, including consensus in 2015 around several norms, such as nonintervention, state responsibility for wrongful acts, and abstention from cyberattacks on critical infrastructure in peacetime.[74] However, efforts to produce further Cyber GGE consensus reportedly were stymied in June 2017 when a small group of countries, including China, rejected three legal principles in the proposed text—states' right of self-defense under the UN Charter, the applicability of international humanitarian law to cyberspace, and the right of states to take countermeasures in response to internationally wrongful acts.[75] China's statements in the recently established Open-Ended Working Group on Developments in the Field of Information and Telecommunications in the Context of International Security[76] similarly indicate a reluctance to be specific about the application of international law to cyberspace.

China's reasons for resisting agreement on such principles could be largely defensive, reflecting wariness at what China views as U.S. hegemony and "militarization" of cyberspace.[77] But as Beijing's global hacking campaign continues to expand,[78] China's reluctance to sign on to basic legal norms leaves gaping questions about its reasons for strategic ambiguity.[79]

It is too early to tell whether a similar dynamic will prevail in the UN Group of Governmental Experts on Emerging Technologies in the Area of Lethal Autonomous Weapons Systems (LAWS GGE).[80] In April 2018, Chinese representatives to the LAWS GGE stated their "desire to negotiate and conclude" a new protocol for the Convention on Certain Conventional Weapons "to ban the use of fully autonomous lethal weapons systems."[81] At the same time, however, China issued a position paper that defined "fully autonomous" weapons so narrowly as to render any ban on such weapons essentially meaningless.[82] Again, such a position leaves myriad questions about the limits China is prepared to place on its international conduct relating to emerging technologies.

CONCLUSION

The examples sketched above are partial illustrations of China's approach toward international law. A more comprehensive treatment would need to cover a host of other issues—from nonproliferation regimes to consular agreements. Nonetheless, a few tentative conclusions can be drawn.

First, China exhibits a flexible approach to international law that enables it to benefit from and exploit the international order without the need to advocate changes to the letter of the law in most areas. In critiquing China's "compliance" with international law, we should be careful not to romanticize the clarity and moral force of existing rules or the necessarily "liberal" nature of international law.

Second, China is increasingly active in seeking to shape legal norms in ways that advance its interests. In some areas, such as trade, Chinese leaders seem to perceive an interest in preserving the status quo. In other areas, such as the law of the sea and human rights, China is advancing positions at odds with U.S.-preferred norms. In other areas, including climate change and the governance of cyberspace, Beijing seems content to maintain legal ambiguity that preserves its freedom of maneuver.

Third, despite its malleability and limitations, international law can also shape the context for the choices of Chinese leaders and their perceptions of their interests. International law can be a source of legitimation or delegitimation. It is a constitutive element of China's interests on important issues such as trade and the South China Sea, where law defines the stakes of competition. In general, Beijing wishes to be seen by the international community as being supportive of international law.

Realism about international law need not collapse into fatalism. U.S. policymakers should revisit the instrumental values of international law: facilitating the peaceful settlement of disputes, promoting positive-sum economic relations, providing a framework for international cooperation, and (hopefully, but not inevitably) promoting human dignity. In response to the China challenge, the United States, in concert with allies and partners, should reengage clear-eyed with international law in an effort to shape rules that are more robust and more effectively enforced in the coming era—however difficult that may be.

NOTES

1. William W. Burke-White, "Power Shifts in International Law: Structural Realignment and Substantive Pluralism," *Harvard International Law Journal* 56, no. 1 (2015): 1, https://harvardilj.org/wp-content/uploads/sites/15/561Burke-White .pdf; Evan A. Feigenbaum, "Reluctant Stakeholder: Why China's Highly Strategic Brand of Revisionism Is More Challenging Than Washington Thinks," Macro Polo, April 27, 2018, https://macropolo.org/analysis/reluctant-stakeholder-why-chinas -highly-strategic-brand-of-revisionism-is-more-challenging-than-washington -thinks/; Evan S. Medeiros, "The Changing Fundamentals of US-China Relations," *Washington Quarterly* 42, no. 3 (2019): 93–119, www.tandfonline.com/doi/full/10 .1080/0163660X.2019.1666355; Graham Allison, "The Myth of the Liberal Order," *Foreign Affairs*, June 14, 2018, www.foreignaffairs.com/articles/2018-06-14/myth -liberal-order.

2. Graham Allison, "Of Course China, Like All Great Powers, Will Ignore an International Legal Verdict," *The Diplomat*, July 11, 2016, https://thediplomat.com/ 2016/07/of-course-china-like-all-great-powers-will-ignore-an-international-legal -verdict/.

3. Tim Rühlig, "How China Approaches International Law: Implications for Europe" (Brussels: European Institute for Asian Studies, May 2018), www.eias.org/ wp-content/uploads/2016/03/EU_Asia_at_a_Glance_Ruhlig_2018_China_Inter national_Law.pdf; Vijay Gokhale, "China Doesn't Want a New World Order. It Wants This One," *New York Times*, June 4, 2020, www.nytimes.com/2020/06/04/ opinion/china-america-united-nations.html. This is not to suggest that China endorses international law in toto. As will be shown in this chapter, China is seeking to advance its own preferred norms in many areas, but generally these efforts do not require formal changes to the law itself.

4. Jamie P. Horsley, *Party Leadership and Rule of Law in the Xi Jinping Era: What Does an Ascendant Chinese Communist Party Mean for China's Legal Development?* (Washington, DC: The Brookings Institution, September 2019), www.brookings .edu/research/party-leadership-and-rule-of-law-in-the-xi-jinping-era/; Taisu Zhang and Tom Ginsburg, "China's Turn toward Law," *Virginia Journal of International Law* 59, no. 2 (2019): 306, https://vjilorg.files.wordpress.com/2019/10/ ginsburg-zhang-chinas-turn-toward-law-final-v3-1.pdf; Susan H. Whiting, "Authoritarian 'Rule of Law' and Regime Legitimacy," *Comparative Political Studies* 50 (2017): 1907, http://faculty.washington.edu/swhiting/wordpress/wp-content/ uploads/2016/12/Authoritarian-Rule-of-Law-and-Regime-Legitimacy.pdf.

5. Congyan Cai, *The Rise of China and International Law: Taking Chinese Exceptionalism Seriously* (Oxford: Oxford University Press, 2019), 41–54.

6. Louis Henkin, *How Nations Behave* (Washington, DC: Council on Foreign Relations, 1979), 110.

7. Xue Hanqin, *Chinese Contemporary Perspectives on International Law: History, Culture, and International Law* (The Hague: Pocketbooks of the Hague Academy of International Law, 2012), 23.

8. Ibid., 54–55.

9. Julia Ya Qin, "Trade, Investment and Beyond: The Impact of WTO Accession on China's Legal System," *China Quarterly* 191 (September 2007): 720–741, www.jstor.org/stable/20192817?seq=1; Donald C. Clarke, "China's Legal System and the WTO: Prospects for Compliance," *Washington University Global Studies Law Review* 2, no. 1 (January 2003): 97, https://openscholarship.wustl.edu/law_global studies/vol2/iss1/4/.

10. Xue Hanqin and Jin Qian, "International Treaties in the Chinese Domestic Legal System," *Chinese Journal of International Law* 8, no. 2 (July 2009): 299, 302, https://academic.oup.com/chinesejil/article/8/2/299/310810; Björn Ahl, "Chinese Law and International Treaties," *Hong Kong Law Journal* 39, no. 1 (2009): 737, 749–750, www.law.hku.hk/hklj/2009-Vol-39.php.

11. It bears noting that the Chinese judiciary explicitly lacks independence from the party-state. Lucy Hornby, "China's Top Judge Denounces Judicial Independence," *Financial Times*, January 17, 2017, www.ft.com/content/60dddd46-dc74 -11e6-9d7c-be108f1c1dce.

12. Congyan Cai, "International Law in Chinese Courts during the Rise of China," *American Journal of International Law* 110, no. 2 (April 2016): 269, 270–271, https://doi.org/10.5305/amerjintelaw.110.2.0269.

13. Yaroslav Trofimov, Drew Hinshaw, and Kate O'Keeffe, "How China Is Taking Over International Organizations, One Vote at a Time," *Wall Street Journal*, September 29, 2020, www.wsj.com/articles/how-china-is-taking-over-international -organizations-one-vote-at-a-time-11601397208; Tung Cheng-Chia and Alan H. Yang, "How China Is Remaking the UN In Its Own Image," *The Diplomat*, April 9, 2020, https://thediplomat.com/2020/04/how-china-is-remaking-the-un-in-its-own -image/; Kristine Lee, "Coming Soon to the United Nations: Chinese Leadership and Authoritarian Values," *Foreign Affairs*, September 16, 2019, www.foreignaffairs .com/articles/china/2019-09-16/coming-soon-united-nations-chinese-leadership -and-authoritarian-values.

14. Congyan Cai, *The Rise of China and International Law*, 101.

15. Liu Xiaofeng, "New China and the End of American 'International Law,'" *American Affairs* 3, no. 3 (Fall 2019), https://americanaffairsjournal.org/2019/08/ new-china-and-the-end-of-american-international-law/.

16. Wang Yi, "China, a Staunch Defender and Builder of International Rule of Law" (speech, October 24, 2014), www.fmprc.gov.cn/mfa_eng/wjb_663304/wjbz_ 663308/2461_663310/t1204247.shtml.

17. James A. Lewis ed., *Meeting the China Challenge: Responding to China's Managed Economy* (Washington, DC: Center for Strategic and International Studies, January 2018), www.csis.org/analysis/meeting-china-challenge.

18. "Joint Statement of the Trilateral Meeting of the Trade Ministers of Japan, the United States, and the European Union," European Commission, January 14, 2020, https://trade.ec.europa.eu/doclib/docs/2020/january/tradoc_158567.pdf; Jim Brunsden, "US, Japan and EU Target China with WTO Rule Change Proposal," *Financial Times*, January 14, 2020, www.ft.com/content/8271be9a-36d6-11ea-a6d3 -9a26f8c3cba4; "2019 Report to Congress on China's WTO Compliance," (Washington, DC: Office of the U.S. Trade Representative, March 2020), https://ustr.gov/sites/default /files/2019_Report_on_China%E2%80%99s_WTO_Compliance.pdf.

19. Mark Wu, "The 'China, Inc.' Challenge to Global Trade Governance," *Harvard International Law Journal* 57, no. 2 (2016): 261, 323, https://harvardilj.org/ wp-content/uploads/sites/15/HLI210_crop.pdf ("Over the past decade, we have witnessed the rise of 'China, Inc.,' a form of economic exceptionalism with intertwined linkages between the state, the [Chinese Communist] Party, and public and private enterprises. This system is giving rise to continued trade frictions between China and her trading partners. The WTO possesses limited ability to resolve such frictions. While the WTO may trumpet its successful resolution of over forty cases involving China, other issues go unaddressed."); Hao Chen and Meg Rithmire, "The Rise of the Investor State: State Capital in the Chinese Economy," *Studies in Comparative International Development* 55 (2020): 257, www .hbs.edu/faculty/Publication%20Files/20-120_882c50c2-53f2-40fd-975d -dbfccde4d45e.pdf.

20. Yang Guohua, "China in the WTO Dispute Settlement: A Memoir," *Journal of World Trade* 49, no. 1 (2015): 18, www.researchgate.net/publication/279329158_ China_in_the_WTO_dispute_settlement_A_Memoir; James Bacchus, Simon Lester, and Huan Zhu, "Disciplining China's Trade Practices at the WTO: How WTO Complaints Can Help Make China More Market-Oriented," Policy Analysis 856 (Washington, DC: Cato Institute, November 15, 2018), www.cato.org/sites/cato .org/files/pubs/pdf/pa856.pdf.

21. Ka Zeng, "China, America, and the WTO," *The Diplomat*, February 7, 2013, http://thediplomat.com/2013/02/china-america-and-the-wto/.

22. Timothy Webster, "Paper Compliance: How China Implements WTO Decisions," *Michigan Journal of International Law* 35, no. 3 (2014): 525, https:// repository.law.umich.edu/mjil/vol35/iss3/2/; Romi Jain, "China's Compliance with the WTO: A Critical Examination," *Indian Journal of Asian Affairs* 29, no. 1 (2016): 57–84, www.jstor.org/stable/44123129?seq=1.

23. For an argument about the limits of WTO remedies, see Mark Wu, "A Free Pass for China," *New York Times*, April 2, 2014, www.nytimes.com/2014/04/03/ opinion/a-free-pass-for-china.html ("The approach typically involves contravening trade rules just long enough to allow domestic players to build up their market position without incurring W.T.O. sanctions. China then undoes the policy and claims that it is respectful of W.T.O. judgments. But undoing China's gains afterward often proves difficult.").

24. Xi Jinping, "Opening Ceremony of 1st China International Import Expo" (speech, Shanghai, November 5, 2018), www.xinhuanet.com/english/2018-11/05/

c_137583815.htm; "Wang Yi Attends the 9th East Asia Summit Foreign Ministers' Meeting," Ministry of Foreign Affairs of the People's Republic of China, August 2, 2019, www.fmprc.gov.cn/mfa_eng/wjdt_665385/wshd_665389/t1686515.shtml.

25. Robert E. Lighthizer, "How to Set World Trade Straight," *Wall Street Journal*, August 20, 2020, www.wsj.com/articles/how-to-set-world-trade-straight-1159 7966341; Philip Blenkinsop, "U.S., EU, Japan Agree New Subsidy Rules with China Trade in Focus," Reuters, January 14, 2020, www.reuters.com/article/us-trade-wto -subsidies/us-eu-japan-agree-new-subsidy-rules-with-china-trade-in-focus-idU SKBN1ZD1RM; Silvia Amaro, "'A Reform-or-Die Moment': Why World Powers Want to Change the WTO," CNBC, February 7, 2020, www.cnbc.com/2020/02/07/ world-powers-us-eu-china-are-grappling-to-update-the-wto.html.

26. Antara Ghosal Singh, "What Does China Want from WTO Reforms?" *The Diplomat*, May 21, 2019, https://thediplomat.com/2019/05/what-does-china-want -from-wto-reforms/; Huo Jianguo, "如何应对WTO改革的复杂博弈" [How to deal with the complex game of WTO reform], Huanqiu, January 8, 2019, https://opinion .huanqiu.com/article/9CaKrnKgKX5.

27. Ben Dolven, Susan V. Lawrence, Thomas Lum, and Ronald O'Rourke, *Arbitration Case between the Philippines and China under the United Nations Convention on the Law of the Sea (UNCLOS)* (Washington, DC: Congressional Research Service, July 6, 2016), https://crsreports.congress.gov/product/pdf/R/R44555/4.

28. Robert D. Williams, "Tribunal Issues Landmark Ruling in South China Sea Arbitration," *Lawfare* (blog), July 12, 2016, www.lawfareblog.com/tribunal-issues -landmark-ruling-south-china-sea-arbitration.

29. Ibid.

30. United Nations Convention on the Law of the Sea, opened for signature Dec. 10, 1982, 1833 U.N.T.S. 397 [hereinafter, UNCLOS], article 296, www.un.org/Depts /los/convention_agreements/texts/unclos/unclos_e.pdf.

31. UNCLOS articles 55–58.

32. Peter Dutton, "Three Disputes and Three Objectives—China and the South China Sea," *Naval War College Review* 64, no. 4 (2011): 42, https://digital-commons .usnwc.edu/nwc-review/vol64/iss4/6/.

33. Oona A. Hathaway and Scott Shapiro, *The Internationalists: How a Radical Plan to Outlaw War Remade the World* (New York: Simon & Schuster, 2017), 362–363.

34. Ngo Minh Tri, "China's A2/AD Challenge in the South China Sea: Securing the Air from the Ground," *The Diplomat*, May 19, 2017, https://thediplomat.com/ 2017/05/chinas-a2ad-challenge-in-the-south-china-sea-securing-the-air-from-the -ground/.

35. Paul Gewirtz, *Limits of Law in the South China Sea* (Washington, DC: The Brookings Institution, May 2016), www.brookings.edu/research/limits-of-law-in -the-south-china-sea/.

36. English translation of the Law of the People's Republic of China on Safeguarding National Security in the Hong Kong Special Administrative Region, *Xinhua*, June 30, 2020, www.xinhuanet.com/english/2020-07/01/c_139178753.htm.

37. "Hong Kong: The Joint Declaration," House of Commons Library, July 5, 2019, https://commonslibrary.parliament.uk/research-briefings/cbp-8616/.

38. Basic Law of the Hong Kong Special Administrative Region of the People's Republic of China, www.basiclaw.gov.hk/en/basiclawtext/images/basiclaw_full_text_en.pdf; Alvin Y. Cheung, "Road to Nowhere: Hong Kong's Democratization and China's Obligations under Public International Law," *Brooklyn Journal of International Law* 40, no. 2 (2015): 465, 470, 477, https://brooklynworks.brooklaw.edu/bjil/vol40/iss2/3/.

39. Javier C. Hernandez, "Harsh Penalties, Vaguely Defined Crimes: Hong Kong's Security Law Explained," *New York Times*, June 30, 2020, www.nytimes.com/2020/06/30/world/asia/hong-kong-security-law-explain.html.

40. Vivian Wang and Alexandra Stevenson, "In Hong Kong, Arrests and Fear Mark First Day of New Security Law," *New York Times*, July 1, 2020, www.nytimes.com/2020/07/01/world/asia/hong-kong-security-law-china.html; Vivian Wang, Austin Ramzy, and Tiffany May, "Hong Kong Police Arrest Dozens of Pro-Democracy Leaders," *New York Times*, January 5, 2021, www.nytimes.com/2021/01/05/world/asia/hong-kong-arrests-national-security-law.html; "Implementation Rules for Article 43 of the Law of the People's Republic of China on Safeguarding National Security in the Hong Kong Special Administrative Region" (Hong Kong: The Government of the Hong Kong Special Administrative Region of the People's Republic of China, July 6, 2020), www.gld.gov.hk/egazette/pdf/20202449e/es220202449139.pdf.

41. "MEPs Call on EU to Consider Lawsuit against China over Hong Kong," European Parliament, June 19, 2020, www.europarl.europa.eu/news/en/press-room/20200615IPR81235/meps-call-on-eu-to-consider-lawsuit-against-china-over-hong-kong.

42. Jerome A. Cohen, "Law and Power in China's International Relations," *New York University Journal of International Law and Politics* 52 (2019): 123, 146 https://papers.ssrn.com/sol3/papers.cfm?abstract_id=3373792; Joyce Ng, "Sino-British Joint Declaration on Hong Kong 'No Longer Has Any Realistic Meaning,' Chinese Foreign Ministry Says," *South China Morning Post*, June 30, 2017, www.scmp.com/news/hong-kong/politics/article/2100779/sino-british-joint-declaration-hong-kong-no-longer-has-any.

43. Basic Law of the Hong Kong Special Administrative Region of the People's Republic of China, articles 13–14; Sino-British Joint Declaration, article 3(2), www.cmab.gov.hk/en/issues/jd2.htm.

44. Basic Law of the Hong Kong Special Administrative Region of the People's Republic of China, article 23.

45. U.N. Expert Communique, note 82. International Covenant on Civil and Political Rights (entry into force March 23, 1976) [hereinafter, ICCPR], articles 9, 19, 21, 22, www.ohchr.org/en/professionalinterest/pages/ccpr.aspx.

46. ICCPR articles 4, 12, 19, 21.

47. Robert D. Williams, "The 'China, Inc.+' Challenge to Cyberspace Norms," Aegis Series Paper 1803 (Stanford, CA: Hoover Institution, February 2018), 5–6,

www.hoover.org/sites/default/files/research/docs/williams_webreadypdf1.pdf
(discussing China's expansive official conception of national security); Ankit
Panda, "The Truth about China's New National Security Law," *The Diplomat*, July 1,
2015, https://thediplomat.com/2015/07/the-truth-about-chinas-new-national
-security-law/.

48. Ted Piccone, *China's Long Game on Human Rights at the United Nations*
(Washington, DC: The Brookings Institution, September 2018), www.brookings
.edu/research/chinas-long-game-on-human-rights-at-the-united-nations/
(arguing that China pursues a "two-part strategy that seeks to 1) block international
criticism of its repressive human rights record, and 2) promote orthodox interpretations of national sovereignty and noninterference in internal affairs that
weaken international norms of human rights, transparency, and accountability");
Yu-Jie Chen, "China's Challenge to the International Human Rights Regime," *New
York University Journal of International Law and Politics* 51 (2019): 1179, https://
papers.ssrn.com/sol3/papers.cfm?abstract_id=3308205.

49. Margaret K. Lewis, "Why China Should Unsign the International Covenant
on Civil and Political Rights," *Vanderbilt Journal of Transnational Law* 53, no. 1
(2020): 131, 142–143, https://papers.ssrn.com/sol3/papers.cfm?abstract_id=3375182;
Jerome A. Cohen, "Law and Power in China's International Relations," 152.

50. Jerome A. Cohen, "Law and Power in China's International Relations," 158
(citing Jerome A. Cohen, "Law's Relation to Political Power in China: A Backward
Transition," *Social Research: An International Quarterly* 86 (2019): 231, https://
papers.ssrn.com/sol3/papers.cfm?abstract_id=3354939). Nor can Chinese courts
directly apply rights enshrined in China's Constitution. Keith Hand, "Resolving
Constitutional Disputes in Contemporary China," *University of Pennsylvania East
Asia Law Review* 7 (2011): 51, https://scholarship.law.upenn.edu/ealr/vol7/iss1/2/.

51. Fu Hualing, "Duality and China's Struggle for Legal Autonomy," *China
Perspectives* 1 (2019): 3, www.researchgate.net/publication/332932787_Duality_
and_China's_Struggle_for_Legal_Autonomy.

52. Kenneth Roth, "China's Global Threat to Human Rights," Human Rights
Watch, 2020, www.hrw.org/world-report/2020/country-chapters/global; *2019
Annual Report* (Washington, DC: Congressional-Executive Commission on China,
2020), www.cecc.gov/publications/annual-reports/2019-annual-report; Jerome A.
Cohen, "Law and Power in China's International Relations," 159–160.

53. Austin Ramzy and Chris Buckley, "'Absolutely No Mercy': Leaked Files
Expose How China Organized Mass Detentions of Muslims," *New York Times*,
November 16, 2019, www.nytimes.com/interactive/2019/11/16/world/asia/china
-xinjiang-documents.html; Austin Ramzy, "How China Tracked Detainees and
Their Families," *New York Times*, February 17, 2020, www.nytimes.com/2020/02/17
/world/asia/china-reeducation-camps-leaked.html.

54. Adrian Zenz, "Sterilizations, IUDs, and Mandatory Birth Control: The
CCP's Campaign to Suppress Uyghur Birthrates in Xinjiang," The Jamestown
Foundation, June 2020, https://jamestown.org/product/sterilizations-iuds-and
-mandatory-birth-control-the-ccps-campaign-to-suppress-uyghur-birthrates-in

-xinjiang/; "China Cuts Uighur Births with IUDs, Abortion, Sterilization," Associated Press, June 29, 2020, https://apnews.com/269b3de1af34e17c1941a514f78d764c.

55. Convention on the Prevention and Punishment of the Crime of Genocide, entry into force January 12, 1951 [hereinafter, "Genocide Convention"], article II, www.un.org/en/genocideprevention/documents/atrocity-crimes/Doc.1_Convention%20on%20the%20Prevention%20and%20Punishment%20of%20the%20Crime%20of%20Genocide.pdf (defining genocide to include "any of the following acts committed with intent to destroy, in whole or in part, a national, ethnical, racial or religious group, as such: (a) Killing members of the group; (b) Causing serious bodily or mental harm to members of the group; (c) Deliberately inflicting on the group conditions of life calculated to bring about its physical destruction in whole or in part; (d) Imposing measures intended to prevent births within the group; (e) Forcibly transferring children of the group to another group."); Lisa Reinsberg, "China's Forced Sterilization of Uyghur Women Violates Clear International Law," Just Security, July 29, 2020, www.justsecurity.org/71615/chinas-forced-sterilization-of-uyghur-women-violates-clear-international-law/; James Millward, "The Uighurs' Suffering Deserves Targeted Solutions, Not Anti-Chinese Posturing," The Guardian, July 27, 2020, www.theguardian.com/commentisfree/2020/jul/27/the-uighurs-suffering-deserves-targeted-solutions-not-anti-chinese-posturing.

56. "China Forcing Birth Control on Uighurs to Suppress Population, Report Says," BBC, June 29, 2020, www.bbc.com/news/world-asia-china-53220713; Mimi Lau and Linda Lew, "China Defends Its 'Vocational Training Centres' in Xinjiang White Paper," South China Morning Post, September 17, 2020, www.scmp.com/news/china/politics/article/3101986/china-claims-vocational-training-given-nearly-13-million-people.

57. Lisa Reinsberg, "China's Forced Sterilization of Uyghur Women Violates Clear International Law."

58. Jerome A. Cohen, "Law and Power in China's International Relations," 153; Congyan Cai, The Rise of China and International Law, 137–145.

59. Margaret K. Lewis, "Why China Should Unsign the International Covenant on Civil and Political Rights," 138–140.

60. Yu-Jie Chen, "China's Challenge to the International Human Rights Regime," 1221; Andréa Worden, "China's Win-Win at the UN Human Rights Council: Just Not for Human Rights," Sinopsis, May 29, 2020, https://sinopsis.cz/wp-content/uploads/2020/05/worden-unhrc-win-win.pdf.

61. Leslie Hook and Lucy Hornsby, "China Emerges as Powerbroker in Global Climate Talks," Financial Times, November 16, 2018, www.ft.com/content/7c1f16f8-e7ec-11e8-8a85-04b8afea6ea3.

62. Chloe Farand, "China and India Demand Cash for Climate Action on Eve of UN Summit," Climate Home News, September 17, 2019, www.climatechangenews.com/2019/09/17/china-india-demand-cash-climate-action-eve-un-summit/.

63. Mark Landler and Jane Perlez, "Rare Harmony as China and U.S. Commit to Climate Deal," New York Times, September 3, 2016, www.nytimes.com/2016/09/04/world/asia/obama-xi-jinping-china-climate-accord.html.

64. U.N. Framework Convention on Climate Change Conference of the Parties, Twenty-First Session, Adoption of the Paris Agreement, U.N. Doc. FCCC/CP/2015/L.9/Rev.1 (December 12, 2015) [hereinafter, "Paris Agreement"], article 4, https://unfccc.int/files/meetings/paris_nov_2015/application/pdf/paris_agreement_english_.pdf; "The Paris Agreement: Nationally Determined Contributions (NDCs)," U.N. Framework Convention on Climate Change, https://unfccc.int/process-and-meetings/the-paris-agreement/the-paris-agreement/nationally-determined-contributions-ndcs.

65. Henry Fountain and John Schwartz, "Climate Accord Relies on Environmental Policies Now in Place," *New York Times,* November 12, 2014, www.nytimes.com/2014/11/13/world/climate-pact-by-us-and-china-relies-on-policies-now-largely-in-place.html.

66. Xi Jinping, "Secure a Decisive Victory in Building a Moderately Prosperous Society in All Respects and Strive for the Great Success of Socialism with Chinese Characteristics for a New Era" (speech, Beijing, October 18, 2017), www.xinhuanet.com/english/download/Xi_Jinping's_report_at_19th_CPC_National_Congress.pdf.

67. Somini Sengupta, "China, in Pointed Message to U.S., Tightens Its Climate Targets," *New York Times*, September 22, 2020, www.nytimes.com/2020/09/22/climate/china-emissions.html.

68. Muyu Xu and David Stanway, "China CO2 Emissions from Energy Sector Still on Rise—Researchers," Reuters, November 14, 2019, www.reuters.com/article/us-china-coal-carbon/china-co2-emissions-from-energy-sector-still-on-rise-researchers-idUSKBN1XO0QL.

69. Sagatom Saha, "China's Belt and Road Plan Is Destroying the World," *National Interest*, August 18, 2019, https://nationalinterest.org/feature/chinas-belt-and-road-plan-destroying-world-74166 ("That China has been supporting coal abroad while canceling coal projects at home is simple self-interest: Beijing sees coal equipment exports as a solution for excess industrial capacity. Beijing must keep legacy coal manufacturers afloat because the Chinese coal industry and steel industry, which depends on coal, supply roughly twelve million Chinese jobs."

70. David A. Wirth, "While Trump Pledges Withdrawal from Paris Agreement on Climate, International Law May Provide a Safety Net," *Lawfare* (blog), June 2, 2017, www.lawfareblog.com/while-trump-pledges-withdrawal-paris-agreement-climate-international-law-may-provide-safety-net.

71. For an argument regarding the strategic benefits of greater U.S. action on climate change, see James A. Baker III, George P. Shultz, and Ted Halstead, "The Strategic Case for U.S. Climate Leadership," *Foreign Affairs*, April 13, 2020, www.foreignaffairs.com/articles/united-states/2020-04-13/strategic-case-us-climate-leadership.

72. Regarding applicability of the U.N. Charter to cyberspace, see "Report of the Group of Governmental Experts on Developments in the Field of Information and Telecommunications in the Context of International Security," A/68/98, United Nations General Assembly, June 24, 2013, sec. 2, para. 19, www.un.org/ga/search/view_doc.asp?symbol=A/68/98&referer=/english/&Lang=E.

73. "Group of Governmental Experts," United Nations Office for Disarmament Affairs, www.un.org/disarmament/group-of-governmental-experts/.

74. "Report of the Group of Governmental Experts on Developments in the Field of Information and Telecommunications in the Context of International Security," A/70/174, United Nations General Assembly, July 22, 2015, www.un.org/ga/search/view_doc.asp?symbol=A/70/174.

75. Michael Schmitt and Liis Vihul, "International Cyber Law Politicized: The UN GGE's Failure to Advance Cyber Norms," Just Security, June 30, 2017, www.justsecurity.org/42768/international-cyber-law-politicized-gges-failure-advance-cyber-norms.

76. "Open-Ended Working Group," United Nations Office for Disarmament Affairs, www.un.org/disarmament/open-ended-working-group/.

77. Greg Austin, "International Legal Norms in Cyberspace: Evolution of China's National Security Motivations," in *International Cyber Norms: Legal, Policy & Industry Perspectives*, ed. Anna-Maria Osula and Henry Rõigas (Tallinn: NATO Cooperative Cyber Defence Centre of Excellence, 2016), https://ccdcoe.org/uploads/2018/10/InternationalCyberNorms_Ch9.pdf.

78. "Fact Sheet: President Xi Jinping's State Visit to the United States," The White House, September 25, 2015, https://obamawhitehouse.archives.gov/the-press-office/2015/09/25/fact-sheet-president-xi-jinpings-state-visit-united-states; Jack Goldsmith and Robert D. Williams, "The Failure of the United States' Chinese-Hacking Indictment Strategy," *Lawfare* (blog), December 28, 2018, www.lawfareblog.com/failure-united-states-chinese-hacking-indictment-strategy.

79. Ben Buchanan and Robert D. Williams, "A Deepening U.S.-China Cyber-security Dilemma," *Lawfare* (blog), October 24, 2018, www.lawfareblog.com/deepening-us-china-cybersecurity-dilemma (responding to Lyu Jinghua, "A Chinese Perspective on the Pentagon's Cyber Strategy: From 'Active Cyber Defense' to 'Defending Forward,'" *Lawfare* (blog), October 19, 2018, www.lawfareblog.com/chinese-perspective-pentagons-cyber-strategy-active-cyber-defense-defending-forward).

80. "2019 Group of Governmental Experts on Lethal Autonomous Weapons Systems (LAWS)," United Nations Geneva, www.unog.ch/80256EE600585943/(httpPages)/5535B644C2AE8F28C1258433002BBF14?OpenDocument.

81. Elsa Kania, "China's Strategic Ambiguity and Shifting Approach to Lethal Autonomous Weapons Systems," *Lawfare* (blog), April 17, 2018, www.lawfareblog.com/chinas-strategic-ambiguity-and-shifting-approach-lethal-autonomous-weapons-systems.

82. "Position Paper Submitted by China to the Group of Governmental Experts of the High Contracting Parties to the Convention on Prohibitions or Restrictions on the Use of Certain Conventional Weapons Which May Be Deemed to Be Excessively Injurious or to Have Indiscriminate Effects," United Nations Geneva, April 11, 2018, www.unog.ch/80256EDD006B8954/(httpAssets)/E42AE83BDB3525D0C125826C0040B262/$file/CCW_GGE.1_2018_WP.7.pdf.

35

China's Expanding Influence at the United Nations—and How the United States Should React

JEFFREY FELTMAN

A simplistic quip about the UN contains some truth: "The United States undervalues multilateralism. Europeans overvalue multilateralism. And China wishes to change multilateralism." With China now the second-largest provider of assessed contributions to the UN's regular budget (12 percent compared to 22 percent from the United States) and peacekeeping budget (15 percent compared to 27 percent from the United States),[1] China legitimately expects a greater voice.

Angst about the growing Chinese role[2] usually cites the four (out of fifteen) UN specialized agencies—the Food and Agriculture Organization, the International Civil Aviation Organization, the International Telecommunications Union, and the United Nations Industrial Development Organization—now headed by Chinese nationals.[3] But China is also upping its game in UN political work. As UN under-secretary-general for political affairs (2012–2018), I witnessed China's expanding interest in peace and security issues under two secretary-generals, Ban Ki-moon and António Guterres.

BEYOND A DEVELOPMENT FOCUS

China's traditional focus at the UN was on development issues.[4] President Xi Jinping's 2015 General Assembly speech signaled a shift, in announcing a $1 billion "peace and development" fund and $100 million to support an African Union's standby peacekeeping force.[5] Xi's January 2017 Davos remarks reinforced China's aspirations for a more assertive international profile.[6]

INCREASING THE VETO TEMPO

China has exercised its Security Council veto sixteen times, less than any other permanent member (the "P5"—the United States, the United Kingdom, Russia, France, and China) which holds that power.[7] But the frequency is rising. For thirteen vetoes, China joined with Russia. The Chinese-Russian bilateral relationship remains complex and marked with mutual suspicion, as Moscow's allegations that a Russian scientist spied for Beijing reveal.[8] But inside the council, Beijing and Moscow together downplay human rights, play up sovereign rights, and vex the United States.

With China and Russia's strong "P2" alliance, the "P3" (U.S., France, U.K.) should be a counterweight and coordinate outreach to the ten members elected for two-year terms (the "E10"). The P2, however, exploited dysfunction in the P3 stemming from Trump administration policies. Moreover, if a P5 country can deny the adoption of a draft resolution (which requires at least nine affirmative votes out of the fifteen total), it can avoid exercising its veto. China counts on support from the three African council members through commercial and financial leverage and by aligning positions on Africa-related issues with the African states. If China and Russia stay aligned and are confident of A3 support, they only need one other council member to side with them to block a resolution without using the veto.[9]

CHINA AND PEACE OPERATIONS

UN peace operations—peacekeeping and special political missions (including special envoys)—operate under Security Council mandates and General Assembly–approved budgets. Thus, while Chinese oversight is not new, China's previously quiet approach to peace operations has become less muted.

China starts from a strong position as the second-largest funder of UN dues. China's credibility is enhanced by having skin in the game: China's

2,500-plus peacekeepers exceed those of the other P5 combined.[10] Allied with Russia, China uses mandate renewals and budget debates to try to strip out human rights monitors from peace operations. In September 2019, China threatened to veto the renewal of the UN's Afghanistan mission in an unsuccessful attempt to insert praise of the Belt-and-Road Initiative into the mandate.[11] In June 2020, China for the first time blocked Guterres's appointment of a UN special representative (mimicking what other P5 members have done for years).

In addition, in 2019, Huang Xia, a Chinese diplomat, became the first Chinese national to lead a UN peace operation. His appointment as special envoy for Africa's Great Lakes region was in part due to Chinese lobbying. In 2020 Guterres named Chinese national Guang Cong as the deputy special representative for the UN's South Sudan mission. While Cong has served in UN missions since 2002, it is unusual to have a peace operation in sub-Saharan Africa with both its head (from New Zealand at the time of Cong's appointment) and the political deputy from outside the continent: Chinese influence likely explains the absence of African insistence on an African national.

CHINA AND UN POLITICAL WORK

While the UN's peace operations focus on specific conflicts, UN political officers monitor global developments to try to prevent or resolve conflict. As with peace operations, Chinese interest in this political work has grown under Xi.

Unlike Washington, Beijing now provides annual voluntary contributions to the UN Department of Political Affairs (DPA, now the Department of Political and Peacebuilding Affairs). Chinese financial support, while modest, allowed DPA to combat the perception that its work was backed only by Western states. Chinese analysis contributed to DPA's understanding of specific situations and helped determine whether there was a potential UN role. Before my December 2017 trip to Pyongyang, at a time of alarming tension, no country provided better guidance about dealing with North Korean counterparts.

In 2016, DPA received its first Chinese junior professional officer, with a second added later. In 2017, China blessed DPA's proposal to open a liaison office to the Shanghai Cooperation Organization (SCO), headquartered in Beijing. While Washington may dismiss the SCO—a forum established by China, Russia, and most Central Asian states—links to other regional organizations are key to UN legitimacy and credibility with the countries involved. A less confident China, wary of UN "spying," would likely have resisted hosting a UN liaison officer. This growing DPA-Chinese relationship reflected the higher profile China was adopting throughout the UN system.

PRESERVING VALUES-BASED MULTILATERALISM

As a UN official, I wanted deeper relations with China on peace and security matters. Now, outside the UN, I view China's growing power in the multilateral system with concern.

But (take a deep breath) China has not imposed a hostile takeover: UN data indicate that, as of April 2020, among UN senior leaders, there are twenty-six Americans compared to three Chinese, in addition to those Chinese heading the four specialized agencies.[12] As of 2017 (the most recent statistics available), the UN reports 5,274 Americans and 1,114 Chinese nationals in full-time positions.[13]

For all its faults and weaknesses, the UN and the multilateral system under U.S. leadership have largely served as a force multiplier for American interests while producing global benefits. But Americans need to be realistic. With its greater global weight today, China will inevitably assume a larger role in the UN.

China's desire for increasing influence in the UN is preferable to Beijing-designed alternatives that exclude or disadvantage the United States. China has not tabled a peace and security equivalent to the Asia Infrastructure Investment Bank. Having China operate within a long-established system established under U.S. leadership provides us a home field advantage. And Beijing and Washington might discover some common interests—China is far more attentive to budget expenditures now than when its dues were insignificant. China's interests in access for markets, investment opportunities, and natural resources are more readily realized with peace and stability. This differs from Russia's promotion of instability in Georgia, Ukraine, Syria, and Libya.

But to prevent China from changing the multilateral system by substituting Chinese rules for those we wrote, we cannot abandon the playing field. We need to cultivate allies to confront Chinese-Russian attempts to strip out or distort normative principles of the UN, such as human rights. As Bruce Jones, Will Moreland, and I argued in September 2019, one element of a multipronged U.S. strategy to maintain leadership in a revitalized multilateral system is to compete within the existing structures for what matters to us.[14]

Yet the Trump administration created vacuums that facilitate Chinese inroads. The game does not cease when we stomp off the field. The Chinese and the Russians must be delighted to see our absence ease their goal in swapping out our values for theirs.

Then there is the money. Even under the Trump administration, the United States remained the top provider in dollar terms of voluntary contributions for UN activities such as humanitarian assistance. But the United States is also the top debtor in terms of its assessed, or mandatory, contributions: $1 billion and counting in arrears. With the UN Secretariat in a financial crisis that the United States could unilaterally solve by paying its dues, Americans should not be surprised by less patience with, and deference to, U.S. demands in Turtle Bay. It is not in our interest to be perceived as the scofflaw when China is on the move.

Given unease in many capitals about Chinese intentions, the potential for renewed cooperation to preserve a values-based approach to the UN and multilateralism exists. Indeed, the Trump administration successfully tapped into shared concerns about Chinese intellectual property practices to tip the elections for head of the World Intellectual Property Organization away from the Chinese candidate.[15]

Yes, China's influence inside the UN is expanding. We cannot stop that. But we can end the current absurdity by which our absence facilitates China's ability to promote its own operating system in place of the universal values enshrined in the UN Charter, the Universal Declaration of Human Rights, and multiple conventions.

ACKNOWLEDGMENTS: Ted Reinert edited this chapter.

NOTES

1. U.N. General Assembly, A/74/11 (June 3–21, 2019), https://undocs.org/en/A/74/11.

2. Ben Evansky and Adam Shaw, "Chinese Influence Surges at UN, as US Warns of 'Concerted Push' to Advance Agenda," Fox News, July 13, 2019, www.foxnews.com/politics/chinese-influence-surges-un.

3. Colum Lynch and Robbie Gramer, "Outfoxed and Outgunned: How China Routed the U.S. in a U.N. Agency," *Foreign Policy*, October 23, 2019, https://foreignpolicy.com/2019/10/23/china-united-states-fao-kevin-moley/.

4. Since 2007, three successive Chinese nationals have headed the UN Secretariat's Department of Economic and Social Affairs. In the same period, three successive Americans have served as under-secretary-general for political affairs. By comparison, French nationals have led the UN's Department of Peacekeeping Operations (now renamed the Department of Peace Operations) continually since 1997, leading to jokes that DPKO (now DPO) is a "French-occupied zone."

5. Xi Jinping, "Working Together to Forge a New Partnership of Win-Win Cooperation and Create a Community of Shared Future for Mankind" (speech, New York, September 28, 2015), https://gadebate.un.org/sites/default/files/gastatements/70/70_ZH_en.pdf.

6. Xi Jinping, "Opening Plenary" (speech, Davos, January 17, 2017), www.weforum.org/agenda/2017/01/full-text-of-xi-jinping-keynote-at-the-world-economic-forum.

7. "Security Council—Veto List," Dag Hammarskjöld Library, United Nations, https://research.un.org/en/docs/sc/quick/veto.

8. Mary Ilyushina, "Russia Accuses Leading Arctic Researcher of Spying for China," CNN, June 17, 2020, https://edition.cnn.com/2020/06/17/europe/russia-china-spying-allegation-intl/index.html. See also Pavel K. Baev, *The Limits of Authoritarian Compatibility: Xi's China and Putin's Russia* (Washington, DC: The Brookings Institution, June 2020), www.brookings.edu/research/the-limits-of-authoritarian-compatibility-xis-china-and-putins-russia/.

9. While the A3 are usually united, which at least in its current configuration often seems to serve Chinese-Russian interests, there are times when Paris can rely on close relations with Francophone countries to peel one or more A3 member to French positions.

10. "Contributors to UN Peacekeeping Operations by Country and Post," United Nations Peacekeeping, March 31, 2019, https://peacekeeping.un.org/sites/default/files/msrs_march_2019.pdf.

11. Michelle Nichols, "China Signals Veto in Standoff with U.S. over Afghan U.N. Mission—Diplomats," Reuters, September 16, 2019, https://af.reuters.com/article/worldNews/idAFKBN1W1279.

12. "Senior Officials of the United Nations and Officers of Equivalent Rank Whose Duty Station Is New York," United Nations Protocol and Liaison Service, June 15, 2020, https://protocol.un.org/dgacm/pls/site.nsf/files/SeniorOfficials/$FILE/ListofUNSeniorOfficials.pdf.

13. "Human Resources by Nationality," United Nations System Chief Executives Board for Coordination, www.unsystem.org/content/hr-nationality.

14. Bruce Jones, Jeffrey Feltman, and Will Moreland, *Competitive Multilateralism: Adapting Institutions to Meet the New Geopolitical Environment* (Washington, DC: The Brookings Institution, September 2019), www.brookings.edu/research/competitive-multilateralism/.

15. Daniel F. Runde, "Trump Administration Wins Big with WIPO Election," *The Hill*, March 9, 2020, https://thehill.com/opinion/international/486590-trump-administration-wins-big-with-wipo-election.

36

China's Influence on the United Nations Human Rights System

SOPHIE RICHARDSON

In recent years, the Chinese government has become considerably more active in a wide range of United Nations (UN) and other multilateral institutions, including in the global human rights system. It has ratified several core UN human rights treaties,[1] served as a member of the UN Human Rights Council (HRC), and seconded Chinese diplomats to positions within the UN human rights system.

This new activism by one of the most consequential actors in the international system, if underpinned by a serious (albeit unlikely) commitment among senior Chinese leaders to uphold human rights, could have been transformative. But the opposite has happened.[2] Particularly under President Xi Jinping's leadership, the Chinese government does not merely seek to neutralize UN human rights mechanisms' scrutiny of China, it also aspires to neutralize the ability of that system to hold any government accountable for serious human rights violations.[3]

It is crucial—particularly for people who live in democracies and enjoy the rights to political participation, an independent judiciary, a free media, and other functioning institutions—to recall why the international human rights system exists. Quite simply, it is because states often fail to protect and instead violate human rights, particularly in countries that lack systems for redress and accountability. People need to appeal to institutions beyond their government's immediate control.

Beijing is no longer content simply denying people accountability inside China: it now seeks to bolster other countries' ability to do so even in the international bodies designed to deliver some semblance of justice internationally when it is blocked domestically.[4]

Beijing's resistance to complying with global public health needs and institutions in the COVID-19 crisis,[5] and its blatant violation of international law with respect to Hong Kong,[6] should not be seen as anomalies. They are clear and concerning examples of the consequences for people worldwide not only of a Chinese government disdainful of international human rights obligations but, increasingly, also seeking to rewrite those rules in ways that may affect the exercise of human rights around much of the world. Chinese authorities fear that the exercise of these rights abroad can directly threaten the party's hold on power, whether through criticism of the party itself or as a result of holding Beijing accountable under established human rights commitments.

CHINA AND THE UN HUMAN RIGHTS SYSTEM

In June, HRC member states adopted China's proposed resolution on "mutually beneficial cooperation" by a vote of 23–16, with eight abstentions.[7] This vote capped a two-year effort that is indicative of Beijing's goals and tactics of slowly undermining norms through established procedures and rhetoric, which have had significant consequences on accountability for human rights violations. The effort became visible in 2018 when the Chinese government proposed what is now known as its "win-win" resolution,[8] which set out to replace the idea of holding states accountable with a commitment to "dialogue," and which omitted a role for independent civil society in HRC proceedings. When it was introduced, some member states expressed concern at its contents. Beijing made minor improvements, and, along with the perception at the time that the resolution had no real consequences, it was adopted 28-1. The United States was the only government to vote against it.

China's June resolution seeks to reposition international human rights law as a matter of state-to-state relations, ignores the responsibility of states to protect the rights of the individual, treats fundamental human rights as subject to negotiation and compromise, and foresees no meaningful role for civil society. China's March 2018 resolution involved using the council's Advisory Committee, which China expected would produce a study supporting the resolution. Many delegations expressed concern but gave the resolution the benefit of the doubt, abstaining so they could wait to see what the Advisory Committee produced.

China's intentions soon became clear: its submission[9] to the Advisory Committee hailed its own resolution as heralding "the construction of a new type of international relations."[10] The submission claims that human rights are used to "interfere" in other countries' internal affairs, "poisoning the global atmosphere of human rights governance."

This is hardly a coincidence: China has routinely opposed efforts at the council to hold states responsible for even the gravest rights violations, and the submission alarmingly speaks of "so-called universal human rights." It is nonetheless encouraging that sixteen states voted against this harmful resolution in June 2020, compared with only one vote against it in 2018, signaling increasing global concern with China's heavy-handed and aggressive approach to "cooperation."

That the resolution nonetheless passed reflects the threat China poses to the UN human rights system. In 2017, Human Rights Watch documented China's manipulation of UN review processes, harassment, and intimidation of not only human rights defenders from China but also UN human rights experts and staff, and its successful efforts to block the participation of independent civil society groups, including organizations that do not work on China.[11]

In 2018, China underwent its third Universal Periodic Review (UPR), the process for reviewing all UN member states' human rights records. Perhaps because Chinese authorities had since China's previous review opened an extraordinary assault on human rights, Chinese diplomats did not just resort to some of their past practices, which had included providing blatantly false information at the review, flooding the speakers' list with friendly states and government-organized civil society groups, and urging other governments to speak positively about China.

This time around China also pressured UN officials to remove a UN country team submission from the UPR materials (ironically that report was reasonably positive about the government's track record),[12] pressured Organisation of Islamic Cooperation member states to speak positively about China's treatment of Uyghur Muslims, and warned other governments not to attend a panel event about Xinjiang.

China has so far fended off calls by the high commissioner for human rights and several HRC member states for an independent investigation into

gross human rights abuses in Xinjiang, the region in China where an estimated 1 million Uyghurs and other Turkic Muslims remain arbitrarily detained.[13] Typically, violations of this magnitude would have already yielded
actual accountability proceedings, but China's power is such that three years
into the Xinjiang crisis there is little forward movement.

In July 2019, two dozen governments sent a letter to the HRC president—
though they were unwilling to make the call orally on the floor of the
HRC—urging an investigation.[14] China responded with a letter signed by
thirty-seven countries, mostly developing states with poor human rights
records. In November, a similar group of governments delivered a similar
statement at the Third Committee of the UN;[15] China responded with a
letter signed by fifty-four countries.[16]

Beijing also seeks to ensure that discussions about human rights more
broadly take place only through the human rights bodies in Geneva, and
not other UN bodies, particularly the Security Council. China contends
that only the HRC has a mandate to examine them—a convenient way of
trying to limit discussions even on the gravest atrocities. In March 2018,
it opposed a briefing by then high commissioner for human rights Zeid
Ra'ad al Hussein to the Security Council on Syria,[17] and in February 2020
it blocked a resolution at the Security Council on the plight of Myanmar's
ethnic Rohingya.[18]

UN human rights experts, typically referred to as special rapporteurs,
are key to reviews and accountability of UN member states on human rights
issues. One of their common tools is to visit states, but China has declined
to schedule visits by numerous special rapporteurs, including those with
mandates on arbitrary detention, executions, or freedom of expression.[19] It
has allowed visits by experts on issues where it thought it would fare well:
the right to food in 2012, a working group on discrimination against women
in 2014, and an independent expert on the effects of foreign debt in 2016.[20]
In 2016, China allowed a visit by Philip Alston, then the special rapporteur
on extreme poverty and human rights, who ended his visit early when authorities followed him and intimidated people he had spoken to.[21] Since that
time, China has only allowed a visit by the independent expert on the rights
of older people in late 2019.

China also continues to block the Office of the UN High Commissioner
for Human Rights from having a presence in China. While there are two
dozen other UN agencies in China, they have rarely invoked their mandate
to promote human rights.

In late June, fifty UN current and former special procedures—the most prominent group of independent experts in the UN human rights system—issued a searing indictment of China's human rights record and call for urgent action.[22] The experts denounced the Chinese government's "collective repression" of religious and ethnic minorities in Xinjiang and Tibet; the repression of protest and impunity for excessive use of force by police in Hong Kong; censorship and retaliation against journalists, medical workers, and others who sought to speak out following the COVID-19 outbreak; and the targeting of human rights defenders across the country. The experts called for convening a special session on China, creating a dedicated expert on China, and asking UN agencies and governments to press China to meet its human rights obligations. It remains to be seen whether and how the UN secretary-general, the high commissioner for human rights, and the HRC will respond.

Despite its poor human rights record at home, and a serious threat to the UN human rights system, China was reelected to the HRC in October, though with a significant drop in votes (from 180 down to 139), the lowest of any elected government in the Asia region. Absent a critical mass of concerned states committed to serving as a counterweight to both problems, people across China and people who depend on this system for redress and accountability are at serious risk.

WHAT HAPPENS IF CHINA'S POLICIES ARE NOT REVERSED—AND WHAT TO DO

The consequences for failing to stop China's assault on the international human rights system are simple and stark. If these trends continue unabated, the UN Security Council will become even less likely to take action on grave human rights crises; the fundamental underpinnings of a universal human rights system with room for independent actors will further erode; and Chinese authorities' (and their allies') impunity will only grow.

Serious rights-violating governments will know they can rely on Beijing for investment and loans with no conditions. People around the world will increasingly have to be careful whether they criticize Chinese authorities, even if they are citizens of rights-respecting democracies or in environments like academia, where debate is meant to be encouraged.

Chinese government conduct over the first half of 2020—its stalling in an independent investigation into the COVID-19 pandemic, its blatant rejection of international law in deciding to impose national security legislation on Hong Kong, even its manipulation of Tiananmen commemorations for people in the United States—appears to have galvanized momentum to push back. Parliament members from numerous countries are calling for the appointment of a UN special envoy on Hong Kong and/or a standing mechanism at the HRC to examine and report regularly on human rights violations by the Chinese government.

But this is far from creating the kind of counterweight necessary to curb Beijing's agenda, whose threat can now be seen clearly. To protect the UN human rights system from Chinese government erosions, rights-respecting governments should urgently form a multiyear coalition not only to ensure that they are tracking these threats but also to prepare themselves to respond to such threats at every opportunity to push back. This means nominating candidates for UN expert positions and calling out obstructions in the accreditation system.This means canvassing and organizing objections to norm-eroding resolutions, and mobilizing allies to put themselves forward as candidates for the HRC or other selections made by regional blocs. China has the advantages of deep pockets and no periodic changes in government to encumber its ability to plan; democracies will struggle with both. But here the stakes could not be higher—not just for the 1.4 billion people in China, but for people around the world.

Finally, it is critical that none of these efforts to limit the Chinese government's threats to human rights rebound on people across China or of Chinese descent around the world. The rapid spread of COVID-19 triggered a wave of racist anti-Asian harassment and assaults, and an alarming number of governments, politicians, and policies are falling into Beijing's trap of conflating the Chinese government, the Chinese Communist Party, and people from China.[23] They are not the same, and the human rights of people in China should remain at the core of future policies.

ACKNOWLEDGMENTS: Emilie Kimball and Anna Newby edited this chapter.

NOTES

1. "UN Treaty Body Database: China," United Nations Human Rights Office of the High Commissioner, https://tbinternet.ohchr.org/_layouts/15/TreatyBodyExternal/Treaty.aspx?CountryID=36&Lang=EN.

2. Kenneth Roth, *China's Global Threat to Human Rights* (Washington, DC: Human Rights Watch, 2020), www.hrw.org/world-report/2020/country-chapters/global.

3. *The Costs of International Advocacy: China's Interference in United Nations Human Rights Mechanisms* (New York: Human Rights Watch, September 5, 2017), www.hrw.org/report/2017/09/05/costs-international-advocacy/chinas-interference -united-nations-human-rights; Ted Piccone, *China's Long Game on Human Rights at the United Nations* (Washington, DC: The Brookings Institution, September 2018), www.brookings.edu/research/chinas-long-game-on-human-rights-at-the -united-nations/.

4. Ted Piccone, *China's Long Game on Human Rights at the United Nations*.

5. Sarah Zheng, "Why Is China Resisting an Independent Inquiry into How the Pandemic Started?" *South China Morning Post*, May 16, 2020, www.scmp.com/ news/china/diplomacy/article/3084602/why-china-resisting-independent-inquiry -how-pandemic-started.

6. "Hong Kong: Beijing Threatens Draconian Security Law," Human Rights Watch, May 2, 2020, www.hrw.org/news/2020/05/22/hong-kong-beijing-threatens -draconian-security-law.

7. "States Should Oppose China's Disingenuous Resolution on 'Mutually Beneficial Cooperation,'" Human Rights Watch, June 16, 2020, www.hrw.org/news /2020/06/16/states-should-oppose-chinas-disingenuous-resolution-mutually -beneficial-cooperation.

8. John Fisher, "China's 'Win-Win' Resolution Is Anything But," Human Rights Watch, March 5, 2018, www.hrw.org/news/2018/03/05/chinas-win-win-resolution -anything.

9. "The Role of Technical Assistance and Capacity-Building in Fostering Mutually Beneficial Cooperation in Promoting and Protecting Human Rights," United Nations Human Rights Council, www.ohchr.org/EN/HRBodies/HRC/ AdvisoryCommittee/Pages/TheRoleTechnicalAssistance.aspx.

10. Andrea Worden, "China's Win-Win at the UN Human Rights Council: Just Not for Human Rights," Sinopsis, May 28, 2020, https://sinopsis.cz/en/worden-win -win/.

11. "UN: China Blocks Activists, Harasses Experts," Human Rights Watch, September 5, 2017, www.hrw.org/news/2017/09/05/un-china-blocks-activists-har asses-experts.

12. "UN: China Responds to Rights Review with Threats," Human Rights Watch, April 1, 2019, www.hrw.org/news/2019/04/01/un-china-responds-rights-re view-threats.

13. "UN: Rights Body Needs to Step Up on Xinjiang Abuses," Human Rights Watch, March 12, 2020, www.hrw.org/news/2020/03/12/un-rights-body-needs -step-xinjiang-abuses.

14. "UN: Unprecedented Joint Call for China to End Xinjiang Abuses," Human Rights Watch, July 10, 2019, www.hrw.org/news/2019/07/10/un-unprecedented -joint-call-china-end-xinjiang-abuses.

15. Sophie Richardson, "Unprecedented UN Critique of China's Xinjiang Policies," Human Rights Watch, November 14, 2019, www.hrw.org/news/2019/11/14/unprecedented-un-critique-chinas-xinjiang-policies.

16. Louis Charbonneau, "China's Great Misinformation Wall Crumbles on Xinjiang," Human Rights Watch, November 20, 2019, www.hrw.org/news/2019/11/20/chinas-great-misinformation-wall-crumbles-xinjiang.

17. "Procedural Vote Blocks Holding of Security Council Meeting on Human Rights Situation in Syria, Briefing by High Commissioner," United Nations, March 19, 2018, www.un.org/press/en/2018/sc13255.doc.htm.

18. UN Fails to Take Action on Order against Myanmar on Rohingya," Al Jazeera, February 4, 2020, www.aljazeera.com/news/2020/02/fails-action-order-myanmar-rohingyas-200205020402316.html.

19. "View Country Visits of Special Procedures of the Human Rights Council since 1998: China," United Nations Human Rights Office of the High Commissioner, https://spinternet.ohchr.org/ViewCountryVisits.aspx?visitType=all&country=CHN&Lang=en; "Thematic Mandates," United Nations Human Rights Office of the High Commissioner, https://spinternet.ohchr.org/ViewAllCountryMandates.aspx?Type=TM&lang=en.

20. "Human Rights by Country: China," United Nations Human Rights Office of the High Commissioner, www.ohchr.org/EN/countries/AsiaRegion/Pages/CNIndex.aspx.

21. "Report of the Special Rapporteur on Extreme Poverty and Human Rights on His Mission to China," United Nations Human Rights Office of the High Commissioner, https://ap.ohchr.org/documents/dpage_e.aspx?si=A/HRC/35/26/Add.2; Philip Alston, "End-of-Mission Statement on China," United Nations Human Rights Office of the High Commissioner, August 23, 2016, www.ohchr.org/en/NewsEvents/Pages/DisplayNews.aspx?NewsID=20402&LangID=E.

22. "UN Experts Call for Decisive Measures to Protect Fundamental Freedoms in China," United Nations Human Rights Office of the High Commissioner, June 26, 2020, www.ohchr.org/EN/NewsEvents/Pages/DisplayNews.aspx?NewsID=26006&LangID=E.

23. "Covid-19 Fueling Anti-Asian Racism and Xenophobia Worldwide," Human Rights Watch, May 12, 2020, www.hrw.org/news/2020/05/12/covid-19-fueling-anti-asian-racism-and-xenophobia-worldwide.

37

How to Curb China's System of Oppression in Xinjiang

DAHLIA PETERSON
JAMES MILLWARD

The genocide crisis in Xinjiang represents the convergence and culmination of failed development efforts, increasingly aggressive assimilationist policies, and a cycle of repression-resistance-repression that has played out in Xinjiang since the 1990s.[1] Xinjiang's network of internment camps has deprived more than 1 million people of their liberty.[2] Turkic Muslim internees have not been tried, but simply accused of extremism. Signs of supposed extremism, published in a police list to identify "pre-crimes" in potential detainees, include commonplace Islamic practices, such as avoiding alcohol, fasting, veiling, wearing a beard, or owning a Quran. Foreign travel or contacts and having "too many children" are also justifications for detention.[3] Within the camps, internees are subjected to regimented daily routines, political indoctrination, some Mandarin language training, and forced renunciations of Islam and Uyghur culture. Former detainees who have managed to leave China report crowded cells, unsanitary conditions, poor food, beatings, physical and psychological torture, and systematic rape, as well as forced birth control.[4]

Although People's Republic of China (PRC) authorities insist that the camps are "vocational training centers," a leaked template specifies that "students" must complete at least one year of "concentrated educational transformation" and pass a strict evaluation of their political thinking and discipline before they proceed to a further three to six months of "vocational" factory skills training.[5]

SURVEILLANCE COMPANIES INVOLVED

Chinese and non-Chinese companies alike are involved in Xinjiang's system of surveillance, implicating them in all these forms of repression. Such companies benefited financially and reputationally in 2015 from the central government's policy of prioritizing "stability" in Xinjiang and the construction of the national rural-focused Sharp Eyes surveillance program.[6] By 2018, nearly 1,400 Chinese companies were competing for lucrative contracts in Xinjiang—of these, around 1,000 were Xinjiang-based.[7]

From the perspective of policy options, these companies fall into three groups: Chinese firms that have landed on the Bureau of Industry and Security (BIS) Entity List for their harms to human rights in Xinjiang; active Chinese players in Xinjiang that have so far evaded U.S. sanction; and Western companies selling core hardware to either of the two preceding groups.

ENTITY LIST COMPANIES AND IMPACT

In October 2019, the United States began to use human rights to justify adding Chinese companies and government bodies to the BIS Entity List in order to cut off these entities' access to imported components. However, many offending Chinese firms remain unlisted.[8] BIS selected eight companies and twenty Xinjiang government institutions, pointing to their "implementation of China's campaign of repression, mass arbitrary detention, and high-technology surveillance" against Uyghurs, Kazakhs, and other Turkic Muslim groups in Xinjiang.[9] The list included video surveillance companies Dahua, Hikvision, Megvii, Yitu, Sensetime, and Yixin Science and Technology Co. Ltd; voice recognition firm iFlytek; and digital forensics firm Xiamen Meiya Pico Information Co. Ltd.[10] The role these companies play in Xinjiang will be discussed in the sections that follow.

In May 2020, BIS added eight more Chinese firms and China's Ministry of Public Security's Institute of Forensic Science to the list under the same justification.[11] The additions included Aksu Huafu Textiles, likely due to forced labor concerns, facial recognition companies CloudWalk, Intellifusion, IS'Vision, NetPosa and its subsidiary SenseNets, and information technology infrastructure company FiberHome Technologies Group, along with its cloud and big data subsidiary Nanjing FiberHome Starrysky Communication Development.[12]

Many of the sanctioned Chinese companies are also on the Chinese Ministry of Science and Technology's national "AI Champions" list.[13] Artificial intelligence (AI) champions have a voice in national technical standards setting. They also have relative freedom from competition with state-owned enterprises and are meant to help China lead the world in AI technologies by 2030.[14] Of the fifteen national champions, five have been placed on the Entity List for human rights violations in Xinjiang: iFlytek, Hikvision, Yitu, Megvii, and SenseTime.

China's facial recognition giants form the backbone of its surveillance system in Xinjiang and exercise great influence across China and the globe. Hikvision and Dahua supply around one-third of the global market for security cameras and related goods like digital video recorders.[15] From 2016 to 2017, eleven Hikvision and Dahua Public-Private Partnership Safe Cities and public security checkpoint projects in Xinjiang totaled more than 7 billion yuan ($1.2 billion).[16] One Hikvision project in Ürümqi was worth $79 million, with a network of 30,000 security cameras, video analytics hubs, intelligent monitoring systems, big data centers, police checkpoints, and drones.[17] Another Hikvision project in Pishan County included the installation of a surveillance system in a re-education camp and mosques.[18]

Facial recognition companies, such as Yitu, Cloudwalk, and Intellifusion, actively market their products for public security use. At "anti-terrorism" expos held in Xinjiang in August 2017, CloudWalk demonstrated its Fire Eye (火眼) product, capable of twenty-four-hour monitoring and immediate police notification upon detection of fugitives or persons of interest.[19] At the same expos, Intellifusion demonstrated Deep Eye (深目), purportedly customizable for antiterrorism needs.[20] Yitu launched a similar project called Dragonfly Eye (蜻蜓眼), capable of performing static photo-based face comparisons or video-based dynamic comparisons in both residential and public areas.[21] All of the aforementioned companies' products could be used to identify subjects of interest among the Uyghur population, referred to by the authorities as "focus personnel."[22]

Beyond facial recognition, longtime voice recognition player iFlytek collaborated with hardware and service providers Meiya Pico and Fiberhome to develop tools automating transcription and translation of Uyghur language audio into Mandarin. This product enables authorities to scan for "pre-criminal" and criminal content.[23] After iFlytek established a subsidiary and laboratory in Xinjiang to develop speech recognition technology focusing on non-Chinese languages, authorities in the region adopted the tool for tracking and identifying non-Han populations.[24]

Placement on the Entity List has not yet significantly slowed the development of these companies, as they have claimed to source supply chain alternatives and have received renewed demand under COVID-19.[25]

NON–ENTITY LIST COMPANIES AND IMPACT

Several technology companies not yet placed on the Entity List have perpetuated both overt and indirect human rights harms in Xinjiang. Longtime Xinjiang-based Leon Technology, for example, oversaw half of the Safe City projects in Ürümqi by the end of 2017.[26] The firm also launched a joint venture with SenseTime called Tang Li Technology, increasing surveillance through "convenience police stations" in Kashgar and expanding monitoring to thousands of video access points in the city's rural areas.[27]

Data doors, manufactured by companies, such as Pingtech, CETC, and Dilusense, have also been integral to data collection efforts in Xinjiang.[28] The entryways have facial recognition capabilities and ID card verification, and can lift electronic device identifier numbers; how they source their components is often unclear.[29] When collected data are combined with data from facial recognition, surveillance cameras, license plates, phone records, and social media posts, authorities can track individuals with alarming clarity.[30]

WESTERN COMPANIES' ROLE

An underexamined question is how Western companies have bolstered China's surveillance state and Xinjiang operations through investment and financing, academic and research partnerships, intellectual property transfer, medical equipment export for surveillance (as in the case of Thermo Fisher), or hardware exports.[31] These firms provide a technical basis for China's unprecedented mass racial profiling and ethnic oppression, especially in hardware, as Chinese companies largely cannot provide homegrown substitutions and rely on the West for the chips that enable deep learning and storage hard drives designed for surveillance.[32]

U.S.-based companies such as Intel, NVIDIA, Xilinx, Seagate, and Western Digital have sold hardware used in Chinese surveillance operations.[33]

According to Chinese sources, graphics processing units (GPU) from Intel and NVIDIA have delivered direct benefits to Chinese surveillance companies.[34] Hikvision and Dahua both rely on these chips for their servers, cameras, and safe city applications.[35] Hikvision and Dahua also depend on leading American hard drive companies, such as Seagate and Western Digital; a company active in Xinjiang stated that it only uses products from Western Digital and Seagate.[36]

It is also possible that NVIDIA and Intel hardware have contributed to detection of Uyghurs in video surveillance systems outside Xinjiang, as at least eight nationwide Ministry of Public Security (MPS) projects require NVIDIA and Intel chips to perform Uyghur detection.[37] The MPS mandated this capability in its December 2017 draft facial recognition guidelines— which were met by Hikvision, Yitu, Megvii, SenseTime, and CloudWalk.[38]

RECOMMENDATIONS

The following sections offer policy recommendations for the United States, allies, and multilateral actors.

Policy Recommendations for the United States
Related to Surveillance Technology

- The United States should propose alternative surveillance technology standards at the UN's International Telecommunications Union, where Chinese companies have been the only submitters since 2016, and therefore the only major player shifting normative goalposts.[39]

- BIS and the State Department, along with academics, researchers, and nongovernmental organizations, should publicly disclose knowledge of Chinese surveillance companies' supply chains, and determine how many suppliers are from the United States and other democracies.

- The aforementioned groups should create a public repository of rights abuses in Xinjiang, modeled off databases such as the California Proposition 65 list or the Environmental Protection Agency's Toxics Release Inventory Program, to further scrutinize and identify underexamined companies for the Entity List.[40]

- Congress should prevent Chinese surveillance companies from selling their technology in the United States, beyond current bans on use by U.S. government customers.

- BIS and the interagency process should disclose if the earlier inclusion of Huawei on the Entity List has arrested its surveillance activities in Xinjiang, even if that was not why Huawei was initially sanctioned.[41]

General Policy Recommendations for the United States Regarding Repression of Turkic Muslims in Xinjiang

- The United States should more clearly articulate the intended aims of its policy actions on Xinjiang to include the closure of internment camps; reduction of surveillance and elimination of "pre-criminal" profiling of Xinjiang indigenous peoples; an end to family separation and birth suppression targeted at Uyghurs and other non-Han groups; return to previous PRC support and promotion of the identity and culture of Xinjiang's non-Han groups; and encouragement of a Xinjiang economic development program prioritizing indigenous conditions and human rights.

- The U.S. Citizenship and Immigration Services should address its asylum backlog for the hundreds of Uyghurs settled in the United States who face deportation risk and near-certain internment if returned to China.[42]

- The United States should enhance its position to advocate for human rights and fair economic practices in Xinjiang and the PRC more broadly by joining and/or reenergizing its role in Asia-Pacific regional multilateral organizations and meetings (Trans-Pacific Partnership, Asia-Pacific Economic Cooperation, Association of Southeast Asian Nations), and by rejoining the UN Human Rights Council.

- The Labor Department's Bureau of International Labor Affairs (BILA) should prioritize investigating and publicizing the Xinjiang issue and be provided with requisite funding to do so.[43] BILA should investigate not only Xinjiang-based factories but commercial and carceral operations of Xinjiang-related activities of Chinese municipalities, provinces, and corporations involved, and other arrangements by which the PRC state channels Xinjiang labor into manufacturing. The BILA should publish and frequently update lists of goods and enterprises of concern.

- Potential U.S. importers of goods from China should strengthen their due diligence in scrutinizing supply chains for involvement in the Xinjiang surveillance, internment, and involuntary labor complex.

- U.S. Customs and Border Protection, as informed by the BILA and private actors, should robustly enforce forced labor restrictions to block imports of goods associated with the Xinjiang surveillance, internment, and involuntary labor complex.

Policy Recommendations for Global and Multilateral Actors

- Other nations should coordinate with the United States to identify, publicize, and sanction officials and corporations associated with the repression in Xinjiang. Chinese and international corporations should redouble their diligence efforts to avoid direct or indirect association with the Xinjiang surveillance, internment, and forced labor complex. All nations should denounce the repressive policies in Xinjiang during interactions with PRC interlocutors.

- All nations should provide asylum and support to Turkic Muslims fleeing oppression in the PRC, in adherence to the principle of non-refoulement.

- Corporations and nations should collectively signal to PRC authorities that their sponsorship and participation in the 2022 Beijing Olympics will be impossible if the current treatment of Xinjiang peoples continues.

ACKNOWLEDGMENTS: The authors would like to thank Julian Gewirtz for helpful discussions, Shelton Fitch, Igor Mikolic-Torreira, Ted Reinert, Lynne Weil, and Remco Zwetsloot for editing assistance, and anonymous peer reviewers for comments on the draft.

NOTES

1. Editorial, "What's Happening in Xinjiang Is Genocide," *Washington Post*, July 6, 2020, www.washingtonpost.com/opinions/global-opinions/whats-happen ing-in-xinjiang-is-genocide/2020/07/06/cde3f9da-bfaa-11ea-9fdd-b7ac6b051dc8_ story.html; Yuhui Li, *China's Assistance Program in Xinjiang: A Sociological Analysis* (New York: Lexington Books, 2018), 103–106. Regarding the failures of development, see also Ilham Tohti, "Present-Day Ethnic Problems in Xinjiang Uighur Autonomous Region: Overview and Recommendations," trans. Cindy Carter, Ilham Tohti

Initiative, September 2016, https://ilhamtohtisite.files.wordpress.com/2016/09/
ilham-tohti_present-day-ethnic-problems-in-xinjiang-uighur-autonomous-region
-overview-and-recommendations_complete-translation3.pdf. Regarding
intensified securitization and assimilative policies, see Darren Byler, "Spirit
Breaking: Uyghur Dispossession, Culture Work and Terror Capitalism in a Chinese
Global City" (PhD diss., University of Washington, 2018), https://digital.lib.wash
ington.edu/researchworks/bitstream/handle/1773/42946/Byler_washington_
0250E_19242.pdf; David Tobin, *Securing China's Northwest Frontier: Identity and
Insecurity in Xinjiang* (Cambridge, UK: Cambridge University Press, 2020).
Regarding Uyghur birthrate suppression, see "China Cuts Uighur Births with
IUDs, Abortion, Sterilization," Associated Press, June 29, 2020, https://apnews.com
/269b3de1af34e17c1941a514f78d764c; Adrian Zenz, *Sterilizations, IUDs, and
Mandatory Birth Control: The CCP's Campaign to Suppress Uyghur Birthrates in
Xinjiang* (Washington, DC: The Jamestown Foundation, June 2020), https://
jamestown.org/product/sterilizations-iuds-and-mandatory-birth-control-the-ccps
-campaign-to-suppress-uyghur-birthrates-in-xinjiang/.

2. Adrian Zenz calculated the initial estimates of numbers interned on the
basis of camp size, local quotas, and Chinese documents. Ibid. In February 2018, a
Uyghur activist media outlet in Turkey released a document it says was leaked by a
"believable member of the security services on the ground" in Xinjiang. The document, dating from late 2017 or early 2018, tabulates precise numbers of internees
in county-level detention centers, amounting to 892,329 (it excluded municipal-
level administrative units, notably the large cities of Ürümqi, Khotan, and Yining).
Naoko Mizutani 水谷尚子, "ウイグル絶望収容所の収監者数は89万人以上" [The
number of Uyghurs interned in re-education camps exceeds 890,000], *Newsweek
Japan*, March 13, 2018. www.newsweekjapan.jp/stories/world/2018/03/89-3_1.php.
Though the document's provenance cannot be confirmed, if genuine it supports the
estimates of a million or more total internees. Randall Schriver, then assistant secretary of defense for Indo-Pacific Security Affairs at the U.S. Department of Defense,
estimated that up to 3 million Xinjiang Muslims were interned in the camps. Phil
Steward, "China Putting Minority Muslims in 'Concentration Camps,' U.S. Says,"
Reuters, May 3, 2019. These figures and figures quoted in media accounts generally
do not include over 300,000 newly put in prison in 2017–2018, though they are also
victims of the algorithm-aided roundup of supposed extremists. Shawn Zhang and
other researchers gathered further evidence of the internment system's scale from
satellite images and coordinates from Google Earth and other open sources. Journalists were able to confirm the identification of sites as internment camps by visiting some of them on the ground. See Shawn Zhang, "List of Re-education Camps
in Xinjiang 新疆再教育集中营列表," Medium, May 20, 2018, https://medium.com
/@shawnwzhang/list-of-re-education-camps-in-xinjiang-%E6%96%B0%E7%96%8
6%E5%86%8D%E6%95%99%E8%82%B2%E9%9B%86%E4%B8%AD%E8%90%A5
%E5%88%97%E8%A1%A8-99720372419c; Shawn Zhang, "Xinjiang Re-education
Camps List by Cities," Medium, May 20, 2019, https://medium.com/@shawnw-

zhang/xinjiang-re-education-camps-list-by-cities-f4ed0a6e095a; and other photo essays posted on by Zhang on Medium, https://medium.com/@shawnwzhang. A more extensive Buzzfeed investigation identified through satellite imagery 268 compounds with prison features built since 2017 in Xinjiang and through other sources verified 92 of these as detention centers. Megha Rajagapolan, Alison Killing, and Christo Buschek, "China Secretly Built a Vast New Infrastructure to Imprison Muslims," August 27, 2020. www.buzzfeednews.com/article/meghara/china-new-internment-camps-xinjiang-uighurs-muslims.

3. For more on the punishments for having "too many" children, see "China Cuts Uighur Births with IUDs, Abortion, Sterilization," Associated Press.

4. Maya Wang, *"Eradicating Ideological Viruses": China's Campaign of Repression against Xinjiang's Muslims* (New York: Human Rights Watch, September 9, 2018), www.hrw.org/report/2018/09/09/eradicating-ideological-viruses/chinas-campaign-repression-against-xinjiangs; "China Cuts Uighur Births with IUDs, Abortion, Sterilization," Associated Press; Adrian Zenz, *Sterilizations, IUDs, and Mandatory Birth Control*.

5. Zhu Hailun, "Opinion on Further Strengthening and Standardizing Vocational Skills Education and Training Centers Work," Autonomous Region State Organ Telegram, 2017, www.documentcloud.org/documents/6558510-China-Cables-Telegram-English.html. Document published by International Consortium of Investigative Journalists as part of "The China Cables." Original Chinese version: www.documentcloud.org/documents/6558509-China-Cables-Telegram-Chinese.html.

6. Danielle Cave, Fergus Ryan, and Vicky Xiuzhong Xu, *Mapping More of China's Tech Giants: AI and Surveillance* (Barton, Australia: Australian Strategic Policy Institute, November 28, 2019), www.aspi.org.au/report/mapping-more-chinas-tech-giants; Dahlia Peterson and Josh Rudolph, "Sharper Eyes: Shandong to Xinjiang," China Digital Times, September 13, 2019, https://chinadigitaltimes.net/2019/09/sharper-eyes-shandong-to-xinjiang-part-3.

7. Darren Byler, "The Global Implications of 'Re-education' Technologies in Northwest China," Washington, DC, Center for Global Policy, June 8, 2020, https://cgpolicy.org/articles/the-global-implications-of-re-education-technologies-in-northwest-china; Danielle Cave, Fergus Ryan, and Vicky Xiuzhong Xu, *Mapping More of China's Tech Giants*.

8. Placement on the Entity List means companies are subject to additional license requirements and limited availability of most license exceptions for exports, reexports, and in-country transfers to entities on the list. See "Addition of Certain Entities to the Entity List," *Federal Register*, October 9, 2019, www.federalregister.gov/documents/2019/10/09/2019-22210/addition-of-certain-entities-to-the-entity-list; Amy K. Lehr and Efthimia Maria ("Mariefaye") Bechrakis, "The United States Blacklisted 28 Chinese Entities over Repression of Muslim Minorities in Xinjiang. What Does This Mean for Human Rights?" Center for Strategic and International Studies, October 11, 2019, www.csis.org/analysis/united-states-blacklisted-28-chinese-entities-over-repression-muslim-minorities-xinjiang.

9. "Addition of Certain Entities to the Entity List," *Federal Register*.

10. AFP, "China's Blacklisted AI Firms: What You Should Know," *Bangkok Post*, October 13, 2019,

www.bangkokpost.com/business/1771179/chinas-blacklisted-ai-firms-what -you-should-know.

11. "Commerce Department to Add Nine Chinese Entities Related to Human Rights Abuses in the Xinjiang Uighur Autonomous Region to the Entity List," U.S. Department of Commerce, May 22, 2020, www.commerce.gov/news/press-releases /2020/05/commerce-department-add-nine-chinese-entities-related-human-rights.

12. Ibid.; Simon Glover, "BCI Slammed for Refusing to Quit Xinjiang," EcoTextile News, January 29, 2020, www.ecotextile.com/2020012925609/materials -production-news/bci-slammed-for-refusing-to-quit-xinjiang.html.

13. The national team was first launched in November 2017 with five members, and has since expanded to fifteen total. See Jeffrey Ding, "China's AI National Team," ChinAI, May 20, 2019, https://chinai.substack.com/p/chinai-51-chinas-ai -national-team; "科技部扩容'AI国家队名单，十家新公司入选" [The Ministry of Science and Technology expands the list of 'AI National Team,' 10 new companies are selected], 电子工程专辑 [EE Times China], August 30, 2019, www.eet-china .com/news/201908301010.html.

14. Gregory C. Allen, *Understanding China's AI Strategy* (Washington, DC: Center for a New American Security, February 6, 2019), www.cnas.org/publications /reports/understanding-chinas-ai-strategy.

15. Charles Rollet, "In China's Far West, Companies Cash in on Surveillance Program That Targets Muslims," *Foreign Policy*, June 13, 2018, https://foreignpolicy .com/2018/06/13/in-chinas-far-west-companies-cash-in-on-surveillance-program -that-targets-muslims.

16. A big contributor to the discrepancy between Hikvision and Dahua's shares of the $1.2 billion is Dahua winning the $686 million Safe County project for Yarkant County, the location of the July 2014 rioting. See Charles Rollet, "Dahua and Hikvision Win over $1 Billion in Government-Backed Projects in Xinjiang," IPVM, April 23, 2018, https://ipvm.com/reports/xinjiang-dahua-hikvision.

17. Charles Rollet, "In China's Far West, Companies Cash in on Surveillance Program That Targets Muslims."

18. Charles Rollet, "Evidence of Hikvision's Involvement with Xinjiang IJOP and Re-education Camps," IPVM, October 2, 2018, https://ipvm.com/reports/ hikvision-xinjiang.

19. The expos were the 4th China-Asia-Europe Security Expo and the 13th Xinjiang Police Anti-Terrorism Technical Equipment Expo. See "共筑平安新疆 云 从科技携人脸识别亮相亚欧安防展览会" [Building safety in Xinjiang: CloudWalk Technology debuts face recognition at the Asia-Europe Security Exhibition], CTI Forum, August 24, 2017, https://web.archive.org/web/20200623203839/ www. ctiforum.com/news/guonei/519237.html; "商汤、旷视、云从、依图，究竟谁将在人 脸识别领域独领风骚？" [Sensetime, Megvii, Cloudwalk, Yitu, who will be the leader in face recognition?], 新鲜事研究社 [What's New Research], May 19, 2013,

https://web.archive.org/web/20200623212409/https://baijiahao.baidu.com/s?id=16 33414565832463606&wfr=spider&for=pc.

20. "云天励飞"深目"动态人像识别解决方案将亮相亚欧安博会" [Intelli-fusion's 'Deep Eye' Dynamic Portrait Recognition Solution will debut at Asia-Europe Expo], 中国安防展览网 [China Security Exhibition Network], August 8, 2017, https://archive.vn/OZkfO.

21. Cao Yiqing, "从依图科技看中国AI的弯道超越" [Seeing the acceleration of Chinese AI from Yitu Technology's perspective], Yu De, October 11, 2019, https://web.archive.org/web/20200623212059/https://baijiahao.baidu.com/s?id=16470583 44062254767&wfr=spider&for=pc.

22. The "focus personnel" label is likely similar to the seven groups of "focus personnel" highlighted by Human Rights Watch: petitioners, those who "undermine stability," those who are involved in terrorism, major criminals, those involved with drugs, wanted persons, and those with mental health problems who "tend to cause disturbances." See "China: Police 'Big Data' Systems Violate Privacy, Target Dissent," Human Rights Watch, November 19, 2017, www.hrw.org/news/2017/11/19 /china-police-big-data-systems-violate-privacy-target-dissent.

23. Darren Byler, "The Global Implications of 'Re-education' Technologies in Northwest China"; Meiya Pico was also responsible for the intrusive spying app MFSocket. Celia Chen and Meng Jing, "What You Need to Know about Meiya Pico, China's Low-Profile Forensics Champion Named in Data Privacy Scandal," *South China Morning Post,* July 9, 2019, www.scmp.com/tech/start-ups/article/3017688/ what-you-need-know-about-meiya-pico-chinas-low-profile-forensics.

24. Danielle Cave, Fergus Ryan, and Vicky Xiuzhong Xu, *Mapping More of China's Tech Giants.*

25. "'实体清单'事项 海康威视、大华股份最新、全面回应" [Hikvision, Dahua share their latest and comprehensive response to the 'Entity List'], 中国安防行业网 [*China Security Industry Network*], October 10, 2019, https://web.archive.org/web/ 20200623220513/http://news.21csp.com.cn/c34/201910/11389485.html.

26. This includes one of the eleven Dahua and Hikvision Xinjiang projects highlighted by IPVM worth $1.2 billion. Leon was one of the awardees alongside Dahua in the Qiemo Safe County project in 2017. See Charles Rollet, "Dahua and Hikvision Win over $1 Billion in Government-Backed Projects in Xinjiang"; Jeffrey Ding, "Complicit—China's AI Unicorns and the Securitization of Xinjiang," ChinAI, September 23, 2018, https://chinai.substack.com/p/chinai-newsletter-29 -complicit-chinas-ai-unicorns-and-the-securitization-of-xinjiang.

27. Jeffrey Ding, "Complicit—China's AI Unicorns and the Securitization of Xinjiang."

28. Masha Borak, "China's 'Data Doors' Scoop Up Information Straight from Your Phone," *South China Morning Post*, May 7, 2019, www.scmp.com/abacus/tech /article/3029333/chinas-data-doors-scoop-information-straight-your-phone.

29. Ibid.

30. Ibid.

31. For more on how Thermo Fisher enabled biometric surveillance in China,

see Sui-Lee Wee, "China Is Collecting DNA from Tens of Millions of Men and Boys, Using U.S. Equipment," *New York Times,* June 17, 2020, www.nytimes.com/2020/06/17/world/asia/China-DNA-surveillance.html.

32. These hardware solutions include graphics processing units (GPU) and field-programmable gate arrays (FPGA). See Lorand Laskai and Helen Toner, "Can China Grow Its Own AI Tech Base?" New America, November 4, 2019, www.newamerica.org/cybersecurity-initiative/digichina/blog/can-china-grow-its-own-ai-tech-base.

33. Xilinx provides chips called FPGAs, while Seagate and Western Digital provide AI surveillance-optimized storage solutions. For further details see Dahlia Peterson, "Foreign Technology and the Surveillance State" in *China's Quest for Foreign Technology: Beyond Espionage*, ed. William C. Hannas and Didi Kirsten Tatlow (London: Routledge, September 2020).

34. "AI芯片厂商与传统安防制造企业紧密合作 拓展安防业务" [AI chip manufacturers work closely with traditional security manufacturing companies to expand security business], 中国安防行业网 [China Security Industry Network], December 28, 2017, https://web.archive.org/web/20200630000620/http://news.21csp.com.cn/c34/201712/11365694.html.

35. For further examples see Dahlia Peterson, "Foreign Technology and the Surveillance State."

36. "Congressional Letter Calls Out US Companies Supporting Dahua and Hikvision," IPVM, March 11, 2019, https://ipvm.com/reports/letter-support; Liza Lin and Josh Chin, "U.S. Tech Companies Prop Up China's Vast Surveillance Network," *Wall Street Journal*, November 26, 2019, www.wsj.com/articles/u-s-tech-companies-prop-up-chinas-vast-surveillance-network-11574786846.

37. "China Uyghur Analytic Projects Require Intel And NVIDIA, Intel Condemns, NVIDIA Silent," IPVM, December 2, 2019, https://ipvm.com/reports/uyghur-intel-nvidia.

38. Charles Rollet, "China Government Spreads Uyghur Analytics across China," IPVM, November 25, 2019, https://ipvm.com/reports/ethnicity-analytics; Paul Mozur, "One Month, 500,000 Face Scans: How China Is Using A.I. to Profile a Minority," *New York Times*, April 14, 2019, www.nytimes.com/2019/04/14/technology/china-surveillance-artificial-intelligence-racial-profiling.html. Hikvision is a notable example of a company that actively marketed—then deleted—coverage of its Uyghur detection and analytics capabilities on its website. See Charles Rollet, "Hikvision Markets Uyghur Ethnicity Analytics, Now Covers Up," IPVM, November 11, 2019, https://ipvm.com/reports/hikvision-uyghur.

39. Anna Gross and Madhumita Murgia, "China Shows Its Dominance in Surveillance Technology," *Financial Times*, December 26, 2019, www.ft.com/content/b34d8ff8-21b4-11ea-92da-f0c92e957a96.

40. California Office of Environmental Health Hazard Assessment, "The Proposition 65 List," https://oehha.ca.gov/proposition-65/proposition-65-list; United States Environmental Protection Agency, "Toxics Release Inventory (TRI) Program," www.epa.gov/toxics-release-inventory-tri-program.

41. For example, Huawei reportedly built the police surveillance systems in Karamay and Kashgar prefectures, and was praised by the head of Xinjiang provincial police department for its contributions to the "Safe Xinjiang" program. See Danielle Cave, Fergus Ryan, and Vicky Xiuzhong Xu, *Mapping More of China's Tech Giants*.

42. This logjam is especially prevalent at the Arlington, Virginia, U.S. Citizenship and Immigration Services center, which processes applications in the region where most Uyghurs have settled. See James T. Areddy and Michelle Hackman, "China's Muslim Uighurs Are Stuck in U.S. Immigration Limbo," *Wall Street Journal*, July 28, 2020, www.wsj.com/articles/chinas-muslim-uighurs-are-stuck-in-u-s-immigration-limbo-11595937603.

43. Involuntary labor related to Xinjiang oppression is complex and pervasive, occurring well beyond factories located within or adjacent to internment camps. The U.S. Tariff Act of 1930 defines "forced labor" as "all work or service which is exacted from any person under the menace of any penalty for its nonperformance and for which the worker does not offer himself voluntarily." This could potentially include all Uyghurs and others channeled into state-run and public-private manufacturing arrangements in a context when refusal may result in internment or imprisonment. Tariff Act of 1930, 19 U.S.C. §1307 (1930), https://uscode.house.gov/view.xhtml?path=/prelim@title19/chapter4&edition=prelim.

CONTRIBUTORS

MICHAEL BROWN is the director of the Defense Innovation Unit (DIU) at the U.S. Department of Defense. DIU fields leading-edge capability to the military using commercial technologies rapidly and cost effectively. Previously, he served as a White House Presidential Innovation Fellow, during which he co-authored a Pentagon study on China's participation in the U.S. venture ecosystem, a catalyst for the Foreign Investment Risk Review Modernization Act (FIRRMA). Additionally, he led the initiative for National Security Innovation Capital (NSIC) to fund dual-use hardware technology companies. He spent most of his career in Silicon Valley, where he was the CEO of Symantec Corporation, the global cybersecurity leader, and the Chairman and CEO of Quantum Corporation. He is a member of the Council on Foreign Relations. He received a BA in economics from Harvard University and an MBA from Stanford University.

RICHARD BUSH is a nonresident senior fellow at the Brookings Institution, where he was a scholar from 2002 to 2020. Prior to that, he worked for nineteen years in the U.S. government, first on the staff of the House Foreign Affairs Committee (1983–1995), then as national intelligence officer for East Asia and a member of the National Intelligence Council (1995–1997), and then as the chairman and managing director of the American Institute in Taiwan (1997–2002). He has written books on China-Taiwan relations, China-Japan relations, and Hong Kong. In spring 2021, the Brookings Institution Press will publish his book *Difficult Choices: Taiwan's Quest for Security and the Good Life*, an examination of Taiwan's democratic system.

SHEENA CHESTNUT GREITENS is associate professor at the Lyndon B. Johnson School of Public Affairs at the University of Texas at Austin, and an affiliate of the university's Robert Strauss Center for International Security and Law and Clements Center for National Security. She is also a nonresident senior fellow at Brookings' Center for East Asia Policy Studies. Her research focuses on American national security, East Asia, and authoritarian politics. Her first book, *Dictators and Their Secret Police*, won several awards, and her work regularly appears in academic, policy, and media outlets in the United States and Asia. She holds a PhD from Harvard University; an M.Phil from Oxford University, where she studied as a Marshall Scholar; and a bachelor's from Stanford University. She is currently working on a book manuscript about China's domestic security policies and their importance for China's role in the world.

ERIC CHEWNING is a partner in McKinsey & Company's Advanced Industries practice. His experience spans the public and private sectors. He was the chief of staff to the U.S. Secretary of Defense. In this role he led the secretary's executive team, working across the military services, Joint Staff, Combatant Commands, and senior civilian political appointees. Prior to serving as chief of staff, he was the Deputy Assistant Secretary of Defense for Industrial Policy. In this capacity, he was the principal advisor for analyzing the capabilities, policies, and overall health of the defense industrial base. He is a former U.S. Army military intelligence officer and veteran. Prior to his military service, he was an investment banker at Morgan Stanley, where he focused on corporate finance and M&A in the global industrials sector.

TARUN CHHABRA was a senior fellow at Georgetown University's Center for Security and Emerging Technology, and the director of the Brookings Institution's Project on International Order and Strategy. He previously served on the U.S. National Security Council staff and Department of Defense. He has written on U.S. grand strategy, U.S.-China relations, and U.S.-allied technology cooperation.

DAVID DOLLAR is a senior fellow in the China Center at the Brookings Institution and host of the podcast Dollar & Sense on international trade. He is a leading expert on the Chinese economy and co-author of *China 2049.* From 2009 to 2013, he was the U.S. Treasury's economic and financial emissary to China, based in Beijing. Before his time at Treasury, he worked at the World Bank for 20 years, ending as country director for China and Mongolia. Prior to the World Bank, he was an assistant professor of economics at UCLA, spending a semester in Beijing teaching at the Chinese Academy of Social Sciences in 1986. He has a PhD in economics from NYU and a BA in Asian studies from Dartmouth College.

MEAGAN DOOLEY is a senior research analyst in the Global Economy and Development program at Brookings, where she supports research on poverty and the middle class, development finance reform, migration, and women's economic empowerment.

RUSH DOSHI is a former director of the Brookings China Strategy Initiative and fellow in the Brookings Foreign Policy program. He is also a former fellow at Yale Law School's Paul Tsai China Center. His research focuses on Chinese grand strategy as well as Indo-Pacific security issues. He is the author of *The Long Game: China's Grand Strategy to Displace American Order* and has testified before the Senate Commerce Committee and the U.S.-China Economic and Security Review Commission. Doshi received his doctorate from Harvard University and his bachelor's from Princeton's School of Public and International Affairs with a minor in East Asian studies. He is proficient in Mandarin Chinese.

LEAH DREYFUSS is the associate director of the Center for Security, Strategy, and Technology in the Foreign Policy program at the Brookings Institution. Prior to Brookings, she served as the assistant director of the Homeland Security Program at the Aspen Institute, where she worked on projects including the Aspen Security Forum. She received her bachelor of science in foreign service from the Georgetown University Edmund A. Walsh School of Foreign Service, where she concentrated in international politics, security studies, and international development, and her master of arts in international affairs from the Johns Hopkins School of Advanced International Studies, where she concentrated in strategic studies and international economics.

JEFFREY FELTMAN joined the Brookings Foreign Policy program as the John C. Whitehead Visiting Fellow in International Diplomacy. He is a senior fellow at the United Nations Foundation and a senior advisor to Kissinger Associates. He serves on the Middle East Institute's Board of Governors and on the advisory boards of the European Institute of Peace and the Dialogue Advisory Group. From 2012 until 2018, he was U.N. Under-Secretary-General for Political Affairs. Previously, he was a U.S. foreign service officer. From 2009 until 2012, he was the Assistant Secretary of State for Near Eastern Affairs. Prior to his 2004–2008 tenure as U.S. ambassador to Lebanon, he served in Erbil, Baghdad, Jerusalem, Tel Aviv, Tunis, Amman, Budapest, and Port-au-Prince.

CARRICK FLYNN is a research affiliate with the Centre for the Governance of AI at the University of Oxford, where he was the founding assistant director. He co-authored his piece in this volume while a research fellow at Georgetown's Center for Security and Emerging Technology (CSET). Previously, he worked in human rights and economic development in Africa and Asia. He is a graduate of Yale Law School and the University of Oregon.

SAMANTHA GROSS is director of the Energy Security and Climate Initiative and a fellow in Foreign Policy at the Brookings Institution. Her work is focused on the intersection of energy, environment, and policy, including climate policy and international cooperation, energy geopolitics, and global energy markets. She has been a visiting fellow at the King Abdullah Petroleum Studies and Research Center, where she authored work on clean energy cooperation and post–Paris Agreement climate policy. She was director of the Office of International Climate and Clean Energy at the U.S. Department of Energy, where she directed U.S. activities under the Clean Energy Ministerial. She was also director of Integrated Research at IHS CERA. She holds a BS in chemical engineering from the University of Illinois, an MS in environmental engineering from Stanford University, and an MBA from the University of California, Berkeley.

RYAN HASS is a senior fellow and the Michael H. Armacost Chair in the Foreign Policy program at Brookings. Hass also is a nonresident affiliated fellow at Yale Law School's Paul Tsai China Center, and a senior advisor at McLarty Associates and The Scowcroft Group. His research focuses on policy development on the pressing political, economic, and security challenges facing the United States in Asia.

KEVIN HUGGARD is a senior research assistant in the Center for Middle East Policy at the Brookings Institution. He studied international politics and Arabic at Georgetown University, graduating with a bachelor of science. His research focuses on U.S. policy toward the Israeli-Palestinian conflict and American relationships with nondemocratic governments in the Middle East.

BRUCE JONES is a senior fellow and the director of the Project on International Order and Strategy in the Foreign Policy program at Brookings, where he previously served as vice president. Prior to joining Brookings, he was the director of the NYU Center on International Cooperation. He holds affiliations with Yale and Stanford, and previously taught at Princeton. He has served as a senior advisor to the World Bank and the United Nations, as well as in UN field assignments in the Balkans and the Middle East. He is the author, co-author, or editor of *Still Ours to Lead, Shaping the Emerging World, The Risk Pivot, The Marshall Plan and the Shaping of American Strategy*, and of the forthcoming *To Rule the Waves*.

ELSA B. KANIA is an adjunct senior fellow with the Technology and National Security Program at the Center for a New American Security. Her research focuses on U.S.-China relations, Chinese military strategy, defense innovation, and emerging technologies. She has been invited to testify before the House Permanent Select Committee on Intelligence, the U.S.-China Economic and Security Review Commission, and the National Commission on Service. Her book *Fighting to Innovate* is forthcoming. Currently, she is a PhD candidate in Harvard University's Department of Government.

MARA KARLIN is former director of strategic studies and an associate professor at the Johns Hopkins School of Advanced International Studies, and a former nonresident senior fellow at the Brookings Institution. She served in national security roles for five U.S. secretaries of defense, advising on policies spanning strategic planning, defense budgeting, future wars, and regional affairs. She is the author of *Building Militaries in Fragile States:*

Challenges for the United States and *The Inheritance: America's Military After Two Decades of War* (Brookings).

NATASHA KASSAM is the director of the Lowy Institute's Public Opinion and Foreign Policy program in Sydney, Australia. She is also a fellow of the National Security College's Futures Council 2020–2021 and sits on the advisory board for Melbourne University's Asian Law Centre. She is a former Australian diplomat, working on human rights and legal issues in China, and she drafted the Australian government's 2017 Foreign Policy White Paper. She was also an advisor to the Regional Assistance Mission to Solomon Islands (RAMSI) in Honiara. Her research has appeared on CNN and the BBC and in *Foreign Policy*, the *Washington Post*, and the *New York Times*. She holds a bachelor of laws and a bachelor of international studies from the University of Sydney and speaks Mandarin.

SAIF M. KHAN co-authored his piece for this volume while a research fellow at Georgetown's Center for Security and Emerging Technology (CSET). Previously, he was an intellectual property attorney at Brinks Gilson & Lione and at several technology companies, including Hewlett-Packard. He has a JD from the Ohio State University Moritz College of Law and a BS in physics and an MA in physics from Wayne State University.

HOMI KHARAS is a senior fellow in the Center for Sustainable Development, housed in the Global Economy and Development program at Brookings. In this capacity, he studies policies and trends influencing developing countries, including aid to poor countries, the emergence of the middle class, and global governance and the G-20. He previously served as interim vice president and director of the Global Economy and Development program. He served as the lead author and executive secretary of the secretariat supporting the High-Level Panel, advising the U.N. Secretary General on the post-2015 development agenda (2012–2013). His most recent co-authored/edited books are *Leave No One Behind: Time for Specifics on the Sustainable Development Goals* (Brookings) and *From Summits to Solutions: Innovations in Implementing the Sustainable Development Goals* (Brookings).

EMILIE KIMBALL is an executive assistant in the Foreign Policy program at the Brookings Institution. Prior to working at Brookings, she served as a staff officer on the U.S. National Security Council from 2015 to 2018, where she helped manage the national security decisionmaking process and staffed President Obama on travel around the world, notably to Turkey, the Philippines, and Malaysia in 2015 and Cuba and Argentina in 2016.

LYNN KUOK is Shangri-La Dialogue Senior Fellow for Asia-Pacific Security at the International Institute for Strategic Studies. She is co-editor of the institute's signature publication, the *Asia-Pacific Regional Security Assessment*. She is also a senior research fellow at the University of Cambridge and a visiting professor at Georgetown University's Edmund A. Walsh School of Foreign Service. She is a former Brookings Institution expert and has held fellowships at Yale Law School, Harvard Law School, the Harvard Kennedy School, the Center for Strategic and International Studies, and the Centre for International Law at the National University of Singapore. She served as editor-in-chief of the *Cambridge Review of International Affairs* and the *Singapore Law Review*. Her research focuses on the international relations, security, and law of the Indo-Pacific, with a focus on the South China Sea dispute. She sits on the World Economic Forum's Global Future Council on Geopolitics.

NICOL TURNER LEE is a senior fellow in Governance Studies, the director of the Center for Technology Innovation, and co-editor-in-chief of *TechTank*. Her research explores domestic and global public policies designed to enable equitable access to technology and to harness its power to create change in communities across the world. Her current research portfolio includes 5G, digital divide, online privacy, and artificial intelligence (AI), among other regulatory, legislative, and societal issues. She has a forthcoming book on the U.S. digital divide titled *Digitally Invisible: How the Internet Is Creating the New Underclass* (Brookings, forthcoming). She sits on various U.S. federal agency and civil society boards. She has a PhD and an MA from Northwestern University and a BA from Colgate University.

CHENG LI is director and senior fellow at the Brookings Institution's John L. Thornton China Center. He is also a director of the National Committee on U.S.-China Relations and a distinguished fellow of the Munk School of Global Affairs and Public Policy at the University of Toronto. His recent publications include *Chinese Politics in the Xi Jinping Era: Reassessing Collective Leadership* (Brookings), *The Power of Ideas* (Brookings), and *Middle Class Shanghai: Reshaping U.S.-China Engagement* (Brookings). He is currently completing a book manuscript with the working title *Xi Jinping's Protégés: Rising Elite Groups in the Chinese Leadership*. He received an MA in Asian studies from the University of California, Berkeley and a PhD in political science from Princeton University.

TANVI MADAN is the director of the India Project and a senior fellow in the Foreign Policy program at the Brookings Institution. Her work explores India's role in the world and its foreign policy, focusing in particular on India's relations with China and the United States, and its approach in the Indo-Pacific. She is the author of *Fateful Triangle: How China Shaped U.S.-India Relations During the Cold War* (Brookings). Her ongoing work includes a book project on the recent past, present, and future of the China-India-U.S. triangle, and a monograph on India's foreign policy diversification strategy.

JOSHUA P. MELTZER is a senior fellow at the Brookings Institution, with expertise on international trade law and policy issues, and leads the Digital Economy and Trade Project. He has testified before the U.S. Congress, the U.S. International Trade Commission, and the European Parliament on digital trade issues. He has been an expert witness in litigation on digital trade and privacy issues in the EU and a consultant to the World Bank on trade and privacy matters. He is also a member of Australia's National Data Advisory Council. He teaches digital trade law at Melbourne University and at the University of Toronto Law School, where he is an adjunct professor. Prior to joining Brookings, he was posted as a diplomat at the Australian Embassy in Washington, DC, and prior to that was an international trade lawyer and trade negotiator in Australia's Department of Foreign Affairs and Trade. He has appeared in print and digital media, including the *Economist*, *New York Times*, *Washington Post*, CNN, Bloomberg, MSNBC, CBS, Fox, the Asahi Shimbun, and China Daily. He holds an SJD and LL.M. from the University of Michigan Law School in Ann Arbor and law and commerce degrees from Monash University in Melbourne, Australia.

JAMES MILLWARD is Professor of Inter-societal History at the Edmund A. Walsh School of Foreign Service, Georgetown University, teaching Chinese, Central Asian, and world history. His specialties include the Qing empire, the silk road, Eurasian lutes and music in history, and historical and contemporary Xinjiang. He follows and comments on current issues regarding Xinjiang, the Uyghurs, and other Xinjiang indigenous peoples, as well as PRC ethnicity policy. His publications include *Eurasian Crossroads: A History of Xinjiang, The Silk Road: A Very Short Introduction,* and *Beyond the Pass: Economy, Ethnicity, and Empire in Qing Central Asia.* His articles and op-eds on contemporary China have appeared in the *New York Times, Washington Post, The Guardian, Los Angeles Review of Books, New York Review of Books,* and other media.

SCOTT MOORE is a researcher and policymaker focused on emerging environmental and technological challenges. He is currently director of China Programs and Strategic Initiatives in the Office of the Provost as well as a lecturer in political science at the University of Pennsylvania. He was previously a Young Professional at the World Bank and served as Environment, Science, Technology, and Health Officer for China at the U.S. Department of State. His first book, *Subnational Hydropolitics: Conflict, Cooperation, and Institution-Building in Shared River Basins,* examines how climate change and other pressures affect the likelihood of conflict over water within countries. He holds master's and doctoral degrees from Oxford University and an undergraduate degree from Princeton.

MICHAEL O'HANLON is a senior fellow and director of research in the Foreign Policy program at Brookings. While not a Northeast Asia expert, he has traveled to the region some 50 times in his career, and is author (with Jim Steinberg) of *Strategic Reassurance and Resolve: U.S.-China Relations in the 21st Century.* His latest books are *Defense 101: Understanding the Military of Today and Tomorrow* and *The Art of War in an Age of Peace: U.S. Grand Strategy and Resolute Restraint.* His 2008 report on U.S. military bases abroad was found in Osama bin Laden's library in Abbottabad.

JUNG H. PAK is a former senior fellow and SK-Korea Foundation Chair in Korea Studies at the Brookings Institution, where she focused on Korean Peninsula issues and East Asia regional dynamics. She has held senior positions at the Central Intelligence Agency and has served as a Deputy National Intelligence Officer at the National Intelligence Council. She is the author of *Becoming Kim Jong Un: A Former CIA Officer's Insights into North Korea's Enigmatic Young Dictator,* which draws from her deep knowledge and experience as an intelligence officer. She has been featured on *Face the Nation, This Week with George Stephanopoulos,* and *PBS NewsHour,* and her analysis has appeared in the *New York Times, Wall Street Journal, Financial Times,*

Politico, CNN, Fox News, and *The Atlantic*, as well as major media outlets in Europe and Asia.

DAHLIA PETERSON is a research analyst at Georgetown's Center for Security and Emerging Technology (CSET). She researches China's use of predictive policing algorithms and facial, voice, and gait recognition technologies for its AI-powered surveillance programs; Chinese AI talent development; and threats to American research security. Previously, she interned for the U.S.-China Economic and Security Review Commission (USCC), the State Department's Virtual Student Federal Service, and the Foreign Commercial Service at the U.S. Embassy in Beijing. She holds a BA in economics and Chinese language with a minor in China studies from the University of California, Berkeley, and is pursuing a master's in security studies from Georgetown University.

TED PICCONE is a nonresident senior fellow in the Foreign Policy program at Brookings and the chief engagement officer at the World Justice Project. During his residence at Brookings, he was a senior fellow and the Charles W. Robinson Chair, a visiting fellow at the Robert Bosch Academy in Berlin, and the acting vice president, director, and deputy director of the Foreign Policy program. His research has covered global democracy, rule of law, and human rights; U.S.-Latin American relations, including China's rising profile; emerging powers; and multilateral affairs. He was a senior foreign policy advisor at the State Department, National Security Council, and the Pentagon and holds degrees from Columbia Law School and the University of Pennsylvania.

ESWAR PRASAD is the Tolani Senior Professor of Trade Policy and Professor of Economics at Cornell University. He is also a senior fellow at the Brookings Institution, where he holds the New Century Chair in International Economics, and a research associate at the NBER. He was previously head of the IMF's China Division. He is the author of *The Future of Money: How the Digital Revolution Is Transforming Currencies and Finance*. His previous books include *Gaining Currency: The Rise of the Renminbi* and *The Dollar Trap: How the U.S. Dollar Tightened Its Grip on Global Finance*. His op-ed articles have appeared in the *Financial Times, Harvard Business Review, New York Times, Wall Street Journal*, and *Washington Post*.

JONATHAN PRYKE is director of the Pacific Islands Program at the Lowy Institute. His research is interested in all aspects of the Pacific Islands, including economic development in the region, Australia's relationship with the Pacific, the role of aid and the private sector in Pacific Islands development, and Pacific labor mobility. He joined the Lowy Institute in 2015 from the Development Policy Centre at the Australian National University, where he was a researcher, editor of the *Devpolicy* blog, and a co-convener of the Australasian Aid Conference. He holds a bachelor's of commerce from the University of Sydney, a master's of public policy (development policy), a master's of diplomacy and graduate diploma in international and development economics from the Australian National University.

EVANS J. R. REVERE is a nonresident senior fellow at Brookings' Center for East Asia Policy Studies. He is also senior advisor with the Albright Stonebridge Group. A veteran diplomat, he retired from the U.S. Department of State after a distinguished career as one of the department's top Asia experts. His diplomatic work included service as the acting assistant secretary and principal deputy assistant secretary of state for the Bureau of East Asian and Pacific Affairs. He has extensive experience negotiating with North Korea and once served as the U.S. government's primary day-to-day liaison with North Korea. He is fluent in Chinese, Japanese, and Korean, a graduate of Princeton University, a veteran of the U.S. Air Force, and a member of the Council on Foreign Relations.

SOPHIE RICHARDSON is the China director at Human Rights Watch. A graduate of the University of Virginia, the Hopkins-Nanjing Program, and Oberlin College, she is the author of numerous articles on domestic Chinese political reform, democratization, and human rights in Cambodia, China, Indonesia, Hong Kong, the Philippines, and Vietnam. She has testified before the European Parliament and the U.S. Senate and House of Representatives. She is the author of *China, Cambodia, and the Five Principles of Peaceful Coexistence*, an in-depth examination of China's foreign policy since 1954's Geneva Conference, including rare interviews with policymakers.

BRUCE RIEDEL is a senior fellow at the Brookings Institution and director of its Intelligence Project. Prior to joining Brookings, he spent 30 years in the CIA, including eight years at the White House with the National Security Council. His books include *Kings and Presidents: Saudi Arabia and the United States Since FDR.*

FRANK A. ROSE is a senior fellow for security and strategy in the Foreign Policy program at the Brookings Institution. He focuses on nuclear strategy and deterrence, arms control, strategic stability, missile defense, outer space, and emerging security challenges. Prior to joining Brookings, he served as U.S. assistant secretary of state for arms control, verification, and compliance from 2014 to 2017. From 2009 to 2014, he served as the U.S. deputy assistant secretary of state for space and defense policy. He has also held positions at the U.S. Department of Defense, in the U.S. Congress, and in the private sector. He received his bachelor's in history from American University and a master's in war studies from King's College, University of London.

NATAN SACHS is the director of the Brookings Institution's Center for Middle East Policy. His research focuses on Israel's foreign policy, its domestic politics, and U.S.-Israeli relations. He has taught about the Arab-Israeli conflict at Georgetown University's Government Department and at its Security Studies Program. He has provided congressional testimony, has published widely, including in *Foreign Affairs*, the *Washington Post*, and the *New York Times Global*, and provides commentary for media outlets, including *NBC Nightly News, PBS Newshour,* CNN, MSNBC, the BBC, and NPR. Before joining Brookings, he was a Hewlett Fellow at Stanford's Center on Democracy, Development and the Rule of Law, a Fulbright Fellow in Indonesia, and a visiting fellow at Tel Aviv University's Dayan Center for Middle Eastern and African Studies. He holds a BA from the Amirim Honors Program at the Hebrew University of Jerusalem, and an MA and PhD in political science from Stanford University.

PAVNEET SINGH is a nonresident fellow at Brookings. He is currently a consultant with the Defense Innovation Unit and works with start-up technology companies and investors to explore the nexus of national security challenges and emerging technologies. Most recently, he served on the transition team of President Biden, helping to design the national security and science and technology architecture. He co-authored the Pentagon study on China's participation in the U.S. venture ecosystem and co-led the initiative for National Security Innovation Capital (NSIC) to fund dual-use hardware technology companies. He previously served on the National Security Council and National Economic Council in the Obama administration. Prior to the White House, he was a key member of the executive secretariat of the World Bank's Commission on Growth and Development.

MIREYA SOLÍS is director of the Center for East Asia Policy Studies (CEAP), Philip Knight Chair in Japan Studies, and senior fellow in the Foreign Policy program at Brookings. Prior to her arrival at Brookings, she was a tenured associate professor at American University's School of International Service. She is an expert on Japanese foreign economic policy, U.S.-Japan relations, international trade policy, and Asia-Pacific economic integration. Her most recent book, *Dilemmas of a Trading Nation: Japan and the United States in the Evolving Asia-Pacific Order* (Brookings) received the 2018 Masayoshi Ohira Memorial Award. She earned a doctorate in government and a master's in East Asian studies from Harvard University, and a bachelor's in international relations from El Colegio de México.

ANGELA STENT is professor of government and foreign policy and directs the Center for Eurasian, Russian, and East European Studies at Georgetown University. She is a senior nonresident fellow at Brookings and co-chairs its Hewett Forum on Post-Soviet Affairs. She has served in the State Department's Office of Policy Planning and as the National Intelligence Officer for Russia and Eurasia, and she has been an advisor to NATO. She is a contributing editor to *Survival: Global Politics and Strategy.* She is the author of numerous articles on Russia's relations with the United States and Europe. Her two latest books are *The Limits of Partnership: US-Russian Relations in the Twenty-First Century* and *Putin's World: Russia Against the West and with the Rest.*

TODD STERN is a nonresident senior fellow at the Brookings Institution concentrating on climate change. He served from January 2009 until April 2016 as the Special Envoy for Climate Change at the U.S. Department of State. He was President Obama's chief climate negotiator, leading the U.S. effort in negotiating the Paris Agreement and in all bilateral and multilateral climate negotiations in the seven years leading up to Paris. He is currently focused on writing about the climate negotiations during his time as special envoy as well as on writing, speaking, and advising about ongoing efforts on climate change at both the international and domestic levels. He served under President Clinton in the White House as staff secretary and as counselor to Secretary of the Treasury Lawrence Summers.

CAITLIN TALMADGE is associate professor of security studies in the Edmund A. School of Foreign Service at Georgetown University, and senior non-resident fellow in Foreign Policy at the Brookings Institution. She is also a research affiliate of the Security Studies Program at the Massachusetts Institute of Technology. Her research and teaching focus on U.S. military operations and strategy, civil-military relations and defense policy, nuclear deterrence and escalation, and security issues in Asia and the Persian Gulf. She is author of the award-winning book, *The Dictator's Army: Battlefield Effectiveness in Authoritarian Regimes*, and co-author of *U.S. Defense Politics: The Origins of Security Policy*.

ROBERT D. WILLIAMS is the executive director of the Paul Tsai China Center and a senior research scholar and lecturer at Yale Law School. He is also a nonresident senior fellow at the Brookings Institution and a contributing editor at *Lawfare*. He focuses on U.S.-China relations and Chinese law and policy, with particular interests in technology policy and national security. His recent research and track II dialogues cover issues of cybersecurity, trade and investment policy, technology governance, and international law. He received a BA from Vanderbilt University and a JD from Harvard Law School.

THOMAS WRIGHT is director of the Center on the United States and Europe and senior fellow in the Project on International Order and Strategy at the Brookings Institution. He is also a contributing writer for *The Atlantic* and a nonresident fellow at the Lowy Institute for International Policy. He is the author of *All Measures Short of War: The Contest for the 21st Century and the Future of American Power*. His second book, *Aftershocks: Pandemic Politics and the End of the Old International Order*, is forthcoming. He works on U.S. foreign policy, great power competition, the European Union, Brexit, and economic interdependence.

KETIAN ZHANG is an assistant professor of international security in the Schar School of Policy and Government at George Mason University. She studies rising powers, coercion, economic statecraft, and maritime disputes in international relations and social movements in comparative politics, with a regional focus on China and East Asia. She bridges the study of international relations and comparative politics and has a broader theoretical interest in linking international security and international political economy. Her research agenda emphasizes how globalized production and supply chains affect states' foreign policy and domestic state-society relations, especially regarding coercion and protests. Her book project examines when, why, and how China uses coercion when faced with issues of national security.

INDEX

Italic page numbers indicate tables or figures

Abdallah, King, 245
Abu Dhabi National Oil Company,
    323
academia, superpower marathon and,
    155
Academy of Military Science, 211
"active defense," 272
Aerospace Dongfanhong, 174
"affluents," 309
Africa: bilateral trade relationships
    with, 165; oil exports, *323*
Agreement on Textiles and Clothing,
    315
AI (artificial intelligence), 164, 209,
    297; AI Champions list, 369; and
    "dronifed" weapons systems, 212;
    increasing importance of, 211;
    "intelligent(ized) weapons," 211; and
    kinetic initiative, 211; in military in-
    novation, 209–10; national technol-

ogy standards and, 369; AI weapon,
    211
AI-Based Radar Target Classification
    and Recognition, 214
AidData, 112
Airbus, 35
Aksu Huafu Textiles, 368
al Hussein, Zeid Ra'ad, 362
Alibaba, 154, 313
Alipay, 313
Alliance: climate alliance with, 330
Alston, Philip, 362
American Dream, 309
Andaman and Nicobar Islands, 127
antibiotics, 157
anti-satellite (ASAT) capabilities, 171,
    174–75
Arctic, 134
Argentina, soy crops from, 235
artificial intelligence. *See* AI

ASEAN nations, 38, 112; trade and investment, *113*

Asia Infrastructure and Investment Bank (AIIB), 29, 289

Asia Pacific, oil exports of, *323*

Asian Institute of Policy Studies, 56

Asia-Pacific Economic Cooperation, 115

"aspirants," 309

asymmetric defense, term, 263

AT&T, 165

Atlanticist U.K., 141

augmented and virtual realities (AR/VR), 163–64

Australia: barley tariffs on, 249; and Chinese boundaries, 114; data flow restriction in, 303; Defence Strategic Update 2020, 251; defining identity of, 249; excluding Huawei, 248; exports to China, 248; as Five Eyes member, 251–52; as force multiplier, 249; infrastructure funds with, 116; isolating, 249–50; ODA commitments, *113*; results of Chinese efforts in, 250; and South China Sea, 79; stake in South Pacific, 259–60; struggles of, 252

Austria, *298*

"authoritarian bargain," 315

Aviation Industry Corporation of China (AVIC), 213

Azhar, Masood, 122

Bab al Mandab Strait, 273

Baidu, 154, 166

Bandar, Prince, 244

Bangladesh, military ties with, 124

Basic Law of the Hong Kong Special Administrative Region, 339

basing, 270; Chinese approach to, 271–72; flash points in regard to, 276; plans regarding, 271, 274–78; rumored/real bases, 273–75; studying, 276–78; U.S. approach to, 271–72

BeiDou, 176

Beijing: annual voluntary UN contributions, 355; branding of, 47; "coercion without violence," 72; demonstrating regional leadership, 54; developing base network, 270; exploiting alliance gaps, 54–56; and forced birth control, 340; "free pass," 337; Made in China 2025, 142; "major special projects," 154; military modernization investment, 103; 1C2S blueprint, 69; and persuasion, 70; relations reset, 63; renormalization of relations, 65; and Taiwan, 68–73; Taiwan response options of, 71–72; trade violations, 337; treatment of Uighar Muslims, 143; unification through persuasion, 68–69

Beijing-Pyongyang relations, implications of "renomalization," 65

Beijing-Tianjin-Hebei (*Jing-Jin-Ji*) development strategy, 48

Belgium, Chinese digital economy in, *298*

Belt and Road Forum, 114

Belt and Road Initiative (BRI), 28; and Africa, 165; broadband connectivity as part of, 297; Central Asian investments, 275; conceptual foundation, 29; and developing countries, 290; digital dimension to, 300–301; ensuring sustainability of, 111–12; 5G initiative, 164; fragile projects, 114; inserting praise for, 355; LAC countries joining, 235; memorandum of understanding on, 141; and Middle East, 241; opposing, 122; and overseas bases, 273; and South China Sea, 83; Western debates on, 271

Bhutan-China-India tri-border, 121

Biden administration, 83, 230, 326, 330: and climate cooperation, 329; and South China Sea, 79–80

Biden, Joe, 145; and climate engagement, 326
biotechnology: "beneficial biotechnology," 225; constraints in, 226; policies and actions in, 224–25; "Strategic Emerging Industries," 225
Blue Star, 35
Bo'ao Forum, 29
Bolivia, sanctions against, 237
Bolsonaro, Jair, 236
Borrell, Josep, 144
Brazil: climate alliance with, 330; dialogue with, 127; iron ore in, 235; middle-class expenditures, *311*
breach, incidents of, 55
BRICS (Brazil, Russia, India, China, South Africa), 61
Britain, "golden era" of 141. *See also* United Kingdom
Brown, Michael, 151
Brunei, data flow restriction in, *303*
Bukele, Nayib, 236
Bureau of Industry and Security (BIS) Entity List, 165: adding Chinese firms to, 368–70
Bush, Richard, 68

Cai Qi, 47
Cambodia: potential "bases" in, 274
Cameron, David, 141
Camp Lemonnier, 273, 276
Canada: climate alliance with, 330; data flow restriction in, *303*
capital markets, focusing on, 159
Carnegie Endowment for International Peace, 166
CAR-T therapy, 225
Center for Global Development (CGD), 291
Central Asia, simulating threats in, 135
Central Committee (CC), 44
CGTN (state broadcaster), 248
CH-901 drone, 213
characteristic towns (*tese xiaozhen*), 48

Chen Min'er, 47
Chen Shui-bian, 70
Cheng Lei, 248
Cheng Li, 41
Chewning, Eric, 151
Chiang Kai-Shek, 27
Chicago Council on Global Affairs, 56
Chile: data flow restriction in, 303; metals from, 235
China: achieving state-of-the-art fabrication, 199–201; activism, 28–29; affair with LAC, 234–35; and African council members, 354; ambitions in South Pacific, 256–57; approach to Korean Peninsula, 64; ASEAN trade and investment, *113*; assessing "international balance of power," 26; Australian trust in, 251; ballistic missile defense system, 135; barley tariffs from, 249; bilateral relations, 290–91; biotechnology policies and actions, 224–25; biotechnology shortcomings, 226; blocking UN High Commissioner for Human Rights, 362; carefully defining, 289–90; change in chip fab capacity, *198*; characterizing foreign policy, 272; charting surveillance exports of, 182–84; China-IMF relationship, 289; China-India boundary crisis, 120; chip fab capacity with/without export controls, *202*; chip fab revenue, *200*; chip production in, 196–98; civil space programs, 175–76; clean energy transition, 328; coal infrastructure, 328; coal, 320; Cold War analogy, 151–52; "collective repression" by, 362; competitive engagement and, 120–28; confronting uncomfortable realities, 98; consequences of human rights assault, 363–64; copying Western trends, 312; core Paris commitments, 341; critiquing

China (*cont.*)

compliance with international law, 342; cyber theft, 30; data centers in, 300; data flow restriction in, *303;* declaring Air Defense Identification Zone, 263; defining "core interests," 34; demand for electricity in, 319–21; dependence on computer chips, 193–203; development finance programs, 115; development issues, 354; digital bank currency, 295; digital economy of, 297; digital services, 299–304; domestic politics, 3–5; donations, 289; and East Asia, 5–7; East Wind incident, 244; economic engagement with, 111–18; economic overdependence on, 127; economic potential of 5G networks, 16; economic scale, 152; economic transformation, 153–54; electricity generation, *321;* eliminating poverty in, 43–45; embracing technology fusion, 153; encroaching on EEZs, 77; energy concerns of, 323–24; "Entity List," 80; eroding U.S. influence, 99; establishing "super megacities," 4; evolving posture of, 97; following Cultural Revolution, 336; foray into military basing, 270; forays into Indian Ocean, 124; foreign competition, 297; fossil fuel imports, 319; fuel imports from MENA region, *242;* future aerospace capabilities, 214; GDP per capita, 289; GDP, 225; global chip fab capacity, *197;* global economy and, 18–20; global export drivers, 184–85; global governance and, 20–22; global institutions,153; as global rulemaker, 103–4; goal of imposing sanctions on, 34–36; and gray zone, 263–65 ; and great powers, 7–11; greenhouse emissions of, 326; "hide and bide" strategy,

26; Hong Kong Special Administrative Region, 339; human rights in, 340–41; imports from Australia, 248; in military domain, 2; in South China Sea, 75–83; incorporating international law, 336; increasing chip subsidies, 200; influencing geopolitics, 323–24 ; influencing global middle class, 309; influencing United Nations, 353; initiatives in AI, 210; insufficient consensus on, 153; integration in global economy, 152–53; international economic institutions and, 287; international human rights treaties, 336; and international norms, 304; and international structure, 99; interpreting foreign policy of, 30; investment in India, 122; Israeli-Chinese relations, 243; LAC dependence on, 233; lack of AAIB equivalent, 356; lack of transparency, 290–91; leader's military control, 214; Malacca Dilemma, 28;middle class of, 310–311; and Middle East, 241; middle-class consumption expenditures, *312;* middle-class consumption, 47; middle-class expansion challenges, 314–16; middle-class expenditures, *311;* military spending, *104;* mobile payment values, 299; National Energy Agency, 322; "near seas defense, far seas protection," 274; nine-dash line, 76; nonmilitary advantages of, 78; nonmilitary coercion, 33; normalizing domestic practices, 105; nuclear arsenal, 86; number of chipmakers, *195, 196;* objecting to maritime rights and freedoms, 77; objects in Earth orbit, 174; oil and gas, 322; oil import sources, *323;* on U.S. hegemony, 342; "Open Door" policy, 309; P2 alliance, 354; Pakistan relationship, 121; patrial integration of, 287; peace operations, 354–55; peaceful rise of, 97; "periodic reviews," 340; persuading, 81; persuasion-based approach, 71; policy banks, 235; position as second-largest economy, 95; promoting renminbi, 293–96; regional influence and strategy, 15–17; relations with Saudi Arabia, 243–45; renewable energy sector of, 320; response to LAC diplomacy, 236–37; return of "national rejuvenation," 27; revisionist ambitions, 355; rise in outer space, 171–78; role in rules-based global order, 335–44; Russia-China cooperation, 99–101; Russian oil and gas, 134; sanctions imposed by, 34–36; Security Council veto, 354; 16+1 forum, 141; size of digital economy, 298–99; SME industry barriers, 201; SMEs in, 313; so-called universal human rights, 361; "soft law" norm, 342; sources of leverage, 121; South Pacific aid activities, 257; stripping out human rights monitors, 355; subsidized chip fabs, 200; super metropolises of, 46–48; supporting UNSC resolutions, 61–62; surveillance technology of, 181–82; symbolism of sanctions, 35; taming COVD-19 spread, 55; technology, 12–14; territorial and maritime claims, 76–77; territorial disputes with, 29–30 ; top ten cities of, 47; as torchbearer, 341; "turnkey" platforms, 187; 2010 Nobel Peace Prize, 34–36; 2010 sanctions episode, 34–36; 2021 coast guard law, 77; 2015 Military Strategy, 273; 2007 ASAT test, 172; 2017 THAAD episode, 36–37; 2013 reclamation work, 77; U.S. Nuclear Risk Reduction Center counterpart, 89; U.S.-China nuclear relation-

ship, 86–90; UN activism, 359; UN human rights system, 360–63; and UN political work, 355–56; unification with Taiwan, 70; Universal Periodic Review of, 361; upper hand of, 78; view of Australia, 249; view of South Korea, 53–57; "win-win" economic statecraft, 233; "Wolf Warrior diplomacy," 144; Xinjiang oppression, 367–373

China Aerospace Science and Industry Corporation (CASIC), 213, 214

China Construction & Communications Corporation (CCCC), 80

China Daily, 144

China Electricity Council, 320

China Mobile, 165

China National Electronics Import and Export Corporation (CEIEC), 182

China National Offshore Oil Corporation (CNOOC), 80, 323

China Telecom, 165

China Unicom, 165

"China's National Defense in the New Era" (paper), 210

China-Arab States Cooperation Forum, 323

China-India relations, 120–28; bilateral economic front, 122; Brahmaputra River, 123; competition, 121–23; and Dalai Lama, 123; internal balancing, 124; major standoffs, 123; public diplomacy front, 122; Regional Comprehensive Economic Partnership, 123; senior policymakers, 122

China-LAC relations, implications of, 237–38

China–North Korea relations, 60–66

China-Pakistan Economic Corridor (CPEC), 124, 274

China-Russia relations: asymmetries in, 132; ballistic missile defense system, 135; and Central Asia influence, 136–37; economic relationship, 134;

China-Russia relations (*cont.*)
high-tech cooperation, 134–36; implications of, 137–38; key drivers of, 133–34; military cooperation, 134–36; multilateral fora, 136; political ties, 136–37; and post-West world order, 133; preventing "color" revolutions, 133; U.S. reaction to, 133

Chinese Academy of Sciences, 226

Chinese coercion tactics, implications of, 37–38

Chinese Communist Party (CCP), 4, 68; advancing chip fab capacity, 199; and EU-China relations, 144; command over PLA, 41–42; core interests of, 34; focus on technology development, 155

Chinese Communist Youth League (*tuanpai*), 44

Chinese People's Liberation Army (PLA): and artificial intelligence, 209

Chongqing, branding of, 47

Chongqing-Chengdu corridor development scheme, 48

Cisco, 299

classic deterrence theory, 87

climate change, international law and, 341–42

climate cooperation, 326; additional tools for, 330; bilateral relationship in, 327; climate landscape, 327–29; restarting, 329–30

Clinton, Hillary, 326

CloudWalk, 368

Coats, Daniel, 175

Code of Conduct, negotiations, 82; dismissed by India, 123

Cold War, 33; arms control during, 89–90; call for, 327; post–Cold War, 25, 33, 42, 96; similarities with current competition, 151–52

Colombia, diplomatic activism in, 237

Committee on Foreign Investment in the United States (CFIUS), 268

Comprehensive Agreement on Investment (CAI), 145

Comprehensive and Progressive Agreement for Trans-Pacific Partnership (CPTPP), 117

computer chips: consolidation trends, 196; costs at different transistor sizes, *194*; number of chipmakers, *195, 196*; value of, 194–96

Conference on Interaction and Confidence Building in Asia (CICA), 29

connectivity, rubric of, 137

Convention Against Torture, 340

corporations, orientation of, 155

COVID-19, 46; American response to, 100; Australia reacting to, 247; and compliance resistance, 360; and electricity, 320; and EU-China relations, 143–45 ; impact on China, 311; and Latin America and the Caribbean (LAC), 233; and multilateral networks, 98; post-COVID landscape, 260; recovering from, 250; rushing medical supplies, 238; Russian response to, 132; in Saudi Arabia, 245; scrambling LAC calculus, 236; shocks resulting from, 106; and South China Sea incursions, 79; and South Pacific, 259–60; use of health surveillance, 188; and U.S.-China relations, 107; vaccine for, 225

CSS2 missiles, 244

CTIA (trade association), 166

Cuba, diplomatic activism in, 237

Cuba, sanctions against, 237

Cummings, E. E., 41

cybersecurity, international law and, 342

Czech Republic, 141

Dahua Public-Private Partnership Safe Cities, 369

Dahua, 182, 368

Dai Bingguao, 34

Dalai Lama, 35, 123

data governance, 297–306

Davidson, Phil, 78

Deep Eye, 369

democratic multilateralism, 100

Democratic People's Republic of Korea (DPRK), 60. *See also* North Korea

Democratic Progressive Party (DPP), 70

democratic states, security interests of, 193

Deng Xiaopeng, 26, 289, 309

Denmark, Chinese digital economy in, *298*

denuclearization, 6, 53, 57, 63–64, 66

Development Assistance Committee (DAC), 112, 288, 290

Development Assistance Committee, Diaoyu, 263

Digital Currency/Electronic Payment (DCEP), 294

digital economy, size of, 298–99

digital services: cross-border data flow restrictions, 303–4; governance of, 301–4; restricted domestic market for, 301–2; shaping international environment, 304

Digital Silk Road (DSR), 297; and data governance, 300

Dispute Settlement Body (DSB), 337

Djibouti base, 273

Dollar, David, 287

domestic politics, 3–5

donor-to-donor relations, 115

Dooley, Meagan, 309

Doshi, Rush, 25

Dragonfly Eye, 369

Dreyfuss, Leah, 270

drills, holding, 82

dual circulation (*shuang xunhuan*), 47

Earth orbits, 172

East Asia, 95

East Wind, 244

e-commerce, 313

economic tools/vulnerabilities, reexamining, 267–68

Edelman Trust Barometer, 315

EEZs (exclusive economic zones), 76-80; protecting, 82

18th Central Committee, number of princelings in, 45

18th Party Congress, 44

18th Space Control Squadron, 172

electricity, demand for, 319–21

electronic transactions, regulation of, *302*

Elwood, Tobias, 145

energy/material stockpiles, securing, 266

entity economy (*shiti jingji*), 48

Ericsson, 165

"EU and China: A Strategy Outlook, The," 143

EU-China relations: changes in approach, 140–46; and COVID-19 crisis, 143–45; 5G wireless infrastructure, 141; sudden concessions, 145

Eurasian Economic Union (EAEU), 137

Europe: change in chip fab capacity, *198*; oil exports, *323*

European Think-tank Network on China (ETNC), 144

European Union: and contemporary order, 97; 5G networks in, 165; infrastructure funds with, 116; response to Made in China 2025, 142

exclusive economic zone. *See* EEZs

extreme ultraviolet (EUV) photolithography equipment, 196

fabrication factories ("fabs"), 14, 195-202, *200*

Falun Gong protests, 247

Federal Communications Commission (FCC), 164, 174

Feltman, Jeffrey, 353

Fiberhome, 369

Fiery Cross Reef, 264

15th Party Congress Work Report, 27

fifth-generation wireless technology (5G), 12, 142, 157; American heavy-handedness on, 145; China banned from Japanese government contracts, 118; U.S.-China competition, 162-170. *See also* 5G networks

Financial Action Task Force (FATF), 122

Fire Eye, 369

first and second island chains, 264

Fitch Solutions, 112

Five 5G FAST Plan, 164

5G networks: competition, 105; infrastructure, 55, 141-145, 158; innovations, anticipation for, 167–68; network supply chains, 166–67; setting stage for, 163–64; spectrum management, 164–65; unique architecture of, 164; wireless networks: competition with, 162–68

Five Principles of Peaceful Coexistence, 272

Flynn, Carrick, 193

Ford, Lindsey W., 57

Foreign Affairs, 142

4G Long-Term Evolution (LTE), 164

fragmentation debris, growth of, *173*

France: middle-class consumption expenditures, *312*; middle-class expenditures, *311;* ODA commitments, *113;* and South China Sea, 79; statement on South China Sea, 75

Free and Open Indo-Pacific, coining, 114

Freedom of Navigation Program, 82

future, competing for, 159–60

G-7, 115

G-20, 115

General Motors, 166

General Social Survey, 315

genocide, meeting definition of, 340

German Federation of Industries (BDI), 142

Germany, 45; Chinese digital economy in, *298*; Foreign Affairs Committee, 144; middle-class consumption expenditures, *312*; middle-class expenditures, *311;* ODA commitments, *113;* South China Sea, 75, 79

gigahertz (GHz), 164

gigawatts (GW), 328

GJ-1, 213

GJ-2, 213

"Global China: Assessing China's Growing Role in the World" (project), 1

global institutions, manipulating, 153

global middle class: expenditures, *311*; mobile payment transaction values, *313*; numbers, 310–311; setting trends for, 312–14

Global Positioning System (GPS), 152, 176

global value chains (GVCs), 297

GPS. *See* Global Positioning System

graphics processing units (GPU), 371

gray zone, China and, 263–65

gray-zone conflict, 262; forms of, 263–65; scenarios, 265

great powers: choices of, 98–100; evolving international order, 96–97; key markers, 96; liberal international order, 96–97; multilateral networks of, 97; space and security, 97; strategic competition of, 95–101; and U.S.-China rivalry, 7–11

Great Recession, 288

great-power war, preparing for, 262–63

Greece, 141

Greitens, Sheena Chestnut, 181

Gross, Samantha, 319

Guang Cong, 355

Guangdong Province, 47

Guangdong-Shenzhen-Hong Kong-Macau Bay Area strategy, 48
Guangzhou, branding of, 47
Guterres, Antonio, 353

Halperin, Morton, 89
Hambantota Port, 274
Han Xu, 244
Hass, Ryan, 102
High Ambition Coalition, 330
high-altitude nuclear-induced electromagnetic pulse (HEMP), 266
Hikvision, 182, 368
Hong Kong: and international law, 339–40; data flow restriction in, *303*; national security law of, 117; 1C2S implementation in, 69; "takeover" of, 339; and treason/subversion, 339
Hongyan constellation
Horn of Africa, 276
Hu Jintao: becoming "maritime great power," 28; "going out" policy, 28; link with Xi's foreign policy, 25–27
Hua Hong, *200*
Huang Xia, 355
Huawei, 55, 105, 154; in Africa, 166; Australian exclusion, 248; ban of in U.S., 165, 166; Dutch concerns, 166; engagement with Russia, 135–36; and EU-China relations, 141, 143; 5G patents, 299; in India, 122; U.K. limits, 145, 166; U.S. security concerns, 13
Huggard, Kevin, 241
human rights: assault consequences, 33–64; international law and, 340–41
Hungary, *298*
hydrogen bombs, detonating, 61

Iceland, Chinese digital economy in, *298*
ideological and systems competition, 105–6
iFlytek, 368–70

Impeccable incident, 29
India: anxieties of, 124; avenues of Chinese influence, 127; and Chinese boundaries, 114; Chinese inroads, 127; climate alliance with, 330; and contemporary order, 97; engagement, 121–23; Huawei in, 122; infrastructure funds with, 116; and like-minded balancing powers, 125; managing China, 120–28; middle-class expenditures, *311*; neighbors, 124; opposing BRI, 122; partnership network, 125; partnership with Australia, 251; perception of U.S. alliance, 127; reducing dependence on China, 128; socioeconomic objectives, 121; sources of leverage, 121
India-Japan-U.S. maritime exercise, 127
Indonesia: climate alliance with, 330; COVID-19 response, 79; data flow restriction in, *303*; economic footprint in, 112; middle-class expenditures, *311*; partnership with Australia, 251; and South China Sea, 79
information and communication technology (ICT), 300
infrastructure, regulation of, *302*
innovation-driven development, 166
innovations, anticipation for, 167–68
Intel, 199–200
intellectual property rights (IPR) protection, 290; regulation of, *302*
Intellifusion, 368
Intergovernmental Panel on Climate Change (IPCC), 327
International Covenant on Civil and Political Rights (ICCPR), 339
International Covenant on Economic, Social, and Cultural Rights, 340
international economic institutions, 287; actively participating in, 288–89

international law of the sea, weakening of, 7, 75

international law: Chinese engagement with, 336–37; climate change, 341–42; cybersecurity, 342–43; flexibility toward, 335–56; Hong Kong and, 339–40; human rights; incorporation of, 336; limits of, 341–42; maritime/territorial disputes, 338; new weapons technology, 342–43; preserving "rules-based" form of, 336; trade, 337–38

International Monetary Fund (IMF), 235, 287; including renminbi, 293

international order, evolution of, 96–97

International Telecommunication Union (ITU), 304

Internet of Things (IoT), 299

Investment Bank, 153

iPhone, 310

Iraq, Chinese fuel imports from, *242*

Ireland, Chinese digital economy in, *298*

IS'Vision, 368

ISEAS–Yusof Ishak Institute, 115

Israel: dialogue with, 127; potential "bases" in, 274

Jae-in, Moon, 54–55

Jaish-e-Mohammed (JeM), 122

Japan: ASEAN trade and investment, *113;* change in chip fab capacity, *198;* and Chinese dependence on chips, 201–3; chip fab revenue, *200;* Chinese digital economy in, *298;* climate alliance with, 330; coining Free and Open Indo-Pacific, 114; competition with China, 115; and contemporary order, 97; cybersecurity risk to, 118; data flow restriction in, *303;* development finance programs, 115; drafting international trade rules, 117; economic engagement with, 111–18; Foreign Exchange Law, 117; global chip fab capacity, *197;* manufacturing equipment from, 193; middle class of, 315; middle-class consumption expenditures, *312;* middle-class expenditures, *311;* Ministry of Defense, 78; and national security, 117; number of chipmakers, *195, 196;* ODA commitments, *113;* partnership with Australia, 251; planned contribution to WTO, 117; statement on South China Sea, 75; wielding BRI against, 29; worst state, 98

Japan-China relations, 116

Japanese Air Self-Defense Forces, 264

JCPOA (Joint Comprehensive Plan of Action), 245

Jiang Zemon, 27

Johnson, Boris, 145

Jones, Bruce, 95, 356

Jong Un, Kim, 61

June–August 2017 Doklam crisis, 121

Kagan, Robert, 264

Kania, Elsa B., 209

Karlin, Mara, 270

Kassam, Natasha, 247

Kerry, John, 326, 329

Key Laboratory of Precision Guidance and Automatic Target Recognition, 214

Khalid, Prince, 244

Khan, Saif M., 193

Kharas, Homi, 309

Khashoggi, Jamal, 245

"killer apps," 164

Ki-moon, Ban, 353

Korea, Chinese digital economy in, *298;* data flow restriction in, *303*

Korean Peninsula, 53

Kuok, Lynn, 75

Kuomintang (KMT), 68

Lake Mansarovar, 122

land-based missile force, 87

Latin America and the Caribbean (LAC), 233; affair with China, 234–35; Chinese economic activity in, 235–37; dependency on China, 233; implications of China relationship, 234–35; public opinion regarding China, 236; response to Chinese diplomacy in, 236; "us or them" proposition, 238; as zone of competition, 234

law enforcement, back door for, 185

Lee Teng-hui, 70

Lee, Nicol Turner, 162

"lethal autonomous weapons systems" (LAWS), 210

Li Qiang, 47

Li Wenliang, 42

Li Xi, 47

Li, Keqiang, 55

Libya, Chinese fuel imports from, *242*

Line of Actual Control, 123

lips. *See* North Korea

liquefied natural gas (LNG), 322

Littoral Southeast Asian states, 79

Liu He, 46

Los Angeles Times, 166

Lotte Group, 37

Lotte Mart, 36

Ma Ying-jeou, 70

machine learning (ML), 209

Macri, Mauricio, 236

Macron, Emmanuel, 143

Madan, Tanvi, 120

Made in China 2025, 142; and chip fab capacity, 199; end-state of, 155; strategic technologies, 301

Major Economies Forum, 329

Malacca Dilemma, 28

Malaysia: COVID-19 response, 79; data flow restriction in, *303*; East Coast Rail project, 114; economic footprint in, 112; and South China Sea, 79

Maldives, military ties with, 124

maritime rights and freedoms, asserting, 81

Maritime Rights Protection Leading Small Group, 29–30

Marshall Order, 96

McCarthy, Gina, 329

McNamara, Robert, 289

megacity circles (*teda chengshi qun*), 46

megahertz (MHz), 164

Megvii, 368

Meiya Pico, 369

Melanesia, 259

Meltzer, Joshua P., 297

Mercosur, trade accord with, 237

Merkel, Angela, 141

Mexico: climate alliance with, 330; data flow restriction in, *303*

middle class (China): benefits/disadvantages; changing nature of, 314–16; numbers of, 310–311; planetary boundaries, 314; politics, 315–16; Western trends and, 312

Middle East: Chinese fuel imports from, *242*; and Chinese oil supply, 322; coverage expanding toward, 272; oil exports, *323*; and U.S.-Chinese relations, 243

military clash, unintended, 55–56

Millward, 36

Min Ye, 54

Ministry of Public Security (MPS)

Mischief Reef, 78, 264

missiles, future capabilities of, 214

mission-related debris, growth of, *173*

mmWave, 165

mobile voice communications, evolution of, 166

Modi, Narenda, 120

Moland, Will, 356

moonshots, 158

Moore, Scott, 224

mortality, 315

Mount Kailash, 122

multilateralism, preserving, 356–57

Myanmar, military ties with, 124; potential "bases" in, 275
MYbank, 313

Nanjing FiberHome Starrysky Communication Development, 369
Nathu La mountain pass, 122
National Air and Space Intelligence Center, 176
National Defense Authorization Act, 155, 165
National Defense University, 211
National Energy Commission, 328
National Medium and Long-Term Science and Technology Development Plan Outline, 301
National Security Secretariat, 117
National University of Defense Technology, 211
Nationally Determined Contribution (NDC), 320
NATO, 96
Nepal, military ties with, 124
Netanyahu, Benjamin, 241
Netherlands, 165; and Chinese dependence on chips, 201–3; manufacturing equipment from, 193
NetPosa, 368
network supply chains, 166–67
New Development Bank, 153
New Northern Policy, 56
New Southern Policy, 56
New START inspection, 89
new weapons technology, international law and, 342
New Zealand: and Chinese boundaries, 114; climate alliance with, 330; data flow restriction in, 303; dialogue with, 127
nine-dash line, 264, 338
1992 Consensus, 71
19th Central Committee, number of princelings in, 45
Nobel Peace Prize, 34–36

Nokia, 165
noninterference, discourse around, 272–73
nonlethal weapons, innovating, 267
North America: oil exports, 323. See also United States
North Korea, 36–37; Beijing influence on, 53; and nuclear weapons, 88; as nuclear-armed neighbor, 4; relations with, 60–66
Norway: Chinese digital economy in, 298; and Nobel Peace Prize, 34–36; 34–36; 2010 sanctions episode, 34–36; wielding BRI against, 29
Nuclear Suppliers Group, 124
nuclear weapons: addressing rivalries, 88–89; of China, 86; danger of escalation, 87–88; erosion of perceived position on, 87

O'Hanlon, Michael, 262
Obama administration, 82; responding to Northern Triangle crisis, 237
Obama, Barack: and climate engagement, 326
official development assistance (ODA), 111
oil and gas, dependence on, 322
oil, importing, 243
"1.5°C Report," 327
"One country, two systems" (1C2S), 69
ONE PLUS "1+3+6 formula," 234
OPEC-China Energy Dialogue, 323
Open-Ended Working Group on Developments in the Field of Information and Telecommunications in the Context of International Security, 342
orbital debris, growth of, 172–74, 173
Organization for Economic Co-operation and Development (OECD), 115, 290; Chinese digital economy in, 298; digital services trade index, 301–2); and energy demand growth, 319

Osborne, George, 141

Organization for Economic Co-operation and Development (OECD), 112

other official flows (OOF), 112

Other Transaction Authority (OTA), 155

outer space: challenges to, 173; cooperating with China, 178; developing norms of behavior for, 177; enhancing deterrence in, 177; reinvigorating dialogue on, 177; utilization of, 171

P5, 354, 354

Pacific Alliance, 236

Pacific Deterrence Initiative, 277

Pak, Jung H., 53

Papua New Guinea, 257; data flow restriction in, *303*

Paris Agreement, 20, 320, 327, 329, 341

Paris Club, 288, 290

Partnership for Quality Infrastructure, 115–16

payment systems, regulation of, *302*

Pelosi, Nancy, 158

People's Liberation Army (PLA), 13, 41, 69, 125, 135, 209, 212, 272

People's Liberation Army Air Force (PLAAF), 212

People's Liberation Army Marine Corps (PLANMC), 272

People's Liberation Army Navy (PLAN), 212, 272

People's Liberation Army Rocket Force (PLARF), 212

People's Liberation Army Strategic Support Force (PLASSF), 213

People's Republic of China (PRC), 60, 68; and international law, 336; surveillance exports of, 181. *See also* China

Permanent Court of Arbitration, 264

persuasion, 68–73

Peru, data flow restriction in, *303*

Peterson, Dahlia, 367

Pew Research Center, 106: on Chinese activity in LAC, 236

Philippine National Police (DILG), 185

Philippines: case against China, 76; COVID-19 response, 79; data flow restriction in, *303*; economic footprint in, 112; EEZ of, 78; and South China Sea, 79; wielding BRI against, 29

Piccone, Ted, 233

Pishan County, China, 369

PLAA. *See* People's Liberation Army Army

PLAAF. *See* People's Liberation Army Air Force

PLA Djibouti Support Base, 274

PLAN. *See* People's Liberation Army Navy

PLARF. *See* People's Liberation Army Rocket Force

PLASSF. *See* People's Liberation Army Strategic Support Force

Poland, *298*

Politburo Standing Committee (PSC), 28, 44, 47

Pompeo, Mike, 79–80, 108; trip to Israel, 241

Pony.ai, 166

Portugal, *298*

post–9/11 era, 271

poverty, elimination of, 43–45; expenditures for, *46*

Powell, Colin, 244

Power of Siberia gas pipeline, 134

Prasad, Eswar, 293

precise poverty alleviation (*jingzhun fupin*), 44

"pre-criminal" content, elimination of, 370, 372

princelings, changes in numbers of, *45*

private channels, 37–38

private sector, superpower marathon and, 155

proregress, 41-50; coined, 41
Pryke, Jonathan, 256
pull factor, 184
purchasing power parity (PPP), 309
push factor, 184
Putin, Vladimir, 132; and Xi, 133
Putnam, Robert, 43
Pyongyang: Chinese relief/concern, 62. *See* China: China–North Korea relations; North Korea

Qatar, Chinese fuel imports from, *242*
Qing Dynasty, 136
Quad-plus dialogues, 127
quality infrastructure, 114
quarterly earnings, 155
quiet rebalancing, 38

R&D, 12, 14, 156, 157, 163, 167; bolstering investment in, 158
RAND Corp, 89
Ratner, Ely, 268
Reagan, Ronald, 244
recommendations: against Chinese coercion tactics, 37–38; for biotechnology development, 227; for China–North Korea relations, 60–66; for Chinese global surveillance exports, 185–88; for Chinese space activities, 176–78; for global/multilateral actors, 373; on gray-zone conflicts, 265–68; for great powers, 98–100; for rebalancing U.S.-China relations, 106–9; regarding global economic system, 291–92; regarding South China Sea, 81–83; regarding state-of-the-art chips, 201–203; on responding to data governance practices, 304–6; related to surveillance technology, 371–72; for superpower marathon competition, 157–59; for Xinjiang repression, 372–73
regional capacity, boosting, 82

Regional Comprehensive Economic Partnership, 123
regional security status quo, dissatisfaction with, 103
Reif, L. Rafael, 38
rejuvenation, term, 27
renewable energy, 320
renminbi: hiatus, 294; implications of rise of, 296; promoting, 293; as reserve currency, 295; role in international finance, 294; share of international payments, 294
Repack Airwaves Yielding Better Access for Users of Modern Services Act, 165
Republic of China (ROC), 68
research and development. *See* R&D
resolve dilemma, danger of, 38
Revere, Evans J. R., 55, 60
Richardson, Sophie, 359
Riedel, Bruce, 243
Riyadh, 245
RMB, 225
rocket bodies, growth of, *173*
Rose, Frank A., 171
Rose, Frank, 89
Röttgen, Norbert, 144
Russia: adventurism of, 98; annexing Crimea, 11, 96, 132, 135; ballistic missile defense system, 135; and contemporary order, 97; data flow restriction in, *303*; energy exports, 134; middle-class expenditures, *311*; objects in Earth orbit, *173*; oil exports, *323*; P2 alliance, 354; promoting instability, 356; relations with China, 132–38; Russia-China cooperation, 99–101; stripping out human rights monitors, 355
Russia-India-China trilateral, 123
Russian Cosmos satellite, 172

S-400 surface-to-air missiles, 135
Sachs, Natan, 241

"Safe City" solutions, 182
Safe City Malta, 185
"safe haven" currency, 295
salmon, ban on, 34–36
Samsung, 199–200
sanctions, imposing, 34–36
Santo Island, 259
Saudi Arabia: Chinese fuel imports from, *242*; COVID-19 in, 245; East Wind incident, 244; opposing communism, 244; relations with China, 243–45
Scarborough Shoal, 76; EEZ of, 79; repercussions of building on, 82
Schelling, Thomas, 89
Schlieffen Plan, 263
Second Thomas Shoal, 78
semiconductor manufacturing equipment (SME), 195
Semiconductor Manufacturing International Corporation (SMIC), 195
Senkaku challenge, 263
Senkaku Island, 29, 116
Senkaku Paradox, The (O'Hanlon), 263
SenseNets, 368
Sensetime, 368
sensitive issues with Beijing, 251
September 11, 2001, 96
17+1 format, 142–43
17th Central Committee, number of princelings in, 45
Seychelles, potential "bases" in, 275
Shanghai Cooperation Organization (SCO), 136, 355
Shanghai, branding of, 47
"sharing economy," 164
Shenzhen, branding of, 47
Shinzo Abe, 115
Silk Road Economic Belt. *See* Belt and Road Initiative
Singapore: data flow restriction in, *303*; economic footprint in, 112
Singh, Pavneet, 151
Sino American ties, 25

Sino-British Joint Declaration, 339
Sino-Indian relations, 122
Sino-Japanese relations, limits of, 116–18
situational awareness sensors, 175
six super megacities, granting authority to, 49
Six-Party denuclearization agreement, 63
16th Central Committee, number of princelings in, 45
Slovenia, Chinese digital economy in, *298*
small and medium-sized enterprise (SME), 313
small satellites, mega constellations of, 174
"small town development strategy (*chengzhenhua*), 47
Small, Andrew, 142
social safety net, 107
Solís, Mireya, 111
Solomon Islands, 257
South Africa: climate alliance with, 330
South America: oil exports, *323*
South China Sea: arbitration, 76; HN-1 gliders in, 213; increased presence in, 77; positive development regarding, 80; pursing claims in, 76; resisting militarization in, 79; "rocks," 76; viewing events in isolation, 82–83; worrying developments in, 77–79
South Korea: as alliance linchpin, 53–57; change in chip fab capacity, *198*; Chinese approach to, 53–57; chip fab revenue, *200*; dialogue with, 127; global chip fab capacity, *197*; number of chipmakers, *195*, *196*; 2017 THAAD episode, 36–37; worst state of, 98
South Pacific: and Australia, 258; China's ambitions in, 256–57; Chinese presence in, 257; establishing military base in, 258; governance

South Pacific (*cont.*)
  institutions, 258–9; risks of China
  in, 257–60; strategic significance of,
  257–58
Southeast Asia: boosting support for,
  80; change in chip fab capacity, *198*;
  reassuring, 80
Soviet Union, 152
Space X, 174
spacecraft, growth of, *173*
Space-Track.Org, 173
Spain, *298*
Special Drawing Rights (SDR), 293
spectrum management, 164–65
Spratly Islands, 76–78; EEZ of, 79
Sprint, 165
Sri Lanka, 274; military ties with, 124
stability-instability paradox, 87
Starlink satellites, 174
statecraft strategy, developing, 159
state-owned enterprises (SOEs), 117
STEM (science, technology, engineer-
  ing, and mathematics), 155; human
  capital in, 158–59
Stent, Angela, 132
Stern, Todd, 326
Stilwell, David, 80
Strait of Malacca, 78, 274
strike platforms, privatizing, 266
Su-35 fighter jets, 135
Subi Reef, 264
sub-Saharan African, peach operation
  in, 355
suicide drones, 213
Sullivan, Jake, 145
Sultan, Prince, 244
Sunflower Movement, 70
superpower marathon (U.S.-China):
  Cold War analogy, 151–52; Cold
  War contrast, 153–54; ideological
  conflict in, 152–53; preparing for,
  154–57
surveillance and public security tech-
  nology platforms: charting exports

of, 182–84; growth in adoption of,
  183; presence of, *183*
SWIFT (Society for Worldwide Interbank Financial Telecommunications), 268, 295
Switzerland, *298*

Taiwan: attempts to persuade, 68–73;
  change in chip fab capacity, *198*;
  chip fab revenue, *200*; democratization of, 69–70; global chip fab capacity, *197*; limited military campaign
  against, 71; "national treatment,"
  72; number of chipmakers, *195, 196*;
  "opposing independence" of, 70;
  persuading, 69; rejecting 1C2S, 71;
  responding to "coercion without
  violence," 73; use of force against,
  68–69
Tajikistan, "initial presence" in, 275
Talmadge, Caitlin, 86
Tanzania, potential "bases" in, 275
Tao Guang Yang Hui, modifying, 26.
  See also China: "hide and bide"
  strategy
Technology C. Ltd, 368
technology, 12–14; competition in, 105;
  fusions, 153; in U.S.-China superpower marathon, 151–60
teeth. *See* China: China–North Korea
  relations
Tencent, 166, 313
Terminal High Altitude Area Defense
  (THAAD), 3; and Australia, 250;
  deploying, 36–37
Tesla, 166
Thailand: data flow restriction in, *303*;
  economic footprint in, 112
13th Five-Year Plan (13th FYP), 224,
  320
Thousand Talents, 226
"three evils," 136
3GPP (3rd Generation Partnership
  Project), 304

Tianjin Binhai Artificial Intelligence Military-Civil Fusion Center, 214
Tianjin, branding of, 47
Tibet, 123, 249, 321, 363
Timor-Leste, 259
T-Mobile, 165
total objects, growth of, *173*
traditional military capabilities, retaining, 267
Trump administration: public bullying, 165; UN activities, 357; creating vacuums, 357
Trump, Donald, 140; and Australia, 251; and climate engagement, 326; Huawei ban under, 164; meeting Kim Jong Un, 62; tweets of, 61. *See also* Trump administration
Tsai Ing-wen, 70–71
Tsentr (Center), 135
Tsinghua Unigroup, *200*
TSMC, *194*, 199–200, *200*
Turkey, 98
Turkic Muslims, 340, 362, 372–73
Turnbull, Malcolm, 248
12th Five-Year Plan, 320
2020 Munich Security Conference, 158
2+2 dialogue, 115
2+2 meeting, 127
2010 sanctions episode, 34–36
2017 Cybersecurity Law, 117
2017 National Intelligence Law, 185
2017 THAAD episode, 36–37
2018 National Defense Strategy, 262
2018 Shanghai Biennale, naming, 41
2018 Winter Olympics, 62
2019 Defense White Paper, 77
2019 Worldwide Threat Assessment, 105
two-level games, 43

U.N. Debris Mitigation Guidelines, 173
U.S. Air Force Ventures, 155
U.S. Army Futures Command, 155
U.S. Defense Intelligence Agency, 171

U.S. Freedom of Navigation Operations, 82
U.S. Nuclear Risk Reduction Center, 89
U.S. Pacific Command, 78
U.S. Trade Representative (USTR), 158
U.S.-China Climate Change Working Group, 326, 329
U.S.-China relations, 1; bilateral relationship, 327; climate relationship, 326–30; downward trajectory of, 102–6; Europe's role in, 145–46; 5G competition, 162–68; great-power rivalry, 7–11; ideological and systems competition, 105–6; joint communiques, 103; "Mar-a-Lago sprit," 122; and Middle East, 243; military competition, 215; new equilibrium for 102–9; player gap, 97; policy principles for, 30–31; present order and, 97–98; pursuing strategic competition, 100; regional security statis status quo and, 103; restoring sources of comparative advantage, 108–9; "return of the jungle," 95; reversing fatalism, 108; right-sizing risks, 106–7; shared framework for, 107; strategic competition, 185; technological rivalry, 118; technology competition, 105
U.S.-India relations: agreements, *126*; defense trade, *126* dialogues, *126*; exercises, *126*; liaisons, *126*; quadrilateral, *126*; recent developments in, 125, 127–28
U.S.-Indian Malabar military exercises, 115
U.S.-Japan Mutual Security Treaty, 263
U.S.-Philippines Mutual Defense Treaty, 82
U.S.-South Korea alliance, friction in, 55
U.S.-South Korea-Japan security cooperation, erosion of, 55

UN Commission on the Limits of the Continental Shelf, 79

UN Convention on the Prevention and Punishment of the Crime of Genocide

UN Framework Convention on Climate Change, 330

UN Group of Governmental Experts on Advancing Responsible State Behavior in Cyberspace in the Context of International Security (Cyber GGE), 342

UN Group of Governmental Experts on Emerging Technologies in the Area of Lethal Autonomous Weapons Systems (LAWS GGE), 342

UN High Commissioner for Human Rights, 362

UN Human Rights Council (HRC), 359

UN Security Council (UNSC), 121; resolutions, 61–62

Un, Kim Jong, 54

UNCOPUOS Long-Term Sustainability Guidelines, 173

United Arab Emirates, Chinese fuel imports from, *242*

United Kingdom: Chinese digital economy in, *298*; climate negotiations, 328; and contemporary order, 97; middle-class consumption expenditures, *312*; middle-class expenditures, *311*; and South China Sea, 79; statement on South China Sea, 75

United Nations Committee on the Peaceful Uses of Outer Space (UN-COPUOS), 173

United Nations Convention on the Law of the Sea (UNCLOS), 76–77, 79, 82, 338

United Nations: Chinese influence at, 353; Department of Political Affairs (DPA), 355; human rights system, 359–64, *360–63*; peace operations, 354–55; political work, 355–56; preserving values-based multilateralism, 356–57; quip about, 353; regular budget of, 353; specialized agencies of, 337, 353, 356

United States: abandoning alliance commitments, 98; alliance architectural linchpin of, 53; ASEAN trade and investment, *113*; and BIS Entity List, 368; change in chip fab capacity, *198*; and China-Russia relations, 133, 137–38; and Chinese boundaries, 114; and Chinese dependence on chips, 201–203; Chinese digital economy in, *298*; chip fab revenue, *200*; Cold War analogy, 151–52; consistency in rule of law, 82; continued scale and weight of, 97; countering false narratives, 80; data flow restriction in, *303*; Department of Defense (DOD), 155; Department of the Treasury, 288; DPRK-U.S. diplomacy, 62; exploring autonomy and AI, 210; global chip fab capacity, *197*; in technology competition, 157; infrastructure funds with, 116; leadership vacuum created by, 104; manufacturing equipment from, 193; manufacturing erosion, 155–56; middle class of, 315; middle-class consumption expenditures, *312*; middle-class expenditures, *311*; and Middle East, 242; national mobile infrastructure, 164; number of chipmakers, *195, 196*; objects in Earth orbit, 173; ODA commitments, *113*; perceived position of nuclear advantage, 87; policymakers, 88; position on maritime claims, 79; possibility of competition, 154–55; as "powerful adversary," 210; pursuing damage limitation, 86; renewed alliance focus from, 98; responding to coercion tactics, 37–38;

responding to data governance practices, 304–6; responding to digital services trade, 297; revisionist ambitions, 355; Sino-American ties, 25; statement on South China Sea, 75; strategic competitor of, 1; ties with Philippines, 82; U.S. Navy's Sixth Fleet, 274; U.S.-China nuclear relationship, 86–90; U.S.-Israeli partnership, 241; U.S.-LAC relations, 237–38; warships, 77

Universal Periodic Review (UPR), 361

unmanned aerial vehicles (UAVs), 213

unmanned underwater vehicle (UUVs), 213

Uyghurs, 22, 327, 340, 362, 368, 371–72

Vandenberg Air Force Base, 172

Vanuatu, 274

Venezuela, diplomatic activism in, 237; sanctions against, 237

Verizon, 165

vessels, collision of, 29

veto tempo, increasing, 354

Vietnam: data flow restriction in, *303;* dialogue with, 127; economic footprint in, 112; and South China Sea, 79

Vladivostok, 136

Vostok 2018, 135

warfare education, strengthening, 265

Waymo, 166

WeBank, 313

WeChat Pay, 313

Western Hemisphere, 271

Western Pacific, 95

"whole of society" threats, 107

Williams, Robert D., 335

Wolf Warrior diplomacy, 144

Woody Island, 96

World Economic Forum: on 5G networks, 164

World Health Assembly, 247

World Trade Organization (WTO), 287; Beijing access to, 336; rules, 288

World War II, superpower glow following, 270

Wright, Thomas, 140

Wright, Tom, 100

WS-43 drone, 213

Xi Jinping, 1; addressing Australia Parliament, 247; appeal for green development, 48; assuming party chairmanship, 43–44; born "red," 43; "bugs" in power consolidation, 25; calling Moon, 55; carbon neutrality pledge, 329; "catch up and surpass" United States, 157; coining terms, 44; and climate engagement, 326; contradictory clues by, 42; and control of media, 42; contradictory moves of, 42; elite discontent of, 99; expenditures on poverty alleviation under, *46;* exporting governance model, 105; first term, 44–45; focus on "national rejuvenation," 27; granting authority to megacities, 47–48; January 2017 Davos remarks, 354; Mao Zedong legacy and, 42; on military innovation, 211; policy on territories, 29; and poverty elimination, 43–45; power consolidation, 42; and private-sector development, 42; protégés of, 47; and Putin, 133; and renewable energy, 322; and rural population, 46–48; seizing pandemic opportunity, 55; six super megacities under, 47–48; solidifying command of, 42; and Trump administration, 42; two centenary goals, 27, 30; and "two-level games," 43; 2009 Ambassadorial Conference of, 29; visiting North Korea (2019), 63; Xi-Kim meeting, 63

Xi Zhongxun, 43

Xiamen Meiya Pico Information Co. Ltd, 368

Xie Zenhua, 326

Xinjiang Uyghur Autonomous Region, 2

Xinjiang: and entity list companies in, 368–70; genocide in, 367; non-entity list companies in, 370; prioritizing "stability" in, 368; surveillance companies involved in, 368; vocational training centers, 367; Western companies' role in, 370–71

"Yellow Peril" racism, 107

Yitu, 368

Yixin Science, 368

yuan, 45

yubu, 41–43

Zeman, Miloš, 141

Zhang, Ketian, 33

Zhejiang Province, 47

Zheng Wang, 27

Zhou Enlai, 43

ZTE, 164